Networked Governance of Freedom and Tyranny
Peace in Timor-Leste

Networked Governance of Freedom and Tyranny
Peace in Timor-Leste

John Braithwaite, Hilary Charlesworth
and Adérito Soares

E PRESS

Published by ANU E Press
The Australian National University
Canberra ACT 0200, Australia
Email: anuepress@anu.edu.au
This title is also available online at http://epress.anu.edu.au

National Library of Australia Cataloguing-in-Publication entry

Author: Braithwaite, John.

Title: Networked governance of freedom and tyranny : peace in Timor-Leste / John Braithwaite, Hilary Charlesworth and Adérito Soares.

ISBN: 9781921862755 (pbk.) 9781921862762 (ebook)

Series: Peacebuilding compared.

Notes: Includes bibliographical references.

Subjects: Timor-Leste--Politics and government.
Timor-Leste--Autonomy and independence movements.
Timor-Leste--History.
Timor-Leste--Relations--Australia.
Australia--Relations--Timor-Leste.

Other Authors/Contributors:
Charlesworth, H. C. (Hilary C.)
Soares, Adérito.

Dewey Number: 320.95987

All rights reserved. No part of this publication may be reproduced, stored in a retrieval system or transmitted in any form or by any means, electronic, mechanical, photocopying or otherwise, without the prior permission of the publisher.

Cover design and layout by ANU E Press

Cover photo: Veronica Pereira Maia, Sydney, 1996. 'I wove this tais and wove in the names of all the victims of the massacre in Dili on 12 November 1991. When it touches my body, I'm overwhelmed with sadness. I remember the way those young people lost their lives for our nation.' Photo: Ross Bird

Printed by Griffin Press

This edition © 2012 ANU E Press

Contents

Dedication	vii
Preface	ix
Advisory Panel	xv
Glossary	xvii
Map	xxi
1. A Political Puzzle	1
2. A Brief History of Timor	9
3. Unprincipled Engagement and Misplaced Realism from 1974	17
4. Not So Networked Warfare, 1975–1999	47
5. Networked Solidarity, International and Clandestine	61
6. Santa Cruz Massacre, 1991	79
7. *Reformasi* and Referendum, 1998–1999	91
8. Transitional Governance	111
9. Transitional Security	135
10. Transitional Justice and Reconciliation	175
11. Transitional Social and Economic Development	235

12. Women in Networked Governance	263
13. Republican Networked Governance of Transition	279
Appendix: Methodology for Peacebuilding Compared	307
References	311
Index	343

We dedicate this book to Nina de Jesus Soares (five years old) who died in Batugade town, near the border with Indonesia, in 1975. She was among thousands of Timorese children who died after 1975 as a consequence of the war in Timor-Leste.

Preface

This book is about the ethical limits of state sovereignty. It explores these limits in two ways. One is a critique of realism as a theory of international affairs. The second is about the limits of reforming tyranny through the centralised agency of a state sovereign who is a progressive leader or a political party responsible for overthrowing a tyrant.

Realist international relations theory explains the world as if it were a billiards table with one kind of actor that matters: billiard balls, each representing a unitary state. These balls vary in size depending on the economic and military power of that state. So the world is understood under this metaphor as one in which little balls do not shape history; they are constantly pushed aside by the bigger and especially the biggest ones, the great powers. This realist metaphor is challenged as an explanatory account in this book. It is a story of a tiny, non-unitary ball of a million people with no state military, no economic clout—Timor-Leste—pushing aside the will of the world's greatest powers: the United States, the European Union, and also the fourth-largest country in the world, an emerging economic powerhouse with a formidable and dominant military, Indonesia.

There are many versions of realist international relations theory. For our analytic purposes, we settle on four features as definitional. One is that unitary nation states shape history. Two is that the states that shape history most are those with the most economic and military power. Three is that world affairs are understood as unitary states pursuing their national interests as states, where the key national interests are the very economic and military assets that constitute realist power. These first three defining features of realism are explanatory claims. Realism is also the dominant ethos of diplomatic practice across recent centuries and therefore has a strong normative underpinning in the minds of its practitioners. Diplomats should see themselves as custodians of their national interest and should seek to maximise that national interest. This normative assertion is our fourth defining feature of realism.

More extreme versions of realism, which have been particularly prominent in the thinking of recent Republican administrations in the United States, see the interjection of international values and rights and building international institutions as causing irresponsible commitments, rigidity in diplomacy and escalation of conflict. They disparage this as Wilsonian idealism—a reference to Woodrow Wilson, the American President who was instrumental in creating the League of Nations that failed to prevent World War II. This more extreme form of realism is not taken as definitional for the analytic purposes of this book. In part, this is because the targets of our critique are not Bush–Cheney realists of this extreme kind, but leaders like Presidents Jimmy Carter and Bill Clinton of the United States and Prime Ministers of Australia Gough Whitlam, Malcolm Fraser, Bob Hawke and Paul Keating, whom the authors view as mostly admirable leaders who were strong supporters of international institutions, peacemaking, human rights and the United Nations. In spite of this, our book shows that the behaviour of all these leaders towards Indonesia and Timor-Leste reflected the view, as expressed in the words of former US Ambassador Stapleton Roy, that 'Indonesia matters, East Timor does not' (Roosa 1999:1). Their conduct of Timor diplomacy satisfied all four of our defining features of realism in international affairs. One objective of our book is to understand the politics needed to keep admirable leaders more consistently admirable in the face of realist pressures.

This book is not about adjudicating the nuances, revisionist versions or extremes of realist international relations theory; rather it is a critique of these four core tenets. One nuance that is particularly important to our narrative is that sometimes great powers outsource regional security to a middle power of that region. Once the Soviet Union withdrew from Afghanistan, the successive administrations of Presidents Reagan, George H. W. Bush and Clinton (until 1997) no longer viewed Afghanistan as important and outsourced its stability to Pakistan. This proved a disastrous blunder. A less well understood blunder was that for a period after the Vietnam War, the United States withdrew from interest in South-East Asian and South Pacific diplomacy, outsourcing responsibility for the so-called 'arc of instability' around Australia to Australia and Indonesia. We will argue that Australia and Indonesia proved as incompetent and venal with Timor as did Pakistan with Afghanistan, causing catastrophe and immiseration for the peoples of those lands.

The family of one of our authors, Adérito Soares, suffered greatly from this venality, though no more than most Timorese families. This book is dedicated to Adérito's tiny sister Nina who died as a result of one tragedy of the war in Timor. Adérito played his part in the clandestine movement in Renetil, became a key drafter of the post-conflict Constitution as a member of the constitutional assembly that also became a de-facto first parliament of the first new nation of the twenty-first century. Today he has left politics and is Timor-Leste's Anti-Corruption Commissioner. Adérito also married into an Australian family. So all three authors write partially from an Australian vantage point.

We will argue in Chapter 3 that on no issue in its history has Australia had more influence on world affairs than on Timor-Leste because of the way US Secretary of State Henry Kissinger decided to opt out of Timor diplomacy, entrusting it to Jakarta, Canberra and Lisbon. European powers did likewise, while China only feigned interest. Just as the focus of the book is on Timor as a case study, it is also on Australia as a case of realism in international affairs, illustrating the swampy moral ground that realism created.

The university with which we are all affiliated, The Australian National University, has been for decades the most distinguished centre of scholarship on Indonesia outside Indonesia itself. Just as we are grateful to Australia and the Australian Research Council for nurturing our research, so we thank the wonderful community of scholars, including many amazing students from our region, at The Australian National University who have nourished us. On the republican themes of this book, we particularly single out the inspiring influence of Philip Pettit. Yet there have also been aspects of realism in the scholarly climate at The Australian National University at times and this is reflexively part of our account at certain moments of the history.

The second analytic focus of our book casts a critical light on different leaders we admire: Xanana Gusmão, José Ramos-Horta and Mari Alkatiri. We are grateful to them for agreeing to be interviewed and for the way their struggle has inspired the world. The virtue of their political project that caught our interest is that it was networked. Networks among weak actors ultimately defeated the strong in this story. The way networked governance by the weak can overwhelm great powers, rendering realist international relations theory predictively false, has long been a focus of our research group (Braithwaite and Drahos 2000). So have been several other theoretical frameworks we deploy in this book to shape our understanding of how weak networks can control strong tyrannies: the nodal governance of networks (Drahos 2004; Johnston and Shearing 2003; Shearing et al. 2003) and principled engagement (Pedersen 2008) informed by responsive regulation (Ayres and Braithwaite 1992; Braithwaite 2002) as an alternative to the unprincipled engagement and disengagement that are recurrent fruits of realism.

Our second analytic focus is on how nodes of networks against domination become sources of domination from the moment they assume sovereignty over a state. Our conclusion is that public policy—state policy—is not the crucial solution to both the challenges we seek to understand. Rather it is the policies of civil society organisations organised into networks. In the Timor narrative, the key actors in the defeat of realist Western power and Indonesian power were in the clandestine network, the diplomatic front of the resistance and the international solidarity network. According to our analysis, the crucial failure in building the Democratic Republic of Timor-Leste after the conflict was that it was not republican enough. It was too focused on building a state controlled by the three greatest leaders of the resistance and the party of the resistance. The networks that made the triumph over realist forces possible were dispensed with when they were most needed to act as checks and balances on the new executive.

So the second contribution we seek to make is to republican political theory—again, this has long been a focus of our research network at The Australian National University (Ayres and Braithwaite 1992; Braithwaite and Parker 1999; Braithwaite and Pettit 1990; Pettit 1997)—and in particular a focus on reframing the republican ideal of the separation of powers (Braithwaite 1997). Our argument is that republics must radically pluralise their vision of how to separate powers within the state, so the state has many branches of separated powers rather than just the traditional three (legislature, judiciary and executive). The new Anti-Corruption Commission that Adérito Soares leads is just one of those branches. Even more important than variegating separations of powers within the state is enrolling networks of checks and balances from civil society outside the state. In a society like Timor-Leste, these must go beyond capital-city non-governmental organisations (NGOs) in the Western mould and include rural indigenous networks as checks on state power.

So these are the senses in which our title, *Networked Governance of Freedom and Tyranny*, has meaning. Networks restraining excesses of realist international diplomacy and networks checking excesses of executive domination within a state are what deliver republican freedom. We define networked governance as plural actors linked by coordinating dialogue that constitutes both interdependence and sufficient autonomy for different nodes of the network to check and balance other nodes of power. While networked governance has a more variegated horizontal architecture than state governance (Castells 1996), networks of capacity and accountability are linked to every layer of subnational, national and international hierarchy. Sometimes they are coordinated by state regulation, sometimes not.

We distinguish republican freedom from other conceptions by characterising it as freedom as non-domination (Braithwaite and Pettit 1990; Pettit 1997). It is freedom from arbitrary power secured by networks of checks and balances that include much more than a rule of law. According to this conception, republicanism is a philosophy of how to maximise freedom as non-domination. Republicans do not think non-domination is the only value that matters. We just say that a good strategy of institutional design is to ask the question: which political arrangements will maximise freedom as non-domination? Our conclusion is that they are often networked arrangements. Networked accountabilities that humble power enable regimes to change in ways that ensure one form of enslavement is not replaced with another. Domination can be continuously challenged by networks that renew themselves with novel ways of checking power that are not confined to enduring constitutional balances.

Here there is common ground with other theoretical traditions, such as the notion of 'destabilization rights' that Roberto Unger (1986, 1987) introduced to critical legal studies. Charles Sabel and William Simon (2004) further developed the concept of destabilisation rights within the tradition of 'democratic experimentalism'. These are rights to unsettle and open up state institutions that persistently fail to fulfil their functions. Destabilisation rights are dynamic checks on failures of institutionalised checks to do their job. Rights to public law litigation can destabilise defunct structures, as can rights of oppressed minorities to appeal for redress to UN institutions. Destabilisation rights enable a politics of dis-entrenchment. Networks can deliver experimental innovation in the invigoration of separations of powers. The state is often too paralysed for innovation and democratic experimentalism. Western doctrine on the separation of powers has stultified, we hope to show, because it has not been open to learning from the democratic experimentalism in civil separations of powers revealed in non-Western histories such as that of Timor-Leste.

Finally, our research community has long had an interest in feminist theory in international affairs, particularly on questions of justice (Braithwaite and Daly 1994; Charlesworth 2010; Charlesworth and Chinkin 2000; Charlesworth et al. 1991). Throughout history, the domination of women has been a feature of successor regimes that lifted other forms of enslavement. The regime led by the big three men of the liberation of Timor is no exception. Yet we also discovered women's narratives of networked resistance to male domination that are distinctively Timorese. These, we argue, might be productively 'vernacularised' (Merry 2006) into Western feminist wisdom.

Feminist politics has been more successful than in most countries at getting women into Timor-Leste's Parliament. Yet our analysis concludes this is not the main game. Networked governance for freedom is not mainly about replacing political leaders who believe in a politics of domination with politicians who do not, desirable as this is. It is not about replacing business leaders who ruthlessly exploit workers, consumers and the environment to maximise profits with disciples of corporate social responsibility—good thing though that is. The main game is a vibrant civic republican politics of networked checks that humble state dominations and rapaciousness in markets. That is the game we seek to understand and diagnose from the lessons of Timor's history.

Our research ethics protocols do not allow us to acknowledge the greatest debts we owe, which are to the many Timorese, Indonesian, UN and international voices heard in our interviews. We thank you for your openness and generosity. Our ethical obligations under The Australian National University's Research Ethics Committee approval were explained to all participants. These included an obligation to report quotes and insights from each informant without identification unless they specifically indicated that they wanted to be quoted as the source. We also thank the members of our Advisory Panel listed on the next page who in most cases assisted by both suggesting folk we should interview and commenting wisely and critically on long drafts with great generosity of spirit. They bear no responsibility for the ways we failed to learn from their counsel. Likewise, we thank three referees appointed by ANU E Press for their helpful comments. We particularly thank Kate Macfarlane, manager of the Peacebuilding Compared project, for her endless kindness and dedication and our ANU E Press mentors, Margaret Thornton, Duncan Beard and Jan Borrie. We thank Kate's predecessor, Leah Dunn, with whom we did many Timor interviews in 2006, and Andrew Goldsmith with whom we also had much fun in the field as he used interviews we conducted jointly for his own project on policing with Sinclair Dinnen.

We use Timor-Leste to refer to the twenty-first-century state formed by the constitution of the Democratic Republic of Timor-Leste. For its sixteenth to twentieth-century history, we use East Timor or Portuguese Timor (before 1975).

John Braithwaite
Hilary Charlesworth
Adérito Soares

Advisory Panel, Timor-Leste Case of Peacebuilding Compared

Michael Barnett, University of Minnesota

James Fox, The Australian National University

Daniel Fitzpatrick, The Australian National University

Helen Hill, Victoria University

Lia Kent, The Australian National University

Damien Kingsbury, Deakin University

Gordon Peake, The Australian National University

Philip Pettit, Princeton University

Dionisio Babo-Soares, Co-Chair, Truth and Friendship Commission

Patrick Walsh, Commission for Reception, Truth and Reconciliation, Dili

Glossary

acolhimento	welcome and reintegration ritual commonly used to reintegrate former militia members into the community
adat	Indonesian term for customary village law still widely used in Timor-Leste. It is for Timorese a synonym of the Tetum word for customary village justice, *lisan*
aldeia	hamlet
APEC	Asia Pacific Economic Cooperation
Apodeti	Associação Popular Democrática Timorense (Timorese Popular Democratic Association): pro-Indonesian party formed in 1974
ASDT	Associação Social-Democrata Timorense (Timorese Social Democratic Association)
ASEAN	Association of South-East Asian Nations
BAKIN	Badan Koordinasi Intelijen Negara (State Intelligence Coordinating Agency of Indonesia)
barlaque	bride price
CAVR	Comissão de Acolhimento, Verdade e Reconciliação (Commission for Reception, Truth and Reconciliation)
CEDAW	Convention on the Elimination of All Forms of Discrimination against Women
CEP	Community Empowerment Project
chefe	traditional chief, leader
chefe de posto	subdistrict leader
chefe de suco	village leader
Clandestinos	network of people who provided food, shelter, intelligence and logistical support to Falintil
CNRM	Conselho Nacional da Resistência Maubere (National Council of Maubere Resistance)
CNRT	Conselho Nacional de Reconstrução do Timor (National Congress for Timorese Reconstruction)
CNRT	Conselho Nacional de Resistência Timorense (National Council of Timorese Resistance)
CRP	Community Reconciliation Process

CRRN	Conselho Revolusionário da Resisténsia Nasional (Revolutionary Council of National Resistance)
Falintil	Forças Armadas da Libertação Nacional de Timor-Leste (Timorese Armed Forces for the National Liberation of East Timor)
FRELIMO	Frente de Libertação de Moçambique (Liberation Front of Mozambique)
Fretilin	Frente Revolucionária do Timor-Leste Independente (Revolutionary Front for an Independent Timor)
F-FDTL	Falintil-Forças de Defesa de Timor Leste (Timor-Leste Defence Force)
GMPTL	Grupo das Mulheres Parlamentares de Timor-Leste (Women's Parliamentary Group of Timor-Leste)
Golkar	Golongan Karya (Indonesian Golkar Party)
ICRC	International Committee for the Red Cross
IMF	International Monetary Fund
INTERFET	International Force for East Timor
IDP	internally displaced person
ISF	International Stabilisation Force
JSMP	Justice System Monitoring Programme
juramento	blood oath
Kopassus	Komando Pasukan Khusus (Special Forces Command of the Indonesian Army)
lia nain	literally, 'keepers of the word', men of law
lisan	authority of traditional elders; customary village justice
liurai	traditional king, traditional chief
MAG	martial arts groups
nahe biti	traditional justice carried out on the mat
NGO	non-governmental organisation
OMT	Organização de Mulher Timor (Organisation of East Timorese Women)
OPEC	Organisation of Petroleum Exporting Countries
OPMT	Organização Popular de Mulher Timor (Popular Organisation of East Timorese Women)

POLRI	Kepolisian Negara Republik Indonesia (Indonesian National Police)
PNTL	Policia Nacional de Timor-Leste (National Police Force of Timor-Leste)
PSHT	Persaudaraan Setia Hati Terate (Brotherhood of Pentjak Silat)
Renetil	Resistencia Nacional dos Estudantes de Timor Leste (Timor-Leste Students' National Resistance)
SRSG	Special Representative of the Secretary-General of the United Nations
suco	village
tais	cloth made from traditional weaving methods
TNI	Tentara Nasional Indonesia (Indonesian Armed National Forces)
UDT	União Democrática Timorense (Timorese Democratic Union)
uma lulik	shared sacred house
UN	United Nations
UNAMET	United Nations Mission in East Timor
UNDP	United Nations Development Programme
UNHCR	United Nations High Commissioner for Refugees
UNIFEM	United Nations Development Fund for Women
UNMIT	United Nations Integrated Mission in Timor-Leste
UNMISET	United Nations Mission of Support in East Timor
UNOTIL	United Nations Office in Timor-Leste
UNPOL	United Nations Civilian Police
UNTAET	United Nations Transitional Administration in East Timor
WTO	World Trade Organisation

Map of Timor-Leste

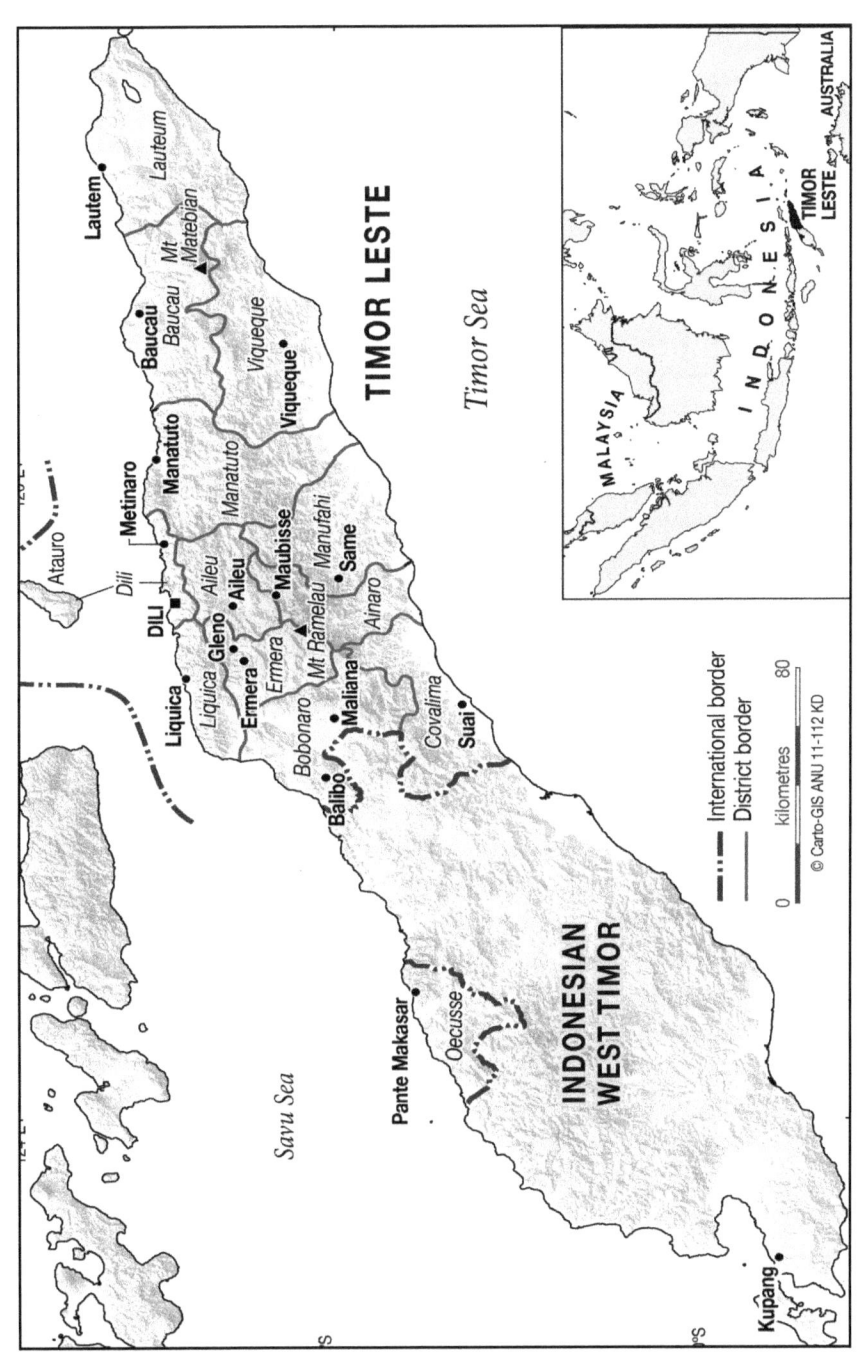

1. A Political Puzzle

This book starts with a political puzzle. When John Braithwaite and Hilary Charlesworth were young, Gough Whitlam was a breath of fresh air, a great political intellect and reformer in the long years of conservative rule in Australia. In 1972, he finally led a social-democratic party to power with a progressive political agenda. His government survived only three years. Social democrats look back on them as years of great reform when Australia withdrew from the Vietnam War, recognised China, resisted colonialism, handing independence to its own colony of Papua New Guinea, increased aid to the poor internationally and domestically, recognised Aboriginal land rights for the first time, took women's equality seriously and much more.

On the conservative side of politics, the Whitlam Government is of course seen differently: as fiscally undisciplined wreckers of economic growth. In retrospect, we see some merit in the argument that Whitlam's arrogance led him to breach checks and balances his own Treasury sought to put in his path. But we see him more as unlucky in coming to power in the year of the first Organisation of Petroleum Exporting Countries (OPEC) oil shock, when both inflation and unemployment began to rise across the globe.

The puzzle of Gough Whitlam is of a leader who introduced major reforms to increase freedom and equality at a more rapid pace than any Australian prime minister before or since, yet who did a great injustice that cost more than 100 000 lives, causing starvation, torture and tyranny in East Timor.

The next generation of Australian social-democratic leaders displayed similar contradictions. One was Bill Hayden, who became the second most influential member of Whitlam's Government in its final year when the decisions on the Indonesian invasion of Timor were made by Australia, who succeeded Whitlam as leader and became Foreign Minister in the next social-democratic government in 1983. Another was Hayden's successor as Foreign Minister, Gareth Evans. They both made great contributions to UN peacebuilding in Cambodia. After politics, Evans became an influential player on the international stage as President of the International Crisis Group and as a midwife of the Responsibility to Protect doctrine. Hayden and Evans were critics within their party of Whitlam's failure to take his East Timor policy to cabinet for approval and critics of the 1975 Indonesian invasion. Had Whitlam taken it to cabinet, many would have passionately opposed his policy. Yet Hayden and Evans opted to become realists on this issue after 1975. Much as they disapproved of the invasion, it had become a fact on the ground; Indonesia was a powerful neighbour which was not to be trifled with on Timor. More fundamentally, Hayden and Evans believed that to do anything to encourage resistance of Indonesian rule in East Timor would simply increase and prolong the suffering of the Timorese people. So they tended to see the idealists of the Timor solidarity movement as irresponsible.

Their realist analysis seemed from 1975 to 1998 to be almost obviously right, sounding like commonsense. Even if Australia had become an active supporter and fomenter of Fretilin's struggle against Indonesia, the United States and other major players would never turn on Indonesia. Indonesia was of utmost geopolitical significance during the Cold War, having in the 1960s the largest communist party in the world outside China and Russia. It had the largest Muslim population of any country; the West wanted it as an ally in the next great divide in global politics: between radical Islam and the West. If the United States, China, the Soviet Union, Iran and Iraq agreed on anything, it was that Indonesia must be cultivated diplomatically, not crossed.

While the analysis of leaders like Hayden and Evans seemed at the time to fit with the international political context, events proved them wrong. There was a realistic hope for a referendum for the people of East Timor to vote whether they wanted the alleged benefits of integration into Indonesia. That referendum occurred in 1999 and Timor-Leste won its independence. Evans' comment on a draft of this book was that as José Ramos-Horta 'has said to me a number of times since, until Habibie's extraordinary turnaround in 1997 he and his colleagues really believed that substantial autonomy was the only achievable game in town'. Moreover, Ramos-Horta had publicly as well as privately expressed appreciation for the 'behind-the-scenes' work Evans had done at the United Nations towards that objective. In a paper that appeared only in part in *The Australian* newspaper on 27 September 1999, Evans articulated his position as a kind of balanced realism:

> In Australia's Asian environment, playing to the gallery won't keep you out of trouble: most of the time you can be expected to be booed for your idealism by your foreign audience and for your realism by the domestic one. The intelligent course is not to opt for one or the other, but to steer a balanced course between both…Always give pre-eminence to Australia's national interests, but define those interests broadly, as including not only security and economic concerns, but also interests in being, and being seen to be, a good international citizen.

On the occupation, the Evans view in that paper was that

> Australia was in no position militarily to stop or reverse Indonesia's invasion of East Timor in 1975…[and] before the economic crisis of 1997 and its political aftermath changed everything, we all had to live with the fact that there seemed no realistic chance of Indonesia ever agreeing to a fully fledged act of self-determination in which independence was an option.

Yet when the time to replace President Suharto came, Evans argued publicly that Habibie, who had been the member of Suharto's cabinet most open to self-determination options for Timor, and who did in the event support an act of self-determination, was not a sustainable choice, and that a 'military leader' was the best hope 'to end the civil and political crisis'. He thought 'either Wiranto or possibly Prabowo' the likely military leader to take over (Fernandes 2011:172–3), but he hoped for a moderate military leader. This when none of the leading generals of this period, and certainly not these two, would let Timor go on the basis of a referendum, not without leaving it awash with blood. Yet the survival of Indonesian democracy as well as the survival of Timor-Leste were better served by the succession of Habibie and Wahid as non-military presidents who insisted on reform of the role of the military in the democracy.

At another level, foreign ministers like Evans and Hayden, who evinced this kind of balanced realism, are as good as Australian foreign ministers get. Both were peacemakers who believed in what Evans called 'cooperative security' that refuses to privilege military solutions and seeks to prioritise 'habits of dialogue' (Evans 1993; Salla 1997b). As Evans warned, we cannot be so idealist as to think that foreign ministers can survive politically without spending much of their time in realist pursuits, any more than we can expect business leaders to survive without pursuing profits. Yet we can struggle for a republican polity that puts politicians under maximum pressure to eschew war making that might serve some national interest and to honour rights when that comes at a national cost, and for business leaders to act with corporate social responsibility. In other words, Australians can struggle for the kind of networked politics that delivers them foreign ministers that are more like Norwegian foreign ministers than Australian ones, tycoons that are more like Warren Buffet[1] than Australian business leaders.

The argument of this book is that the error of otherwise good leaders was one of misplaced realism. It was the error of discounting a networked politics of hope, discounting patience in politics. It was a failure to understand weapons of the weak, and how and why the weak quite often prevail over the strong in politics. Part of this was a failure to understand people power and the importance of the crowd in history (Rudé 1964), as we have recently seen again on the streets during the Arab Spring. World leaders particularly underestimated the brilliance and the resilience of the networked diplomacy led by José Ramos-Horta and Mari Alkatiri and of the clandestine movement of Fretilin supporters in Timor, Java and Bali masterminded by Xanana Gusmão. While it is important to understand the qualities of these three Timorese leaders, it is more important to understand

---

1 Buffet has given a large proportion of his profits to the Gates Foundation for the conquest of the diseases of poor nations, and emerged in 2011 as an advocate of wealthy people paying the same proportion of their income in tax as the middle class.

the liberation of East Timor as an accomplishment of networked governance across a galaxy of potent nodes. Such nodes included Ramos-Horta's office, the Maputo hub and Xanana Gusmão's prison cell—nodes that tied disparate strands of the network into a coherent fabric. That is what we will describe in the early chapters of this book: the network analysis of power that made the realist analysis a tragic political error.

We will argue that networked struggles for justice, peace and freedom are the mainstay of progressive politics in the kind of world we inhabit today. Bold and brilliant social-democratic reformer though he was, Gough Whitlam wrote a less important page in history than José Ramos-Horta. We will try to show how and why there is much to learn from Timor-Leste on the networked governance of freedom.

Then, from Chapter 4, we describe the networked governance of tyranny in Timor. In politics, there is commonly a tipping point where a networked governance of freedom becomes a networked governance of tyranny. This of course most often happens when a networked revolutionary vanguard of any complexion actually takes over a state. Whether it is a Lenin with a more progressive politics than the aristocracy he helped overthrow, or a Yeltsin with a more progressive politics than the party machine he helped displace, the networked power that is a force for liberation quickly becomes one for oppression when the key node of the oppositional network absorbs the commanding heights of the state. As Hannah Arendt (1963:86) put it: 'Politically speaking, one may say that the evil of Robespierre's virtue was that it did not accept any limitations.'

Our normative analysis, based on civic-republican political theory, is that when networks of freedom fighters take over a state, as in several 'Arab Spring' states today, the transition is always dangerous. Timor-Leste illustrates the danger as a politics of hope soured to a politics of despair, particularly in 2006, when the chatter of automatic weapons once more dominated the capital and people fled burning homes once more. Our theory is first that networked countervailing power must always be quickly asserted against a vanguard that captures a state, whether it is the state captured by Gough Whitlam or Xanana Gusmão. We will argue that between 1999 and 2002 the encompassing network infrastructure of the Conselho Nacional de Resistência Timorense (CNRT: National Council of Timorese Resistance) was dismantled too quickly; political participation networks were narrowed around the leadership, instead of expanding to embrace wider circuits of civil society. Memories of the trauma of civil war between Frente Revolucionária do Timor Leste Independente (Fretilin: Revolutionary Front for an Independent Timor) and União Democrática Timorense (UDT: Timorese Democratic Union) in 1975 fuelled fear of political-party pluralism initially, with some members—though by no means all—of the Fretilin elite manoeuvring for a one-party state.

However progressive the politics of the leader, civic republicans can never hold firm in their faith in a leader. It is not only that power tends to corrupt anyone; it is also that power in the hands of a deft practitioner of networked resistance from below is particularly likely to corrupt. Decades of evading intelligence networks are good preparation for running a secret police that is effective in intimidating people. We see this throughout history as networked resistance of historical tyrannies in the hands of Lenin in Russia, Mao in China and Sukarno in Indonesia became more terrible tyrannies in their politically skilful hands. Our theory is further that networked resistance to the good leader who can control bad forms of power is not enough. There is also a specific imperative for networked campaigning for separations of powers that progressively become more separated. We make a case from the history of Timor-Leste for progressive struggle for continuous improvement in securing ever more separated powers; not just for a classical republican tripartite separation of powers between an executive, legislature and judiciary, but for much more variegated and indigenously attuned separations of ever more powers; not just separations of government powers, but division of both private and public powers. Eisenhower's concept from the 1950s of breaking up the military-industrial complex in the United States captures part of this idea. Not just struggle for a new democratic constitution that guarantees for all time a separation of powers, but for an ever evanescent constitutionalism that struggles to continuously deepen separations of powers at every stage of a nation's history.

This is the theoretical prism through which we see the political successes and failures of UN peacebuilding and state-building in Timor-Leste (Chapters 8–13). We find fault in the way the United Nations failed to coax and caress separations of powers that might work in post-conflict Timor. Yet there are revealing strengths as well as weaknesses in Timorese peacebuilding: a politics of hope is alive and kicking in Timor-Leste. Chapter 13 concludes that in future we might evaluate international peace operations according to

- how well they fix problems
- how much of the responsibility over the fix they shifted to locals
- how they have contributed to separations of the power to fix.

We consider in Chapter 8 the challenges of transitional governance, in Chapter 9 of transitional security, in Chapter 10 of transitional justice and in Chapter 11 of transitional social and economic development. Chapter 12 focuses the republican analysis on feminist politics of non-domination. Chapter 13 considers the prospect that precisely because Timor-Leste has been so tested by tyranny and so resilient in resistance to it, we should not discount the possibility that one day it will take separations of powers up through the current ceiling to a new global benchmark.

In our history, we consider the failures of the Indonesian state to grapple with the 'realities' (non-realist realities!) of the networked warfare choreographed by the genius of Xanana Gusmão. This is an irony as Indonesia itself was a creation of networked insurgency. The Indonesian military continued to use a networked warfare strategy against Fretilin, by enrolling martial arts groups and indigenous Timorese militias into the conflict. We study the failures of the Indonesian state to grasp how the East Timor clandestine network (Rede Clandestina) could enrol[2] the Indonesian democracy movement by being a major contributor to its student front (Chapter 5). We consider how that democracy movement could enrol even Suharto's Vice-President to its project of *reformasi*, where part of the *reformasi* package became a referendum for East Timor. Vice-President Habibie became convinced that *reformasi* would enable him to succeed Suharto as President. We ponder the networking paradox that the very gang networks (militias and martial arts groups) enrolled by the Indonesian military on its side of the conflict were differentially enrolled by competing Timor-Leste factions that split Timor open in the violence of 2006–08. We analyse the contemporary corruption of economic development in Timor-Leste. It includes enrolment by the current Timor-Leste political elite of business elements from Suharto's crony capitalism and business entrepreneurs from the Indonesian military who once dominated Dili (Chapter 11).

Rule of law is analysed as an accomplishment that can be forged by networked politics (Chapter 10). Concrete experience also shows networked politics to be a principal threat to the rule of law. Hence, a crucial question becomes what kind of networked politics can realise its promise for the rule of law while transcending its corruption of the rule of law. Networked governance for the rule of law that also regulates networked corruption of the rule of law takes a particular form that we attempt to describe. In the context of Timor-Leste, this is a form that is about village justice contesting state justice and vice versa.

We do not see networked governance for freedom that is then corrupted to become networked governance of tyranny as just a problem of the constitutional moment in the history of a nation when the oppressed become the rulers. Chapter 6 discusses the hard case for republican theory of the politically decisive Santa Cruz Cemetery massacre of 1991. Santa Cruz was at the same time a dazzling accomplishment of networked governance for freedom, and for tyranny (perpetrated by the forces of freedom). Santa Cruz was the most terrible transitional moment a republican or a liberal could imagine. And new challenges arise a decade after peace and democracy, and continuously after that, as we illustrate throughout the book.

---

2   Our use of the concept of enrolment in this book leans theoretically on Bruno Latour's (1986, 1987) translation theory of power as enrolment of other actors.

We seek to make a contribution to the political theory of why realism is so often misplaced, why networked governance is a more important vehicle for freedom than realist power. At the same time, we seek to show through the Timor-Leste case why networked governance can be freedom's greatest enemy. And we seek to develop an argument about what can be done about it. It is an argument for a contemporary civic-republican politics of endless struggle for networked governance of freedom and for continuous improvement in separations of powers. Principled engagement and responsive regulatory theory provide a philosophy in our work for developing practical tools of nonviolent struggle for non-domination and separations of powers. These ideas are developed in Chapter 3.

Chapter 12 considers feminist politics in Timor-Leste as a case of networked governance of freedom (and tyranny). We suggest a feminist politics in the civic-republican tradition first recorded by Mary Wollstonecraft is evident in the concrete struggles of many Timorese feminists. We find in contemporary Timorese feminist praxis a path and a vision for continuous networked struggle for emancipation. Chapter 12 shows that the women of Timor-Leste have not surrendered meekly to their exclusion from power. We argue that feminist struggle is like social-democratic politics in that concentrations of (male) power are resilient, which means that gains are never consolidated permanently. Nevertheless, institutionalised separations of powers can increase the durability of gains. Checks and balances, institutionalised through bureaucracies that enforce women's rights for example, make it harder for entrenched male power to dominate totally.

At its foundation, civic-republican theory is about continuous struggle towards a society without domination, where no men or women are slaves to others (Pettit 1997). This is a destination that can never realistically be attained, but is more closely approached in some societies than others. Our book contributes to republican and feminist theory by showing that non-domination for women requires a much more variegated set of separated powers than simply a separation of the executive, legislature and judiciary and requires a networked as opposed to a statist pursuit of non-domination. For example, we find in Chapter 12 that women's clandestine networks during the long conflict, often organised through churches (as we also found in Bougainville and Solomon Islands), women's rights networks at the United Nations, international women's non-governmental organisations (NGOs) and an electoral architecture that guarantees women at least one-third of parliamentary seats all played parts in supporting the struggles of Timorese women for non-domination.

The networked governance tradition in political theory is primarily a descriptive one. It is about the empirical observation in a world of global business networks, trans-governmental networks (Slaughter 2004) and global NGO networks that governance can be more important than government (by a state), that networked power can be more important than hierarchical bureaucratic power. One reason for this is that nodes in a network often enrol (Latour 1986, 1987) bureaucratic hierarchies to their projects, as Ramos-Horta ultimately came to enrol key bureaucracies of the Portuguese state, then the Australian state, then the United States and the United Nations. Fretilin enrolled even key concentrations of power within the Indonesian state at points in this history, illuminating the consummate power of networked jujitsu that flips the bureaucratic power of an adversary against itself. Scholars such as Sorensen (2006; Sorensen and Torfing 2006) and Rhodes (1997; Bevir and Rhodes 2003) worry that the explanatory theory of networked governance is not paralleled by a normative theory of dangers that tempers its strengths. We hope this book will prove a constructive contribution to forging such a theory by bringing the explanatory power of networked governance (Castells 1996) together with republican and feminist normative theories and with concrete historical praxis in Timor-Leste. We hope the result is a novel amalgam of explanatory and normative theories that illuminates emancipatory politics.

That foreshadows our conclusions. First, in Chapter 2, we briefly summarise the history of Timor-Leste that is the political crucible for these lessons. And at the last, the Appendix describes the Peacebuilding Compared project that led to the collection of our data in Timor-Leste, and some details of the wider ambitions and methods of this project that will see us monitor Timor-Leste and 50 other conflicts until 2030.

2. A Brief History of Timor

Knowledge of the ancient indigenous history of the island of Timor is limited. Prior to colonisation, Timor was divided into dozens of small kingdoms ruled by traditional kings called *liuri*. They were reliant on slash-and-burn agriculture. The Dawan or Atoni, who might have been the earliest settlers of the islands from mainland Asia, came to occupy the 16 local kingdoms (*reinos*) in the west of Portuguese Timor at the time of colonisation. The Belu or Tetun migrated to Timor in the fourteenth century, creating 46 tiny kingdoms in the east of the island by pushing the Dawan to the west (Fox 2004; Therik 2004:xvi).

Perhaps as early as the seventh century, Chinese and Javanese traders were visiting Timor with an interest in the plentiful sandalwood on the island. This was the same resource that attracted the Portuguese a millennium later, as well as trade in Timorese slaves (Kammen 2003:73). Coffee was introduced as a significant export after 1815. The Chinese, Javanese and later the Portuguese continued as the dominant international influences in Timorese history. James Dunn (2003:9) reports that ethnic Chinese dominance of commerce was formidable in East Timor prior to the Indonesian invasion: 'In the early 1960s, of the 400 or so wholesale and retail enterprises in the Portuguese colony all but three or four were in Chinese hands. The latter were controlled not by Timorese but by Portuguese.' The Chinese, on Nicol's (2002:44) estimate, controlled 95 per cent of all business in East Timor in April 1974. Coffee production, however, was dominated by a Portuguese corporation, SAPT (Hill 2002:8–9). Much of the Chinese elite was slaughtered or fled in the Indonesian invasion[1] or the UDT–Fretilin fighting that preceded it (Dunn 2003:178), their commercial dominance supplanted by a Javanese elite of cronies of President Suharto, many of whom were also Chinese.

The Portuguese were the first European arrivals on Timor, in 1511 establishing a foothold in what is the contemporary enclave of Oecussi when Dominican friars started creating converts to Catholicism. The Portuguese capital shifted to Dili in 1769. Dutch colonisation started in 1568, with the Dutch East India Company building a fort and trading centre during the seventeenth century in Kupang—today the largest city in Indonesian West Timor. While the Dutch and Portuguese arm wrestled across several centuries for notional sovereignty, neither had significant sway over the kingdoms outside their trading ports. Portuguese interest was limited; the colony was administered from Goa until

---

1   Dunn (2003:245) reports that in the invasion hundreds of Chinese were killed—often just the men, after being separated from their families. In one large slaughter, 'a group of Chinese community leaders who, it seems, had come out into the street to offer some kind of welcome to the vanguard of the "New Order" were gunned down'.

1896, with Chinese traders always more influential forces on the ground than the Portuguese. The 1859 Treaty of Lisbon ended the intermittent conflict between the proxies of the Portuguese and Dutch on Timor. It gave the eastern half of the island plus the enclave of Oecussi to Portugal, the rest to the Dutch.

Portuguese colonialism to some seemed benign in Timor compared with its other colonies only because it was on such a loose rein. As Wise (2006:20) points out, it included a substantial slave trade and common use of forced labour for cash crops, road construction and other purposes right up until 1974. In the early twentieth century, the Portuguese took slightly more interest in consolidating their limited control, especially over taxation. This provoked a rebellion led by Manufahi *liurai*, Dom Boaventura, in which forced labour was an important grievance. His rebellion won significant support across the territory. It was put down after a loss of possibly 25 000 lives in 1912.

Japan drove Australian troops from Kupang in 1942. Surviving Australian forces fled across the border into the neutral Portuguese territory of East Timor. This drew Portuguese Timor into the conflagration, with an invasion of 20 000 Japanese troops who were harassed by the hit-and-run tactics of Australian forces and East Timorese allies. Until this happened Japan had had no intention of invading East Timor (Scott 2005:7), partly because Germany was concerned that Portugal not be drawn into the war on the Allied side. By the end of the war, perhaps 40 000 to 60 000 East Timorese had lost their lives (Dunn 2003:22) and many women had experienced sexual slavery. At the end of a guerilla campaign, most of the Australians escaped back to Australia with the loss of only 40 men (Pilger 1994:237).

Scott describes this terrible suffering after Australia's intentional strategy of dragging East Timor into World War II as the first of four Australian betrayals of the people of East Timor in recent history. The second was Prime Minister Gough Whitlam's declared support for the integration of East Timor into Indonesia long before a reluctant President Suharto had been persuaded of this course. The third betrayal was when the United Nations, with prominent involvement from Australia, guaranteed the people of East Timor that they could vote for independence or for autonomy within Indonesia without fear. When widespread killing broke out after the result was announced, predominantly Australian UN personnel were ordered back to the greater security of Dili and then were evacuated from the country. As in World War II, many individual young Australians showed extraordinary acts of bravery in defending Timorese, as in unarmed Australian police officers standing between a militia member with a weapon and the Timorese citizen he was about to shoot. The dishonesty and duplicity of Australia as a nation were what betrayed Timor through its leaders, not the magnificent young people who went to do the impossible job on the ground in East Timor. David Scott nominates as the fourth betrayal that Australia knew from its intelligence intercepts that the Indonesian Army planned the 1999 slaughter and scorched-earth policy that it implemented; yet Prime Minister John Howard failed to press the Indonesian leadership forcefully enough on this and convinced himself that Australian intelligence might prove incorrect.[2] A fifth betrayal in our view that occurred since Scott's book was published was the coercive negotiation of oil and gas rights with Timor-Leste over the disputed aspects of the post-independence border with Australia, as discussed in Chapter 11. A related sixth betrayal that Scott did not highlight was the refusal at various stages to grant asylum to desperate Timorese who fled to Australia:

> With all this high level political maneuvering aimed at positioning to take advantage of these rich oil reserves, Australia began to refuse asylum to East Timorese refugees so as not to cause offense to Indonesia. There was a sense in Canberra that it was time to 'put the East Timor issue to bed'. When 1,200 refugees arrived in September 1994, Australian immigration authorities took the cynical position that, because the East Timorese held Portuguese citizenship and were not facing persecution in Portugal, they were therefore not entitled to claim the protection of Australia. This was a bizarre and contradictory position, given that Australia had argued forcefully in the International Court of Justice against any claim by Portugal to speak for the East Timorese when the Portuguese challenged the legality of the Timor Gap Treaty…In 1996, one East Timorese asylum seeker appealed the Refugee Review Tribunal's adverse finding on his claim for asylum. As a consequence of the Federal Court judgment in his favor, in three other East Timorese cases the tribunal deemed that Portuguese nationality was inapplicable and ruled in favor of the East Timorese concerned. However, the Australian government appealed these decisions in July 1997. After deliberately dragging out the appeal process until the end of 1999, the government decided to drop its appeal in the Federal Court against the asylum seekers, opting to return to the normal refugee determination process. By this time, however, the referendum in East Timor had taken place, and this group no longer had any claim to asylum. (Wise 2006:46)

The Carnation Revolution

The Portuguese dictatorship of Antonio de Oliveira Salazar, succeeded by Marcelo Caetano, was overthrown by the peaceful 'carnation' revolution of 1974—named after the flowers placed in the military's guns by demonstrators.

---

2   This is discussed in more detail in Chapter 7.

Because decolonisation was part of the spirit of the revolution, a space was created in East Timor for liberation movements and political associations. The two main parties to emerge were the Associação Social-Democrata Timorense (ASDT: Timorese Social Democratic Association), later renamed Frente Revolucionária do Timor Leste Independente (Fretilin: the Revolutionary Front for an Independent East Timor), and União Democrática Timorense (UDT: the Timorese Democratic Union). The founders of Fretilin were mostly very young, and included Nicolau Lobato, Mari Alkatiri and José Ramos-Horta. Francisco Xavier do Amaral was invited by the founders to join them because he was older (Hill 2002:62–61). UDT initially favoured 'progressive autonomy' under Portugal with a right to self-determination, though it then moved to support for independence when it became clear that this was a more popular policy with the people of East Timor.

Figure 2.1: Democracy demonstrators lead the carnation revolution in Portugal by placing flowers in the barrels of soldiers' guns

Photo: Reuters/Picture Media

In the context of the Cold War and its own recent purges of communists, Indonesia worried that communist elements in Fretilin might establish a communist satellite or a base for insurgency in its midst. Another specific fear of the Indonesian intelligence establishment was a Soviet naval base in the midst of Indonesian waters. Indonesian intelligence operatives in Dili were active both in a failed attempt to establish an influential party supportive of integration with Indonesia (Apodeti: Associação Popular Democrática Timorense/Timorese Popular Democratic Association) and in persuading UDT that they should shun democratic alliance with Fretilin. The Indonesian intelligence agenda was to divide pro-independence forces and create internal chaos. This succeeded in ultimately enabling them to justify to Western allies that an Indonesian takeover was necessary to prevent Marxist rule.

On 11 August 1975, UDT broke a four-month coalition government with Fretilin, mounting an armed movement to control the territory and exclude Portuguese and Fretilin influence in order to assure Indonesia that East Timor would not be a breeding ground for communism. This followed a meeting of UDT with General Ali Murtopo in which he conveyed a message from his leadership that a communist government would not be tolerated, but that there might be support for independence under a staunchly anti-communist government (Bertrand 2004:137). In addition, Indonesian intelligence fed UDT the line that Fretilin was planning a coup that would exclude them from power, so they had better get in first.

Within 10 days of UDT's attempted coup, Fretilin reversed UDT's attempt to seize armed control. Most Timorese within the colonial military were successfully recruited by Fretilin to reverse the UDT insurrection. Leaders of all the significant non-Fretilin parties, including UDT and Apodeti, fled across the border into West Timor. Some forged common cause with Indonesian invasion plans, though most did not, realising by this stage they were being used by Indonesian intelligence. UDT and Apodeti fighters made almost no military contributions to the invasion. For weeks before the full-scale invasion, Indonesian Special Forces pretended to the United States to be UDT and Apodeti troops engaging in armed incursions across the border into East Timor. One reason for this was to create the impression that the UDT–Fretilin civil war that had ended was ongoing. The intent was to manufacture a pretext for an Indonesian occupation to end the chaos. The full-scale invasion arrived on 7 December 1975. When it did, Fretilin members killed large numbers of UDT prisoners.

Richard Woolcott (2003:158–9), while not conceding that Australia made any mistakes in its own realist diplomacy of 1975, quotes with relish the generous way Ramos-Horta has acknowledged mistakes on his side:

> [W]e the East Timorese, in 1974 and 1975, were inexperienced, immature and irresponsible in not grasping the opportunity of independence with wisdom. Instead we engaged in civil war…thus we played into the hands of the hardliners in Indonesia…so blaming Australia and the United States is a bit one-sided. I always hope that the East Timorese side can be humble enough to say that we were inexperienced, immature and stupid.

Woolcott goes on to quote Ramos-Horta as saying that Fretilin's unilateral declaration of independence in November 1975 was 'a tactical political error', though on Woolcott's own account an error made long after invasion was inevitable and indeed clandestinely under way.

During the mid-1970s, there were atrocities by Fretilin against UDT, and vice versa. As we have found in all cases of Peacebuilding Compared to date, the conflict created opportunities to settle scores that had nothing to do with the war. In his testimony to the Comissão de Acolhimento, Verdade e Reconciliação (CAVR: Truth and Reconciliation Commission), President of Fretilin in 1975, Francisco Xavier do Amaral, said that some used the conflict to seek vengeance against those responsible for firing them from their jobs (CAVR 2006:Part III, p. 47). Current Prime Minister, Xanana Gusmão, put the diverse drivers of score settling in the UDT–Fretilin conflict this way:

> Sometimes this wasn't because they had a problem with them about this [political] situation, but from an old problem. I know that sometimes it was because someone had taken someone else's girlfriend and so now he used it as a chance to beat him. I know this. People took advantage of this war to beat others and to take justice into their own hands. But some did beat others because they were angry at them due to the war… [I] want to say that in this process of war so many died…it is true that Fretilin killed many UDT prisoners…UDT also killed Fretilin prisoners. (CAVR 2006:Part III, p. 43)

In June 1974, East Timor's Foreign Affairs spokesman, Ramos-Horta, had pulled off the first of a long list of diplomatic triumphs. He obtained a letter signed by Indonesian Foreign Minister, Adam Malik, welcoming the prospect of an independent East Timor (Dunn 2003:54). The letter assured that 'the government as well as the people of Indonesia have no intention to increase or expand their territory'. It was not long before Malik was forced to retreat from this view by the more powerful intelligence lobby in the Indonesian polity. While military defeat was the short-term upshot of Ramos-Horta's consummate networking between friends in different Timorese factions and potential enemies in Jakarta, his gifts at grafting power by networking others to do his running for him, rather than by thrusting himself forward as a supreme leader, were evident from the beginning. On some accounts, Ramos-Horta was the most influential force in shaping ASDT and Fretilin (and their coalition with UDT) because he had the ability to listen, be responsive and harness both the radical and the more conservative elements in Fretilin (Nicol 2002:135–53). He also worked with Timorese student leaders returning from Portugal (Hill 2002) to arrange new organisational bases of influence, helping to inspire the formation of the National

Union of Timorese Workers, the National Union of Primary School Teachers, the National Women's Organisation and the National Youth Organisation (Nicol 2002:153).

While the networking strengths that in the long run saw Fretilin prevail to create an independent Timor-Leste were palpable in 1975, so was its intolerance of difference and of differentiated power. This was manifest in the murder of UDT prisoners. Fretilin declared from the outset that it was 'the only legitimate representative of the people' (Dunn 2003:25). It disagreed with the Portuguese Governor's pleas for the army to remain impartial guarantors so 'that the people of Timor will be able to freely choose their future' (Nicol 2002:170). At every stage, the Fretilin view was that the military (Falintil) must become a pillar of unity with Fretilin in pursuit of national liberation. Dalliance with communism was always less of a political danger in Fretilin than interest in the ideology of a one-party state. Western diplomats persistently misdiagnosed these dangers in reverse importance, even after Mikhail Gorbachev came to power in Moscow in 1985, and the Cold War began to thaw.

3. Unprincipled Engagement and Misplaced Realism from 1974

I know that I am recommending a pragmatic rather than a principled stand but this is what national interest and foreign policy is all about.

— Australian Ambassador to Indonesia, Richard Woolcott, 17 August 1975, advice to Prime Minister Whitlam that the gap in Australia's Timor Sea border that was vital to settling offshore petroleum rights could be more easily settled with Indonesia (quoted in CAVR 2006:Part 7, p. 28)

[M]y overall assessment of that policy [Australian policy towards East Timor] during the 25 years under consideration is that it was mostly a failure. There was failure to support an underlying principle of the United Nations and of international law and justice: the right of all people to self-determination. And there was failure to work to restrain Indonesia from the path of military intervention and aggression in 1975.

— Former Australian Foreign Affairs official Dr Henry Chan (quoted in CAVR 2006:Part 7, p. 32)

This chapter characterises the diplomacy of Australia and the West more broadly towards Timor as realist and unprincipled. Then it seeks to develop the road not taken as 'principled engagement' (Pedersen 2008). This alternative path is illustrated by the Obama–Clinton diplomacy towards Burma and Arab states. The chapter then argues that responsive regulatory theory is helpful in revealing the mechanisms that can give principled engagement both bite and integrity. Responsive regulatory theory seeks to transform institutions while minimising resort to either violence or stigmatisation of adversaries. Without being pacifist, responsive regulatory theory renders 'violence as a last resort' as more than just a slogan. It develops a philosophy and a practice of exploring alternatives to violence in a sequenced and principled way, avoiding stigmatisation of adversaries at every layer of a regulatory pyramid.

Unprincipled Australian Engagement

Australian Prime Minister Gough Whitlam in 1975 believed in and practised decolonisation (in Papua New Guinea, for example). Yet he and his advisors worried that the decolonisation occurring in the hundreds of smaller islands in the oceans around Australia was leading to many new nations of fewer than a million people that would not be economically viable even with decades of foreign aid. Whitlam saw East Timor as another of these island micro-states that would find it hard to lift its people out of poverty.

The boundaries the colonial powers drew between the Dutch East Indies and Portuguese Timor in the 1859 Treaty of Lisbon did not track any clear cultural lines; they simply split the island down the middle and also carved out the western Portuguese enclave of Oecussi, where the Portuguese had a trading centre.[1] In Australian eyes, there were no mature political parties or political movements in the early 1970s that had crystallised public opinion. There were certainly many new young leaders who advocated an independent East Timor, but others spoke for joining Indonesia. Whitlam felt integration would be best for the economic future of the people of East Timor. President Suharto seemed to be doing a good job of stabilising the Indonesian economy after the unsteady hand of the Sukarno years. Corruption might have been rife at the top, but at the same time the conditions of the poor were improving. Considering as well that Indonesia had proved resiliently inclusive of Christians, and that there were large numbers of Christians in West Timor, embrace within the same province of this developing republic seemed the best outcome to Whitlam.

Whitlam's opponents accused him of being soft on communism because he consistently opposed the Vietnam War and withdrew Australia's participation in it as soon as he came to power. In fact, Whitlam was a solidly anti-communist social democrat. There was a determined revolutionary socialist minority within Fretilin, and Whitlam became open to some of the misinformation Indonesian intelligence agents within East Timor were generating that these elements were much more in charge of Fretilin than they really were. Whitlam, however, did not believe the Indonesian intelligence fabrications that China and the Soviets, even Vietnamese military advisers, had infiltrated East Timor in ways they had not. Whitlam listened to the concerns of the Indonesian intelligence establishment that a pro-communist regime in the midst of the Indonesian archipelago would be destabilising, and a Soviet naval base in Dili would be a particularly large strategic setback,[2] given the importance of the deep ocean trough north of Timor for nuclear submarines to slip undetected between the Indian and Pacific oceans. BAKIN (Badan Koordinasi Intelijen Negara: State Intelligence Coordinating Agency), the Indonesian Army's central coordinating intelligence agency from 1969, had been patiently floating the idea of integrating Portuguese Timor into Indonesia (Taylor 1999:23), and in mid-1974 developed a plan, Operasi Komodo (Operation Giant Lizard),[3] to destabilise and take Timor (Taylor 1999:31), with the academic think tank the Centre for Strategic and International Studies (CSIS) (Fernandes 2011:26–8).

---

1   There was actually local support for the enclave remaining Portuguese (Farram 1999).
2   That this would divide Indonesian waters into two zones was a particular concern of Lieutenant-General Benny Moerdani (CAVR 2006:Part I, p. 22).
3   One Timorese civil servant who was working at brokering peace agreements between gangs on the streets of Dili in 2006 made the interesting point that 'they should admit that Operation Komodo was very successful in that it turned them against each other'.

3. Unprincipled Engagement and Misplaced Realism from 1974

Figure 3.1: Toasting series: Whitlam toasts Suharto

Photo: National Archives of Australia

In September 1974, Whitlam met with BAKIN officers on the way to a meeting with President Suharto (Taylor 1999:32). At that point BAKIN was making more headway with persuading Whitlam that an independent East Timor would be a political threat to the region than it was with its own president. Suharto and Foreign Minister Malik were taken aback with how forthrightly aligned Whitlam's views were with those of BAKIN at their subsequent meeting. Indeed, influence between BAKIN and Whitlam was likely two-way. A 14 October 1974 cable to Canberra from Austalia's Ambassador in Lisbon quoted BAKIN General Ali Murtopo as saying 'that until Whitlam's visit to Djakarta they had been undecided about Timor. However the Prime Minister's support for the idea of incorporation into Indonesia had helped them to crystallise their own thinking and they were now firmly convinced of the wisdom of this course' (Documents on Australian Foreign Policy 2000:119). Murtopo was not an advocate of full-scale invasion during 1974 and the early part of 1975 in the way Benny Murdani and some other generals were. Until the time of the invasion, President Suharto rejected the counsel of the latter group and supported Murtopo's thinking that Special Forces destabilising Fretilin would ultimately allow Indonesia to engineer something like the fraudulent Act of Free Choice that allowed the United Nations to deliver West Papua to Indonesia in 1969 (Fernandes 2011:20, 30). Perhaps Whitlam was influenced by the belief that this was what Murtopo and Suharto were aiming for rather than an invasion.

Networked Governance of Freedom and Tyranny: Peace in Timor-Leste

3. Unprincipled Engagement and Misplaced Realism from 1974

Figures 3.2a–c: Fretilin supporters rally in Portuguese Timor, 1975

Photos: Penny Tweedie/Panos

The stories of Chinese, Vietnamese and Soviet military infiltration of East Timor were so inconsistent that it did little credit to Western nations that they did not dismiss Cold War security concerns about Timor as fanciful or exaggerated. Former Australian consul in Dili James Dunn (2003:187) sees the Whitlam Government as particularly culpable in allowing Indonesia to paint the false picture in late 1975 that a destabilising civil war was raging inside East Timor, when in fact the short UDT–Fretilin war was over:

> [I]n late September when Indonesia was trying to maintain the fiction that the civil war was still raging, the Australian government could have exposed it as a lie. Not only did the Whitlam government not do this; as we have seen, official spokesmen went out of their way not to discredit

the accounts from Jakarta which they knew to be fabrications. In a way
the Whitlam government joined with Indonesia to prevent Fretilin from
gaining international credibility. (Dunn 2003:187)[4]

Whitlam communicated his view to Suharto and other world leaders that the
best interests of the people of Timor, Indonesia and Australia and of their
alliance with the United States would all be served by the island of Timor being
unified within Indonesia. As soon as Fretilin gained control of Timor, Australia
cut off most shipments of petroleum to Timor on grounds that Fretilin might
use them militarily (Kohen and Taylor 1979:104). Until August 1975, President
Suharto had been resisting the advice of his military leadership for more than
a year that integration of East Timor into Indonesia—by force if necessary—
was the best course (Scott 2005:106–7). Whitlam might have been advised that
Indonesia was more firm in its resolve to annex East Timor than it was (CAVR
2006:Part I, p. 19). Suharto and a number of senior generals were opposed to
an invasion; their view changed only after Fretilin had soundly defeated UDT.[5]
The invasion of West Papua had come at a cost, particularly diplomatically and
in world opinion of Indonesia, which did seem to Suharto to be worth the fight.
But would the forced integration of East Timor be worth it, given that Timor did
not seem to have the resource riches in gold and energy that were apparent in
Papua? Suharto's reluctance proved prudent in retrospect because the economic
cost of development transfers to Timor became huge (several times as high as for
other provinces), as did the military cost of thousands of Indonesian soldiers'
lives, and a diplomatic cost that was so high that the integration could not be
sustained in the medium term. Suharto was also worried that an invasion could
bring US modernisation of his armed forces to a halt (Documents on Australian
Foreign Policy 2000:376). The Indonesian intelligence establishment, particularly
BAKIN, was whipping the Indonesian public into a state of indignation with
fabricated stories such as of a Fretilin cross-border attack that killed seven

---

[4] Gerard Stone's account in *The Times*, as the first journalist to enter East Timor after the civil war broke out, put it this way: 'Strangely, it is in the interest of all three governments—Portuguese, Indonesian and Australian—to make the situation appear as chaotic and hopeless as possible: Portugal: To explain away its loss of face and inability to pursue any further colonial responsibilities. Indonesia: To justify intervention and the eventual forced reunion of the island. Australia: To conceal its shameful rejection of a cry for help. In that light, I am convinced that many of the stories fed to the public in the past two weeks were not simply exaggerations: they were the product of a purposeful campaign to plant lies' (*The Times*, 2 September 1975). As far as we can tell, Australian parliamentarian Ken Fry, who went to Timor with a cross-party committee, was accurate in his UN testimony when he said that all Australians who actually went to Timor during the months of the Fretilin Government were impressed at the way it had stabilised the country: 'Like all other Australians who visited Timor during this period, I came away full of admiration for the Central Committee of the Fretilin party. I was tremendously impressed by their moderation, by their integrity and by their intelligence in dealing with a very difficult situation' (Kohen and Taylor 1979:27).

[5] An Australian Foreign Affairs cable reported Bian Kie, the Private Secretary of the Indonesian military commander, as providing intelligence that '[a]s recently as National Day celebrations on 17 August [1975] the President had refused to give the green light to a deputation of top generals who sought a ruling on East Timor policy. Indeed, according to Bian Kie, the President made some disparaging remarks about Murdani's desire for a military solution' (Scott 2005:106).

villagers in West Timor (Taylor 1999:59). Even much later than August 1975, Suharto's reluctance was still in play. Australian Ambassador Richard Woolcott reported that: 'As a senior general remarked to me in an unguarded moment early in November 1975: "We have to act but we still have to persuade the old man to agree"' (2003:138).[6]

Whitlam's enthusiasm for integration helped persuade Suharto to back his military leadership's plan to prepare for invasion.[7] In 1975 Saigon fell—the high point of US disengagement from Asia. The United States had long respected Australian intelligence assessments of its own region. More than at any time before or since, in 1975 the United States was willing to defer to Australia as the Western experts on Indonesia. Other Western governments similarly 'looked to Canberra for intelligence and policy advice on the issue' (CAVR 2006:Section 7.1, p. 23). Commentators on different sides, such as Richard Woolcott (2003:151–2) and Desmond Ball and Hamish McDonald (2000), could agree that the Australian Embassy in Jakarta was better informed than any other about Indonesian plans for East Timor during 1975, even more than the Indonesian Foreign Ministry and all other Indonesian agencies outside the inner circle of top generals and intelligence officials.

US President Ford and Secretary of State Kissinger had no stomach for muscular intervention in the East Timor question.[8] Yet Whitlam's analysis made sense to the US intelligence community. So when Ford and Kissinger visited Indonesia on 6 December 1975—the day before the invasion—they did not object, indeed said they understood Indonesia's good intentions, but asked that the invasion not commence until they had left Jakarta. Kissinger also warned that 'the use of US-made arms could create problems'[9] (Scott 2005:112; see also Burr and

---

6 An 18 August 1975 Woolcott cable said: 'Receiving reports from his senior advisers twice daily, the President is at present firm in his attitude that Indonesia should not intervene militarily in Portuguese Timor at this stage. Concern about Australia's reaction, the Non-Aligned meeting in Lima, the forthcoming session of the General Assembly, and his wish to concentrate his resources on Repelita II [the national economic plan] are all factors in his present attitude' (Taylor 1999:52).

7 Leadbeater (2006:35) found that '[o]n 14 October 1974, the Australian Ambassador in Lisbon was told by General Ali Mortopo that Australian support for the idea of incorporation helped his team "crystallise their own thinking" and overcome indecision about East Timor. After the Whitlam visit they were "now firmly convinced of the wisdom of this course".' They then used Whitlam's support as one of their arguments with Suharto.

8 The Kissinger papers include a report of a meeting of Kissinger with his closest advisors on 12 August 1975: 'We have taken the position that the US should eschew involvement in the Timor situation and leave its resolution to the Indonesians, Portuguese, Australians and the Timorese themselves' (Scott 2005:107). Indeed, a 17 August 1975 cable from Richard Woolcott said that the US Ambassador to Indonesia had told him that 'he is under instructions from Kissinger not to involve himself in discussions with the Indonesians… and to cut down its reporting on Timor' (Documents on Australian Foreign Policy 2000:314). The British Ambassador similarly advised his government: 'Britain's interest is that Indonesia integrates that territory…if there is a crisis and a debate in the UN we shall all keep our heads down and avoid taking a position against Indonesia' (quoted in CAVR 2006:Part I, p. 19). In addition to the realist interests the United Kingdom shared with Australia, British companies became major suppliers of the weapons used in that reign of terror over the people of East Timor.

9 On the same day, waiting in an outside hall while the two presidents met, Brent Scowcroft from the US National Security Council asked Indonesian military commander Benny Moerdani straight out: 'Will you be

Evans 2001). The Ford–Kissinger visit to Jakarta resulted in the doubling of US military assistance to the Indonesian Government for the following year (Kohen and Taylor 1979:35).

What Australia's Western allies probably did not understand at that time was that, unlike them, Australia saw itself as having a profound economic interest in the integration of Portuguese Timor into Indonesia. Australia, in the words of an Indonesian Foreign Minister we interviewed, had irrevocably taken them 'to the cleaners' in a 1972 seabed agreement with Indonesia. Portugal, in contrast, was adopting a much tougher negotiating position on licensing petroleum exploration off the Timor coast that would be in Australia's part of the Timor Sea bed under the terms of the Indonesian agreement.[10] When Indonesia took over East Timor, Australia believed this contested oil-rich seabed would fall into the lap of Australia (Cleary 2007:12–14). Indonesia actually toughened its negotiating position after the invasion, but eventually Australia did secure most of the rights to the Timor Sea oil that it coveted. After the invasion, Australian oil interests successfully lobbied for Australia to be the first country to recognise Indonesian sovereignty over Portuguese Timor (Taylor 1999:75).

Whitlam did not urge an invasion of East Timor. He simply articulated a preference for integration and then showed a reluctance to urge his friend Suharto *not* to invade, even in October 1975 after the killing in Balibo of five journalists from Australian media organisations covering the armed encroachments of Indonesian forces across the border (Scott 2005:107). Instead of defending the human rights of its journalists, and protesting publicly when it was well aware that the journalists were killed because they were exposing an Indonesian invasion dressed up as a civil war, the Australian Government opted for a cover-up. While Whitlam always made it clear he did not support enforced integration, but integration 'in accordance with the properly expressed wishes of the people of Portuguese Timor' (Scott 2005:147), he continued to back integration when it was clear this would occur at the point of a gun without the support of the people of East Timor. In 1982, as a former prime minister—notwithstanding the fact that an act of self-determination by the people of East Timor had never occurred—Whitlam pressed: 'It is high time that the question of East Timor was voted off the United Nations agenda and ceased to preoccupy and distract the nations of South-east Asia and the Pacific' (quoted in CAVR 2006:Ch. 7.1, p. 84).

---

using US weapons?' The General knew it was illegal to do so under the terms of their sale, but gave an honest answer: 'our military is built largely around US systems. We have no choice' (Conboy 2003:242).

10   'It would seem to me that this Department might well have an interest in closing the present gap in the agreed seabed border and that this could be much more readily negotiated with Indonesia by the closing [of] the present gap than with Portugal or an independent Portuguese Timor' (Australian Ambassador to Indonesia, Richard Woolcott, Cablegram to Canberra, 17 August 1975).

Australian Labor Party policy was self-determination for the people of East Timor. Whitlam never took the question of the likely invasion of East Timor to cabinet, or, as far as we know, confided with any member of his cabinet about the nature of the conversations he was having with Suharto. Whitlam knew that the invasion was going to occur, but he was looking the other way, declining to raise his voice against it, in violation of the policy of his party. Had Whitlam decided to defend the principles of the UN Charter, and persuaded the United States and the United Nations to warn Suharto off the invasion, as James Dunn (2003) and Matthew Jardine (2000) have argued, Indonesia might have been persuaded to abandon it. Indeed, given how uncertain Suharto himself was as to whether the invasion was prudent, it is possible that had Whitlam discouraged rather than encouraged it in his conversations with Suharto, and made it clear that Australia would oppose an illegal invasion at the United Nations, this might have been enough to tip the Indonesian policy scales against the invasion. José Ramos-Horta (1987:78) put it more strongly when he referred to a US Central Intelligence Agency (CIA) analysis of this question: 'There is no doubt in my mind that if Australia and the United States had cautioned Suharto against invading unilaterally in East Timor, the invasion wouldn't have taken place.' As Ball and McDonald (2000:23) put it:

> [F]or a self-perceived statesman anxious to project Australia as an independent actor in its region, Whitlam showed a remarkably pessimistic assessment of Canberra's ability to sway the Indonesians from their path, exert positive influence in East Timor itself or marshal support for a principled approach among friendly countries. Deriding the motives of all suggesting otherwise, he saw no way between the two stark alternatives of facilitating an Indonesian takeover—by any plausible means that could be sold to the Australian public—or going to war.

When Bill Hayden first took over from Whitlam as Labor leader in opposition, he found the forced integration of Timor 'inexcusable, unjustifiable, illegal and immoral' (Scott 2005:169). He reversed this posture as Foreign Minister in the Hawke Labor Government from 1983, concluding that self-determination for East Timor was a hopeless cause, and less important than securing Indonesian support for an Australian-led peace initiative for Cambodia.[11] Hayden's successor as Foreign Minister in the Hawke Government, Gareth Evans, also thought that Whitlam had erred in not being faithful to Labor policy of self-determination in 1975, but, like other Western foreign ministers, he froze out Ramos-Horta, accepting the invasion as a fact on the ground. He gave priority to good relations with Indonesia, which were critical to the considerable accomplishment of

---

11 In this period, Cambodia also caused the Soviet Union to further soften its support for Fretilin when it sought Indonesian backing to replace the pro-China Khmer Rouge with the pro-Soviet Heng Samrin Government in 1979 as Cambodia's representative to the United Nations (CAVR 2006:Part 7.1, p. 46).

launching the first genuinely multidimensional UN peacekeeping operation in Cambodia. Prime Minister Bob Hawke similarly endorsed a pragmatic recognition of the importance of maintaining warm diplomatic collegiality with Indonesia, and with President Suharto in particular. Likewise with his Labor prime ministerial successor, Paul Keating. During the Liberal Government of 1975–83, Prime Minister, Malcolm Fraser, and Foreign Minister, Andrew Peacock, also legitimated East Timor's integration (Woolcott 2003:161).

There is realist contagion in diplomacy. Once Australia had become a firm supporter of legitimating the occupation, a realist argument for the United States doing likewise was that this would consolidate its regional alliance with Australia, and, more fundamentally, once the United States was locked in to the legitimacy of the occupation, a realist concern for Australia was to continue to support the United States in this. The testimony of Assistant Secretary of State Richard Holbrooke to Congress in 1981 not only made this point, but also canvassed a host of realist arguments (that mostly also applied to Australia) for the United States to support Indonesia on East Timor

- Indonesia is strategically important because it is such a large, influential yet moderate member of the Non-Aligned Movement
- it is an 'important oil producer—which plays a moderate role in OPEC'
- there are important US business and trade interests in Indonesia
- it 'occupies a strategic position astride the sea lanes between the Pacific and Indian Oceans'
- it is an influential Muslim country whose leaders 'have publicly called for the release of our hostages in Iran'
- its influence in the Association of South-East Asian Nations (ASEAN) is important, particularly with potentially destabilising developments in Indochina (CAVR 2006:Ch. 7.1, p. 59).

In its about-face on Australian Labor Party policy on self-determination for East Timor, the Labor elite set itself on a course that would become out of tune with the feelings of most Australians, whose hearts became very much with the people of East Timor. The Australian people over time came to see the East Timorese as underdogs crushed by an illegal invasion that their Australian Government was too weak to stand up to.[12] Australia did not get the realist pay-off of the warm relationship with Indonesia in the months after the invasion that was the

---

12 Indeed, this was an elite-citizens tension evident from the beginning. A 31 March 1975 Foreign Affairs brief for Prime Minister Whitlam stated: 'A trade union and student group, led by Mr Jim Roulston, has also recently returned from Timor. Ministerial correspondence on the subject is increasing; it invariably calls on the government to adopt a robust stand with Indonesia over Timor. Another strand of opinion has stressed the special obligation we have to the Timorese because of the help extended to the Australian "Sparrow Force" during the war…In the last few weeks too the Australian press has descended on Timor; its reporting

objective of its diplomacy. Suharto became extremely angry that an Australian government, wary of the negative reaction of its electorate to the invasion, did not speak and vote as strongly in support of Indonesia at the United Nations as it did privately to them. Moreover, 'Jakarta appeared to hold the Australian government responsible for the activities of "its" public and press, sections of which vociferously opposed the invasion' (Kohen and Taylor 1979:105).

The Fraser Government that succeeded Whitlam persisted with a low-integrity realism. This realism was recurrently lose-lose for Fraser's relationships with Indonesia and with the Australian people. For 11 months, the Fraser Government angered the Suharto regime with its protests that it had no legal basis for shutting down a Darwin radio that was the only way for the resistance to get information out of East Timor to the United Nations and the world's media on the atrocities that were occurring there. Then in October 1976, Fraser enraged many Australians and the media when he ordered the Commonwealth Police to seize the transmitter. Realism is a theory that becomes untrue in practice when a democratic government seeks to implement a realist agenda that its people do not share. There is no fact of the matter of what the national interest is; the national interest is what people think it is. As Robert Putnam's study of the Bonn G-7 economic summit showed, international relations is not a simple realist game of balancing the power and rational interests of the national players; it is a two-level game (Putnam 1988) that must simultaneously be played across the table of international politics in front of each diplomat and across their own table of domestic politics that sits behind each nation's diplomats. Politicians can play hands that lose them a lot of chips at both tables. On Timor, Australian leaders certainly lost at both international and national tables between 1975 and 1999.

In Chapter 5, we will see how Australian public opinion sympathetic to East Timor was cultivated by a solidarity network inspired by Ramos-Horta and by outraged veterans who had only survived World War II with the support of East Timorese fighters and helpers against the Japanese. Tom Uren, a senior and admired figure in Whitlam's cabinet, was one of them. Uren was perhaps one reason Whitlam never took East Timor to cabinet.

Australian political and diplomatic leaders saw themselves as being more worldly wise and responsible than the Australian people, whom they saw as led by their hearts more than their heads. Prime ministers and foreign ministers drew support from what has often been disparagingly called the 'Indonesia lobby' among Canberra policy elites. Benedict Anderson (1996) was one of the first to use the term 'Indonesia lobby', in a 1986 paper that described the efforts

---

has occasionally been tendentious and it has overdrawn the Indonesian threat…as well as the attitude of groups like Amnesty International…But domestic political factors may be nudging us further into the Timor quagmire' (Documents on Australian Foreign Policy 2000:233).

of Ali Murtopo, Benny Murdani, Harry Tjan and Jusuf Wanandi (a CSIS group instrumental in planning the takeover of East Timor). This group made a 1975 visit to the United States to cultivate a network of pro-Indonesia academics and diplomats, dangling research visas, among other incentives. As with Anderson in the United States, in Australia there were many scholars of Indonesia such as Herb Feith who were consistently outspoken critics of Indonesian policy in East Timor, and Australian diplomats such as James Dunn, who took a similar line. It is fair to say, however, that the dominant ethos of Australian diplomats who were experts on Indonesia—of whom the most influential was Richard Woolcott—was of engagement with Indonesia that was uncritical, indeed supportive, of East Timor's integration into Indonesia. The leading Canberra scholars of the 'Indonesia lobby' were likewise uncritical on this issue, even if they were critically engaged on other issues.

The authors are friends and admirers of many of the scholars in our college, the then Research School of Pacific and Asian Studies (now the College of Asia and the Pacific) at The Australian National University, who were the intellectual defenders of what we call unprincipled engagement with Indonesia over East Timor. They formed a distinguished and decent group of people who sincerely believed that they were advocating an engagement between Indonesia and Australia that was in the best interest of the peoples of the two nations by ensuring productive trading and security relationships. Scholarly critics of the pro-Indonesia policy network in the East Timor solidarity movement have argued that they were excluded as critics from the funding opportunities, the influence with Canberra–Jakarta elites, and even from access to Indonesia, which the scholars of the Indonesia lobby enjoyed between 1975 and 1999. While this might be true, we do not see unprincipled engagement as venal and careerist, but as an error of analysis of what was best in the long run for Indonesia, for Australia and for East Timor.

Nor was the pro-Indonesia policy network monolithic; it was as riddled with factions and hard-fought differences of opinion as the solidarity network. Most members, among both its diplomats and its scholars, thought that both Whitlam and Woolcott went too far in urging integration so early and so strongly; some offered written advice to that effect. What distinguished the approach of one network from the other was the willingness to confront Indonesia at every opportunity over its human rights abuses. The pro-Indonesia network did not; its members felt nothing would be achieved by resisting an invasion that would never be reversed, that harm would be done to Australian interests by offending Indonesia.

The Idea of Principled Engagement

Before concluding that Australian policy on East Timor from 1975 to 1999 was one of unprincipled engagement with Indonesia, let us recount the history of the idea of principled engagement. It is an idea that has been applied to how corporations might engage with authoritarian or military regimes while sustaining fidelity to principles of corporate social responsibility (Holliday 2005), to how NGOs with a commitment to peace might engage with militaries as partners in humanitarian and development work in poor countries (Thompson 2008), but most widely to how democratic states committed to human rights might engage with states that are the worst abusers of human rights.[13]

The history of different states' engagement with Burma since the arrest by its military junta of Aung San Suu Kyi following her 1990 election victory has defined the development of the concept. Under pressure from human rights groups, and general outrage in Western public opinion, the imprisonment of the charismatic Oxford-educated, Westernised Suu Kyi led most Western nations to renounce Burma as a pariah state. From 1991, ASEAN, of which Burma became a member in 1997, aggressively rejected Western stigmatisation of Burma, announcing its alternative policy of 'constructive engagement' (Malik 2000:247). Indonesia has always been the most influential member of ASEAN, no less so than in development of the policy of constructive engagement with Burma. This began in the year of the Santa Cruz massacre in East Timor, which led to Indonesia for a short period in 1991 becoming almost the pariah in Western public opinion that Burma had continuously been. But all ASEAN states to varying degrees resented the sanctimonious way the West stigmatised them as states that did not take human rights seriously. In the 1990s Prime Minister Mahathir of Malaysia was outspoken in this regard, particularly against Australia. Singapore's Lee Kuan Yew was a prominent interlocutor with the view that Asian values were different from Western ones. 'Asian values' included the idea of respectful acceptance of one another regardless of records on human rights.[14] Asian values were said to imply stronger responsibilities to states and weaker rights against the state. In a sense, what happened with Burma is that the West so overplayed its hand in stigmatising the regime as a human rights pariah that the majority of the world that is Asia (with China and India[15] being

---

13   See the research project Principled Engagement: Promoting Human Rights by Engaging Abusive Regimes. This joint project between the United Nations University, Sydney University and the Australian Defence Force Academy is co-directed by Morten Pedersen and David Kinley. It will involve a dozen leading scholars and practitioners from around the world and will address an important gap in the academic literature on international statecraft, as well as provide concrete lessons and recommendations for policymakers. It will develop a theoretical model of principled engagement and undertake a series of case studies to elucidate how it works in practice.
14   For a discussion of the 'Asian values' debate, see Boll (2001); Milner (1999); Sen (1997).
15   India decided to abandon its isolation of Burma by allowing it to join ASEAN in 'constructive engagement' from 1994 (Malik 2000:247).

particularly sympathetic to ASEAN constructive engagement on Burma, and Japan not unsympathetic) dealt a global setback to the legitimacy of the global human rights regime.[16]

What happened to the human rights regime has parallels with Western–non-Western diplomacy on all the central issues, such as democracy, that define the Western good governance canon of late modernity. So when Australia and New Zealand treated Fiji as a pariah following each of its three coups since 1987, mobilising support to exclude it from the South Pacific Forum, the Pacific Island Forum and the Commonwealth, Melanesian neighbours, notably Vanuatu and Papua New Guinea, dissented from Western stigmatisation of Fiji. They maintained warm relationships of 'Melanesian brotherhood' with the coup leaderships, embracing them within the bosom of the Melanesian Spearhead Group of states, believing that Melanesian ways of not cutting off wrongdoers were a more effective approach to the shared objective of restoring democracy in Fiji.

The problem with ASEAN's (and India's and China's) constructive engagement with Burma of course was that it gave the message that the rest of Asia did not care if Burma abused human rights. This was different from the more principled engagement of Vanuatu with Fiji, which was very much about saying that democracy matters, but our brotherhood with each other also matters. Morten Pedersen (2008) has developed theoretically the policy of principled engagement with Burma. It means friendly diplomatic and trading relationships with Burma that are also unremittingly firm in protesting the imprisonment of democracy advocates and in communicating disagreement with all specific human rights abuses as they arise. Such a relationship with the West is believed by principled engagement advocates to have the advantage of persuading Burma to allow Western NGOs to operate inside the country. By supporting bottom-up engagement of Burmese civil society with their country's profound problems of delivery of health, education and anti-poverty programs, small steps are taken towards Burmese civil society learning to be democratic. The problem of completely cutting off Burma from the West is not only that its sick and poor are also cut off from donor help. It is also that Burma is cut off from the nurturance of civil society, from the development of social capital (Putnam 1993), so that if one day the junta steps aside in favour of genuine democracy, there will be people and institutions ready to lead the democracy from below. There will be the resources for a networked governance of freedom to resist post-junta nodes of tyranny.

---

16 On the unproductiveness of the 'Asian values' debate, see Bell (2000); Ghai (1994); Hanreich (2009); Sen (1997); Thompson (2001).

Educational development of elites in waiting is particularly critical here. Education helps economic development under a junta, which on the one hand supports the survival of the junta; on the other hand, education is an immediate assistance to the poor of Burma, contributing to the alleviation of their poverty and suffering. In addition, it lays a foundation for a future democracy that might actually work rather than disintegrate, and creates an educated constituency that might demand democracy at the ripe moment for transformation. The rational contemporary incumbent of the junta can look at this proposition and calculate that education spending makes the people better off in the short term, thereby shoring up in the short term the legitimacy of a junta that makes him rich and powerful. At the same time, he might calculate that a more educated community increases long-run prospects of democratic transition. His rational calculation can be that enhanced short-term survival prospects certainly benefit him, while reduced long-term prospects of survival might be more likely to hurt his junta successors after he retires. At least, he might calculate that way if he is not a young junta member.

The International Crisis Group (ICG), for which Morten Pedersen worked on Burma, became the most internationally influential vehicle for the doctrine of principled engagement. As early as 2002, it applied principled engagement to peacebuilding in Liberia (ICG 2002). During this period, the International Crisis Group was led by none other than Gareth Evans, the very Australian Foreign Minister from 1988 to 1996 who we conclude continued the unprincipled engagement of his predecessors Bill Hayden and Andrew Peacock with Indonesia over East Timor.

In 2009, the doctrine of principled engagement came of age when US Secretary of State, Hilary Clinton,[17] and President, Barack Obama, gave prominent speeches in which they argued for principled engagement as the new US policy towards Arab and other states such as Burma with whom their relationship was fraught (MacAskill 2009). In late 2010, the Burmese junta seemed to respond in a limited way, releasing Aug San Suu Kyi unconditionally (while continuing the confinement of some 2000 other political prisoners) and holding flawed elections that were boycotted by Suu Kyi's National League for Democracy. Since then there has been some further gradual but significant progress towards democratic institutions.

---

17 'We will pursue principled engagement with those who disagree with us' (Hilary Clinton, viewed 9 May 2011: <http://www.state.gov/secretary/rm/2009a/july/126071.htm>), also a theme in President Obama's landmark Cairo speech (viewed 9 May 2011: <http://www.whitehouse.gov/the-press-office/remarks-president-cairo-university-6-04-09>). Harold Koh (2010) has described 'principled engagement' as the first of four commitments of an emerging 'Obama–Clinton Doctrine'.

Responsive Regulatory Theory and the Principled Engagement Debate

Responsive regulatory theory is helpful in clarifying some of the dilemmas of engagement in diplomacy. Our analysis here distinguishes three options: one is tolerance and understanding of violation of an international norm, of a criminal state and its crime (such as a crime against humanity or a crime of aggression such as an illegal invasion); a second is stigmatising a crime and a criminal state (as in treating Burma as a pariah state, or defining Iran as a rogue state—part of an 'axis of evil'); a third is respectful engagement with the state and its people while firmly disapproving its crime. This third option is principled engagement. This way of describing the compliance method of principled engagement reveals that compliance method to be reintegrative shaming. Reintegrative shaming theory (Ahmed et al. 2001; Braithwaite 1989, 2002) argues that if a society shows tolerance and understanding towards a form of criminal behaviour, that form of crime will increase. So if a society gives a green light to family violence by never confronting it with disapproval, family violence will be rife; if citizens just laugh when their friends and neighbours are heard to have cheated on tax then tax cheating will become widespread.

Yet reintegrative shaming theory asserts that shaming crime is not necessarily a superior policy to tolerance and understanding. It all depends on how the shamefulness of crime is communicated. Stigmatising shaming makes crime worse; reintegrative shaming reduces crime. Stigmatisation treats the criminal as a bad actor who has committed a bad act. Reintegrative shaming treats the criminal as a good actor who has committed a bad deed. Stigmatisation is disrespectful shaming (as in treating Burma as a pariah); reintegrative shaming communicates disapproval within a continuum of respect for the offender (as in principled engagement that sustains a respectful relationship with Burma). Stigmatisation has rituals that certify criminality (like the pronouncement of guilt in a courtroom) without rituals to de-certify deviance (like a truth and reconciliation hearing and report in which some victims forgive the criminal). Reintegrative shaming places importance on the termination of the certification of criminality by various kinds of restorative justice rituals that de-certify deviance, and that embrace the offender back into the community of the law abiding. This de-certification of deviance might or might not depend on expressions of remorse by the wrongdoer, listening to victims, apology and offers of reparation. We will not sidetrack here onto the various ways this is done. The point is that a third distinction between stigmatisation and reintegrative shaming is that reintegrative shaming pays a great deal of attention to ceremonies to de-certify deviance once remorse, reform and repair occur.

Reintegrative shaming theory has been applied to both individual and organisational law breaking. Makkai and Braithwaite (1994) found that 331 nursing homes inspected by inspectors with a reintegrative shaming philosophy experienced 39 per cent improved compliance with the law in a follow-up inspection two years later. Nursing homes inspected by stigmatising inspectors suffered an equivalent drop in compliance two years later, while homes checked by tolerant and understanding inspectors suffered an intermediate fall in compliance (see Figure 3.3). Obviously, the data suggest that this is a major issue with inspection effectiveness—the difference between making things 39 per cent better and 39 per cent worse. It seems that both being nasty and being nice to lawbreakers can be counterproductive, while being firm but fair in a respectful way can work. When this result was first published, one referee wondered whether inspectors 'can really have such an impact in one inspection'. The qualitative fieldwork for that nursing home compliance research suggested they often have even larger effects than a 39 per cent improvement when respectful confrontation of nursing home crime is a catalyst of a major process of corporate deliberation.[18] It is not just the single encounter; the subsequent staff meetings and the soul-searching at subsequent quality-assurance committee meetings are what can be triggered when inspection is firm, respectful and forgiving.

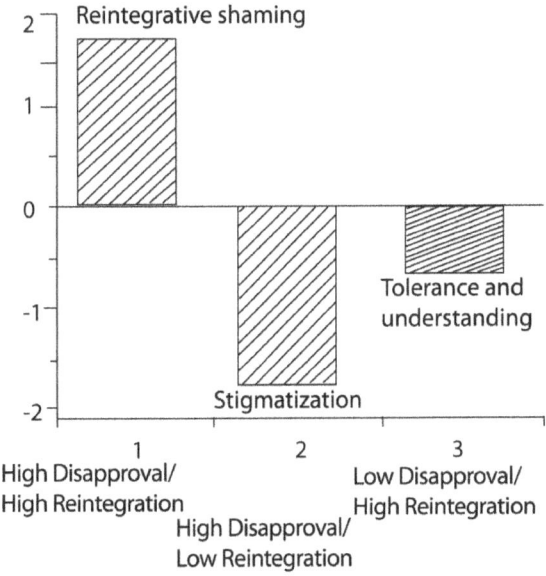

Figure 3.3: Improvement in compliance. Mean improvement in compliance for nursing homes where inspectors used high disapproval and high reintegration styles; high disapproval and low reintegration styles; low disapproval and high reintegration styles

Source: Makkai and Braithwaite (1994)

---

18   See Braithwaite et al. (2007:Ch. 3).

Low disapproval/high reintegration (unprincipled engagement) maps onto the way Australia responded to Indonesian crimes in East Timor between 1975 and 1999. None of the Australian Prime Ministers of this era gave speeches firmly disapproving the illegal invasion of East Timor and the human rights crimes that followed the invasion; all of them made it a priority to have a close and friendly relationship with President Suharto, the youngest of them (Keating) respectfully addressing him as *bapa* (father). High disapproval/high reintegration maps onto the Obama–Clinton policy of principled engagement with Burma. High disapproval/low reintegration maps onto the old US policy of stigmatising Burma as pariah state, just as with the 'axis of evil' states. The Makkai and Braithwaite (1994) data also showed that respectful confrontation of the seriousness of non-compliance works best when inspectors know the chief executive of the nursing home well. This tracks the conventional diplomatic wisdom that if a head of state has a warm and respectful personal relationship with another head of state, he or she will be better able to communicate disapproval of specific conduct of concern by that state. Of course, states are larger, more complex organisations than nursing homes. Yet we do think there are some principles of respectful engagement with leaders of general relevance to steering any complex organisation that breaks a law. Even more broadly, the reintegrative shaming literature argues that whether it is parents raising children or inspectors regulating businesses, nattering at bad behaviour does not work;[19] what works is a history of respectful engagement that allows us to face bad behaviour and engage the wrongdoer by making a case that this is not something that should be tolerated in a civil society.

While this is far too sweeping a generalisation, there is something to the hypothesis that Western social control is much more prone to oscillate between liberal tolerance and understanding and stigmatising outcasting[20] than non-Western social control. Certainly, non-Western audiences are regularly perplexed by sudden shifts to stigmatise them—for example, Saddam Hussein of Iraq. In the 1991 war, the articulated US policy was to humiliate Saddam Hussein so he could not rise again with a reputation as a dogged fighter in the Arab world. Saddam actually thought the United States would respond to his invasion of Kuwait in the same way as it responded to Suharto's invasion of East Timor: public denunciation for the benefit of human rights critics, with a nudge and a wink to him (Simpson 2004:458). The error of diplomacy with Saddam Hussein was that the US Ambassador to Iraq in a critical meeting failed to communicate

---

19 For the negative impact of 'nattering' by parents who scold their children often but do not follow through to ensure compliance, see Patterson (1982). A nattering parent might tell their son to stop hitting his sister as they walk from dining room to kitchen without stopping to ensure the violence stops and to ensure it is understood how important this is.

20 This is tempered by the fact that non-Western societies have been greatly influenced by globalisation of the Western mentalities of the core outcasting institutions invented by the West: stigmatic criminal law and the prison.

to him that the United States was prepared to escalate up the kind of regulatory pyramid discussed in the pages that follow. Indeed it was prepared to escalate right up to war, but it did not convince Saddam of that until he had already committed his troops to battle. Reintegrative diplomacy is most likely to work when it occurs in the shadow of the political capacity and will to escalate. That is why the diplomacy of Hans Blix and Kofi Annan with Saddam Hussein later in the 1990s can be seen in retrospect as so effective in persuading him to dismantle his considerable weapons of mass destruction program. Kofi Annan said to him, reintegratively, in one meeting for which we have a transcript:

> You're a builder, you built modern Iraq. It was destroyed once. You've rebuilt it. Do you want to destroy it again? Look how you talk about the suffering of your people. It's in your hands, we can do something about this. If we can work out an agreement that will prevent military action and you would undertake to comply, it will save the day. (Shawcross 2000:241)

This was a good example of principled engagement with a ruthless tyrant that worked, just as it seems to be working for the moment in Burma and in various places across the Arab Spring. It worked without escalation in Tunisia and Egypt, and with escalation in Libya. With hindsight, Kofi Annan's principled engagement with Iraq (backed by the implied threat of force) seemed effective. UN inspections and sanctions worked; Iraq had ceased to pose any kind of credible military threat to Kuwait, Israel, the United States or even to the state the United States had wanted Iraq to threaten, Iran, where the United Nations and its peacekeepers had also effectively brokered a peace. President George W. Bush and his American mass media organisations believed, and internationally promoted the belief, that President Hussein's performances for the 'dangerously naive' Annan and his weapons' inspector, Hans Blix, were a charade. Annan and Blix for their part believed in a trust-and-verify presumption that Saddam could be persuaded to walk his talk. They believed war would make the world less safe by risking new cycles of violence in the Middle East.

On our theoretical view, stigmatisation reduces the prospects of a dangerous leader becoming a more democratic political leader, of decreasing domination, renouncing terrorist violence. Most bouts of twentieth-century terrorism ended with the integration of some terrorist leaders into legitimate politics after they renounced violence (Karstedt 2005)—whether it was terrorism in Northern Ireland, Israel or South Africa, or the terrorism of the Italian Red Brigades, the Baader–Meinhof gang in Germany, militias in East Timor, or the Bougainville Revolutionary Army in Papua New Guinea. It simply does not help to label an Israeli prime minister a terrorist because he once committed terrorist acts. Even if there is some truth in the view that his renunciation of political violence is hypocritical, a performance for Western publics, we do better to eschew scoffing at his talk of nonviolence; we want him to walk the talk. Hence, the stupidity of

Western leaders like Dick Cheney in opposing the release from prison of Nelson Mandela because he had been an advocate of armed struggle against an elected government—Mandela the terrorist who had blown things up.

Asian leaders particularly do not warm to being constantly niggled over their human rights record in ways that do not amount to sincere, problem-solving communication. Interestingly, the Peacebuilding Compared project has concluded that Indonesian social control over terrorism has been unusually effective, with Indonesia experiencing sharp reductions in terrorism that other Muslim societies have not yet seen. Indonesia was the nation in the world with the biggest terrorism problem at its peak in 2002; today Indonesia experiences low rates of violence of all forms (Braithwaite et al. 2010a:Ch. 1). One of the strategies that has helped accomplish this has involved showing respect and kindness to convicted terrorists, engaging them with religious leaders whose theology and practice they respect in every way other than the renunciation of violence, helping their families and helping them to find productive alternative forms of employment on their release from prison. At last, the West is learning from this Indonesian wisdom in the way it is conducting what the West disastrously called the 'War on Terror'.

When the West stigmatises a society like Indonesia or Burma—because of differences between Western and Asian modalities of social control—the outcome can be particularly counterproductive. One of the counterproductive effects of stigmatisation demonstrated by criminological research is that those who are rejected reject their rejectors. Being rejected, they have a status problem. They then solve that status problem collectively with others who have been similarly rejected. They turn to find support in a community of the similarly rejected; they find respect in a criminal subculture precisely because they are so rejected by mainstream society. The tragedy is that this oppositional subculture further reinforces criminality, excuses it, and teaches methods for executing crime with greater professionalism and impunity.

This is the same general social dynamic that occurs when Asian societies rejected by the West band together to reject their rejectors by glorifying 'Asian values' and vilifying Western human rights discourse. It is the dynamic of certain members of Muslim societies together turning to excuse violence against the West, together seeking to build a new caliphate, after generations of humiliation and stigmatisation by the West. Our hypothesis is that Western stigmatisation of non-Western actors is even more likely to strengthen collective cultures of resistance to Western norms than Western stigmatisation of Western actors. Obversely, the request of the Non-Aligned Movement, which Indonesia had helped form and which Suharto aspired to chair, that Indonesia withdraw from East Timor (at its 1975 Colombo summit and subsequent summits) was an accomplishment of young Ramos-Horta's diplomacy that did not run this risk. It was, therefore, a particularly strategic form of shaming (Ramos-Horta 1987:160–2; Schwartz 1999:194–229).

In Chapter 11, we apply Sally Engle Merry's (2006) approach of 'vernacularising' rights discourse into local non-Western discourses as a technology of respect. Even more respectful is vernacularising Eastern and southern discourses into global human rights discourse. So we conceive bubbling up influences from non-Western sources into global discourse as part of what is required by principled engagement. Principled engagement, we argue, does not mean abandoning rights universals. It means embedding them more respectfully. It does not mean watering them down; it means infusing them with diverse flavours that help them become more tasty beverages.

Principled Engagement and Sanctions

The debate on principled engagement has been entangled with the debate on sanctions in the case of Burma. Responsive regulatory theory separates these issues in the following way. Responsive regulation means attempting at first to secure compliance with a norm by persuasion, praise for improvement, education, capacity building, restorative justice and other mechanisms of principled engagement with respect and without recourse to sanctions. Then, if principled engagement without sanctions fails and fails again and again to persuade, escalation to sanctions is considered, and when that fails, escalation to tougher sanctions is foreshadowed, then implemented. This is the idea of the regulatory pyramid illustrated in Figure 3.4.

So, responsive regulatory theory certainly positions persuasion, capacity building and other mechanisms of principled engagement as alternatives to sanctions at the base of the pyramid. And the idea of responsive regulation is that most of the regulatory action should occur at the base of the pyramid. Yet it is also part of the theory of responsive regulation that by signalling (without threatening) a credible capacity to escalate to increasingly onerous sanctions, right up to shutting down the criminal organisation, principled engagement without sanctions or threat of sanctions can be more effective at the base of the pyramid. Hence, responsive regulatory theory does not pose a choice of principled engagement versus sanctions. The question is whether principled engagement can work without sanctions, and, if it cannot, what potency of sanctions is required to change behaviour? Then there is a logically prior empirical question of whether principled engagement is more often effective in changing behaviour than stigmatisation or unprincipled tolerance and understanding.

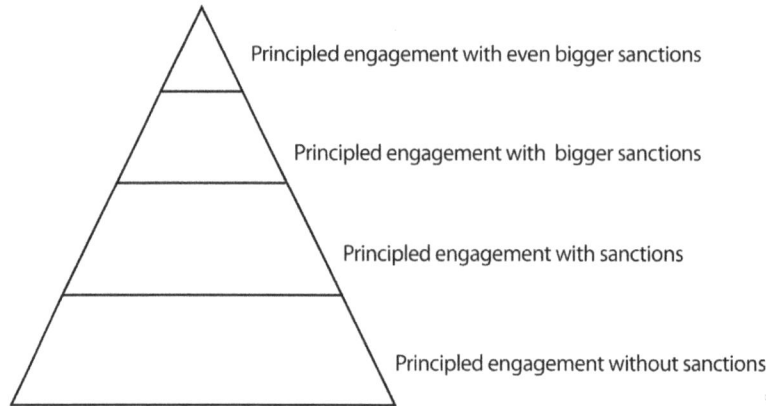

Figure 3.4: A responsive regulatory pyramid with principled engagement and sanctions

In practice, responsive regulation of states that perpetrate human rights abuses tends to be accomplished by escalated networking of informal sanctioning by more network partners in the international system—states, businesses, media organisations, human rights NGOs, traditional chiefs, UN agencies, foundations and other donors—becoming enlisted in a widening web of sanctions against the rights-abusing state: naming and shaming, withdrawal of donor support, trimming trade links, cutting defence support, cutting diplomatic support, terminating the membership of international organisations, and so on. This networked escalation approach to responsive regulation is illustrated in Figure 3.5. When international society finds a way to signal the inexorability of escalation up a credible pyramid of networked regulation, cooperation with principled engagement (without sanctions) can become more effective and widespread.

Unprincipled Engagement with Indonesia

Not only did the Australian Government and Australian scholars of Indonesia succumb to unprincipled engagement with Indonesia after the crime of aggression of 1975, so did the United States, the United Kingdom, other Western and Eastern powers, and the United Nations. None of these actors in the pro-Indonesia network would refer to the invasion as a crime, when clearly it was as a matter of law, no less so than the crime of aggression for which many of these same state actors hanged Prime Minister Tojo of Japan in 1948, or the human rights crimes for which they hanged President Saddam Hussein of Iraq in 2006.

Our first argument is that at least this unprincipled engagement with Indonesia's leadership was not as bad a policy as the stigmatisation directed at Burma. The door was at least kept open to Indonesia and respectful diplomatic relationships were sustained. In the long run, however, if Gough Whitlam had opted for principled engagement, had seriously confronted President Suharto with the view that an invasion would be illegal and that Australia would call on the United Nations to have it reversed by an Indonesian withdrawal, if this had been done from their earliest meeting, and at each subsequent meeting, in circumstances where Suharto and his Foreign Minister, Malik, at first resisted an invasion, it is possible that the United States and European powers would have supported this Australian position, and the spectre of resolute UN opposition to an invasion might have meant it would not have occurred. That principled engagement might then have saved not only more than 100 000 Timorese lives, but also the lives of thousands of Indonesian soldiers, which was a huge drain on the Indonesian budget for 24 years and prevented the international humiliation of Indonesia in 1999 when the occupation ultimately was reversed.

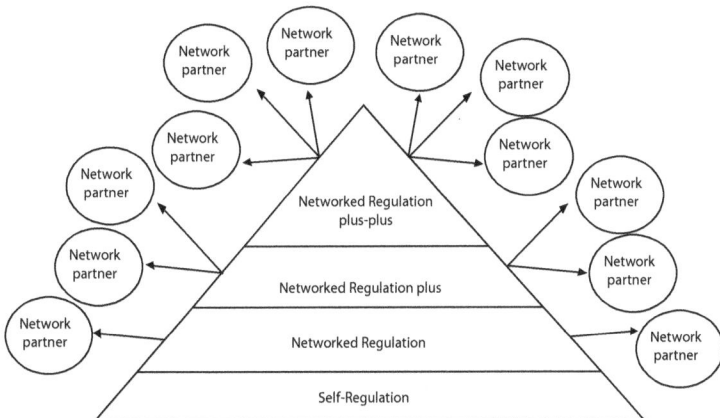

Figure 3.5: An example of a pyramid of networked escalation. This pyramid picks up Peter Drahos's (2004) idea of nodes that tie together networks at each layer of a pyramid

Australia allowed itself to be a bad friend of Indonesia in the medium term by this unprincipled engagement.[21] Our argument is that it served Indonesia poorly because of an error of misplaced realism. At first, Whitlam believed

---

21   Rodney Tiffen (2001:104) concluded one of the more perceptive analyses of the politics of principle versus pragmatism on Timor with: 'Nearly all the assumptions in 1974 and 1975—about what would constitute a pragmatic policy—were proven false over the following quarter of a century. The Indonesian annexation did not produce stability. Australia's pre-emptive acquiescence in Indonesian designs did not produce harmonious relations with Indonesia. East Timor remained a vexatious issue in Australian domestic politics. And the toll in human suffering was horrendous.'

that because Indonesia had the military might to pull off a quick, clean victory over Fretilin forces and because its military leadership wanted to do just that, therefore Suharto wanted to invade (when he did not) and would inevitably either do that or engineer destabilisation that would lead to a West Papua Act of Free Choice fraud. Second, the argument of the rest of this book is that because Whitlam's successors (and US President Gerald Ford's successors, including the human rights champion, President Jimmy Carter) succumbed to the misplaced realism of seeing Indonesia as too important to cross, and their foot as too firmly planted on the throat of East Timor, unprincipled engagement became the policy. While these heads of state were not willing to cross Indonesia, the international solidarity movement, the international media and, ultimately, international society were. The foot Indonesia was believed to have so firmly on Fretilin's throat began to shake after Santa Cruz and more so after the Asian financial crisis, until finally it was removed because of an escalation of networked pressure. Belatedly, after Santa Cruz, Western democracies did begin to move up the two pyramids of Figures 3.4 and 3.5, especially through cutting off new defence technologies and training to the Indonesian military, who cared about these things. And belatedly, it worked. The illegal invasion was reversed and Indonesian crimes against the human rights of Timorese ceased from late 1999.

As influential a network as the pro-Indonesia diplomats, think tanks and scholars was in Australia and across the globe, ultimately it was defeated by a more powerful network of rather hairy people in the clandestine movement domestically and the solidarity movement internationally. Our argument in Chapters 5 and 6 will be that this network mobilised a most effective pyramid of networked escalation that finally caused Indonesian resolve to crumble. Second, we will argue that unwaveringly principled engagement that two hairy young men started in a marginalised mission ended in the office of the President of Timor-Leste. Those men, Xanana Gusmão and José Ramos-Horta, over decades of struggle, manifested the power of principled engagement. They never stigmatised Indonesia or Indonesians; they persistently chastised any racist vilification of the invaders by their followers; they eschewed terror tactics; certainly, they waged a war in defence of their country against the invasion, but it was a war in which they progressively came to opt for minimalist as opposed to maximalist violence. At the end, both quickly forgave Indonesian leaders, even General Wiranto, in open rituals of embrace. They surprised supporters and enemies alike by apologising for the killing they had inflicted on young Indonesian soldiers. Their reintegrative shaming of Indonesia in the 1980s and 1990s was infectious in inspiring ever expanding networks of supporters of East Timor in a way that bore similarities to the way Nelson Mandela inspired both anti-apartheid networks and reconciliation with his white oppressors.

In the film *Invictus*, Mandela flips black support behind the (overwhelmingly white) South African rugby team in its 1995 World Cup campaign. His aide says the experts give South Africa no chance of surviving the quarterfinals. Mandela replies: 'If we believed the experts you and I would still be in prison.' The celebrations after the World Cup victory in South Africa unify the nation in the way Mandela hoped. When the white South African captain accepted the cup, he said that the team was inspired by Mandela—'we won it for our President'[22]—and many of us who were watching wept.

Our argument is that leadership for networked escalation of pressure against human rights crimes can be an accomplishment of inspiring leadership based on principled engagement. But that leadership need not come from international leaders like Gough Whitlam. It can come from a black man in a prison cell on Robben Island; it can come from a junior officer remote in the mountains who takes over the Timorese resistance when all the senior leaders are dead, and later leads from a prison cell in Jakarta; it can come from a Timorese man in his mid-twenties with a limited high school education who works as a cleaner in New York to support his UN networking by day; it can come from young Timorese women who as refugees in Australia and Portugal inspired the patience of the solidarity movement. We argue, however, that unlike Mandela, Gusmão and Ramos-Horta have not yet moved to depersonalise power through humility.

Misplaced Realism

Realist international relations theory does not see refugee women, imprisoned bombers and lobbyists funded by employment as a cleaner as important to shaping history. History according to realist international relations theory is shaped by states in proportion to the military and economic power those states control. It models international affairs as a billiards table on which the bigger billiard balls with more force behind them invariably push aside smaller balls. We can immediately see in responsive regulation's pyramid of networked escalation (Figure 3.4.) why that will recurrently prove to be false. The weak often prevail over the strong in the world system because they can inspire the enrolment of many organisational actors who are stronger than themselves to their cause (Braithwaite and Drahos 2000). Notwithstanding its massively larger military and economy, Indonesia did not prevail over tiny Timor-Leste. As we see in the next chapter, even the purely military part of the invasion was costly. Indonesia did not prevail even though it was supported with military equipment and diplomatically by the United States and all its allies, and by ASEAN in its own region.

---

22 This at least was what he actually said in 1995. He said something a bit different in the film.

That support, and the 1975 victory it delivered in Dili, was pyrrhic precisely because it was based on realism rather than principle. These allies who were supporting Indonesia diplomatically and with weapons and military training were democracies. Australian activists and a good many ordinary citizens look back with distaste on what our country has done on East Timor. Many Labor Party activists who were devotees of Gough Whitlam stood with East Timor once they realised the handiwork of their leaders. Equally, we would expect, though we do not know, that many around US President Jimmy Carter were moved to support the international solidarity movement on East Timor when they discovered that the administration of the human rights president was sending Bronco aircraft armed with napalm to maim and starve ordinary villagers of East Timor. In other words, when realism is too palpable, when engagement is too unprincipled, the kind of people power that is a subject of the rest of this book can swing in to outflank realist power, so long as it is resilient and patient.

This anti-realist analysis applies with special force to democracies when it becomes clear to citizens who believe in human rights, in international law and in the principles of the United Nations that their leaders are flouting these principles for realist reasons. Yet this analysis also applies to non-democracies, the leaders of which must also bring their cadres with them. China was one of the few states to consistently support Fretilin at the United Nations and provide limited resources to Ramos-Horta's diplomacy—though it was realist enough to shy off supplying weapons to Fretilin; Indonesia was after all a major force in Third-World diplomacy networks on which the increasingly soft power of China depended. Fretilin visited Beijing seeking military support on 29 December 1975. Australian Ambassador to China, Stephen FitzGerald, reported on the request for military aid. FitzGerald noted that when the Chinese Foreign Minister said at the opening banquet that 'the East Timorese people…would surely win the final victory on national independence so long as they persevere in self-reliance and hard struggle', he meant 'no' (CAVR 2006:Part 7.1, p. 41). The irony was that the Foreign Minister proved to be right in this utterance that was infected with duplicitous realism. British Ambassador to China, John Ford, opined in a cable of 2 January 1976 that China's strong language in support of Fretilin in the Security Council should not be taken at face value (CAVR 2006:Part 7.1, p. 41):

> Apropos the Fretilin delegation's visit to Beijing and the Chinese ostensible support of Fretilin, the Chinese had apparently commented to the effect that too much notice should not be paid to their support of Fretilin: there were occasions when cannons need to be fired even if only paper balls were shot.

The error of misplaced realism is nicely palpable in this quote now that we can see that the paper balls Ramos-Horta and his network were able to mobilise from widening circles of cardboard cannons ultimately proved more potent than military hardware.

The Character of a Deeper 'Realism'

So what is the opposite of this realism? In Chapters 5 and 6, we will argue that it is patient networking of weapons of the weak. Hard-headed diplomats might say that the opposite of realism is romanticism. There is something to this; yet there is more. That extra element that was manifested by the people of Timor and the international solidarity movement that supported them is a commitment of character, a commitment to sacrifice oneself if necessary to do what is right and just, rather than what is realistic. It involves the unwavering resilience that led so many foreigners who visited places like Vietnam during the US occupation, Afghanistan during the Soviet occupation, East Timor during the Indonesian occupation, and the United States during the Revolutionary War to conclude that these people would never give in. This is well illustrated by the story of Shirley Shackleton, Australian wife of one of the 'Balibo Five' journalists, when she arrived in 1989 to plant a tree in Balibo to honour her husband. Indonesian authorities refused permission to plant it near the place of his death. Finally, a priest offered a place to plant the tree behind his church. Troops sealed off the vicinity to prevent any Timorese witnessing the planting. Shirley Shackleton then described what happened:

> They had not allowed any Timorese to be there…But as I knelt, saying a few words to Greg, the most wonderful singing washed over me. On the other side of the road, a young people's choir had timed its practice to my being there. I shall never forget those beautiful voices. They came through the barrier the Indonesians had set up between us,[23] and they comforted me. You see, that's how the resistance works; everything is pre-arranged but never appears to be. They will never be defeated. (Pilger 1994:273)

---

23 This does not mean the children literally broke through, just their voices (see also Shackleton 2010:241–3).

Figure 3.6: Shirley Shackleton sits next to the grave of her husband, Greg, 9 July 2010

Photo: Adek Berry/AFP

This book is about the difference in character between people who never surrender to crimes against humanity and pragmatists who do give in to what is a realistic pursuit of national interest. The key Australian and American realists who are the lead characters of our drama are old men now. Diplomats like the former Australian Ambassador to Indonesia and Head of the Department of Foreign Affairs Richard Woolcott and former US Secretary of State Henry Kissinger doubtless comfort themselves with the belief that in their time, on questions like Timor, they took the tough decisions in the national interest. Yet they also know that the people of the nations in whose interest they acted do not see it that way. Most of these citizens do not want to be the kind of nation that is duplicitous in betraying innocents. They do not agree that a nation like Australia is better off to be the kind of nation that repeatedly betrays its friends.

Gough Whitlam seems to realise in his old age that he is a greatly revered Australian, but nevertheless perceived as having left one great blemish on our national character. Like Gough Whitlam, Gareth Evans can take satisfaction in his old age that his contributions to humankind have been profound on many fronts. In spite of that, he must know that he is not a figure of affection among the Australian people, that the images that stick in the nation's consciousness are much more of him clinking champagne glasses with the Indonesian Foreign Minister after concluding the Timor Gap Treaty (which would allow drilling for oil to proceed to benefit Australia and Indonesia). They are much more of Evans excusing the Santa Cruz massacre as an 'aberration' from an improving Indonesian rights record. At the end of the day, it is not very realistic for these individuals (or for their nation) to lose their repute as a person of character who hails from a nation of character. They as individuals and their nations as nations come to value more their character and the repute it enjoys than the short-term national objectives pursued with 'realism'.

Figure 3.7: Toasting Series: Gareth Evans toasts Indonesian Foreign Minister, Ali Alatas, flying over the Timor Sea to celebrate signing the Timor Gap Treaty, 1989

Photo: National Archives of Australia

If these men wish to look at the executors of a deeper long-term realism that nations of democratic citizens really do value, they should look to figures they would have called romantic in their time like Nelson Mandela, Helen Suzman, Mahatma Gandhi and Thomas Jefferson who in earlier times were scoffed at as romantics by the diplomatic realists of London and other imperial capitals. All the world's great religions, and a great deal of contemporary psychological evidence, teach paradoxically that we are better off if we do not live a life of maximising our wealth (or power or other realist assets). It is not just that it is right for us to be givers rather than takers; it is that we are better off when we are givers. When realist thinkers about international affairs refuse to apply this insight to the interests of nations and their leaders, they perpetrate a deep error in their understanding of where reality resides in the long run of history.

4. Not So Networked Warfare, 1975–1999

Indonesia's Timor campaign started with a limited form of networked warfare in the latter months of 1975. The main objective of the cross-border military incursions in these months was to sustain an impression of internal conflict by Indonesian soldiers pretending to be Timorese opponents of Fretilin. Their orders were to create 'terror and intimidation'. Small numbers of UDT and Apodeti refugees did accompany them in mainly non-fighting roles; they were networked with the Indonesian forces as 'Partisans'. Actually, Indonesia had been giving military training to Apodeti in West Timor since December 1974 and had been conducting covert operations in East Timor with the support of local intelligence operatives throughout 1974 (CAVR 2006:Part I, p. 5). Except in the latter stages of the cross-border campaign, Fretilin forces acquitted themselves well, inflicting losses on Indonesian forces that found themselves bogged down in the wet season.

Figure 4.1: José Ramos-Horta, second from left, after Indonesian cross-border attacks had begun, but just before the full invasion of Dili, with Xavier do Amaral, second from right, Alarico Fernandes shaking his hand and Xanana Gusmão to his left

Photo: Penny Tweedie/Corbis

The Indonesian military's conception of the real invasion was that it would be a frontal exhibition of overwhelming force to take Dili first. There would be quick capitulation, they thought, in the face of a massive show of force. Well in excess of 20 000 troops landed in Timor during December 1975, later increased to 40 000 (Kohen and Taylor 1979:39) and possibly increasing to 60 000 for certain high points of the deployment (Smith with Dee 2003:41), in addition to large numbers of (former US) naval vessels offshore and air support. General Ali Murtopo confided to a US source before the invasion that 'the whole business will be settled in three weeks' (Burr and Evans 2001:7). Indonesian generals had the more colourful way of putting the shock-and-awe plan: 'breakfast in Dili, lunch in Baucau and dinner in Lospalos' (CAVR 2006:Ch. 7.9, p. 12).

The resistance from Fretilin forces was stronger than expected. The initial landing by many hundreds of paratroops went badly; many were shot by Fretilin forces in buildings along the seafront as they came down; others drifted out to sea and drowned; others landed behind Fretilin lines. Perhaps shock and anger at these early losses contributed to the wanton slaughter that then occurred on the dock and on the streets of Dili, even of Chinese business leaders who came out to welcome them. Chinese families managed to get letters out through places like Kupang to reveal probably hundreds of Chinese killed in the first two days (Kohen and Taylor 1979:78). One of the letters said: 'At 2 pm, 59 men, both Chinese and Timorese, were brought on to the wharf…These men were shot one by one, with the crowd, believed amounting to 500, being ordered to count' (Taylor 1999:68).

Spies identified Fretilin members to be shot; entire families were executed if they had a Fretilin flag at the front of their house; many women were taken out to the warships to be raped and killed. Rosa Muki Bonaparte, charismatic Secretary of the Popular Organisation of Timorese Women, was shot when she resisted being taken to a warship. Others were shot to enable looting of their possessions. The widespread atrocities made no political sense; they were hardly likely to win hearts and minds. Some argue that it was a result of the propaganda that some commanders fed their young charges of the devilish communists and Christians who were the enemy. Whatever the reason, the barbarism and indiscipline, combined with the Indonesian losses and the fact that most Fretilin forces escaped in well-prepared plans to convene in the mountains where their weapons and food were hidden, strengthened the commitment of the resistance. For the next two years, Fretilin controlled most of the country and most of the population fled to these Fretilin-controlled areas. Fretilin claimed 80 per cent of the population under their control in 1976 and 1977.

Figure 4.2: Rosa Muki Bonaparte, second from left, with, from left to right, Mari Alkatiri, Nicolau Lobato and Mau Laka, 1975

Photo: Jill Jolliffe

Fretilin's military wing, Falintil, avoided head-on confrontations with massed Indonesian forces after that first day of the invasion, but inflicted great damage by ambushing small groups of Indonesian troops as they moved around the country in hit-and-run attacks on bases and by sniper fire. Their tactics would seek to split a smaller group of Indonesian soldiers away from the main group, then hunt and kill that smaller group (Interview with Falintil officer, September 2009). Bahasa-speaking Falintil troops dressed in captured Indonesian uniforms would walk into a camp to check that only a small number were there at the time of a planned attack (Interview with Falintil fighter, November 2006). Indonesia was most unwilling to reveal to the world or to its own people how great were the losses it was suffering in those early years. In 1977 a senior Indonesian officer confided to a Dutch official that 5000 casualties had been inflicted by Fretilin (Dunn 2003:267). The morale of fearful Indonesian soldiers soon fell. This low morale inevitably filtered back home to sap the spirit of a nation that had been led to expect quick victory. Estimates of total Indonesian lives lost in the fighting range from 4000 to 20 000 and of its cost from US$1 million to $3 million per day (Salla 1997a:450). This cost burden foreclosed opportunities for development projects and also sapped the morale of the Indonesian elite. The international media began to discuss the conflict as 'Indonesia's Vietnam' (*The Times*, 18 August 1976). In the long run, it was no Vietnam because Falintil had no external patron supplying arms and cash.

Figure 4.3: Desperation in the face of famine

Photo: Peter Rodgers/Fairfax Media

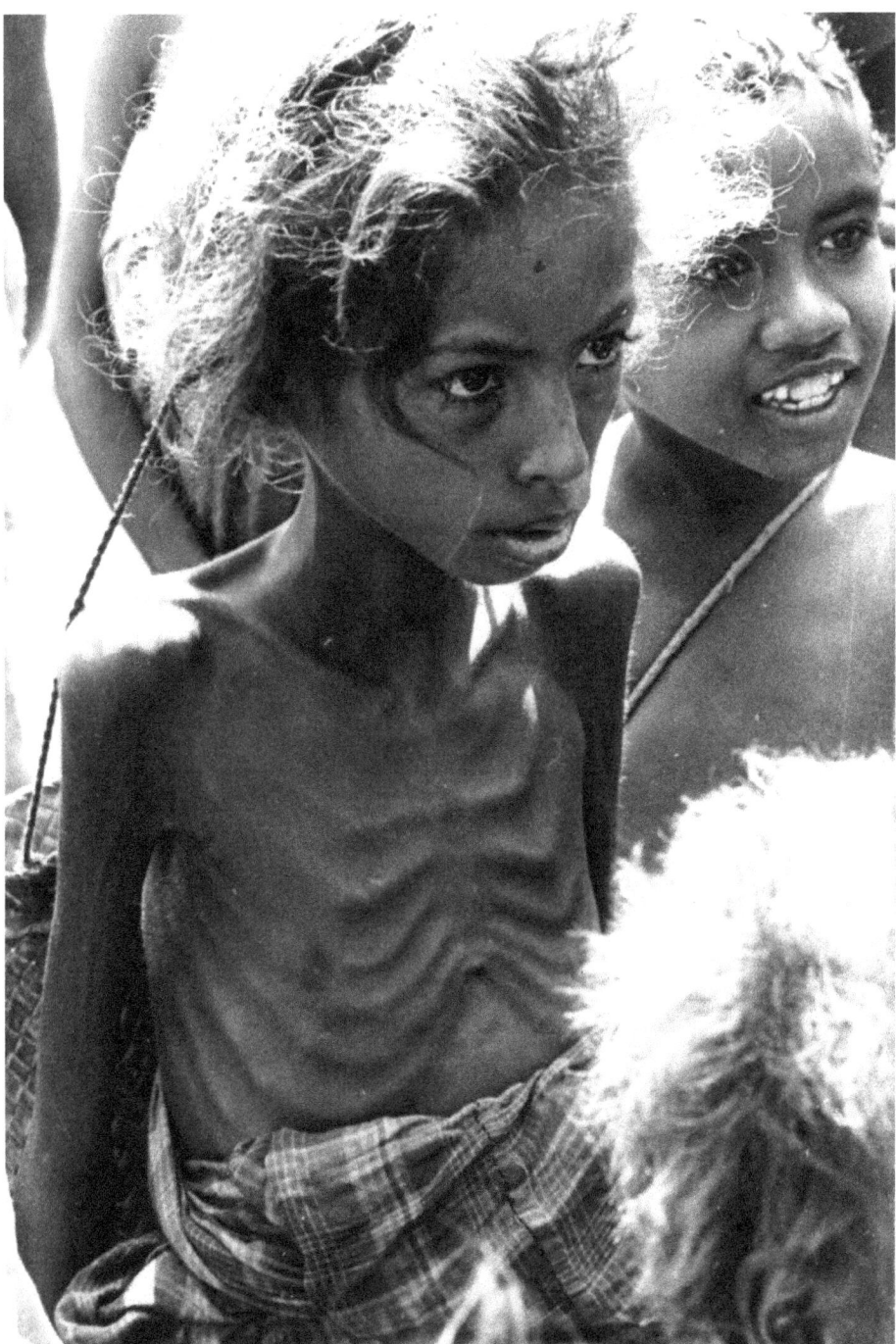

Figure 4.4: Resilience in the face of famine

Photo: Peter Rodgers/Fairfax Media

Because all six foreign journalists who remained in the country were shot when Indonesian forces arrived in the areas where they were reporting, the invasion was a success (compared with Vietnam) in deterring foreign media organisations from sending journalists to East Timor for many years unless they were specifically invited to cover something of interest to Indonesia. Indonesia also banned the International Committee of the Red Cross (ICRC) and indeed all international relief, human rights and development agencies from East Timor during the early years of the conflict—a decision with terrible consequences once mass starvation was caused by defoliation from the air of the large swathes of the country that were Fretilin controlled. When the ICRC was allowed in from September 1979, their relief work saved large numbers of lives, but they were allowed to distribute food only in military-controlled areas (Robinson 2008:97) and only Indonesian Red Cross workers were permitted. The policy was an explicit one of starving civilians into surrendering to camps where they knew many more would die. The West was again deeply culpable over this intentionally induced famine. 'According to one reliable account, the US ambassador to Indonesia, Edward Masters, failed to report the famine in East Timor for a full nine months after he had witnessed it firsthand' (Robinson 2008:97). Western leaders did not want to look and were not shown what they did not want to see.

When Rockwell OV-10 Bronco aircraft arrived with infrared detectors, rockets and napalm, designed for counterinsurgency against an enemy without anti-aircraft weapons, Indonesian fortunes began to improve. Starvation became a weapon of war as defoliants destroyed the gardens feeding the large numbers of people supporting the fighters in the mountains. For the first two years of fighting, Fretilin was still running a revolution, educating the people to a new democratic, egalitarian, non-feudal society, as well as running a war. This education also prepared the young for participation in the clandestine network (Chapter 5) in the next phase of the conflict after armed resistance had substantially collapsed. But starvation and constant bombing and artillery attacks led to civilian surrenders to Indonesian transit camps. The Indonesian strategy was then to use these large camps to segregate the insurgents from their civilian supporters ('separate the water from the fish'). The insurgents also began to run out of ammunition. Divisions opened up, particularly over policy on civilian surrender, including violent divisions that resulted in the execution as traitors of some leaders who wanted to allow civilians to surrender. For communist supporters of Fretilin in Australia and elsewhere there was disappointment that the Fretilin leaders progressively moved further away from a communist ideology. Communications out of East Timor on the internal divisions went to the Australian communist activist Denis Freney, who was the designated recipient of radio messages. This gave him an opportunity to move against the social-democrat leader of the diplomatic front, Ramos-Horta, using his crucial leverage of control of the radio communications to distort the situation and declare Ramos-Horta a traitor. Ramos-Horta and other Fretilin leaders were imprisoned for a period in Maputo, Mozambique, in 1978 at the behest of those seeking a more radical leadership. After Xanana Gusmão took over leadership of the insurgency, he interpreted the divisions, detentions and executions as a result of political hubris, domination and intolerance of a plurality of voices:

> This senseless radicalism paid no attention to our concrete conditions and limitations. It made us intolerably overbearing and led us to put many compatriots on the same footing as the criminal aggressor. We have committed crimes against our own brothers and, during this difficult war, we have spent more time in arresting and assassinating compatriots than thinking about capable defence of the Homeland, the results of which were evident in the events of 1978. (Xanana Gusmão, 7 December 1987, in Gusmão 2000:132)

These words show the struggle inherent in being embattled to survive domination, the struggle against oneself dominating to crush diversity. Xanana on the one hand was such an admirable figure in that he opened up the resistance to participation from all political factions, including former UDT members, who wanted independence for East Timor. On the other hand, an important observation of our analysis will be that in government he still fell prey himself to the very tendency he struggled against throughout his life as a leader of his people. In combination, all these forms of new adversity encountered by Fretilin caused its substantial decimation, including the loss of almost all the top leaders, in encirclement campaigns between late 1977 and early 1979.

Gradually, the strategy of having most of East Timor's civilian population living with Falintil in some 30 movable bases collapsed after a troop surge with improved air support from 1977. One by one, the bases succumbed to the new campaign of 'encirclement and annihilation'. The Fretilin leadership finally changed policy and allowed civilians to surrender. This was but the beginning of their suffering as they endured starvation, torture and many hardships first in 'transit' camps, then in 'resettlement' areas that ultimately came to house 300 000 civilians (Robinson 2008:87). Tens of thousands died in them.

Indonesian military training manuals for the East Timor campaign outlined a strategy of physically separating insurgents from their 'network' of civilian support (Robinson 2008:96). US military aid spiked in 1978 to fund the hardware to deliver 'encirclement and annihilation'. The starvation and forced displacement of hundreds of thousands of civilians were not 'unfortunate but inevitable by-product[s] of war'; they formed a conscious Indonesian policy facilitated by the United States (Robinson 2008:98). It was also Fretilin policy that civilians should live with them and sustain their independence in the mountains, but that was a defensive policy of preventing civilians from being captured by invading forces. They were in no sense human shields because Indonesian policy tolerated the killing of civilians.

While Indonesia declared East Timor pacified in March 1979, one surviving Falintil unit staged an audacious attack on Dili in June 1980, demonstrating that the insurgency lived. In the next phase, the Indonesian military organised civilians in 'fence of legs' campaigns during 1981, harnessing tens of thousands—on one estimate, 80 000 (Sebastian 2006:134)—women, men, children and the elderly, to march across the island in front of units of soldiers, flushing out insurgents before them. Xanana Gusmão was the principal target; his mystique increased when he escaped the net. 'Fence of legs' had been used successfully against the Darul Islam insurgency in the 1950s, as had the counterinsurgency strategy of targeting and assassinating leaders (Sebastian 2006:141). Only modest numbers of Falintil fighters were netted in 1981. Stories abounded of civilians in the fence of legs allowing them to slip through. Many civilians were caught, however, many of whom were massacred, creating the impression that the campaign was a success (CAVR 2006:Ch. 3.9, p. 92).

In 1980 Xanana Gusmão took charge and began to rebuild Falintil as a fighting force of several hundred on the ashes of the thousands of fighters who had perished. Apart from himself, only one other member of the Fretilin Central Committee still in Timor after the occupation had survived into 1980. In the reorganisation he put in place, the Conselho Revolusionário da Resisténsia Nasional (CRRN: Revolutionary Council of National Resistance) took command. CRRN was to be an umbrella that embraced all political factions who favoured independence, not just Fretilin. This was a decisive move away from Marxist–Leninist influence; CRRN became a more pluralist national unity movement. Xanana was elected to all the leadership positions, however: National Political Commissar, Commander-in-Chief of Falintil and President of CRRN. This concentration of power in the hands of one man reflected the admiration most of the survivors had for Xanana and their view of him as their last hope. The separation of Falintil from Fretilin went a step further in 1988 with the resignation of Falintil Commander, Xanana Gusmão, as a member of Fretilin, and the formation of the Conselho Nacional da Resistência Maubere (CNRM: National Council of Maubere Resistance), replacing CRRN as the supreme body of the resistance, with Xanana its President. Fretilin, in 1987 in the lead-up to this change, finally renounced its claim to be the only legitimate representative of the Timorese people. On the eve of Suharto's fall in April 1998, CNRM was renamed again, as the Conselho Nacional de Resistência Timorense (CNRT: Council of Timorese Resistance), and was joined by Apodeti Party members, again with Xanana Gusmão as President.

4. Not So Networked Warfare, 1975–1999

Falintil forces were radically dispersed across the country by Gusmão into many pockets, often with only two or three fighters at shifting bases assigned to hit-and-run attacks on bases of perhaps 15–30 Indonesian soldiers (Pinto and Jardine 1997:52). There were, however, mobile forces of the best armed and trained fighters who could arrive to support local pockets who were in trouble or who sought to overwhelm a modest Indonesian force.

Gusmão also held meetings with the leadership of the Catholic Church, which by 1980 had shifted profoundly from being a conservative bulwark of Portuguese colonial rule to being the advocate for downtrodden Timorese and a rock to which most Timorese could cling. In 1975, the Church leadership had been much more supportive of UDT than of Fretilin because of fears of communism. Xanana's masterstroke of forming the CRRN enrolled the Church as a cover for a great deal of the clandestine activity, discussed in Chapter 5.

By this time, the Indonesian military had coopted large numbers of Timorese to work alongside them in various capacities, including auxiliary forces who mobilised violence. East Timorese Hansip (civil defence) units were established from late 1976. Hansip members were used to organise civilians in the fence-of-legs campaigns. Some of the Hansip groups became the militias formed by the military to intimidate the population before and after the independence referendum of 1999. The rape and pillage of 1999 were the culmination of a progressive process of the military enrolling Timorese to intimidate and regulate Timorese.

In the early days of the Timor campaign the invaders suffered from having failed to educate their soldiers that this had to be a very different fight from the genocidal slaughter that had been waged against communists in the mid-1960s, wiping out half a million of them so they could no longer be a political force in Indonesia. At first, it did look like a genocidal campaign. In addition to the slaughter both of numbers of Timorese civilians that was quite unnecessary to securing major towns and of the Chinese business elite, transmigration programs began to swing into action to bring large numbers of Javanese to East Timor to dominate its civil service and to control its commercial life. Many in the international solidarity movement began to campaign against what was happening in East Timor as genocide, highlighting behaviour such as the widespread secretive use of the injectable contraceptive Depo-Provera against Timorese women. But the objectives of the New Order Indonesian leadership in East Timor were different from the anti-communist campaign. They were certainly to utterly dominate the East Timor resistance and to make the East Timor economy a wholly owned subsidiary of the crony capitalist system linked to the Suharto family. The objective was not to wipe out the Timorese; Timorese who collaborated with the New Order were embraced; the education of locals at universities in Java and Bali was supported. It was a regime of remorseless brutality against enemies of the New Order but of generosity towards those who supported it. In addition to enrolling Timorese in various forms of auxiliaries who could support the military from time to time in their work, as with the fence-of-legs work, the New Order invested hugely in enlisting Timorese youth in paramilitary youth groups, scouting organisations, martial arts groups and youth organisations under the wing of Golkar (Suharto's political party). Indonesian domination of the province suffered because at first the rank and file of the Indonesian military did not understand—had not been adequately trained to understand—that quite unlike the anti-communist campaign of the 1960s, this was a campaign to win the hearts and minds of most Timorese, killing only the hold-outs among them.

While this was a much more sophisticated and effective strategy of networked counterinsurgency, in the long run of the Timor campaign two further things went wrong. First, as we will document in Chapters 5 and 6, the young people of Timor had been educated well in their two years of survival in the mountains to their revolutionary emancipation from colonial control. We will see that the clandestine network joined in droves the organisations that were approved by the Indonesians and then used them as a cover to organise against the Indonesians. Second, the policy of sustained violence only against those who openly defied the New Order backfired once it became impossible to prevent video evidence of atrocities finding its way onto Western television screens. We will see in Chapter 6 that this undermined the pro-Indonesia network in the West.

In Australia, it was particularly Foreign Minister Gareth Evans who walked into this trap. There was a certain injustice in this because Evans was rather more assertive than most in the pro-Indonesia network in communicating concern over respect for human rights. He was sensitive in 1991 to the fact that signing the Timor Gap Treaty—while an economic coup for Australia—would be regarded as a betrayal of the East Timorese by many Australians, including in his own party. Visiting Indonesia in February 1991 to finalise the treaty, he said:

> I have taken the view that Australia does have a duty as an international good citizen to go on raising [human rights] issues…The truth of the matter is that the human rights situation [in East Timor] has, in our judgment, conspicuously improved, particularly under the present military arrangements. (Pilger 1994:312)

Evans was right: for some years the incidence of forced disappearances, torture and other human rights abuses had been greatly reduced (see Figure 4.6). Then in 1991 the Santa Cruz massacre (Chapter 6) was captured on Western television cameras and Evans was pilloried by commentators like John Pilger for statements such as those above. It did not help that Evans was quick to defend Indonesia after the 1991 massacre, describing it as 'an aberration, not an act of state policy' (Pilger 1994:312). It was state policy to be ruthlessly brutal with those who openly resisted it, while seeking to respect human rights, and enrol and win the hearts and minds of those who collaborated with it. While this was a great improvement from the indiscriminate violence of the 1970s, human rights abuses became a problem for Indonesia in the 1990s that they had not been in the 1980s. In a context where the Suharto regime was increasingly under challenge even in Jakarta, in a world of more miniaturised media technology, it became impossible to prevent damaging images of atrocities in Indonesia from reaching a Western media that had been persuaded by the international solidarity movement to become more interested in covering it. Strategies like networking indigenous militias to do some of the regime's dirty work were partially successful in the 1980s, and certainly an advance on the tactics of the 1970s that gave the appearance of genocide. Networking indigenous militias also backfired in the 1990s. In 1999, the undisciplined violence of militias guided by the Indonesian military leadership was to bring utter international disgrace to their nation.

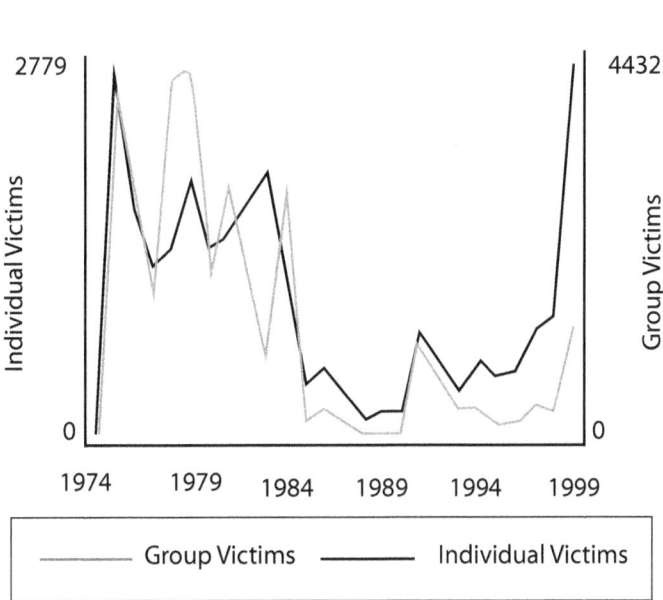

Figure 4.5: Individual and group victims of human rights violations across time in East Timor

Source: Database of Narrative Statements Given to the CAVR. CAVR (2006)

So our conclusion is that, while the Indonesian military adapted its strategies to new realities of new decades with success in the medium term, it did so more slowly than the East Timor clandestine and international solidarity movements. As a consequence, the Indonesian military was ultimately outmanoeuvred by its enemies.

As early as the late 1970s, the leaders of the insurgency were clear that they could not hold out militarily for many years on as small an island as Timor with no international border to escape across and no-one supplying them with military hardware. Nor did they wish to surrender. They wished to keep reinvigorating the insurgency as a card in their negotiating armoury. It was a useful card with Indonesian elite and public opinion because they had killed so many Indonesian soldiers and imposed such costs on the national budget to fight them.

Xanana Gusmão wanted to stem the needless waste of the lives of young Timorese and Indonesian fighters (especially as more of the latter became Timorese themselves). Yet he was reported to be brimming with confidence when he negotiated a ceasefire with the Governor of East Timor in 1983. One report had him saying 'oil prices were down and Indonesia could not afford to keep troops in East Timor' (Conboy 2003:299). In a June 2011 interview with Adérito Soares, Gusmão said that he used the ceasefire to regroup for the next Indonesian assault that he knew was coming. The ceasefire broke down, but nevertheless both sides came to realise that they were better off refraining from all-out assault on the other. There were assorted agreements between local Falintil and local Indonesian military commanders that they would seek to avoid killing of one side by the other. While the Indonesian military had secured effective control of almost all the country, and while they knew there were only a few hundred insurgents left, they knew the cost of going after them would be high because there were thousands of young men and women in the clandestine network who would lay down their lives to join Xanana in the fight. It was not a hurting stalemate, but rather in some ways a non-hurting stalemate. This freed Xanana to focus on his real campaign, which was in mobilising a clandestine network that would undermine Indonesian legitimacy in East Timor, link up with a democracy movement in the rest of Indonesia to help overthrow the New Order, and link up with an international solidarity movement that would support Ramos-Horta's leadership on the diplomatic front. An ongoing function of the armed resistance from remote camps was to provide somewhere for members of the clandestine network to escape to when their identities became known and their lives imperilled. Because the military card had become no more than a background option for Falintil and a niggling nuisance for the Indonesian military (that still tied down a number of watchful battalions), it was no real setback for the resistance when Xanana was captured in his Dili hideout in November 1992 and exiled to prison in Jakarta. From his Jakarta prison cell, it became much easier for him to lead the more important struggles of the clandestine network within the heartland of Indonesia and to develop an understanding of the pressure points on the increasingly fragile Suharto regime. Even Nelson Mandela was able to visit Xanana when he was assertive enough to ask President Suharto for a meeting. Xanana had no problem sending messages back to East Timor in the hands of Timorese students and others who visited him in prison and through encrypted emails. For Xanana, like Mandela, some of his prison guards came to admire him. Others took bribes to look the other way as he went about his subversive networking.

The 1983 ceasefire was seen by the Catholic Church and by many moderates in Jakarta as a welcome pause in suffering and an opportunity for lasting peace and reconciliation. Many military leaders, in contrast, saw the ceasefire at worst as a display of weakness, at best as an opportunity to photograph and identify the numbers and location of Falintil fighters as they enjoyed the freedom to visit their families and villages. The much more total control the military enjoyed over East Timor and its economy than any other province allowed its officers to benefit financially from the conflict. Coffee growers, for example, were forced to sell the province's largest export through an army-controlled monopoly at much less than half the market price (Kingsbury and McCulloch 2006:217). Profits earned by lower ranks had to be shared up the chain of command. Many junior officers ran small local businesses through local men or engaged in extortion from other businesses. Senior officers also controlled many larger monopolies and used violence to force out competitors (Kingsbury and McCulloch 2006:218). In this financial sense as well, until 1998 the military did not see itself as in a hurting stalemate, but in a highly lucrative stalemate. They could not imagine what their enemy could do to break up their country or their profits. Here, as we will see in the next chapter, the CNRM leadership had a more politically creative imagination.

5. Networked Solidarity, International and Clandestine

This chapter describes how the clandestine movement worked inside Timor and across Indonesia. Its links to the Church and to a politics of nonviolence are then discussed. Then the chapter considers the links between the clandestine movement, the international solidarity movement and the diplomatic front to form a complex, partially integrated network.

The Clandestinos

A revealing interview was with a Timor-Leste police officer who had served in the Indonesian police (then part of the military) in the 1980s and 1990s. His job in the clandestine network was to be Xanana Gusmão's driver around Dili.[1] He could take the Commander-in-Chief to his home for a meeting with others in the clandestine network without the meeting being monitored because he was a trusted member of the Indonesian military. An error of misplaced realism discussed in Chapter 4 that many in the Indonesian security sector made was that the 1983 ceasefire, while distasteful because it appeared weak, could do more good than harm because it would allow them to photograph and locate Falintil members and their relatives. Realistically, there was no harm in leaders like Xanana Gusmão being given an opportunity to make a case for a referendum to Timorese or Indonesians, because the latter would never be persuaded to agree to it and Timorese would never win it. This of course did prove erroneous as the Indonesian cabinet was persuaded to support a referendum in 1999. More importantly, Falintil leaders used the ceasefire to recruit Timorese deep within the Indonesian state and security apparatus, such as the commander's police driver, to the clandestine network. It gave young urban Timorese such hope and inspiration to see Xanana move about safely and seemingly invincibly after all those years in the mountains. It gave their leader a network of loyal support that allowed him to live in the capital while planning the bold demonstration that became the Santa Cruz massacre (Chapter 6).

---

1   In debates in which people say it was a policy mistake to recruit some of the new Timor-Leste police from the ranks of those who served in the Indonesian police it is often forgotten that many of the latter were heroes of the fight for democracy. One Australian United Nations Civilian Police (UNPOL) officer told us how his local POLRI (Kepolisian Negara Republik Indonesia: Indonesian National Police) commander tipped him off after the referendum result was announced in 1999: 'Tomorrow I've been told to remove your security at midday and not see what happens.' The Australian added that the local militia had a list of priority targets for assassination that he himself was on, but the POLRI commander was number one on that list.

At this point in the Timorese struggle, the years of revolutionary education in the mountains in the late 1970s when most of the population of East Timor lived under the protection of Fretilin provided a solid foundation for clandestine recruitment. Before civilians, particularly young people who had lost close relatives to Indonesian atrocities, were allowed to surrender, they were prepared for later service in the clandestine network. The 1983 ceasefire established continuity with that educative project of the young to the possibility of a long-term struggle in which they would one day prevail. During the ceasefire, Falintil leaders were able to make contact with the youth leaders they had prepared ideologically for clandestine leadership. The education that the Indonesians provided to the brightest and best of the young Timorese only assisted in their preparation for clandestine leadership. Timorese youth leaders made high schools and universities primary recruiting nodes for the clandestine network. The clandestine movement infiltrated Indonesian security and governmental organisations to gain intelligence, provided food and other supplies to Falintil, and organised demonstrations and educational and outreach activities to advance the independence struggle.

The clandestine movement had a cellular structure, with each village having a network known as *nucleos de resistencia popular*, which became known as *nurep*. *Nurep* coordinated hamlet-level networks: the *selcom* (McWilliam 2005:35). Even within the same cell, members had little knowledge of who beyond their immediate contact was in the clandestine movement, so they were not in a position to give up comrades under torture. McWilliam's (2005) research showed how traditional kin-based 'house' communities thwarted Indonesian eradication of armed and clandestine resistance. One account has the clandestine network ultimately growing to 1700 cells (Scott 2005:3). When Indonesian intelligence realised this was the case, it partially mirrored the clandestine structure, locating a *babinsa* (village guidance noncommissioned officer) in each village, with more restive villages having a 'village guidance team' and armed village guards often called *hansip* (CAVR 2006:Ch. 3.9, p. 97).

We must be careful not to essentialise the clandestine network. There were many in the clandestine movement who also assisted the Indonesian military to save themselves or hedge their bets. Some saved themselves by giving the Indonesians intelligence that was occasionally valuable, but that wilfully put them off the scent on things that were important. Other Timorese who, on balance, were pro-integration, nevertheless helped the resistance. A good example is provided by Janet Steele's (2007) work on the journalists of the newspaper *Suara Timor Timur*, which was controlled by pro-integration interests and approved by Indonesia. These journalists 'recall with pride practicing a kind of subterranean journalism that presented subtle challenges to the government's point of view' (Steele 2007:262). They had a commitment to journalistic professionalism that

5. Networked Solidarity, International and Clandestine

led them to get facts to the people, often by educating an acquired capacity to 'read between their lines'. When they discovered facts they could not publish, for example because they came from an interview with a Falintil leader, they would regularly be sent to Reuters, AP or the BBC, so others could publish them. Sophisticated Indonesian observers could see that Timorese in many walks of life were neither black nor white, but were seeking to achieve as dark a shade of Fretilin grey as they could manage safely. Until Santa Cruz, Indonesian strategists thought they were doing well in lightening that shade of grey as increasing numbers of Timorese fell for the error of misplaced realism, seeing integration as the only pragmatic path for improving conditions and relieving the suffering of the Timorese people.

Martial arts groups with a long pedigree in Indonesia as nationalistic organisations, and a great variety of other Java-based youth groups with appeal to young women as well as young men, were seeded in East Timor. Some had strong links with and received material support from the military, others from Suharto's party, Golkar. One of the activities of such groups was to persuade citizens to get out to vote for Golkar candidates at elections in which their opponents could not win. Clandestine youth often used the resources of these youth organisations—the paper, the food and the transport—to support their resistance work. The lesson for occupying powers is that unless hearts and minds are genuinely won, the resistance will find ways of appearing to capitulate while capturing the rewards of capitulation for the resistance.

Just as Xanana Gusmão gained great legitimacy with the Catholic Church by embracing UDT members in CNRM,[2] distancing Falintil from communism and persuading Fretilin to step back from its claim to be the only true representative of the Timorese people, the Catholic Church was also impressed by the ceasefire as a genuine attempt to engage Indonesia in dialogue towards a peaceful settlement. When the ceasefire broke down, this meant that the Catholic Church was more committed than ever to the travails of the Timorese people and to providing cover for the clandestine movement.

The Church, Nonviolence and the Clandestine Network

The resistance 'slowly changed its strategy from armed struggle to a nonviolent struggle, discovering along the way, perhaps to its surprise, that the nonviolent

---

2   The CAVR (2006:Ch. 3.9, p. 98) suggests that at a meeting with Xanana Gusmão in September 1982, the head of the Catholic Church in Timor, Monsignor Lopes, 'highlighted the need for national unity between Fretilin and UDT', and that Xanana indicated that he was listening to this by the national unity changes of 1983.

struggle was more effective and more powerful than the armed struggle had been' (Hallett and Summy 2000:10). One reason nonviolence was more effective was that it forged common ground with the Church. The Church in Timor was more organisationally effective than either CNRM or the Indonesian state, at least in the rural areas where most people lived. The Church had an infrastructure of land, buildings, resources from the Church internationally and from humanitarian donors and an infrastructure of leadership that had genuine legitimacy and mass civil society participation. Local church leaders witnessed a virtuous circle between their defence of common Timorese people from the human rights abuses of the military and a growth in attendance at mass and spiritual commitment to the Church as a rock to which the people could cling. In the time of Portuguese Timor, the church leadership stood above the people; during the Indonesian time, it stood with the people, and people rallied to it. The Indonesian Ministry of Religious Affairs' policy, which required people to register their religion, also helped the Church. Many of the lapsed Catholics, agnostics and much larger numbers of animists who had never connected to Catholicism, when forced to choose, registered as Catholics, and many became committed Catholics when they saw the Church as the bulwark of sanctuary and of the survival of Timorese identity. This was reinforced by the decision that the official language of the liturgy would be Tetum. Joining the Church thus became a private gesture of resistance to perceived Muslim invaders and an affirmation of Timorese identity. In 1973, 28 per cent of the population described themselves as Catholic; in 1980, the Indonesian statistics office listed 80 per cent of the population as Catholic (CAVR 2006:Ch. 3.9, p. 99), and by independence it was 90 per cent (Wise 2006:31).

Catholic youth rallies and Youth Cross marches from village to village became venues where young people from many districts mixed together and Falintil members could join the rally or march and conduct a meeting with clandestine youth leaders as they walked for miles behind the cross. Particularly in the early years of the conflict, letters written to members of the international solidarity movement by nuns and priests inside East Timor were the principal means of getting information about Indonesian abuses to the outside world.

Indonesian security forces worried about the strengthening ties between Falintil and the Church. Hallett and Summy (2000:10) argue that this helps explain why elements of the Indonesian military, particularly Kopassus (the Special Forces), might have shifted strategy in the 1990s to arming militias 'not so much to provoke and plunder as to tempt pro-independence forces to abandon their effective nonviolent struggle for a return to the ineffective armed struggle'. This is a particularly apt analysis of the difficulties the leadership had in 1999 to persuade Falintil commanders to keep their men in cantonment while their families were being killed and homes razed by militias they easily could have cut down in most areas. One member of the Falintil high command described cantonment as 'an extreme humiliation for us as guerilla fighters' (Interview, September 2009). José Ramos-Horta told this story in our September 2009 interview when we asked him what contribution he was able to make that he was particularly proud of (as recorded in our fieldnotes):

> One 'small contribution' he was able to make in 1999 arose when Xanana called him in New York in tears, totally distraught, saying Taur Matan Ruak [the Falantil Commander] would only hold his men in cantonment for two more days. Horta said to his leader that 'you cannot show weakness now; this is the last time for you to show weakness. Now is when we need your strongest leadership. Pull yourself together.' Horta pulled strings with the US security sector to arrange a phone line that would get him through to Ruak. Horta said to Ruak, 'This is the time to close ranks. I never intervene in the chain of command. But it is critical that you follow Xanana's orders. Please don't leave the cantonments. If we do that now, support from the international community will evaporate quickly. I will deliver the UN; we are almost there.' Ramos-Horta then told us: 'I was lying when I said that; we were nowhere near being there.' Ruak had replied in Portuguese to Xanana 'shit to the international community' and hung up on him. The problem was that the families of the Falintil troops were being slaughtered by the militias and their homes burnt to the ground. Falintil could have cut through the militias like a knife. TMR [Taur Matan Ruak] conceded in the conversation with Horta that he must follow Xanana's orders and hold them in cantonment.

It seems to some commentators that the Indonesian generals behaved in an irrational fashion in 1999. Yet had Falintil not been as disciplined as it was at this point, Falintil might have been drawn into what the world would have seen as a civil war, instead of the slaughter of innocents instigated by Indonesian soldiers that they in fact saw. Our analysis here is not quite that nonviolence was more effective than violence, but that nonviolent struggle to convert the enemy who were killing them, and their enemies in the United States, the United Kingdom and Australia who were arming and training their killers, backed by a residual capacity to reinvigorate the insurgency that gave the clandestine youth hope, was effective. It was the shift to nonviolence without abandoning the diplomatic card of a return to armed violence that was effective. Without the option of armed escalation, the financial cost of containment would have been much less for Indonesia, the belief in the possibility of ultimate victory would have been less for the clandestine youth, and the concern of the international diplomatic community that Timor could turn disastrously embarrassing again would have been less.

The Vatican was in the grip of a similar realist analysis to that of the Governments of Australia and the United States, though it was not willing to recognise Indonesian sovereignty over East Timor. This meant that the leadership of the Church in East Timor answered directly to the Vatican rather than through the Indonesian Church leadership. Nevertheless, the Vatican was focused on adverse repercussions for Catholics in the rest of Indonesia of any human rights activism and support for the resistance in East Timor. So the Vatican discouraged such advocacy. Under Indonesian pressure, it ultimately forced the resignation of Monsignor Lopes, who had been meeting with and encouraging the resistance rather too much for Jakarta's liking (Lennox 2000). The replacement was Bishop Belo. When Pope John Paul II visited in 1989, both Indonesia and the resistance were able to interpret it as a vindication of the legitimacy of their position in East Timor. Yet it was obviously a deeply moving experience for the 100 000 Timorese who attended the Pope's main mass to have their suffering acknowledged by the Pontiff. And it was an embarrassment for Indonesian authorities that young people at the mass unfurled banners and raised chants for independence and human rights when given this opportunity for the international media to notice. The brutal response of the Indonesian military to the demonstration was recorded by the foreign media and witnessed by the Pope and his entourage.

Students, Youth and the Clandestine Network

While an estimated 13 000 Timorese men and women were killed fighting with Falintil and more than 20 000 others suffered great hardship in doing so (Scott 2005:3), most who lost their lives were civilians—many killed on suspicion of being part of the solidarity movement. The clandestine student movement Renetil (Resistencia Nacional dos Estudantes de Timor Leste: Timor-Leste Students' National Resistance) was formed in Bali in 1988. Adérito Soares was a member. Renetil operated among Timorese university students in Java as well. Students in the clandestine movement also infiltrated the government-approved student association in which membership was compulsory for Timorese students, Impettu (the East Timorese Students and Youth Association), and ultimately came to control it. Meeting was a problem—always something that could attract surveillance from the security forces—so a good way for clandestine students to meet was under the auspices of Impettu, whose activities were approved by the regime. Through Impettu, Renetil used to organise an annual Christmas party. This was formally supported by the head of the military in each region who would offer some financial assistance to Impettu to host the party. Prior to the party, Impettu invited Timorese students from around Indonesia to attend. So, every Christmas, Impettu was able to bring together between 300 and 400 East Timorese students from all over Java and Bali. Prior to the Christmas party,

Impettu also organised a soccer competition that ran over four or five days. At the Christmas party, Impettu would invite the regional military commander to give a speech. The military commander looked on this as an event at which he could supervise the students. For the students themselves, however, this formal gathering, which had the blessing of the military, was a great opportunity for the clandestine network from Bali and Java to coordinate activities such as the embassy fence-jumping discussed below, underground activities and contact with Falintil.

The philosophy of the student resistance in Java and Bali was Gandhian: to use nonviolence, risky demonstrations and courageous sacrifice with the ultimate objective of persuading Indonesians to support their cause. This they did, particularly in the form of Indonesian students who were part of a democracy movement committed to bringing down Suharto. Timorese students supported the Indonesian democracy movement in its clandestine activities and in pro-democracy and human rights demonstrations where Fretilin flags would often be seen in the crowd. In turn, Indonesian students supported them. The two social movements persuaded each other that they were struggling against the same root cause of a diverse set of problems that included injustice for East Timor. That root cause was the Suharto New Order regime. The clandestine network had forged links with Indonesian human rights activists from the early 1980s when Timorese political prisoners began to be sent to Java in large numbers. The prisons became networking sites between the two resistance movements. The Timorese resistance leadership believed that a likely path to independence for East Timor lay in an Indonesian democracy movement with a student vanguard destabilising the Suharto regime and replacing it with a democratic regime that would respect the human rights of the Timorese people. Winning the trust and respect of the Indonesian democracy movement in this way being such a key objective, the leadership absolutely forbade and prevented the formation of terrorist cells that might harm the people of Java. 'Ramos-Horta quickly showed the door to terrorist groups offering to take hostages and plant bombs. I saw him do it once in New York' (Scott 2005:5). Renetil came to call its strategy 'Indonesianisation' of the conflict. In this context, Xanana Gusmão described war as 'the art of living side by side with the enemy' (McLeod 2008). Indonesian pro-democracy activist Coki Nai Pos Pos, who spent time in prison with Xanana, said: 'The Indonesian pro-democracy movement used the East Timorese international contacts and exposure to advance their agenda and the East Timorese used us to influence domestic politics' (McLeod 2008:4).

In the mid-1990s, the Timorese students in Jakarta invented a new strategy to attract international attention through nonviolence. This was mass fence jumping into embassies to seek asylum (see Fernandes 2011:130–6; Sword Gusmão 2003:56–66). The most publicised Renetil fence-jump occurred into the US Embassy at the time of the Asia Pacific Economic Cooperation (APEC) meeting of 1994 when the international media was assembled in Jakarta. The students achieved front-page attention around the world for days as 29 of them sat in the embassy demanding an audience with President Clinton. They did not win that, but they were shunted off to asylum in Portugal to get them out of the way, only to generate more publicity there. While embassy security tightened after this, there were a dozen subsequent successful mass fence-jumps in 1995 and 1996 into the embassies of the Netherlands, the United Kingdom, Japan, Australia, New Zealand, Poland, Russia and France. There were also six attempts that were foiled; these included some with more than 50 students attempting to jump embassy fences (Singh 1996:364).

Many young people of the clandestine movement sacrificed their lives, not only at Santa Cruz as we discuss in the next chapter, but mostly quietly, not returning one day, never returning to the embrace of their families. Larger numbers sacrificed their university studies, seeing university enrolment in Indonesia as an opportunity to dedicate themselves to liberation for their country rather than to advancement of their careers.

The International Solidarity Movement

The international solidarity movement was a small number of people in a tiny number of nations who played a critical role in connecting the sacrifices of the clandestine movement to wider audiences. For international solidarity movements to work, it is not necessary for all concerned people to contribute to all struggles against oppression, just for some of them to contribute to one. Many of the dedicated people of the solidarity movement were inspired by José Ramos-Horta's charisma, charm, hope, vision and tenacity.

One delightful story of how individuals in the solidarity movement enrolled the most implausible of allies to help to get the story of Timor's suffering out is told by one of its members, David Scott:

> Rupert Murdoch had been a friend in the 1950s and '60s through the marriage of his sister, Helen, to my close friend, Geoffrey Handbury. In early January 1976 I called at his Fifth Avenue office…he bounded out of his office and greeted me warmly. 'Come in and meet some of the boys', he said. With a big grin he introduced me to his colleagues: 'Meet my friend from Australia', he said, 'who's here trying to establish a communist base north of Darwin.' Despite the edge of the bonhomie, Rupert arranged for *The Australian* correspondent in New York to send

an article by me for publication in *The Australian*. And when I went to Washington later, he gave me an introduction to the editor of *The Washington Post*. (Scott 2005:52–3)

The most amazing story of how the solidarity movement lit up with imaginative activism after the Santa Cruz massacre involves four women from Ploughshares for Peace who slipped into British Aerospace premises and used hammers to disarm a British Hawk jet fighter headed for delivery to Indonesia. The Hawks had been used to terrifying effect against the villagers of East Timor. What was most remarkable was that a jury in Liverpool acquitted them, finding that they had acted to prevent the greater crime of genocide (CAVR 2006:Ch. 7.1, p. 111; for a firsthand account, see Zelter 2004).

Figure 5.1: The Ploughshares for Peace Four at a reunion

Photo: Pat Gaffney/Pax Christi

Another imaginative, information-age strategy was the Portuguese Hackers Against Indonesia. They dispersed propaganda across the Indonesian military's web site and the web site of its Department of Foreign Affairs. In August 1998, 45 Indonesian domains were hacked by Timor solidarity supporters. José Ramos-Horta threatened to more seriously unleash this new form of warfare—a 'desperate and ferocious' campaign of Internet sabotage of the Indonesian economy—if it refused to respect the outcome of the August 1999 referendum (CAVR 2006:Ch. 7.1, p. 112).

Figure 5.2: Members of the international solidarity movement occupy an office of the Australian Department of Foreign Affairs and Trade, 1994

Photo: *Northern Territory News*, with thanks to Jude Conway

While the most critical work of the international solidarity movement was done by a small number of dedicated individuals, support from the resources of certain NGOs was also important. Included among these in Australia was the Australian Council for Overseas Aid (ACFOA), now the Australian Council for International Development (ACFID), particularly its Human Rights Office led by Pat Walsh, Community Aid Abroad (now, Oxfam Australia), Action for World Development, the Australian Parliamentary East Timor Friendship Group, Australian Catholic Relief and other Catholic Church networks. In Australia, Darwin, Sydney and Melbourne were the nodes and spiritual heartlands of the pro-Timor lobby, just as Canberra was of the pro-Indonesia lobby. The East Timor Ireland Solidarity Campaign was important, as were East Timor support groups in many other European countries, East Timor Alert Network in Canada, the Catholic Institute for International Relations and the East Timor Action Network (ETAN) in the United States. ETAN, working with Ramos-Horta, built up a network of pro-Timor senators and representatives with influential members like Ted Kennedy, Tom Daschle, Richard Gephart and Nancy Pelosi. ETAN led a successful grassroots campaign to block the transfer of US F-5 fighter aircraft to Indonesia and also successfully campaigned in

Congress against small arms sales to the regime (Simpson 2004:460–1). Such campaigns were also vigorous in European countries that supplied military equipment to Indonesia, including Sweden, Germany and the United Kingdom, where TAPOL (which means political prisoner in Indonesian) became a vital advocacy group. Japanese and British politicians led the formation of the critical international network Parliamentarians for East Timor (Budiardjo 2002:2). The solidarity movement was particularly strong in Portugal (Fernandes 2011:76–8). The International Federation for East Timor was founded to coordinate the campaigns of the solidarity movement which by 1995 spread across more than 20 countries, especially coordination at the United Nations and international forums (Simpson 2004:461). In turn, it spawned regional coordination bodies such as the Asia Pacific Coalition for East Timor.

Figure 5.3: Antonia Maia meets his old friend Paddy Kenneally, an Australian Timor veteran of World War II

Photo: Ross Bird

The solidarity movement was not unified politically and was riven with jealousies and political factionalism. Some members were communist; others were fervently anti-communist. These differences, however, did not prevent Ramos-Horta, Alkatiri and others using them as vehicles to publicise the suffering of East Timor around the globe. The foregoing discussion might mislead readers to think that the international solidarity movement was a transnational advocacy movement in the Western sense that term is often used: organised around groups initiated in the West. In fact, the initial inspiration was African. As the name suggests, Fretilin started as a revolutionary liberation front modelled on FRELIMO (Frente de Libertação de Moçambique: Liberation Front of Mozambique) in Mozambique, and later supported under FRELIMO's wing in Maputo. From its foundation in 1962, FRELIMO fought both militarily and through international networks in churches, trade unions and human rights groups tasked to isolate Portugal, having it expelled from certain international organisations and creating obstacles to ultimate accession to the European Union (Webster 2003:4–5).

The Diplomatic Front

The East Timor solidarity movement was resisted by a much larger, better-placed network of influence, often described as the Indonesia lobby in its Australian incarnation (discussed in Chapter 3). Like the solidarity movement, the pro-Indonesia network was far from ideologically unified, including folk from the right and the left of the Western political spectrum. The belief that warm diplomatic and scholarly exchange with Indonesia should have more prominence unified it. In the Australian context, the idea was that Australian diplomacy and scholarship were far too oriented to other Western nations and insufficiently to the largest Muslim population of any nation in the world. Most members of the Indonesia network between 1975 and 1999 who met at events like the annual Indonesia Update organised by our own school at The Australian National University (now the College of Asia and the Pacific) tended to see the East Timor solidarity movement as irresponsible. The two key nodes of the Australian pro-Indonesia network were in Canberra at the Department of Foreign Affairs (its most important player being Richard Woolcott, former head of that department and former Ambassador to Indonesia) and our former school at The Australian National University (its most senior players being the distinguished political scientist Jamie Mackie and the renowned economist Heinz Arndt). This group of scholars and diplomats included most of the big guns of their professions who specialised in Indonesian affairs. And throughout the 1970s, 1980s and most of the 1990s, they utterly outgunned the mostly more marginal intellectuals who were active in the East Timor solidarity movement. Political leaders of both major political parties in Australia liked the hard-headed political pragmatism of the pro-Indonesia network—well captured by this interview on ABC TV's *Lateline* on 22 March 1994:

> Professor Jamie Mackie (ANU): [I]t's certainly been a tragic and disastrous story. But I think if we were to put East Timor at the top of the agenda and say: 'This is what determines our policy towards the region', we're going to pay a very, very high price. I think we'd be antagonizing countries like Indonesia, Malaysia and, by extension, the rest of ASEAN on issues that matter much—perhaps I shouldn't say much more, but

matter a greater deal, at the moment, like APEC. And with Indonesia chairing the APEC summit later this year, I don't think this is a sensible time to say: 'Let's go out on a limb and pick a fight with Indonesia.'

Margot O'Neill: Is there ever a sensible time?

Jamie Mackie: Probably, not, no. (Aditjondro 1994:54)

It is doubtless hard for readers outside Canberra to understand how anyone could think APEC mattered more than tens of thousands of Timorese deaths. Australia is not a member of the potent regional organisation ASEAN, and suffers a middle-power insecurity syndrome that it cannot wield influence through a regional grouping like the European Union, as most other Western middle powers can. So Australian leaders lobbied in the 1980s and 1990s for APEC. In the late 2000s, Prime Minister Kevin Rudd lobbied (bringing Richard Woolcott out of retirement for the campaign) unsuccessfully for a new Asia Pacific Community. While APEC is not seen outside Canberra policy circles as having made a large contribution to humankind, the very APEC meeting in Jakarta referred to here became at that point the most important occasion since Santa Cruz when the Timor students' movement was able to shine the international spotlight on their country's plight.

Just as it was not necessary for Falintil to be winning more battles than the Indonesian military, so it was not a requirement for ultimate victory that the international Timor lobby was winning more debates than the pro-Indonesia network. In both cases, their job was to be a severe irritant to incumbents of power in Indonesia and their allies who would not go away until major concessions were yielded. Ultimately, the hope was that a moment of political vulnerability, crisis or regime change would come that would bring the enemy to the table for genuine negotiations. The contribution of the international solidarity movement and the clandestine network was to help make Suharto and his military unpopular nationally and internationally, to impose a cost on the good opinion the most outspoken supporters of Indonesia enjoyed within their own parties and their own countries, to win dissenters to military support for Indonesia, particularly in the US Congress, and to win new supporters of Timor in the United Nations. It was to allow the suffering and the injustice inflicted on the people of Timor to be remembered. It was to insinuate doubt into the Realpolitik of seeing the injustice as irreversible.

It was only after the Santa Cruz massacre that the solidarity movement began to be successful in these modest terms. In the late 1970s and 1980s, virtually no-one picked up most of their press releases. Constâncio Pinto and Matthew Jardine (1997:23) use the example of East Timor coverage in the *Los Angeles Times*. It ran 16 stories on East Timor in the five months between August

1975 and the invasion, but none between March 1976 and November 1979—the period when the worst slaughter was occurring in East Timor. John Pilger (1994:316) recorded:

> [*The*] *Australian* sent its Jakarta correspondent, Patrick Walters, on the first shepherded press tour of Dili, accompanied by Indonesian officials. Walters produced a memorable series of disgraceful pieces. Jakarta's 'economic achievements' in East Timor were 'impressive', he wrote, giving official statistics of Jakarta's generous 'development' of the territory. As for resistance, it was 'leaderless' and beaten. Indeed, you wondered what the fuss was all about as 'no one was now arrested without proper legal procedures'. 'The situation regarding human rights', the puppet governor told him, 'is very good at the moment'. (Pilger 1994:316)

Pilger managed to do something himself about breaking through Timor denial by secretly filming inside Timor on the pretext of being a travel agent preparing a tourism promotion. His documentary *Death of a Nation* was widely screened in 1993.

Such efforts were important support for José Ramos-Horta's leadership of what Xanana Gusmão saw as the third front after Falintil and the clandestine front: the diplomatic front. After Santa Cruz gave him a serious platform for international engagement, and even more so after friends in the solidarity movement successfully lobbied for the awarding of the Nobel Peace Prize to him and Bishop Belo in 1996, Ramos-Horta was able to attract some interest in a peace plan. It was called the Timor Talks Campaign, which Indonesia dismissed. It was for a three-phase process. In the first phase there would be two years of dialogue between East Timor, Indonesia and Portugal under the auspices of the United Nations to implement a variety of confidence-building measures, which would include a drastic reduction in Indonesian troops in East Timor and a UN presence. The second phase involved political autonomy under Indonesia and a democratically elected People's Assembly. It would last five to 10 years. Then there would be the third period of a referendum and final transition to a permanent settlement of sovereignty over East Timor.

This kind of talk became vaguely credible in the 1990s in a way it could never have been in the 1980s, because no-one could imagine democratic transformation in Indonesia in the 1980s, whereas in the 1990s cracks were appearing in Suharto's hold on power. So we must go back further to comprehend Ramos-Horta's resilience during his lonely years. Between 1976 and 1984, he was banned from entering Australia for fear this would displease Suharto, and diplomatic doors he sought to enter were slammed in his face all around the world. In the early years, he moved between Mozambique, which was willing to issue visas to the members of the Fretilin Central Committee in exile, and New York.

In New York, Ramos-Horta worked as a UN lobbyist by day and cleaner by night. A critical first objective he secured in early 1976 was to persuade the Secretary-General of the United Nations to keep the door open for dialogue between Indonesia and Portugal over East Timor, though the dialogue itself did not happen until much later. A string of diplomatic successes followed at the United Nations—some close run. Ten General Assembly and Security Council resolutions between 1975 and 1982 taken together 'criticised Indonesia's invasion of the territory, called for the withdrawal of Indonesian troops, and affirmed the right of the East Timorese people to self-determination' (Jardine 2000). Indonesia was reportedly surprised and angered by these UN statements. These resolutions were an important part of laying a foundation for support from international civil society for Indonesian withdrawal. They were steps towards President Habibie ultimately wanting to rid his country of the Timor problem once and for all. Matthew Jardine (2000) argued, however, that independence finally came to East Timor in spite of the United Nations rather than because of it. He observes accurately enough that action flows from UN resolutions only when its most powerful members want it to. In this case, the US Ambassador to the United Nations, Daniel Patrick Moynihan, was undiplomatic enough to say '[t]he Department of State desired that the United Nations prove utterly ineffective in whatever measures it undertook [on East Timor]. This task was given to me, and I carried it forward with not inconsiderable success' (Moynihan with Weaver 1978:247).

Figure 5.4: José Ramos-Horta waves photographs of suffering children at a UN hearing, 1982

Photo: Yutaka Nagata/United Nations Department of Public Information

Communist countries were mostly the ones giving Ramos-Horta limited diplomatic support and resources in the early years. The Communist Party in Australia also lent the vital support of operating a radio and transceiver in Darwin that could communicate with the Fretilin leadership in the mountains of Timor. In the early years of the conflict, doors were mostly closed to Fretilin in Moscow and therefore mostly in Havana. After 1999, Fidel Castro sent large numbers of Cuban doctors to help rebuild the Timor-Leste health system, telling the Fretilin leadership that he felt remorse that he did not help them more during their greatest years of struggle. Because the Soviets were so supportive of Indonesia, China gave considerable rhetorical support and some practical diplomatic assistance to Ramos-Horta in the corridors of the United Nations. As China changed towards becoming the free-market giant of Asia in the 1980s, its relationship with the large Indonesian market became important, and China became more timid in relation to East Timor.

Before the Cold War had ended, Fretilin had shed almost all of its Marxist–Leninist influences and leaders. With the end of the Cold War, Ramos-Horta was prioritising Western support. An international solidarity movement rallied around him in Australia and the United States because of the shame many felt at their countries' complicity in the invasion and subsequent support for the Indonesian slaughter of Timorese civilians.

The feeling of responsibility gradually became even more profound in Portugal—sharply so after Santa Cruz. Portugal worked with the European Union to keep dialogue towards a peace process for East Timor open on the UN agenda. Portugal took Australia to the International Court of Justice in 1991 in an (unsuccessful) attempt to strike down its Timor Gap Treaty to allow exploitation of oil and gas resources in the sea between Australia and Timor. Australia recognised Indonesian sovereignty over East Timor in 1979 so that it could cut its oil deal. One of Portugal's and Ramos-Horta's accomplishments at the United Nations had been to keep Portuguese Timor on the list of non–self-governing territories, with Portugal recognised as the legal administering power.

Portugal, like Australia, was home to many Timorese refugees. Ultimately, it became a base from which support grew not only across the European Union, but also across the Portuguese-speaking diaspora. All parties in the Brazilian Parliament came to contribute to the Sao Paulo Parliamentary Front for East Timor's Independence (Wise 2006:32). Beginning with the votes at the United Nations between 1975 and 1982, Ramos-Horta became adept at calling forth fellow feeling from Mozambique and Angola. These former Portuguese colonies were particularly important in getting African support for East Timor. Mari Alkatiri and Roqué Rodriques led the work of building support in Africa itself.

Kofi Annan's tenure as Secretary-General of the United Nations from January 1997 saw an upgrading of East Timor dialogue on the UN agenda, with Ambassador Jamsheed Marker of Pakistan appointed as the Secretary-General's Personal Representative on East Timor. There were dozens of tripartite meetings involving Portugal, Indonesia and the United Nations between 1976 and 1999. There were also many of these meetings or other gatherings convened by Indonesia alone that East Timor representatives attended. Neither Ramos-Horta nor any of the other recognised leaders of the East Timor resistance attended in this capacity, usually because neither they nor the Indonesians wanted them to be there (Alatas 2006). While peace options such as autonomy within Indonesia were often discussed in these meetings, and while they sometimes included gestures at reconciliation between former Fretilin and UDT leaders, they were not genuine peace talks that included legitimate representatives of the insurgency or of the government deposed by the 1975 invasion. The 1975–99 conflict between East Timor and Indonesia is unusual for Peacebuilding Compared in that we have coded the number of peace talks between the warring parties as just one: the 1983 ceasefire talks. Of course, this is somewhat misleading because there was shuttle diplomacy of the Secretary-General's Personal Representative on East Timor between the Indonesian and resistance leadership, because of peacemaking elements in so many of the tripartite Portugal–Indonesia–United Nations meetings mentioned above, and because of many informal meetings between the imprisoned Xanana Gusmão and Indonesian leaders. Even so, the ultimate peace was not one forged by negotiations.

6. Santa Cruz Massacre, 1991

The Santa Cruz massacre was a turning point in the Timorese struggle. In October 1991, a Portuguese parliamentary delegation, working with the resistance and accompanied by media observers, was due in Dili to see the situation on the ground as part of the tripartite process towards a permanent settlement between Indonesia, Portugal and the United Nations. The Indonesian military set themselves the objective of deterring the kind of demonstrations that had occurred with the Pope's visit in 1989 in front of international media. A campaign of intimidation and harassment was directed at pro-independence groups.

Independence advocates who the military suspected might talk to the delegation were rounded up. Meetings were held all over Timor warning people that if they spoke to the delegation, they would be killed. Bishop Belo told Allan Nairn (1992) of *The New Yorker* that the army was saying that anyone who spoke up or demonstrated in front of the delegation would be hunted down and killed 'to the seventh generation'. On 27 October 1991, the visit was cancelled over a dispute between Indonesia and Portugal as to whether Australian Jill Jolliffe and Portuguese Rui Araujo and Mario Robalo could be among the journalists approved to travel with the parliamentarians. The next day a pro-independence youth, Sebastião Gomes, was hunted by a government agent and killed with a shot in the stomach while he was seeking sanctuary with other young people in the Motael Church in Dili. During the encounter, an Indonesian intelligence agent also suffered fatal injuries inflicted with a sharp instrument.

The plan of Xanana Gusmão and the Executive Committee of the Resistance (CAVR 2006:Ch. 7, p. 28) for the clandestine youth to organise a huge demonstration in front of the Portuguese delegation was then switched to a march after mass from the Motael Church to Sebastião's grave in the Santa Cruz Cemetery. Clandestine youth distributed tapes of Xanana urging people to stand up against the Indonesian military; the tapes were passed on and then the message came that people were to mass for a demonstration at Sebastião's grave on 12 November (Rei 2007:50). We interviewed a member of the clandestine network whose job it was to go to Bali and persuade international journalists to come to Dili for 12 November even though the Portuguese delegation was not visiting, and to help the journalists get in and get out. Key members of the diplomacy front also worked to persuade journalists to attend the Santa Cruz act of defiance.

Indonesian spokesmen claimed two Indonesian soldiers were stabbed during the march that swelled to 3000 or more mostly young people including many children in school uniforms. Journalists present saw a scuffle with a major and another soldier in civilian clothes during the march but doubted there was a stabbing (Nairn 1992). Like others, we have not found any eyewitness accounts of the alleged stabbing (Asia Watch 1991:6). This scuffle occurred half an hour before the massacre. The young people unfurled pro-independence banners and images of Xanana after the march was under way. Banners were pitched at the international media. Their messages included 'Indonesia, Why You Shoot Our Church?' and pleas to 'President Busch' (Nairn 1992). Another banner, filmed by Max Stahl, said: 'Independent Is What We Inspire.' Inspire they did. Jill Jolliffe (2001) argues that Santa Cruz involved a daring new level of defiance never risked before: 'for the first time, they would show the world their support for the guerilla resistance.'

Acting on orders,[1] and without warning the crowd to disperse, troops opened fire on the crowd, driving them into the walled cemetery. They then moved about the cemetery shooting and bayoneting protestors inside. Bodies piled up at the gate to the cemetery as marchers sought to flee back out. There is no doubt from the huge amount of eyewitness evidence collected by the Commission for Reception, Truth and Reconciliation (CAVR) and other investigations independent of Indonesia that this was an intentional, premeditated massacre, as opposed to a panicked reaction to crowd violence. Shooting continued for about 15 minutes on many accounts before there were orders to cease firing and pile the wounded and dead into trucks. On the highest systematic count of the time, 271 East Timorese were killed,[2] 382 wounded and 250 were missing afterwards (ABC News 2006). In April 2009, Australian and Argentine forensic scientists found 16 bodies that they concluded were gunshot victims of Santa Cruz (ABC News 2009). *Anatomy of a Massacre*, an Australian Broadcasting Commission (ABC) documentary on this forensic work first shown in 2010, interprets it as consistent with the 'second massacre' theory promoted by John Pilger (1994), Bishop Belo, Max Stahl and Matthew Jardine (1995:16) among others, and vigorously denied by Indonesia. This was that many who were arrested at the cemetery—some wounded—were taken to a military hospital and other locations and later shot or killed by driving trucks over piles of wounded bodies. The Victorian Institute of Forensic Medicine found there were 'horrific crushing injuries on bones' and bullet wounds to sculls consistent with shooting after the massacre. Eyewitnesses of both the shooting of arrestees and the driving of trucks over them spoke on the documentary, as had other eyewitnesses on the documentary John Pilger made soon after the massacre, *Death of a Nation*.

---

[1] One defence offered by the Indonesian military is that the order 'Don't fire' was misunderstood. This is implausible as an explanation because it does not explain why the firing then continued for 15 minutes or more, followed by bayoneting and smashing the heads of the wounded with rifle butts (as recorded on Max Stahl's video).

[2] The most thorough investigation, the CAVR (2006:Part 3, p. 117), opted for 271 killed and 250 missing as the number—or, that because of the uncertain basis of the evidence, a figure of 200 'is not an unreasonable estimate'. The official Indonesian figure was 19 killed, later increased to 50 (CAVR 2006:Part 3, p. 117).

Some of the 10 foreign journalists who witnessed the massacre were beaten and had their cameras taken. One young New Zealand journalist/student was shot and killed (Severino 2006:124). British cameraman Max Stahl managed to bury a tape at a gravesite before his camera was seized. A Dutch journalist, Saskia Kouwenberg, cut her finger before she went through airport security with the tape. She 'smeared the blood on her underwear, and placed the tape inside. The future history of East Timor was critically influenced by the fact that the Indonesian inspector who made her undress did not insist on checking below her bloodstained underpants' (Federer 2005:36).

The Impact of Santa Cruz

At no point in the history of its struggle was Falintil as desperate and decimated as it was on the eve of Santa Cruz. Gusmão has stated that he was down to fewer than 100 troops, which might have been the case since about 1987 (Smith with Dee 2003:40), and perhaps 45 rifles (CAVR 2006:Part 5, p. 39). After the massacre, Falintil strength is reported by CAVR (2006:Part V, p. 39) to have grown to 245 guerillas with 130 rifles. Santa Cruz also fuelled a huge surge of support for the clandestine movement, notwithstanding increased terror directed against it that drove it further underground at first. The military was 'prepared to kill anyone they had seen at the rally' (Rei 2007:55) in the months after the massacre. Figure 4.7 from the CAVR shows that detention, torture and ill treatment reduced after the level of resistance went down between 1985 and 1990, moving up from 1991 to begin a U-curve of atrocities in Timor. The same CAVR (2006:Part 7, Ch. 4) data also suggest that the struggle became more feminised after Santa Cruz, with the percentage of detention, torture and ill-treatment cases of women increasing markedly from 1991, though never reaching the level they had been between 1975 and the early 1980s.

Notwithstanding the crushing of media coverage of the massacre inside Indonesia, educated public opinion began to know the truth. One way was by reading international newspapers. Underground copies of Stahl's video were widely circulated by the democracy and human rights movements in Indonesia. Informed Indonesian public opinion from this point began to turn against the occupation and the government that was lying about it. Ties between the wider Indonesian democracy and human rights movements and the East Timor clandestine movement strengthened. Indonesian support groups for self-determination for East Timor formed in a number of cities across Java after Santa Cruz. A number of NGOs joined to form the Joint Committee for the Defence of East Timor, among other solidarity groups of Indonesians (CAVR 2006:Ch. 3, p. 119).

The first of many demonstrations of Timorese students in Jakarta occurred a week after Santa Cruz (19 November 1991) to honour the sacrifice of the fallen. Seventy brave Timorese students studying in Jakarta were arrested. They carried banners with slogans such as 'The Mass Murder on November 12 was only a Small Part of the Mass Murder Carried Out for the Last 16 Years'; 'Independence is the Right of all Peoples, Where Are Our Rights?'; 'Better Death than Integration' and 'Where are the Corpses?' (Asia Watch 1991:14). These and the subsequent fence-jumping demonstrations at foreign embassies required young people to take enormous risks. Our interviews reveal that they realised that they were placing their lives and their university enrolments at risk. They worried and discussed among themselves whether their leaders might be putting them in situations where they might be mown down by the military like the young victims of Santa Cruz.

Figure 6.1: The young man filmed by Max Stahl at Santa Cruz who prayed in Portuguese before the life drained from him

Photo: ITV Studios Global Entertainment

The massacre footage galvanised international civil society. As a result, the UN Commission on Human Rights was able to pass a resolution critical of Indonesian practices in East Timor in 1993 (Jardine 2000:58). The US Congress and the European Parliament carried resolutions condemning Indonesia, and Canada, the Netherlands and Denmark suspended aid (Jardine 1995:17). Heads of state of many other countries publicly expressed concern. The impact was especially emotional in Portugal where a national day of mourning was held 19 November. Santa Cruz was an identifiably Portuguese cemetery. One piece of tape showed 'a young man, his profusely bleeding stomach ripped open by bullets and a bayonet, making what appeared to be his last prayer, for which he used the Portuguese language' (Federer 2005:36).

After Santa Cruz, the international media began to seek more images to feed the new interest in East Timor with follow-up stories. The clandestine network was able to supply them. One that was widely distributed (see Aubrey 1998) through the international solidarity movement was a photo of a young girl's corpse, lying naked in her torture cell,

> covered in cuts and horrific wounds. Various profanities written in Bahasa Indonesia are written on her body, and a crucifix has been drawn on her stomach. Stuck to the wall just above her head is a picture of Jesus Christ, and at her feet is a sign in Bahasa, paralleling the death of Christ on the Cross, which translates as 'If you really are God, come down and bring her back to life'. (Wise 2006:110–11)

Solidarity movement web sites later in the 1990s began to distribute a large gallery of images of atrocities. Self-censorship by the media prevented most horrific photographs from being published. Then the international solidarity movement published them in books, and Ramos-Horta presented them to the press in Geneva while appearing before the UN Commission on Human Rights. The forced closure by the police of an exhibition of images that included nails driven through the bodies of raped women created an opportunity for the solidarity movement to ride a censorship/obscenity, 'spectatorial complicity' debate that was covered on prominent Australian current affairs programs such as the *7.30 Report* (McCosker 2004:68).

Santa Cruz gave the Timor lobby a decisive upper hand over the Indonesia lobby for the first time internationally. Attempts by Indonesia's closest friends to defend it were ridiculed. As discussed earlier, critics such as John Pilger (1994:312) excoriated Australian Foreign Minister Evans for saying that the Indonesian human rights record had improved and later that Santa Cruz was 'an aberration, not an act of state policy'. Evans also said the victims who were unaccounted for 'might simply have gone bush' (Pilger 1994:312) when we know today at least some of them turned up in the bush years later with bullet holes in their skulls. While Evans' latter comments are hard to defend, Figure 4.7 suggests that, speaking early in 1991, he was right to say there had been some improvement. Bishop Belo alleged survivors of the massacre were later killed in the military hospital and other places—the 'second massacre' that Pilger referred to in his documentary *Death of a Nation*. In casting doubt on Pilger's evidence, Prime Minister Paul Keating of Australia even cast doubt on the original massacre, saying 'it isn't clear what happened' (Pilger 1994:314). Pilger and the solidarity movement won this contest for Western public opinion resoundingly, and Australian leaders were again seen as apologists for a crime against humanity.

The Indonesian Government attempted to show it disapproved of what happened at Santa Cruz by establishing a National Investigation Commission. While Jakarta blamed the demonstrators for provocation by acting belligerently, the two senior regional military commanders were relieved of their posts as a result of the commission's recommendation. Six senior officers down to battalion commander level were dismissed or demoted (Singh 1996:166). Nine more junior members of the military were court-martialled for disobeying or exceeding orders and sentenced to 8–18 months' prison. This contrasted with the much longer prison terms (nine years to life) given to 13 demonstrators (Singh 1996:167) and the summary death sentence inflicted on uncounted others after they had been interrogated about their involvement in the demonstration. That this was not the work of some rogue junior officers was evident when the commander of the Indonesian military at the time of the massacre, Try Sutrisno (soon to become Vice-President), told graduates at the Indonesian Military Academy that the Timorese 'disrupters' 'must be crushed'. He said: 'Delinquents like these have to be shot, and we will shoot them.' His regional commander for East Timor added: 'We don't regret anything' (CAVR 2006:Part 3, p. 117; Jardine 1995:17). The new commander installed in Dili, Brigadier Theo Sjafei, said: 'If something similar to the 12 November event were to happen under my leadership, the number of victims would probably be higher' (Taylor 1999:xiii).

Damien Kingsbury (2009:60–3) conceives Santa Cruz as perhaps 'the biggest tactical mistake' of the Indonesian military. He tentatively interprets it in terms of anti-Suharto leaders in the Indonesian military wanting to assert a tougher line on military control of Timor and at the same time seeking to embarrass pro-Suharto military leaders by setting them up for culpability.

Was Santa Cruz Intentional Provocation?

Bishop Belo was a strong critic of the murderous behaviour of the Indonesian military before, during and after Santa Cruz and one of the people who argued for the need for an investigation into the possibility of a second massacre of the wounded and the arrested. But he also construed the demonstration as 'a provocative action and uncalled for at that' (Singh 1996:285). Bishop Belo accepted that an Indonesian major had been stabbed during the march—a conclusion that many of the independent observers were uncertain about. Major-General Sintong Panjaitan, the regional military commander based in Bali, in his first military report on the incident also alleged that a grenade had been thrown near the cemetery and that someone fired a pistol in the direction of the soldiers at the cemetery immediately before they fired (Singh 1996:160)—something not reported by any of the Timorese or international observers. A report of the Indonesian Foreign Ministry, however, says: 'A grenade was thrown in the direction of the troops but it didn't explode' (Asia Watch 1991:24). Of course, if it did not explode no-one would have heard it. This report says that at the same time there was the shot 'from a source that could not be determined together with movements and shouts to advance and attack and grab the guns of security forces' (Asia Watch 1991:24). None of the independent observers saw any of this. According to the Associated Press, a Bishop Belo letter six days later said someone had lobbed a grenade at the nearby police station, not in the midst of the troops at the cemetery (Asia Watch 1991:7).

Evidence of violent provocation by the youth in the march is therefore thin and inconsistent. There is overwhelming evidence of efforts by the youth marshals of the march to ensure disciplined nonviolent protest and there is evidence that such discipline was what was ordered by Xanana Gusmão. Views in Timor-Leste differ on whether the intent of the leaders of the resistance in 1991 was to use nonviolent protest to provoke an extremely violent reaction from the military. If the intent was to use the presence of 10 international journalists in Dili—some with an extraordinary level of courage and commitment to getting their tapes out—to get the waning East Timor cause back on the international agenda by provoking violence then it was remarkably successful in achieving that. On balance, we think that probably was the intent of some leaders. This was not a normal context of demonstrating in a way that takes a risk with the patience of the security forces. It was a context where the military had been going from village to village all over the province to get the message across in the clearest possible terms that anyone who demonstrated or spoke out of line while the international media (and the parliamentary delegation) was in town would be killed. And the military was backing this up with violence in advance of 12 November that proved how deadly serious it was.

In this context, pro-independence banners, chants of 'Long live Xanana' and display of Fretilin flags were kinds of nonviolence that were almost certain to provoke violence. Even in the more democratic, more rights-sensitive Indonesia of today, the military in West Papua remains inclined to respond to pro-independence chants in demonstrations and independence flag raisings with deadly force (Braithwaite et al. 2010a:Ch. 2). The military leadership in East Timor promised death to demonstrators; they delivered on that promise; afterwards they said they had no regrets about it and would do it again in the same circumstances. None of this was a great surprise to the planners of the Santa Cruz demonstration. Nor was it to the filmmaker Max Stahl, who said in the documentary *Anatomy of a Massacre* that '[t]hey were prepared to walk into the bullets peacefully'. On Stahl's tape, several young people said as they were filmed preparing banners in the days before the march that they were prepared to die, or were not afraid to die (see Yorkshire Television's *Cold Blood: The massacre of East Timor*). In his interview with us, one senior Falintil commander who remains a major figure in Timor-Leste today described Santa Cruz as an 'intentional sacrifice' to provoke a turning point externally and internally, though he had not expected the violent response would be so extreme. The extent of killing was much greater than in Sharpeville in South Africa 30 years earlier, and the turning point that it delivered was much more decisive.

A youth leader in the clandestine network who was involved in organising the Santa Cruz march told us that leaders of different youth groups were instructed to gather their members together and ask them if they were willing to die or to be tortured or raped for their country; 'If not, go'. Xanana Gusmão's deputy Falintil commander, Mauhudo who was later killed, was said to have been the leader who instructed this and other youth leaders to go to their groups with those fateful questions. Many high school children did leave and declined to participate when they were told this was what they were being asked to risk. On Max Stahl's tape, we see a group of girls in school uniforms looking very afraid and hanging back from joining the march. Later, we see that some did join. And some of these brave and frightened girls were killed. The youth leader said '[i]t was the intention to create an incident in which many would be killed'. He admitted to feeling bad about this in retrospect and acknowledged that it was a human rights violation to sacrifice young peoples' lives. Yet he said the resistance had 'no options' at that time. He felt more stringent criticism should be directed at the West for leaving them in this position, for failing to speak out against the loss of tens of thousands of children's lives in the mountains.

According to a key organiser of the Santa Cruz demonstration, Constâncio Pinto (2009):

> There was [a] strong push from the clandestine youth to carry out the demonstration. The youth even threatened the leadership that if they did not authorize and organize the demonstration, they the youth would organise it by themselves without any coordination from resistance leaders. The demands of the youth to some extent affected the decision of the resistance leadership to decide on the Santa Cruz demonstration… We did not envisage at all that the Indonesian military would launch an attack, going on a rampage and shooting at the peaceful demonstration in Santa Cruz, killing hundreds. What we envisaged was that some youth leaders would be arrested, tortured, and interrogated.

Other senior people we interviewed said it was not the intention for anyone to die, while yet others said it was. It is possible of course that some leaders promoted intentional provocation of loss of life and others believed, or wishfully believed, that the military would not shoot live rounds while they were being watched by the world. Constâncio Pinto said in his memoirs:

> I sent a letter to Xanana, who was still hiding in Dili, asking him if he thought we should go ahead with a demonstration [once the Portuguese delegation had decided not to proceed with their visit]. But before the members of the executive committee made any decision, we received news from Jakarta that the UN Special Rapporteur on Torture, Pieter Kooijmans, was going to arrive in Dili on November 11, 1991. So we decided along with Xanana to take advantage of his visit and hold a peaceful demonstration. We didn't think that Indonesia would take any violent actions against the demonstrators in Kooijmans' presence. (Pinto and Jardine 1997:189)

In the event, Kooijmans was not present. The intent had been to march to his hotel after visiting the cemetery. He was in meetings elsewhere in Dili at the time.

In the Santa Cruz march, as in other demonstrations, schoolchildren whose parents were supportive of Indonesia, in many cases because they were public servants in good jobs, were enticed into the front ranks, sometimes by girlfriends or boyfriends. The idea was that this way they would be most likely to experience the violence of the security forces and this would turn pro-Indonesia families back to the resistance movement. We were told that the way Santa Cruz unfolded, however, as an attack in effect on the rear of the crowd, meant that only 10 to 20 such youth from pro-integration families were killed. A number of key members of the clandestine network were forbidden from attending the march, partly because they were too important to lose, but also for reasons such as not wanting couriers to come under surveillance after being photographed at the march, thereby compromising their effectiveness.

In the months after Santa Cruz, Xanana Gusmão did not grasp at first how effective a turning point this had been. His biographer, Sara Niner (2009:142), says he began to worry that their fight was a 'collective suicide':

> He began to doubt the struggle and all the sacrifices he had overseen as leader. He suffered guilt and depression, displaying an emotional neediness that when met with indifference or rejection, quickly bubbled over into outrage, anger and sarcasm, resulting in further recklessness. Black ironic barbs signaled his frustration.

Constâncio Pinto (1997:195) worried about how he would deal with parents who alleged '[y]ou were the one who gave the order to demonstrate', when he had not participated himself. No Timorese as far as Pinto or we can tell did blame the leaders. Parents blamed the Indonesian military and were proud of their children as martyrs for their country. Their pride was understandable. Without their sacrifice, the torture, rape and disappearances of Timorese might still continue. Of course, the decision to go ahead with this demonstration was putting young people at risk. There might have been different shades of intent to risk but avert death or to actually provoke murder in front of the cameras. For the most part, there was informed consent, although that was imperfect, especially in the case of children.

Xanana Gusmão led his people from violent resistance to the morally preferable path of nonviolent resistance. Yet Santa Cruz shows there is no moral purity to nonviolence. As in war, young people are put in the firing line; some never see their families and parents again. It is worth reflecting that no-one in the United States, not even the parents of white student activists who were murdered in the civil rights campaign of the 1960s, blame Martin Luther King jr (or the Kennedys who supported his reform program in the Capitol) for leading young activists to their death. We might think this is because these leaders, who knew that there were people committed to killing them, sacrificed their own lives as well, rather than retiring from the fight in the face of threats. Perhaps no-one blames Gandhi for the lives lost in the nonviolence against colonialism because he himself was murdered for his nonviolence. Yet equally no-one blames Mandela or the other black South African leaders for the Sharpeville massacre. And no-one—except of course the leadership of the Indonesian army—blamed Xanana Gusmão or his leadership group for Santa Cruz. But Xanana Gusmão was tormented by guilt after Santa Cruz, fuelled by the erroneous belief that Santa Cruz had failed. He wrote, in what Sara Niner (2009:142) described as a 'warm, loving tone', to supporters: 'As a Commander leading an armed struggle I transcend ethics and morals when I encourage my men to face death' (Niner 2009:142).

Nonviolence is a morally preferable path of resistance than violence for consequentialist reasons, particularly because it results in fewer deaths. It is not that it is morally superior because no-one dies in nonviolent struggles. The Indonesian invasion of East Timor was illegal and immoral, and at first armed resistance was somewhat effective in the circumstances. Armed resistance would not be morally justified if it sacrificed young lives with no prospect of forcing the invader into a peace process. The shift Xanana Gusmão led away from violence and towards nonviolence as the primary strategy of resistance was even more morally justified. This was because it achieved more in pursuit of a morally just result at a cost of fewer lives than persisting with fighting a war.

So we do not discuss the shades of moral grey in encouraging children to participate in demonstrations that put them in grave risk to point a finger of blame at Xanana Gusmão or anyone else. He never imagined he would be in a position to reflect for decades on this question. There is plenty of evidence that he imagined he would be killed (probably during one of his visits to Dili) like all his predecessors and his immediate successors in the leadership of the insurgency.

We discuss the shades of moral grey in the complex judgments leaders made at Santa Cruz because, if tactics of nonviolence are to become more decent and effective, we must learn from the decision-making dilemmas they throw up at critical junctures in human history. We must seek to face the truth of what happened and to improve nonviolent strategy in light of cold analysis with warm values. We were particularly struck by the importance of this during our interviews in West Papua in 2007 when West Papuan youth leaders said to us that their strategy was at the right time to trigger a 'super Santa Cruz' to gain the independence of West Papua from Indonesia (Braithwaite et al. 2010a:Ch. 2).

While Santa Cruz was the decisive turning point towards liberty and peace for Timor-Leste, we doubt that the context of media exclusion that was transcended by Santa Cruz could ever be quite the same in the second decade of the twenty-first century, in West Papua or anywhere else. One difference is that modern security forces have learnt lessons from Sharpeville and Santa Cruz. Another is that violence in response to nonviolent resistance can no longer be kept away from the international media by keeping journalists out of conflict zones, as the Indonesians had successfully done for so many years until 1991. As the 2009 demonstrations in Iran and the 2011 demonstrations across the Arab world showed, in contemporary conditions at any large demonstration there are thousands of movie cameras present on young people's mobile phones. They do not need to bury the tape in a grave and then spirit it through airport security. It is much easier to steer the images around the inept Internet security censorship authoritarian regimes seek to impose.

This means there is today less imperative to provoke something special in circumstances where representatives of the international media are physically present. In a place like West Papua, rather than smuggling in foreign journalists and then creating special confrontations for them to film, it is easier for Papuan activists to learn to train all their supporters to become more furtive and efficient at recording on their phones daily acts of violence in response to nonviolence, as well as larger acts of violence in response to mass demonstrations. As cases like Rodney King's beating by the Los Angeles police in 1991, and the 2009 death by heart attack of an innocent passer-by at a demonstration who was assaulted by a British police officer, show, it is not how widespread the scale of violence is that grips the international imagination. It is the narrative of a specific victim, and the momentary grab of violence that changes his or her life, that engages a global audience.

Just as the scale of killing is not the main issue, nor is the horror of the violence. The most horrifying images of state violence in East Timor, such as those of raped women with nails driven through their naked bodies, received little exposure in the international media. Max Stahl's images were widely used because they left something to the imagination. The image of the boy shot and bayoneted in the stomach is awful as he approaches death in the arms of his relative who bravely stays to comfort him. We imagine the relative will also be killed because he does not flee. We never see the horror of the gaping bayonet wound that is draining the boy's life away. They lift the bloodstained shirt to peek at it, but the television audience does not see it. Stahl's other master image was of people, some wounded, running free after clambering over a growing pile of bodies at the entrance to the cemetery. This also only communicates horrific death in our imagination. We do not see any of those piled bodies actually suffer the final crush that kills them. We must imagine that in our engagement with suffering that is not so gross as to cause us to switch to another channel. So the modus operandi of modern nonviolence could be to film furtively many instances of violent response to nonviolence that routinely occur in circumstances of repression. These need to be culled to images that offer the most evocative and personalised narratives, which need to be connected with a structural narrative of oppression for those who wish to engage with root causes and pathways to resistance. This was written before the Arab Spring spread from the narrative of the petrol-doused suicide of vegetable vendor Mohammed Bouazizi, after he could not afford a bribe demanded by a Tunisian police officer. This became the most dramatic illustration in recent history that it is the video-narrative that counts—in this case, assisted by the victim's last Facebook post to his mother asking forgiveness for the suicide, not the horror of the picture.

In other words, West Papua probably does not need the 'super Santa Cruz' the young Free Papua Movement leaders aspire to. Credible insiders like Xanana Gusmão and José Ramos-Horta, reflecting openly on the moral agony involved in putting young people at risk at Santa Cruz, have an important role here. Their reflections on which elements of Santa Cruz would, and would not, translate to a context like West Papua would be a great service to the longsuffering indigenous people of West Papua and also to their Indonesian masters. And such reflection would be a service to learning the lessons of effective nonviolence that pushes the risk of confronting tyranny to its morally acceptable limits. The moral philosophers have special contributions to make to this debate. But first we need richer, more nuanced truth telling about the contested tactics of nonviolence at Santa Cruz that changed the course of history.

7. *Reformasi* and Referendum, 1998–1999

This chapter tells the story of how the patient networked struggle for freedom finally benefited from an external shock that created its moment of opportunity to work not only for freedom for Timor but also for democracy for all Indonesia. It then tells the tale of how militias sponsored by the Indonesian military pushed back murderously but unsuccessfully against democracy.

Renegotiating the Nation

There were two schools of thought within the 1990s East Timor resistance on the potential for the demise of President Suharto. The dominant view was that if Suharto's New Order was displaced in a wave of democratic reform, East Timor might ride that wave by having the democratic aspirations of its people respected through a referendum. The alternative view was that it was best that Suharto be persuaded before he left office that the diplomatic and economic costs of hanging onto tiny Timor did not justify the benefits. This was because any successor to Suharto could never be as capable as Suharto of standing up to the military on an issue as vital to their interests and world view as East Timor. While there was a grain of truth in the second analysis, the first turned out to be true to the way events unfolded.

Others have documented how the Asian financial crisis ushered in the collapse of Suharto's New Order in May 1998 (Aspinall 2005; Bertrand 2004; Rinakit 2005). Braithwaite et al. (2010a) diagnosed anomie—a breakdown of the normative order—in many parts of Indonesia from the late 1990s after the collapse of Suharto's regime in conditions of uncertainty created by the Asian financial crisis. Jemma Purdey (2006:203) articulated this in a slightly different way: 'many Indonesians interpreted *reformasi* [post Suharto] as a new freedom to resolve injustices, perceived or real, by means of mass mobilisation.' The situation in Indonesia in 1998 was that the old rules were swept away for a period. What the new rules of the game would be was up for grabs.

The student pro-democracy movement was emboldening ordinary Indonesians to join them in the streets and then emboldening the business community and growing sections of the military to abandon Suharto (Kingsbury 2009:66). In 1998, Suharto could no longer sustain a balancing act of managing the splits in the military elite, the student-led demonstrations and then anti-Chinese rioting that devastated a large section of the capital. The Asian financial crisis of 1997 and 1998 increasingly wobbled the tightrope on which he balanced until he fell. Suharto was seen as mismanaging the International Monetary Fund (IMF) terms for saving the collapsed Indonesian rupiah. He had mishandled a sequence of different kinds of demonstrations across Indonesia since the mid-1990s, including demonstrations about East Timor or in which Timorese students were vocal. He had stumbled in handling corruption scandals involving himself and his children and another corruption scandal in 1995 that set cabinet ministers against one another in a way that showed that elites 'were beginning to jockey for the post-Suharto period' (van Klinken 2007:23). A group of cabinet ministers threatened to resign if he did not step down. The new president, B. J. Habibie, was a protégé of Suharto who wanted to demonstrate that he would be very different from his mentor: that he would be a democratic reformer who would respond to what the students were demanding on the streets, and a peacemaker. The further debates and demonstrations that *reformasi* engendered about institutional reform also opened new fronts of negotiation over ethnic and religious groups' claims to representation (Bertrand 2004:5). Bertrand's (2004:10) historical institutionalist analysis points out that 'when institutions are weakened during transition periods, allocations of power and resources become open for competition'. At critical junctures, the implicit and explicit ethnic inclusions and exclusions can be contested to 'renegotiate the concept of the nation' (Bertrand 2004:10).

One theme of brand differentiation from Suharto that Habibie explored immediately was his earlier advocacy, when Technology Minister, of an act of self-determination that might get the international community off the nation's back on East Timor. This had been firmly rejected by the military and Suharto at the time. In March 1998, Habibie initiated discussions with Portugal under UN auspices on options for special autonomy for the province that might include a ballot to choose between independence and special autonomy within Indonesia. An offer in the following months of 1998 of special autonomy in return for recognition of Indonesian sovereignty sparked massive demonstrations in East Timor demanding nothing short of a referendum. On 23 June 1998, one-third of the population of Dili was reported to have participated in a street demonstration in support of a referendum (Aspinall and Berger 2001:1009).

Revisionist Howard–Downer Diplomacy

In this climate of renegotiation of the concept of the nation, both domestic and international advocacy became more shrill for a referendum to provide an opportunity for the people of East Timor to redefine their relationship to the nation. On 6 June 1998, the Political and Security Committee of the new Habibie cabinet showed that the rules were changing by supporting a proposal for 'wide-ranging autonomy' for East Timor.

President Habibie was a man easily irritated. One thing he told his staff that recurrently annoyed him was foreign leaders arriving for talks on matters he regarded as important, and then insisting on raising East Timor. The diplomatic front and the international solidarity movement had by 1998 been effective in creating a kind of 'Timor fatigue' among Jakarta elites akin to the Vietnam fatigue in Washington in the 1970s (Webster 2003:24). A letter that arrived from Australian Prime Minister, John Howard (dated 19 December 1998), particularly piqued Habibie, as persons present in the cabinet room when it was discussed attested. Howard himself expressed doubt to us that the letter had angered Habibie, but a number of individuals closer to Habibie were clear it did. The letter indicated a sharp shift in Australian policy towards East Timor. Laurie Brereton, the Australian Labor Party foreign affairs spokesman—against some opposition from figures like the current Foreign Minister, Kevin Rudd (Daley 2008)—had already changed Labor policy back to acknowledging the right of the people of East Timor to self-determination. Howard sensed that this struck an approving chord in the Australian electorate.[1] Moreover, he and his Foreign Minister, Alexander Downer, both told us that they had come to the view that the status quo in East Timor was untenable. Australia's policy position certainly became tricky when it had been asserting a more conservative approach than Indonesia now was itself under Habibie. Howard's preference was for East Timor to stay in Indonesia, but with some special autonomy arrangements, and with a right to vote for independence if the special autonomy package proved unsatisfactory. So he proposed direct Indonesian negotiations with Xanana Gusmão and other leaders from East Timor on an autonomy package that would build in 'a review mechanism along the lines of the Matignon Accords in New Caledonia'. This accord between France and the New Caledonia independence movement deferred a referendum for at least 10 years, during which an autonomy package would be given a chance to work. This was actually the same approach Gusmão and Ramos-Horta had proposed five years earlier.

One thing that irritated Habibie was equating Indonesia with a colonial power, France. When he discussed the letter with his Foreign Minister, he said rhetorically:

> Why should we continue to carry the political and financial burden of governing and developing East Timor, continue to be responsible and blamed by the world whenever something goes wrong and then, after five to ten years, only to be told by the East Timorese: 'Thank you, but now we want to be independent'? (Alatas 2006:149)

---

1 Downer's adviser, Greg Hunt, observed: 'Public opinion probably ran at 90 per cent that Australia had done the wrong thing by East Timor. There was a moral unease, a sense that something should be done. I know that Alexander felt this' (Kelly 2009:488).

Habibie also felt a delayed referendum would be leaving a time bomb for future governments. As Hugh White (2008:74) put it, 'subsequent experience suggests that Habibie was right to say that a protracted period of transition would create an unmanageable security problem in East Timor'. When Habibie sent Howard's letter to cabinet members for discussion, he had scribbled on it:

> [I]f the question of East Timor has become a burden to the struggle and image of the Indonesian Nation and if after 22 years of common history with the Indonesian people…the people of East Timor cannot become united with us, then it would be appropriate and wise if the People's Consultative Assembly were to decide that this 27th Province of East Timor be allowed to separate honourably from the Unitary Republic of Indonesia. (Alatas 2006:151)

Cabinet was surprisingly compliant with this momentous proposal to give East Timor an independence referendum immediately. Most believed that if the right tactics were used, a majority would vote to stay with Indonesia or at least the vote would be close enough to dispute (Chesterman 2002:60). It was a mixture of group-think and limited experience of genuine democracy with international monitors; some key cabinet members assumed it would be possible to put in the fix as had been done with the Act of Free Choice in Papua in 1969 (Fernandes 2008:88). In military interviews, we were told that some generals believed that military intimidation of voters could deliver a voter registration below 60 per cent, in which case the Indonesian Parliament would never vote to endorse independence. The influential economic ministers could see benefits for their tricky task of pruning government expenditure if East Timor were cut off. General Wiranto, who was then both Defence Minister and Armed Forces Commander, might have seen Habibie's decision as a mistake that could prove fatal for Habibie in a future presidential contest with Wiranto, so he held his tongue. Indeed, it did prove to be a terminal political mistake by Habibie. Yet the way Wiranto's armed forces responded to the referendum outcome also destroyed Wiranto's hopes of becoming the next president. Foreign Minister, Ali Alatas, was the only senior cabinet member to raise strenuous objections to the referendum. Even Alatas had cause to ponder clever CNRT footwork to suggest that the ballot might turn out in Indonesia's favour in the end:

> Just before the ballot, in July 1999, Indonesia held its general elections, with East Timor strongly returning the local candidates of the governing party, Golkar. The clear intention of this vote, organized by CNRT, was to allay any fears in Jakarta that the people of the territory might vote other than in favor of the status quo. For some in Jakarta the ploy worked. Indonesia's foreign minister, Ali Alatas, said, 'Up to the balloting, the report we got from our own people, of the prointegration people, including Lopes da Cruz [former Governor and head of the East

Timor Peoples' Front, a political front for the militias] and so on, is that we were going to win'. That Francisco Lopes da Cruz believed that victory was likely showed just how well the CNRT had disguised its intentions. (Kingsbury 2009:71)

Militia Murder

Soon after the announcement of the referendum, violent attacks on independence supporters by military-backed militias began. A massacre occurred on 6 April 1999 of possibly 60 people seeking refuge in a church in Liquica (Robinson 2003:192–6). A New Zealand military officer who was posted in Liquica described the modus operandi of the Indonesian military in 1999. They said to people that they would have to kill someone in their village or the military would kill them. '"You're going to be on our side." They put blood on their hands' (Interview, August 2007). And there were many lesser mass murders. The massive evidence accumulated by the CAVR (2006) makes it clear that there was a conscious military strategy to intimidate people, using Timorese militias armed by the military as proxies, against voting for independence. Quite a lot of terror was executed and directed by the military as well. Many senior military commanders in both Timor and Java believed this would work in securing a vote against independence. Generals behind the plans to move Kopassus troops and trained paramilitaries into Timor in November 1998 included Tyasno Sudarso, head of military intelligence, his predecessor, Zacky Anwar Makarim, and the regional commander, Adam Damiri (Taylor 1999:xix).

Military terror had worked before in other parts of Indonesia in securing election outcomes favoured by the military. The Indonesian military had an investment in East Timor of 'blood and treasure' (Kelly 2009:495). The militarised violence was not only a strike against the support base for independence; the mayhem it created was a strike against Habibie's political survival.[2] Driving people from their homes to flee to the seeming safety of West Timor was also calculated, according to UN analysis, to 'give the impression of a large-scale dissatisfaction with the vote' in the event that it was for independence (Kelly 2009:506; see also McDonald 2002:10–11) and to create various forms of leverage and cross-border discord (Robinson 2008:112). One hope was that this would persuade the Indonesian Parliament 'that a strong enough body of opinion existed to warrant a refusal to endorse the ballot result' (Australian Defence Intelligence Organisation report quoted in Ball 2002:259). Simple vengeance was also a motive.

---

2   An Australian Defence Intelligence Organisation brief of 9 September 1999 linked militia violence to General Wiranto's political ambitions: 'TNI has pursued a centrally conceived and directed strategy throughout the East Timor crisis…Its immediate aim was to retain East Timor as part of Indonesia. Its broader and longer-term aim was to strengthen the position of TNI, and Wiranto, in the Indonesian political system…All necessary force was to be employed, but with maximum deniability…International and domestic reactions to the carnage in East Timor probably exceed TNI expectations and TNI has maneuvered for Habibie to take the blame' (Ball 2002:258–9).

Figure 7.1: UN Secretary-General, Kofi Annan, and his wife, Nane Annan, in 2000 comfort survivors and family members of victims of the 6 April 1999 Liquica church massacre

Photo: Eskinder Debebe/United Nations Department of Public Information

Wiranto hedged his bets in the public eye by presenting himself at times as a peacemaker—for example, in March 1999 organising a reconciliation meeting between Xanana Gusmão and the very militia leaders his organisation was pushing into violent reprisals (Alatas 2006:170), and in April 1999 overseeing the signing of a peace agreement in Dili between independence and autonomy leaders to cease hostilities (CAVR 2006:Ch. 3.19, p. 131). The Bishops of Timor organised further reconciliation meetings in Jakarta in June between Timorese supporters of independence and those supporting integration—a follow-up to a previous one held in September 1998 in Dare (Alatas 2006:197). While they did not accomplish much towards mitigating the violence of 1999, it is an interesting question whether they began to lay a foundation for post-independence reconciliation between Timorese who fought on different sides. At such events it was a shock to the Indonesians to discover that even the militia leaders in their pay had more reverence and respect for Xanana Gusmão than for any Indonesian leader. Gusmão responded to demands from General Wiranto that his men disarm by confining all Falintil troops to cantonment to make it clear that his men were not provoking the violence. He asked Wiranto to reciprocate by disarming the militias and withdrawing his men to barracks. Wiranto refused (CAVR 2006:Ch. 3.19, p. 142). Militias in four districts did respond to the cantonment of Falintil, however, by surrendering their arms in ceremonies with the UN Mission in East Timor (UNAMET). While only a fraction of militia weapons was surrendered, perhaps some further loss of life was prevented in these four districts.

Australian military intelligence was as effective in Indonesia in 1999 as it was in 1975. Messages were intercepted and other intelligence gathered on the ground and from a senior militia leader who defected to Macao to avoid having to go through with the slaughter he was ordered to execute by senior members of the military (Ball 2002:2050–251). Ultimately, sophisticated intelligence was hardly necessary. The head of the Indonesian military in East Timor said on an Australian current affairs television program in June 1999:

> I want to give you this message. If the pro-independence side wins, it's not going to just be the government of Indonesia that has to deal with what follows. The UN and Australia are also going to have to solve the problem and well, if this does happen, then there'll be no winners. Everything is going to be destroyed. East Timor won't exist as it does now. It'll be much worse than 23 years ago [the 1975 invasion]. (CAVR 2006:Ch. 3.19, p. 138)

Militia leaders also gave addresses to large political meetings inside Timor saying quite openly that they would start a civil war if there were a vote for independence (Maley 2000). All this gave a clear picture of the military's scorched-earth plan and the plans to systematically murder independence supporters and their families. The plans were first to attempt to coerce and entice a vote for autonomy within Indonesia. If that failed and a majority voted for independence, there was a plan—'Operation Clean Sweep'—to loot or destroy things of value and execute hundreds of leaders. Part of the idea was to show separatists in other parts of Indonesia such as Aceh, Maluku and West Papua that independence would come at an intolerable price. Fernandes (2005) describes a number of phases in this plan:

> Use the militia proxies to contain and remove foreign observers.
>
> With foreigners unable to report, use the militia to attack the local population and use transport and logistics assets to move them across the border.
>
> Provoke a desperate retaliation from the desperately outnumbered… Falintil, thereby drawing it into a conventional war.
>
> Announce that TNI was forced to intervene between the 'factions', and then, freed from constraints, crush Falintil in conventional warfare.
>
> Create new facts on the ground, ensuring that the results of the ballot were irreversibly overturned. (Fernandes 2005:266)

After as many as 60 people were massacred at Liquica on 6 April 1999 (CAVR 2006:Chs 7.2, 3.19, p. 131), Prime Minister Howard became very concerned about the intelligence Australia was receiving. He asked President Habibie at a one-on-one meeting in Bali on 27 April to support an international peacekeeping force to supervise the independence vote. Howard says Habibie rejected this proposal emphatically. But in a subsequent plenary meeting attended by officials from both sides Habibie softened to agree ultimately to a UN deployment of 300 civilian police advisers, over objections from Wiranto.

Paul Kelly (2009:498) says Habibie had told Howard that 'if a peacekeeping force was imposed on Indonesia then it would abandon East Timor and the ballot and unilaterally withdraw'. Kelly went on to conclude that backdown was the only option because '[h]is threat would have doomed East Timor to civil war between integrationists and separatists'. This is an implausible analysis. Once Indonesian military funding and coercion of the militias to engage in violence ended, most would have stopped fighting. And in the event the militias did stop fighting when the military deserted them. Few of them were fighting out of conviction. Even their most prominent leader, Eurico Guteres, was recorded on camera complaining to a deputy that his men would take the money then most of them would vote for independence. And the militias would have realised that without the protection of the Indonesian military, they would be cut to pieces by Falintil. It would have been a matter of regret by the United Nations and everyone else had Indonesia walked out and washed its hands of the territory. Yet that course probably would have cost a thousand or so fewer lives and a self-determination plebiscite of an appropriately modified sort could still have proceeded under UN supervision.[3]

UN Peacekeepers: Appeasement then assertiveness

Hugh White (2008), Deputy Secretary for Strategy in the Australian Department of Defence in 1999, has been critical of Australia for not pushing much harder and much earlier for UN military peacekeepers in light of the intelligence it had of the likelihood of mass destruction and mass violence (see also Ball 2002; Fernandes 2011:191–206; Maley 2000; Nevins 2002).[4] His argument is that the Australian pressure for peacekeepers should have been applied earlier on the United Nations and Portugal in their Tripartite Agreement negotiation with Indonesia of the terms for the conduct of the referendum. For example, at a meeting in late February 1999, US Assistant Secretary of State, Dr Stanley Roth,

---

3   For a more pessimistic view, see Wheeler and Dunne (2001:815).
4   'We can never know whether, if pushed harder, Indonesia would have acquiesced. But it may well be that by not pushing harder at this time, both directly with Habibie and through others like the UN and the United States, we missed the last best chance to avoid the disasters of September [1999]' (White 2008:80).

pushed for an international peacekeeping force to supervise the elections, but Australia was reluctant at that meeting about such a military commitment. There were also Australia–Indonesia military-to-military leadership meetings, and second-track meetings of that kind as well, in which the Indonesian military was urged to cut its support for the marauding militias (Smith with Dee 2003:405).[5] White (2008:81) said of one of these meetings: 'And even at this late stage, this initiative to confront TNI over its activities in East Timor attracted criticism from inside the government in Canberra as potentially damaging to our relations with TNI.' The UN Secretary-General was aware of the Australian intelligence and secretly urged Australia to prepare for the worst (Nevins 2002:635), which Australia did by moving 2000 troops on alert to Darwin—just a short hop to Dili.

Figure 7.2: A Timorese woman shows her ink-stained finger as she exercises her right to vote

Photo: Glenn Campbell/Fairfax Media

The result of the 30 August 1999 ballot was a 78.5 per cent vote for independence by the remarkable 98.6 per cent of 480 000 registered electors who voted. The scorched-earth policy was implemented immediately after the result was announced by the United Nations on 4 September. Most of the 1200–1500 Timorese who were killed by the Indonesian military or the militias they backed lost their lives after the ballot (CAVR 2006:Ch. 3.19, p. 145). Young men who had

---

5 UNAMET leader Ian Martin also met with General Wiranto on 7 July to urge him to put a stop to the direction and active support his officers were giving in the ordering of militia violence. He presented UN evidence of the relationship between his officers and the militias (CAVR 2006:Ch. 3.19, p. 138).

worked for UNAMET were especially targeted for assassination. The majority of the population fled their homes, 70 per cent of which were razed—whole villages, entire towns. The complete stock of ancient artefacts in the East Timor Museum was taken to Indonesia. The Indonesian military supplied militias with fire engines with their watertanks filled with petrol to do the job (CAVR 2006:Ch. 3.19, p. 147). Recognising the importance of 'seeing like a state' (Scott 1998), every state record of property deeds, tax, marriages, courts—everything was destroyed. Xanana Gusmão's 'victory' speech after the announcement of the vote was one of the great rhetorical pleas for nonviolent struggle:

> I appeal to all the people to hide yourselves, to not go out because the evil people who kill us, within these years still want to continue to do so, seeking to wipe out the Maubere people.[6]
>
> I know, I have heard that Indonesian military in all places are shooting indiscriminately. I appeal that all people remain calm or leave their homes.
>
> Let them burn our homes, it doesn't matter. Let them rob the things that individually we have sweated for, it doesn't matter. I appeal to all the guerrillas, to commander Ruak, to all regional commanders, all my brothers and sisters to maintain your positions to not react to all of these things.
>
> We starve, we thirst, for 23 years and today I appeal, again to my dear brothers and sisters, to continue to endure. Endure the hunger. In order to save the people. Endure the thirst in order to save our country…
>
> I appeal to the commanders of the militias—Joao Tavares, Cancio de Carvalho, Eurico Guterres, Juaniku, Edmandu, and others as well. I appeal to all brothers and sisters to think properly. We can create a new Timor Lorosa'e in love and peace. (Oenarto 2000:2–3, 16)

By 7 September, Falintil Deputy Commander, Taur Matan Ruak (TMR, his *nom de guerre*), was saying to his leaders that he could no longer restrain his men from breaking out of cantonment to save their families. Such a breakout would have caused the civil war the Indonesian military leadership wanted to prevent the international military intervention that was the only hope to save the people (CAVR 2006:Ch. 3.19, pp. 146–7).

At this point, Australian Prime Minister Howard became a bold and decisive supporter of the military intervention that was needed. Now it was US President,

---

6   He was saying this because some of the intelligence that the United Nations and Falintil had received before the vote was for an even worse scenario than occurred. Part of that intelligence was orders dated 17 July 1999 from João da Silva Tavares, Commander-in-Chief of pro-integration forces, in the event of defeat at the ballot to kill 'those 15 years and older, including both males and females, without exception' (Chopra 2000:27).

Bill Clinton, who was hesitant. To Howard's surprise, East Timor was not on Clinton's radar. When he rang Clinton to ask for a commitment of combat troops, Clinton said the US military was heavily stretched elsewhere such as Kosovo, and turned Howard down. Howard and Downer then went public with their criticism of the United States—something that surprised everyone. Howard told us that he let Clinton know that Australia had always supported the United States militarily when it counted and now was the time to reciprocate. Howard and Downer were right, and they were effective in giving the US leadership the message that the Australian people would never forgive the United States if it failed to support a UN peacekeeping mission and failed to prevail on Indonesia to support it. The Portuguese Prime Minister, Antonio Guterres, called Clinton, threatening that Portuguese troops would be pulled out of Kosovo and NATO, and he prevented 16 US military flights from departing from their base in the Azores—a critical logistics base for any US foray to the Middle East (Fernandes 2008:94). He also persuaded British Prime Minister, Tony Blair, to press Clinton. As President Ramos-Horta put it in our interview with him in September 2009:

> Timor was strategically totally unimportant…It was the power of civil society that did the work through the electronic media. What was accomplished in 1999 could not have been accomplished in 1975 even though the slaughter was so much worse in 1975. This media campaign affected and got through to many US members of Congress such as Ted Kennedy and Nancy Pelosi. A group of them harassed the National Security Advisor for more than an hour over East Timor. These were the ones who stood by [Clinton] through the critical days of the efforts to impeach him. Sandy Berger promised he would change Clinton's speech and he did, dramatically. When Clinton walked out onto the White House lawn before heading to New Zealand he said: 'Indonesia must invite UN peacekeepers'.[7]

Solidarity: A resource delivered by Ramos-Horta

Clinton was a responsive politician who was moved not only by the force of the pressure from old friends but also by the quality of the arguments for UN intervention. He responded on 8 September 1999, calling Howard back to say he would support peacekeepers and make a tangible contribution. In the wash-up, these were formidable contributions logistically, but more importantly politically.

---

7   Clinton actually said 'must' twice with emphatic repetition: 'If Indonesia does not end the violence, it must invite, it must invite the international community to assist in restoring security' (Cusack 1999).

Clinton now moved to smash Habibie's resistance to a UN force by mobilizing the might of the United States. The IMF and the World Bank threatened Indonesia's economic lifelines [see also Kivimäki 2003:228]; the State Department went public; the commander of US forces in the Pacific, Admiral Dennis Blair, went to Jakarta and threatened Wiranto to his face; Clinton warned that Indonesia's economy was at risk and declared from the White House lawn that Habibie had to fix the problem or 'invite' the international community to fix it. (Kelly 2009:509)

At the APEC summit in Auckland attended by Ramos-Horta, Indonesian representatives were put under a great deal of pressure; Clinton announced the suspension of US arms sales to Indonesia, as did the British Government and the European Union. Kofi Annan's diplomacy, representing the will of the Security Council, was also relentless. On 12 September, the Indonesian cabinet agreed to an international peacekeeping force. Three days later, the UN Security Council authorised the International Force for East Timor (INTERFET) under the command of Australian Major General Peter Cosgrove. Of the first 7000 INTERFET personnel, 4500 were Australian, ultimately peaking at 11 500, approximately half of which were Australian (Department of Defence 2004:15).

Australia initially sent in just 1500 troops to an East Timor occupied by 30 000 Indonesian troops plus civilian militias. Later, peacekeepers from 22 different UN member states would join them. While this was a peace-enforcement mission, had Indonesia resisted, the 1500 Australians who landed would have been decimated. But it was known by the Indonesians that if they attacked the Australians, the United States would come in to support them. This assurance was requested by Australia, given by the United States and repeated by the United States back to General Wiranto. The US Marine group in the Pacific was moved to the Timor coast to reinforce the assurance that if the Australians were attacked, Wiranto would be taking on the United States—putting a certain end to his political ambitions to become President. US Defence Secretary Cohen said to Wiranto and Habibie in a Jakarta meeting: 'This deployment must not be contested. Any Indonesian forces that contest them will meet US forces' (Kelly 2009:511).

According to Nevins (2002) and Maley (2000), the tragedy is that before the killing started to get out of hand states like the United States and Australia

> did not signal as strongly as they could have to Jakarta that they would not tolerate the commission of any more crimes in 1999. These governments had the power to stop the Indonesian TNI by using the threat of a cut-off of economic and military ties. Because they did not make and thus did not act upon such threats, the TNI assumed that it could act in East Timor with impunity, as it had in the past. (Nevins 2002:625)

One final attempt to appease Indonesia had come from Foreign Minister Downer when he accepted the Jakarta line on 23 February 1999 that only 'rogue elements' in the military were responsible for violence. Australian intelligence already indicated this was absolutely wrong (Kelly 2009:496).[8] The Australian intelligence assessment was also that the Indonesian military was a disciplined force that ultimately followed orders from the top when those orders were unmistakably clear. Once General Wiranto issued clear instructions to General Kiki Syahnakri to go to East Timor and make a declaration of martial law work to restore order, the violence fairly quickly reduced, during the second week of September, and further reduced after INTERFET landed on 20 September 1999. Some officers who resisted General Syahnakri's orders to desist were hauled in and beaten. While General Syahnakri was subsequently indicted in Timor-Leste for his role in planning the 1999 scorched-earth policy, there is no doubt he worked extremely effectively with General Cosgrove and his officers to end nearly all of the violence during September. By 27 September, General Syahnakri was able to formally transfer his martial-law powers to General Cosgrove and complete the evacuation of his troops from the province within weeks.

Even had there not been a lot of intelligence that 'Operation Clean Sweep' (an operation intended to raze the province and target all independence supporters) would result from a vote for independence, it still would have been a mistake to hold a referendum without a substantial international military presence:

> [T]here was no encouraging precedent in the history of the organization [the United Nations] for conducting a vote in the circumstances in which it was attempted in East Timor, that is, with an abundance of spoilers and no credible security guarantees. The conduct of plebiscites to resolve disputes over the status of territory preceded the formation of the UN. The League of Nations conducted six such plebiscites, of which the most famous was that of 1935 which saw the Saarland returned to Germany. For this exercise, a neutral force of 3000 was deployed in order to guarantee an appropriate environment for the vote...What lessons should the UN have derived from these experiences [polls in Namibia, Cambodia, Angola and other cases discussed by Maley]. Three in particular stand out. First, where the interests of all the parties converge in favour of cooperation, it is possible to conduct an election without needing to depend upon the military to enforce a high level of security for voters. Second, where the interests of parties diverge sharply, but a

---

8   Chesterman (2002:61) points out that Timorese themselves evinced little doubt about what was going to happen: 'Across the country there were reports of entire towns packing their belongings and leaving in anticipation of the violence to come. One UN observer in Maliana reported a day before the vote that his entire town [one of the largest in the country] had disappeared, only to find people streaming back from the hillsides from 4 am to queue up, vote, and depart once more. That people anticipated great violence but voted anyway is one of the most remarkable aspects of this story.'

neutral security force is in place, large-scale retribution against voters can be averted. Third, where the interests of parties diverge sharply, and there is no neutral security force, voters are in acute danger. (Maley 2000:67, 69)

Perhaps not many would disagree with this, but at the time UN and Australian officials would argue that, even so, '[i]f the world's fourth biggest country, a respected member of the UN, stands up in New York and promises to look after security, it's very hard to say to them "We don't believe you"' (UN official quoted by Maley 2000:75). In the end, that was precisely what Admiral Blair said to General Wiranto, and more, in their face-to-face meeting in early September after the ballot, according to our interviews. And as Maley (2000:75) points out, the 12 September agreement of Indonesia to UN peacekeepers entering their territory occurred 'in circumstances in which the Indonesian military had far more to hide than had been the case four months earlier'. Engaging Wiranto was critical, because Habibie had effectively failed to do so:

> There was in fact every reason to believe that President Habibie was regarded with deep suspicion by the military, and the manifestly low level of political institutionalisation in the post-Suharto era should have alerted planners to the dangers of making commitments from Habibie the linchpin of a transition process. (Maley 2000:74)

To make Maley's point more theoretically, in conditions of national anomie, which are often the circumstances of armed conflict (Braithwaite et al. 2010a), diplomacy transacted at the level of the head of state involves an undependably Westphalian vision of diplomacy. It is better to conceive the governance of a country as a web of various networks and hierarchies, rather than as a single hierarchy that runs from the head of state down. This is a theme we return to at the conclusion of this book.

INTERFET quickly apprehended militia members who did not flee to West Timor. Up to September 2000, there were 16 or 17 military engagements with militias, 'most of which resulted in injury or death', many of them cross-border incursions (Kingsbury 2009:75). On 22 October 1999, Xanana Gusmão, by then released from prison, was able to return in safety to move among adoring masses of the liberated people of Timor-Leste and deliver in a kind of sonorous wail a deeply moving speech. The depth of Xanana's charisma, his character, his oneness with his suffering people were on display for the world to see in that emotional address. This was a high point of the liberation movement. Our argument now becomes that because that leadership (of Ramos-Horta and Fretilin as well) was so profoundly charismatic, so uninstitutionalised, building a democracy would be difficult.

7. Reformasi and Referendum, 1998–1999

Figure 7.3: Xanana Gusmão comforts an elderly woman after returning to Dili

Photo: Stephen Dupont/Australian War Memorial

Realism at the Two-Level Game of International Politics

Robert Putnam (1988) has argued that international politics is usefully viewed as a two-level game: a game of domestic interest group politics and another of international deal making to avert threats to national interests.

> Each national political leader appears at both game boards. Across the international table sit his foreign counterparts, and at his elbows sit diplomats and other international advisors. Around the domestic table behind him sit party and parliamentary figures, spokespersons for domestic agencies, representatives of key interest groups, and the leader's own political advisors. The unusual complexity of this two-level game is that moves that are rational for a player at one board… may be impolitic for that same player at the other board…On occasion, however, clever players will spot a move on one board that will trigger realignments on other boards, enabling them to achieve otherwise unattainable objectives. (Putnam 1988:434)

At the tables of domestic politics across the West, the international solidarity movement had made some progress by 1999 in raising public concern over East Timor. In a few countries in which the solidarity movement was particularly energetic, such as Ireland and New Zealand, this was a swelling chorus of public concern. But in the United States and the major nations of Europe, East Timor remained a minor public issue. While the solidarity movement did extend to Indonesia's major aid donor, Japan, human rights abuses in Timor were even less of a public issue there, and in Chinese domestic politics it probably did not register at all. Yet in two not-so-important countries—Australia and Portugal, the nations that would come to make the largest contributions to the UN peace operation in East Timor—public concern as the pro-democracy and pro-independence demonstrations of the Timorese and Indonesian students raged in 1998 and 1999 reached the tipping point of becoming a matter of mass outrage at the injustice and at the way their governments had appeased Indonesia. In these two countries, leaders switched the priority in East Timor policy away from concern over what the major players were saying across the international relations table, turning squarely to prioritise the concerns at the table of domestic politics. Mass outrage in Portugal, Australia, Ireland and New Zealand are not things that realist international relations theorists would imagine could change international affairs. They did.

The leaders of Australia and Portugal saw public disgust over East Timor in their electorates that united left and right, young students and old soldiers. In Australia, these groups marched together in the streets in solidarity for action on East Timor in numbers not seen since the Vietnam War. Rank-and-file trade union members put their leaders under pressure to impose bans on trade with Indonesia; as the Victorian Trades Hall Council Secretary put it: 'a lot of these members are ahead of the leadership on this one' (Fernandes 2005:271). In our interviews with Australian Prime Minister Howard and Foreign Minister Downer (from 1996 to 2007), who were the decisive decision makers on Australian Timor policy, it was clear that they saw a domestic political imperative to change that policy. Kelly's (2009) interviews confirm this. They made the change with the same incoherence that characterised Whitlam's policy. Whitlam particularly wanted integration of Portuguese Timor into Indonesia in 1975, but also wanted an act of self-determination, when the latter was utterly incompatible with the former. Howard particularly wanted an act of self-determination, but also wanted Timor to stay in Indonesia, even though his intelligence indicated the latter was incompatible with the former. In rare moments of Australian influence in international affairs, both Whitlam and Howard had quite important sway in delivering their dominant preference from within this incoherent dyad of preferences. Just as Whitlam was not deeply concerned when Timor was integrated into Indonesia without an act of self-determination, Howard was not overly concerned when Habibie agreed to an act of self-determination in circumstances that delivered scant prospect of holding East Timor. It is probable that Habibie would eventually have decided to hold a referendum in East Timor had Howard's letter never been sent, but it is also possible that the abandonment of Australia's policy of unconditional support for the occupation was a final straw, and it was certainly a catalyst for Habibie's announcement of a referendum.

When the Indonesian military unleashed the mayhem of its scorched-earth policy after the referendum in 1999, President Clinton was unmoved at first, not detecting it as a big domestic concern. At first, he heeded the realist advice of his National Security Adviser, Sandy Berger, to avoid entanglement and commitment of resources to a cause that would alienate Indonesia. Then the influential phone calls came in to Clinton from the Australian and Portuguese leaders. While these two countries were not powerful members of the American alliance, these telephone conversations were so emphatic that it was clear that these nations, particularly Portugal, would withdraw significant capital from the bank of that alliance if Clinton remained deaf to their pleas. Moreover, Howard's and Guterres's arguments to Clinton were sound in the terms of this book in making the case that the Sandy Berger line was misplaced realism. UN Secretary-General, Kofi Annan, reinforced this persuasion, also making the case to Clinton that it was against US interests when the United Nations promised people that they could vote in safety under the UN flag, if then the United Nations failed to act in at least an attempt to redeem the promise. Both men were suffering politically from the fall-out of the failure to prevent the genocidal violence in Rwanda, and Annan's message was powerful.

Third, there was an influential group of members of the US Congress, including Ted Kennedy, Patrick Kennedy, Tom Daschle, Richard Gephart and Nancy Pelosi, who were key supporters of Clinton in the battle for survival he was waging over the Monika Lewinsky affair, and indeed many substantive battles, and whose hearts and minds had been captured by Ramos-Horta and the solidarity movement. In the Kennedys' case, the Irish and Catholic Church axes of it were important. Clinton reversed his East Timor policy decisively on 8 September 1999 because he reassessed the balance of political considerations both at his domestic table and at the international table. And he thought it was the right thing to do after listening to the moral force of the arguments put by individuals who were as credible, yet as politically different, as John Howard, Antonio Guterres, Ted Kennedy and Kofi Annan, and in the light of the collective wisdom of the region's leaders at a fortuitously timed September meeting of APEC.

President Habibie had no choice but to turn more of his attention to the international table than Indonesian presidents before and after him. The IMF, the World Bank, the United States, Australia and other major donors were unmistakably signalling the possibility of a withdrawal of support for his beleaguered economy. It was not just a matter of political surrender to the United States and Australia; it was a signal to the international community that Habibie intended to be a genuine democratic change agent in Indonesia. To the domestic audience as well he wanted to distinguish himself from Suharto in his democratic credentials. Unfortunately for him, on the domestic front, giving independence to East Timor in a democratic vote was a step too far for most Indonesians, even though a progressive minority within the elite was supportive at first. Habibie also miscalculated that both the international creditor audience and the economically suffering domestic audience would give more credit than they did to the economic benefits of cutting cross-subsidies to East Timor by the rest of the nation (largely because of high security costs and Timor's low contributions to GDP). The fundamental point for Habibie was that he had to be focused on the international table in a way Suharto refused to, and the politics around the international table changed remarkably in the months before 8 September 1999.

Habibie could not bring the military along with his radical Timor policy shift. He did not really try very hard to bring the military with him. The chaos in Timor during late 1999 and the invective the military and their political supporters directed at Habibie for threatening the unitary state of Indonesia did more to end Habibie's political future than any other factor. The military then turned their blowtorch on Habibie's initially popular successor, President Wahid, for giving away too much in peace talks to end violence in Aceh and West Papua—violence that was also substantially military driven. Yet Wiranto, and Prabowo's even more militant faction of the military, miscalculated at both the international and the domestic tables. They failed to understand that in circumstances where the international community was watching every step they took in East Timor, they could not sell the kind of lies that they had historically pedalled in domestic politics, such as that the violence in Timor was primarily between East Timorese political factions, and that any Indonesian military involvement was minimal and by 'rogue elements' and not centrally directed.

There was too much evidence to the contrary from Australian intelligence, quite a bit of which was leaked, and from Western television cameras capturing members of the Indonesian military issuing orders to marauding Timorese militias, backing them up by firing their weapons at civilians, even of Indonesian soldiers changing out of their uniforms into Timorese civilian garb and wigs to supplant their short-cropped military haircuts with Che Guevara-esque locks. International disenchantment with, and media coverage of, the human rights abuses of the Indonesian military fed into domestic disenchantment with them. Both Wiranto and Prabowo (who was Suharto's son-in-law) no longer enjoyed the protection of the Indonesian elite and both faced indictments—Wiranto over East Timor, Prabowo over the anti-Chinese riots that took 1200 lives in Jakarta in 1998. Later, when the international heat was off, these were dropped.

It was not a terminal political setback for the Indonesian military. Neither Wiranto nor Prabowo went to prison; both staged partial political recoveries as (albeit unsuccessful) presidential candidates in the next decade. Yet the political stars of these men and of the military might have risen much higher in Indonesian politics had the extreme involvement of the military in fomenting violence in Timor and beyond (Braithwaite et al. 2010a) not been exposed after 1999. Instead, the military star that rose to the top of Indonesian politics as President from 2004 until today was General Yudhoyono, the leader of the democratic reform faction within the military.

This was a much preferable outcome to the West than a new ascendancy of a military authoritarianism led by a man who ruled by violence such as Wiranto, or more so Prabowo. Had Timor played out as these men hoped, with chaos spiralling in East and West Timor until they stepped in to end it and reunify the nation as a new president, Indonesia would probably be less democratic and stable than it is today. In this sense as well, the realism of Sandy Berger in the United States and many in Australia's Indonesia lobby was misplaced. Tolerating a period of stormy relations with the Indonesian military leadership, by forcing upon them UN peacekeepers, set Indonesia on a more democratic trajectory towards a preferable leadership for Western interests in a peaceful, flourishing Indonesia. The leadership of the new Timor-Leste reinforced this positive outcome for Western interests by embracing in reconciliation the emerging democratic leadership of the successive presidencies of Wahid, Megawati and Yudhoyono. Timor-Leste's leaders were all careful not to provoke anything that would be destabilising of the maturing Indonesian democracy.

Ordinary people in Timor-Leste also overwhelmingly approved this approach. In our interviews, people repeatedly affirmed their affection for the people of Indonesia, while also communicating their contempt for the military that Wiranto and Prabowo dominated. At the end of the day, the Fretilin generation of 1975, the next generation of Timorese students in the clandestine movement who rallied in Jakarta, the ordinary people of Timor-Leste and the stalwarts of the international solidarity movement might have looked like Che Guevara, but they did not threaten Indonesia with communism. In fact, they made a great contribution to strengthening its democracy. Ramos-Horta and Gusmão are accurate in saying of their people that they did not indulge in a politics of racism against Indonesia, even when Indonesian military leaders afflicted them with a violent form of racism and a pervading paternalism that excluded indigenous Timorese from leadership of the commercial life of the province. Timorese instead proffered a politics of support for the dignity of the Indonesian people and for their aspirations for *merdeka* (freedom from tyranny).

8. Transitional Governance

UNAMET and INTERFET: Redemption and humiliation

This chapter diagnoses some successes and failures of the UN transitional government that was established in Timor. They lead us to contemplate how difficult it is for a peace operation to secure a democratic republic with a separation of powers. We conclude that beyond transition, the pursuit of governance that secures republican freedom from domination and women's rights can keep approaching closer to its final destination, but can never reach it.

INTERFET was an operational success. Much has been written about the splendid job INTERFET troops from 22 countries did in defusing many situations with disgruntled Indonesian soldiers and police who were preparing to pull out, with some militia members, especially near the West Timor border, and with some independence supporters who sought to victimise pro-Indonesia elements (for example, Cosgrove 2006; Martin and Mayer-Rieckh 2005; Ryan 2002; Smith with Dee 2003, 2006). We will not rehearse that literature here. Yet it is important to say that the contribution of General Cosgrove's soldiers was redemptive for an Australian conscience that was ashamed of some or all of the betrayals discussed in Chapter 3. On the other hand, Australia's leaders assumed too much of a sense of ownership of something that was an international accomplishment.

The UN Mission in East Timor (UNAMET) had been an operational success in the conduct of registration of voters for the election and a high-integrity ballot in difficult circumstances. But it failed in preventing the violence. There was little a few hundred unarmed UN police and civilians could do against thousands of armed militia backed by tens of thousands of Indonesian soldiers. Yet the little that could be done they did with great courage. This too was redemptive for Australia's shame over Timor, as the stories emerged of the courage of Australian police in, for example, standing between a militia member and an independence supporter he was about to shoot. Then there was the courage of the UNAMET members and journalists in the besieged UN compound into which 1500 desperate refugees had fled by 5 September 1999, even climbing over its razor wire to get in. When UN Headquarters ordered its staff to evacuate, leaving the refugees to their fate, UNAMET staff voted to stay to protect them as best they could. On 14 September, all 1500 people in the compound were successfully evacuated to Australia.

We interviewed several Australian, New Zealand and non-Australian peacekeepers who today suffer post-traumatic stress disorder, and are unable to work. They paid a heavy price for Australia's national redemption, which in 1999 and 2000 was a profound national emotion. Unfortunately, John Howard overcapitalised on it. His triumphalism in organising what seemed to Indonesians to be a victory march for the troops, and his nationalist bravado, even to the point of suggesting that Australia was now a kind of US 'Deputy Sheriff' in the region, seriously undermined goodwill in Australia's relationship with Indonesia (see Kelly 2009). This aspect of the pro-Indonesia network's warnings came true—at considerable cost to Australian diplomacy (Woolcott 2000:28–9).

Here we have a curious moment in our analysis of intersection with the realist international relations perspective we reject. The theoretical perspective we bring to peacebuilding makes reconciliation and restorative justice central; because war hurts, transition should heal. So national redemption in the wake of betrayal, triumphalism and humiliation is a consequential thing in international affairs. In contrast, realists give short shrift to emotion in international politics, which they see as overwhelmingly about national interests. In this context, it is unusual and perceptive for realists of the pro-Indonesia network such as Richard Woolcott to note John Howard's insensitivity to the healing needed to restore the dignity of the Indonesian people; it is important to recognise the perceptiveness of their analysis.

UNTAET and the Paradoxes of Centralised Power

On 25 October 1999, the UN Security Council adopted a resolution to form the UN Transitional Administration of East Timor (UNTAET). The United Nations saw East Timor as a high-visibility peace operation and sent what Traub (2000:82) dubbed its 'A team'. A great UN diplomat, a charismatic leader, Sergio Vieira de Mello of Brazil, who had recently been a peacebuilding leader in Kosovo, was appointed Special Representative of the Secretary-General (SRSG) at the head of UNTAET. He died in 2003 when a bomb shattered the headquarters of the UN mission to Iraq that he headed.

The magnitude of the job facing UNTAET was daunting. On the positive side, it was not a Somalia with well-armed factions still fighting; the really formidable military protagonist had quit the field of battle. Yet there were residual security problems to fix, and, as we shall see in the next chapter, major new ones brewing. On 6 September 2000, three foreign UN High Commissioner for Refugees (UNHCR) workers were murdered across the border in West Timor. In the early years, the border tensions were a constant distraction from building the new nation (ICG

2006a; Kingsbury 2005). Timor-Leste was not a case of rebuilding a collapsed state. It had never had a state. For 24 years it had been a province of Indonesia effectively ruled by the military. Even the major export industry, coffee, was ruled by a military monopoly. Timorese were excluded for the most part from even the lowest levels of the retail sector of the economy, as they effectively had been by the Chinese during Portuguese colonialism. The professions in East Timor had been totally dominated by Indonesian immigrants who had now fled. Rule from Jakarta and Macau/Lisbon had served the development of Timorese human capital poorly in both commerce and government.

Figure 8.1: Portuguese UNTAET soldiers accompanied by local children in Dili, March 2000

Photo: Eskinder Debebe/United Nations Department of Public Information

Physical capital was also utterly looted or destroyed in 1999. There were no buildings the United Nations could use for offices or accommodation for its staff. Many lived in the cabins of a ship docked at a purpose-built jetty. Other publications have done a fine job of describing the nuts and bolts, the successes and failures, of how UNTAET went about building a new state in Dili. Our focus in this book is rather on one structural feature of the polity that emerged from the peacebuilding: the pluralisation of power for a populace that had been excluded from power by two successive colonial occupations.

UNTAET was a transitional administration. It was not there to support a government, but to be the government, and at the same time, build one to replace it. In the difficult circumstances we have just described, what it built was far too centralised in Dili. The way the United Nations built it was with too heavy an emphasis on consultation with one man, Xanana Gusmão, and too heavy a secondary emphasis on consultation with the survivors of the 1975 generation who fled mostly to Maputo, the pre-eminent members of which were Mari Alkatiri and José Ramos-Horta. Village leaders and youth who played leading roles from before Santa Cruz were excluded from the inner circle. While women ultimately achieved more voice than in many post-conflict governance transitions, they were not in that inner circle where power quickly concentrated.

There is a widespread feeling that the new state has marginalised East Timorese culture and customary life as sources of governance. The crucial misperception—made both by the external actors and by many in the Timorese political elite (who had often spent a long time in exile)—was seeing East Timor after the liberation from Indonesian occupation as a *tabula rasa*: a place void of governance institutions where state building could and would have to start 'from scratch' (see Boege et al. 2008:11).

One thing the *tabula rasa* outlook failed to see was that the clandestine network was a 'resistance that ran parallel to the Indonesian governmental system, and the clandestine system itself was built on traditional socio-political structures' (Caplan 2005:119; Hohe 2002). CNRT—enriched by embracing to it even wider elements of civil society—would have been an apt early vehicle for building on that existing governance capacity. UNTAET, however, eschewed the power sharing with CNRT that CNRT initially proposed (Harland 2005:3).

There was also a language divide. The student leaders of the 1990s had been educated in Indonesian universities. They spoke bahasa Indonesia and Tetum primarily. Many complained in their interviews with us that a measure of their exclusion from the inner circle who made the early decisions was that the language of government and the courts was settled as Portuguese. Court cases were conducted in a language that the youth leaders could not speak—one survey found 92 per cent of Timorese preferred to speak Tetum in court (Asia Foundation 2004:88)—and government documents were written in a Portuguese they could not read. Sergio de Mello was of course fluent in English, but, as a Brazilian, his first language was Portuguese. He was comfortable with a kitchen cabinet that did the deals that mattered face to face in Portuguese. The politics of language was therefore connected to the politics of centralisation; it always is in UN operations. Usually those of the local elite who can converse in English, or sometimes in French, with the UN leadership are the ones who dominate the conversation. Timor-Leste was unique in the way the dynamics of linguistic centralisation of power, and disempowerment of the Tetum-speaking majority, were initially more Portuguese.

Jarat Chopra (2002:981) observed a lot of 'colonial-style behaviour' in a UNTAET in which the 'unprecedented powers to be assumed by the UN attracted the very type of individual who would be intoxicated by that thought':

> Many felt that the Timorese could not be relied on, that they lacked skills and were not ready for self-government, that the UN should stay and its personnel could keep their jobs for longer. Some officials even attempted methodically to prevent the participation of Timorese in the transitional government of the country. They wanted to wield unfettered their newfound authority and spend the hundreds of millions of dollars committed by the world's donors. (Chopra 2002:981)

As a result, according to Chopra, UNTAET did not nurture the emergence of a separation of powers. Space was denied by UN powerbrokers for opposition to the transitional administration. Dissenters were placed on the outer and a culture of freedom of expression and disagreement was not encouraged.

Sergio Vieira de Mello was conscious of the separation-of-powers problem:

> There is no separation of the legislative or judicial from the executive authority. There are no positive models on how to exercise such broad powers…The question remains open how the UN can exercise fair governance with absolute powers in societies recovering from war and oppression. (Vieira de Mello in Beauvais 2001:1101)

While Vieira de Mello was as trusted and revered a peacekeeping leader as the United Nations has had, he was still a child of the Security Council and the pressure it, and the United States, put on its agents to push the reset button on a society as quickly as possible, then get out.

> In response to the United Nations' guiding ideology and UNTAET's primary 'constituencies' (the UN Security Council and donor countries), the mission's approach to state-building has been driven by the need to maintain centralized control, minimize the short-term risk of failure, and maximize short-term visible gains. Only under intense protest from the East Timorese did UNTAET begin to shift its approach toward more long-term development-oriented policies…

> The Security Council's primary interest was to keep UNTAET's involvement 'as brief and tidy as possible' and to avoid the reemergence of hostilities. The emphasis, as with prior peace operations, was to resolve major security issues and move toward 'free and fair' elections

as an exit strategy within a defined time period…[Donor] constituencies provided incentives for UNTAET to minimize the short-term risks of failure (in the form of conflict or crisis) and maximize visible returns on donor investments. These interests militated strongly in favor of central control and allocation of resources to direct service provision. (Beauvais 2001:1106, 1166)

Structurally, the international community provided a lot of money for the United Nations to have transport, offices and other necessities in Dili, but little for the government in the early years. Vieira de Mello told the Security Council: 'Something is clearly not right if UNTAET can cost $692 million, whereas the entire budget of East Timor comes to a bit over $59 million' (Power 2008:314). David Harland concluded that reform of UN budgeting philosophies was a key lesson to be learned from UNTAET:

> The UN assessed budget had no provision for budgetary support to Timorese state institutions. UNTAET was not permitted, under the budget adopted by the UN member states, to buy antiseptic for nurses, pencils for schools, or fix buildings for future Timorese ministries—that was planned to come from local revenues, or from external development assistance, or from a trust fund that couldn't operate without a treasury. But development assistance did not flow, and a stream of revenue could not be generated, and a treasury could not be established, for several months. The UN's inability to bridge the funding gap during this initial period was bad for Timor, and a major public relations failure for the Transitional Administration, which was widely seen by the Timorese as providing strongly for itself, but little for them. Future UN budgets must make provision for budgetary support for an initial period of at least six months in similar circumstances, to cover the period prior to the establishment of full national treasury and budget systems. (Harland 2005:10)

The accountability and institutional incentives encouraged rhetorical flourishes about 'decentralisation', 'Timorisation', 'participation' and 'capacity building', but only ritualistic implementation of such ideals. Until UN missions are subject to independent peer audit and public reporting against these ideals, such ritualism is likely to prevail. This logic likewise compromises concerted UN efforts to take concrete steps towards institutionalising a separation of powers. The best way for missions to be productive is with a period of central UN control, a quick election, then leaving the messy business of separating branches of governance to one of those branches: the elected legislature.

Vieira de Mello did come to concede that '[w]e should have moved more briskly in bringing national partners onboard from the very beginning in a more truly substantive fashion' (Caplan 2005:118). Beauvais (2001:1173) has proposed holding UN peace missions accountable for phased construction of a separation of powers in which an indigenous civil service, news media, judiciary and independent security sector are put in place before the election of a legislature. This means a newly elected sovereign government has these institutional assets at its disposal when it starts work to clean up the national mess that exists after an armed conflict. Second, it means that newly elected politicians are less able to sculpt the civil service, the army, the police and the judiciary, the media and other powerful business interests as its patrimonial ciphers. Table 8.1 represents the four-phased constitution of a separation of powers that Beauvais (2001:1173) proposes as a remedy for the separation of powers UNTAET failed to institutionalise progressively.

Figure 8.2: Sergio Vieira de Mello with José Ramos-Horta returning from exile in 1999

Photo: Andrew Meares/Fairfax Media

Table 8.1: Four-Phase Path Towards Institutionalising a Separation of Powers

	Political authority	Civil administration	Law and order
Phase 1 (emergency intervention)	• Consultative council • Community empowerment and local governance projects • NGO/civil society assessment and development	• Humanitarian aid and basic services • QIPs and TEPs • Preparation of Public Service Commission • Civil service skills assessment	• Applicable law defined • UN CivPol enforcement • Judicial Service Commission (identification and emergency training of judges)
Phase 2 (stabilisation)	• Transitional cabinet • National Council • District councils • Legislative Commission	• Establish decentralised line ministries hired on integrated 'dual-desk' concept • Civil Service Academy	• Establish local police academy • Establish Central Court (international/local)
Phase 3 (transition)	• Civic education • Electoral process • Constitution drafting	• Full recruitment of civil service • Mentoring and on-the-job training	• Establish district courts (local judges and international mentors) • Legal training centre • Local police gradually replace UN CivPol
Phase 4 (independence)	• Ongoing training and technical assistance	• Ongoing training and technical assistance	• Ongoing training and technical assistance

Source: Beauvais (2001:1173)

Stages the UNTAET and UNMISET Transition did Follow

UNTAET's mandate required consultation with the people of East Timor. Initially, CNRT was the vehicle for this consultation. The inner circle of 1975-generation leaders preferred more intimate forms of consultation. Fretilin broke from CNRT in August 2000 and Xanana Gusmão organised for CNRT to be shut down completely in advance of the 2001 elections. UNTAET was also unenthusiastic about CNRT because many of the UNTAET elite were fresh from Kosovo and prone to see CNRT as akin to the Kosovo Liberation Army (KLA), which sought to dominate by excluding anti-KLA elements. It was a poor analogy given that there were no longer any significant elements in the East Timor polity that supported integration with Indonesia.

Paradoxically, marginalising CNRT allowed a small UN and 1975-generation clique to rule. The other early formal consultative mechanism was the 15-member non-elected National Consultative Council created in December 1999 with representatives of both UNTAET and local political factions. The National Consultative Council came in for much criticism for being insufficiently representative and transparent (Chesterman 2002:65). In April 2000, the SRSG announced appointments of local deputy district administrators to operate alongside the 13 international district administrators, and a proposal for new district advisory councils. How much citizen involvement was enabled by these district advisory councils varied from district to district, depending on how empowering individual district administrators were, but it was in general a picture of decentralisation followed by re-centralisation (Chopra 2002:991).

In principle, there was policy learning in this shift to decentralised dual-desk 'co-governance': district personnel reporting directly to their district administrator (who had a local deputy) compared with the situation with the UN Transitional Authority in Cambodia where district-level personnel reported vertically on a department-by-department basis to central administrators. In practice, the decentralisation was grudging, however, with more than 90 per cent of UNTAET positions continuing to be located in Dili (Beauvais 2001:1142). Timorisation was as limited as decentralisation, with Timorese occupying fewer than 10 per cent of management positions 15 months into the UNTAET mandate (Beauvais 2001:1144). The twin failures to decentralise and to Timorise resulted in a fall in UNTAET's local legitimacy once its first six months' honeymoon had ended. It became apparent to Timorese that devolution of political and administrative authority occurred 'in a very limited fashion and only where necessary to defend its [UNTAET's] own legitimacy' (Beauvais 2001:1163).

The World Bank and the Asian Development Bank Community Empowerment Project (CEP), begun in February 2000, was another decentralisation effort that did not succeed as well as the parent efforts in some provinces of Indonesia, including conflict zones such as Aceh (see Braithwaite et al. 2010a). The idea was provision of block grants to subdistricts that would decide development priorities based on proposals submitted by villages. It mostly failed because there was not a subdistrict infrastructure of governance to connect to in the way there was in Aceh. A World Bank official told us that it was planned to start in 1998 just when governance infrastructure was beginning to collapse. Some of the projects CEP supported when it did get going were characterised by waste, embezzlement and poor delivery. Second, Chopra (2002:993) argues that the central-control–personal-control impulses of UN officials frustrated an

Asian Development Bank push for CEP-elected village councils to be a base for elected subdistrict councils that would extend participatory transitional governance up to the district level and ultimately to the National Consultative Council.[1] Chopra and Hohe (2004:295–7) conclude that one reason the promise of the program was never realised was a failure to appreciate the importance of traditional power structures leading to a policy preventing traditional leaders from standing for election to CEP councils. This was perhaps well motivated by a desire to separate powers, but was misunderstood by excluded chiefs and their supporters as an attack on tradition and on them.

These lessons might have been learnt by the time of Law No. 2/2004 for the conduct of elections of *suco* [village] chiefs and *suco* councils (comprising the *suco* chief, the chiefs of all *aldeias* [hamlets] of the *suco*, two women, a 'young person' of each sex and a further *suco* elder). *Suco* elections were held in 2005. Government budgets, however, only go down as far as the subdistrict level. The UN Development Programme (UNDP) now funds a community facilitator in each *suco* who facilitates planning in each *aldeia* within the *suco* to spend $60 000–$80 000 a year on infrastructure projects. So the bottom-up governance killed off by UNTAET is coming back in the nation's second decade.

On 14 July 2000, a broader National Council of 33 was appointed. In making these appointments and in appointing four local 'cabinet' members (including Mari Alkatiri and Ana Pessoa from Fretilin), Vieira de Mello relied heavily on the advice of Gusmão. The practical influence of these 'ministers' was minimal and progress towards Timorisation of the UN civil service continued to be meagre. The *Jakarta Post* gloated with the headline 'The new Timor: a Xanana republic' (Chesterman 2002:69). In this period Adérito Soares spoke out publicly on the need to change the 'culture of command' that had been acquired through the imperative to follow orders in the clandestine movement. One of the few areas where the Timorese cabinet did have influence was on land reform, but it was influence in the direction of the comfortable policy for UNTAET of persuading it to do nothing in this tricky area. Minister for Infrastructure, Joao Carrascalão, from the most powerful property-owning family in the country, 'demanded and obtained control of the Land and Property Unit and then virtually suspended its activities' (King's College Report 2003:316). The post-UNTAET Prime Minister, Mari Alkatiri, was from another wealthy landowning family and the Deputy Prime Minister in the post-2007 administration was another Carrascalão, Mario. This failure left tensions to fester over occupation of properties in Dili by people who had never lived there. These tensions were to explode in 2006.

---

1   CEP was approved only after being rejected twice by UNTAET (Beauvais 2001:1126). 'The CEP was unable to recover from the acrimonious negotiations leading up to its establishment. It continued to be effectively rejected by UNTAET internally, with the consequence that the transitional administration never had much of a presence below the district level, where 80 per cent of the population lives (Hohe 2002)' (Chopra 2002).

Fretilin won 55 of the 88 seats in the Constituent Assembly in August 2001, which became the National Parliament at independence. As soon as the Constituent Assembly was elected, it started consulting on and drafting the Constitution. It was a speedy process, with a final version of the Constitution endorsed by the Constituent Assembly on 9 March 2002. It established a semi-presidential system that circumscribed the powers of the President compared to with those found in fully presidential systems. Smith with Dee (2003:440) describe the powers of the President as 'mainly ceremonial, except in matters of defense, for which he was designated commander in chief of the defense forces'.' Mari Alkatiri attempted to create a 'dominant party system' through the Constitution, with a weak parliament, a weak president and a strong prime minister atop a strong council of ministers (Shoesmith 2008).

The voting system is proportional, with only one single constituency corresponding to the entire national territory (Law 6/2006, Article 9). Voters select parties rather than individual candidates. This has had the advantage of guaranteeing at least one-quarter of the Parliament would be women by mandating that every fourth candidate on party lists are women (Law 6/2006, Article 12[3]). It achieved not only government dominated by the Prime Minister from the most successful party or coalition, but also one centred on Dili, indeed one where parliamentarians were reluctant to leave Dili, where their political fortunes were made or lost: '[Parliamentarians] have no compulsion to listen to an electorate that can vote them in or out of office; they simply have to persuade the party leaders to place them sufficiently high on the party list to gain a seat' (Shoesmith 2008:80).

Xanana Gusmão won 82 per cent of the vote in the first presidential election, in April 2002. Fretilin formed a government headed by Alkatiri as Prime Minister from May 2002. 'Thereafter, a single individual, Mari Alkatiri (to whom the Transitional Administrator now turned his attention, away from Gusmão), from a single party, Fretilin, was poised to control from the capital all aspects of legislative and executive life in the country, inevitably spawning opposition and divisiveness' (Chopra 2002:994).

After the elections, on 20 May 2002, Timor-Leste became the first new independent nation of the twenty-first century and UNTAET ceased to exist as a transitional administration. The UN Mission of Support in East Timor (UNMISET: May 2002 – June 2005) was a successor UN presence established by the Security Council to remain in Timor-Leste to assist the transfer of all operational government responsibilities to the new state. The UN Office in Timor-Leste (UNOTIL: June 2005 – August 2006) was a scaled-down version of UNMISET without a peacekeeping component. Then in August 2006, the UN Integrated Mission in Timor-Leste (UNMIT) reintroduced peacekeepers following the 2006 street violence to be discussed in the next chapter.

Very quickly, resentment became widespread among the young, the educated intelligentsia, church leaders and non-Fretilin politicians over 'Fretilin's exclusivist way of doing politics' (Simonsen 2006:582). Francis Fukuyama (2007:13) described it as 'the secretive and somewhat authoritarian mind-set that the Fretilin leadership acquired during the years of the independence struggle'. An example was the appointment of 65 subdistrict administrators, almost all of whom belonged to Fretilin. Another example was Prime Minister Alkatiri's announcement in February 2005 of a government boycott of the nation's biggest newspaper after it reported alleged deaths from famine in Ainaro District. The Prime Minister also attempted to have the newspaper evicted from its premises (Simonsen 2006:583).

There were many stories of this kind in our fieldwork notes, of Fretilin and the Prime Minister believing they were the law, arbitrarily acting to evict, arrest, dismiss and threaten individuals and businesses who were not to their political liking (see Federer 2005:111–15). The belief of many Fretilin cadres that Fretilin would be the natural party of rule in perpetuity was reinforced by a widespread view in the electorate as a result of the experience of the bloodshed between UDT and Fretilin in 1975 that competition between political parties was a bad thing. A 2003 poll found 45 per cent of the people believed this (Simonsen 2006:584).

The Tension between Peacekeeping and Republicanism

Virginia Page Fortna (2008) has made a profound recent contribution to the peacekeeping literature. Like Doyle and Sambanis (2000, 2006), but on a somewhat different data set, she shows for 95 ceasefires or breaks in fighting (1989–99) that the presence of peacekeepers reduced the risk of recurrence of civil war by at least 59 per cent (all else being equal) in hazard analyses. Her data are also consistent with the common conclusion that when a civil war is still raging, it is difficult to build a democracy. At the top of Figure 8.3, this is the direct explanatory path from peacekeeping to peace to democracy. Data consistent with a peacekeeping-to-democracy path can also be found in Doyle and Sambanis (2006) and Pickering and Peceny (2006), and inconsistent data in Bueno de Mesquita and Downes (2006). But Figure 8.3 hypothesises a second dynamic in play that is well illustrated by our narrative of UN transitional administration in Timor. We have seen that UNTAET (in collaboration with the 1975 generation of three key leaders) dominated diffused indigenous governance capabilities, disempowering civil society leadership, youth leadership and traditional leadership. When Timorese were not genuinely accountable for UN-dominated governance, the habit of blaming internationals for domestic governance failures set in early. Fortna's (2008) quantitative data are consistent with the model in Figure 8.3.

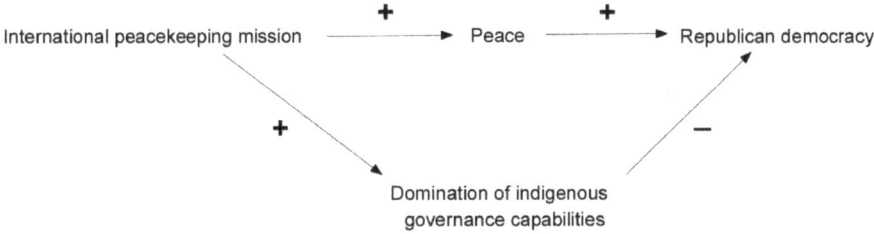

Figure 8.3: Interpretative model loosely based on data in Fortna (2008) from 95 ceasefires or breaks in fighting in civil wars between 1989 and 1999

Figure 8.3 is also consistent with our interpretation of the way compromised or captured governance that disables engagement of pluralised civil society with the republic arises in Barnett and Zürcher's (2009) analysis of peacebuilding. Fortna's (2008:45) account of this dynamic is that 'the very thing that can ensure lasting peace, outside intervention, often reduces the political space available for the emergence of home-grown, domestically legitimate and accountable political institutions'. Fortna interprets her quantitative data as suggesting that peacekeeping fosters conditions for the initial emergence of democracy, 'but at the same time undermines conditions for it to thrive over the longer term', because 'the large footprint of peacekeeping missions may trample and crowd out local democratization efforts as much as empower them' (Fortna 2008:45). Moreover, peacekeepers can implant 'an artificial political structure that collapses when they leave' (Fortna 2008:45). In Fortna's multivariate models, the positive effects of peacekeeping in sustaining a peace that is more fertile soil for democracy than war are cancelled out by other negative effects of peacekeeping on democratisation, freedom and rights. Her data show a very strong association between peacekeeping and peace, but a weak and complex set of relationships that connect peacekeeping to democracy. We hope our Timor narrative will give some context to how such a pattern in the peacebuilding data can make sense. The challenge ahead is to reform peacekeeping so it provides oxygen to the embers of a republic, rather than smothering them, while also maintaining the pacification virtues of peacekeeping.

Paradox in Centralised Excess

Fretilin was formed by the educated youth elite of a rather feudal society in which few young people received an education. In their twenties, Ramos-Horta and Alkatiri were no shrinking violets; they were aware that they were extraordinarily talented young people in comparison with the older uneducated villagers they led. They had a sense that they were born to lead. Xanana Gusmão saw himself more as born to be a poet and forced by circumstances to turn his talents to rule. He used his firm hold on the leadership of the resistance in the 1980s and 1990s to pluralise the politics of resistance. We have seen that he embraced former UDT enemies. This even included the Deputy Prime Minister from 2007 to 2010 and (Indonesian) Governor of East Timor from 1982 to 1992, Mario Carrascalão. He was appointed as a 'silent' (secret) vice-president of CNRT inside Dili in April 1998. The reintegration of Carrascalão began long before this. When Xanana Gusmão met with the then governor to negotiate the 1983 ceasefire, according to a Douglas Kammen (2003:81) interview with Carrascalão, Gusmão proposed a strategic alliance: 'You take care of the people, I'll take care of the *Bapak-bapak* [the Indonesian military].' After Gusmão declared Falintil would be a politically neutral nationalist army and resigned from Fretilin in 1987, Mario Carrascalão said: 'When Xanana said that he wasn't Fretilin, only the commander of Falintil, that's when the war started to be won. Apodeti and UDT people who had been enemies of Fretilin could also join the movement' (Kammen 2003:81).

Ramos-Horta was at one with Gusmão in reconstituting the resistance as social democratic, pluralistic and inclusive. Others in the Fretilin leadership that fled to Maputo clung to the more authoritarian, one-party ideology of Fretilin as the only legitimate government of Timor-Leste. Roque Rodrigues continues to be ideologically Marxist. Mari Alkatiri and Rogerio Lobato were not Marxist in the way Rodrigues was, but were influenced by African revolutionary parties, such as FRELIMO in Mozambique, to believe that centralised control by a party vanguard was needed before people who had lived under feudalism would be ready to rule themselves. Alkatiri told us that he still believed that effective central institutions were needed to prepare people in the villages who were not yet ready for sophisticated participation in government.

On this view, Alkatiri could be said to be modelling his politics on the United Nations. Under UNTAET, sovereignty was placed in the hands of one individual—Vieira de Mello (Chesterman 2002:46)[2]—on the theory that he would orchestrate a transition to a separation of powers into the hands of a plurality of Timorese institutions. One of the lessons of this book is that vanguard theories of political development of any sort are dangerous and require concerted continuous struggle for development of deliberative checks and balances in civil society. Alkatiri as Prime Minister 'personally approved the overwhelming bulk of government spending, especially to the districts, and for amounts as small as hundreds of dollars' (Kingsbury 2009:108). Early in the transition, Alkatiri and Lobato were tolerant of arguments from members of the Fretilin leadership that if Fretilin were defeated at an election, it would be necessary to retake power by force. This was a dangerous tolerance, which as we will see in the next chapter, allowed Rogerio Lobato to regard his secret arming of his police with more sophisticated firepower than the military (whom he saw as supporting his political opponent, Gusmão) as legitimate.

In contrast, Gusmão and Ramos-Horta always rejected such talk, being firm with Falintil members who saw their years of fighting in the mountains as granting a right to govern. Alkatiri's embrace of more genuinely democratic politics came more slowly. As Timor-Leste's first Prime Minister, from 2002 to 2006, he was profoundly centralist in the way he set about constructing a state, frustrated the development of a separation of powers, and abused his power to crush dissent. Alkatiri was also profoundly modernist, often scoffing at supposed virtues of customary law and governance. Xanana Gusmão won overwhelming support in the first presidential election and Fretilin won almost equally overwhelming support in the election for the Constituent Assembly. Gusmão was one of the people Alkatiri then sought to exclude from influence. He very effectively reversed the situation that had prevailed under UNTAET of Gusmão being the pre-eminent Timorese policymaker. Indeed, much earlier, Alkatiri and Fretlilin, realising Gusmão was bound to be elected President, sought to use their numbers to make the presidency impotent in the process of drafting the Constitution.

After Alkatiri lost his prime ministership, and after Fretilin rioting in 2007 failed to destabilise the government, Alkatiri became impressively firm in renouncing violence as a means to power. Following the enormous setback to the nation from the 2006 political violence described in the next chapter, violence became a tainted means to power. Alkatiri lost the prime ministership to Ramos-Horta during the 2006 violence and lost the 2007 election to a coalition led by Gusmão (Ramos-Horta was elected President, so Ramos-Horta and Gusmão switched offices). As leader of the Fretilin opposition in the Parliament since 2007, Alkatiri

---

2 Chesterman (2002:49) points out that UNTAET was the first UN mission with primary responsibility for policing and security, executive power, legislative power, judicial power and treaty-making power, while its predecessor, UNAMET, added primary responsibility for a referendum. UNMIK in Kosovo from 1999 covered all these sovereignties except treaty-making powers and responsibility for a referendum. No mission before 1999 covered legislative and judicial power, except UNTEA in its limited legislative power in West Papua in 1962–63.

has become a democratic critic of the failures of Prime Minister Gusmão to make the separation of powers work. The paradox of Timor-Leste today is that Xanana Gusmão, who led the nation into a politics of democratic pluralism, fought back against his own exclusion by centralising power in his own office as prime minister, and failed to develop separated powers in the new polity. For example, we will see in Chapter 9 that he sought to order police, judges and prosecutors to do his political bidding rather than respect the separation of powers.

It is hard to build a republican democracy with a separation of powers on the ashes of a war. We should not be too critical of Alkatiri, Ramos-Horta, Gusmão and Vieira de Mello as we tell this story of how they created an excessive concentration of power in the hands of a few in Dili and failed at first to build on the institutional strengths that were resilient in the villages. The international community should view Timor-Leste as a learning experience, an experiment in how to do something that is extraordinarily difficult to do. No UN mission ever took on such sweeping sovereign powers as UNTAET to build a state from scratch, so of course there were large mistakes and large learnings to absorb.

While Vieira de Mello had a difficult task, he might have done better to privilege Gusmão rather less as the singular voice of the legitimate aspirations of the people of Timor-Leste. He might have prevailed upon Fretilin and Gusmão not to disband the CNRT so quickly, as this was a functioning transitional institution that embraced youth leaders, women and civil society more broadly. He might have had a more balanced interest in building governance capability up from pre-existing institutions in the villages to complement building governance capability top down from Dili. This is a general dilemma of post-colonial development that was the central issue in the third volume of Peacebuilding Compared, on Solomon Islands (Braithwaite et al. 2010c). Alkatiri might have done better by both the nation and Fretilin for the long run by resisting the temptation to dominate the Constitution-writing process to marginalise Gusmão. Gusmão might have done better by the nation to have worked as hard at reconciliation with Alkatiri as he did at reconciliation with the leaders of Indonesia, and to have resisted the temptation to settle the score with Alkatiri by centralising control of the polity in his hands as much as Alkatiri had done when he was Prime Minister. Ramos-Horta worked much harder than Gusmão as Prime Minister to embrace the Fretilin clique he had replaced.

Yet both Ramos-Horta and Gusmão failed to work at nurturing the next generation of leaders of the nation. Alkatiri was less guilty of this as he cultivated a capable second tier of younger leaders as potential successors to his command of Fretilin. His agenda was to build Fretilin as the second great institutional force at the grassroots of the nation alongside the Catholic Church. Notes from our interview with him in 2009 record:

There were two really well organized institutions in Timor-Leste, the Catholic Church and Fretilin. In 2005 the Catholic Church was able to bring 3 000 out onto the streets in a demonstration against the government. Fretilin decided to demonstrate that its capabilities to mobilize were even greater by holding a demonstration in which 75 000 people participated.

In sum, we have a saga for the most part of institutional centralisation under the charismatic authority of great men from Gusmão and Ramos-Horta to Vieira de Mello, to Alkatiri and back to Gusmão. Part of the greatness of these leaders was the way they mobilised networked influence that engaged civil society across East Timor and around the globe to liberate their nation. Partly because of competition among one another over their roles in shaping the history of Timor-Leste, partly because of centralising imperatives of an overwhelmed United Nations that preferred a narrow circle of interlocutors, CNRT was not expanded as the existing, effective consultative institution to include constituencies excluded from it and then was shut down prematurely before the August 2001 elections. The CEP was white-anted as a vehicle for engaging traditional village leaders to build the democracy from the bottom up as well as the top down. The younger generation was shut out and the cultivation of a robust separation of powers took second place to competition among the 1975 generation to dominate power.

The Fight Back for Separated Powers

No setback is necessarily permanent in history. Good people resist when non-democratic forks in the road are taken. This has been true of the struggle for separated powers in Timor-Leste. Sergio Vieira de Mello, Mari Alkatiri and Xanana Gusmão—the three key players in our narrative of centralising and personalising power—all pluralised to varying degrees from the positions they defended when they were gripping the reins of power tightly. Sergio Vieira de Mello did this in the self-critical post-UNTAET speeches he made before he died. Since Mari Alkatiri has been in opposition, he has been a robust advocate of the separation of powers and as astute a critic of executive domination of the judiciary, the civil service and the security sector as one could hope for in any democratic leader. He is committed to contesting power through the ballot box and rejecting the path to power that Rogerio Lobato pursued of capturing the security sector as the supporter of 'a natural party of government'. The younger generation of Fretilin leaders shares this view.

Prime Minister, Xanana Gusmão, and his government continue to breach the separation of powers in important ways on a fairly regular basis. As one senior civil servant put it in November 2006: 'Xanana and other leaders were not used to leading society through institutions. They led through direct interface between leader and community. The way the state works is different from the way a guerilla works.' At the same time, the enduring contribution of Gusmão as a leader who used personalised power to pluralise the resistance in an inclusive way shows signs of being reasserted. We see this in the appointment of as prominent a Fretilin leader as Ana Pessoa to the critical independent office of Prosecutor-General in 2009. She is not the only Fretilin leader, and counts alongside many pro-integration leaders who Gusmão has embraced in his post-2007 administration. Notwithstanding that progress, we will see in the next chapter continuing separation-of-power deficits that have been in play since 2007.

One of the reasons the three leaders of whom we have been most critical on the centralised power issue have moved towards being more supportive of separations of powers is that they have come in for so much criticism from Timorese and international civil society on this issue. We say separations of powers because the Democratic Republic of Timor-Leste is constitutionally a republic and we interpret republican philosophy as requiring a much richer separation of powers than simply Montesquieu's tripartite one of legislature, executive and judiciary (Braithwaite 1997). It also means prosecutors being independent of the judiciary and the police; an ombudsman, an auditor-general and an anti-corruption commissioner who can call all these independent officers to account under a rule of law; an independent media and a broader business community that can also do so because they are not dominated by the executive government.

Politically, we conceive republicanism as a political philosophy of continuous struggle for more effectively separated powers (Barnett 2006). It is a struggle towards a polity where each separated power has sufficient clout to exercise its own functions with support to do so from other separated powers. A republic is a polity where no one centre of power is so dominant that it can crush any other separated power without the other separated powers mobilising to defeat that domination from the centre.

Republicanism does not require powers that are so diffused that separated powers cannot act decisively. The executive is empowered to declare war, the judge to declare guilt, the legislature to declare laws. Decisiveness for the judge is actually enhanced by the knowledge that only an appellate court can overturn her decision on an error of law; she cannot be dominated by a prime minister who demands the acquittal of a political crony. Decisiveness for a constable on the street is knowing that she is the one with the power to decide whether to arrest a judge who appears to assault his wife; then it is no longer in her hands but in the hands of the separated powers of a prosecutor. Decisiveness for a general is knowing that once the executive declares war, she can conduct it in accordance with laws of war approved by the legislature, without interference from politicians who think of themselves as armchair generals.

Of course, a mature constitutional debate is needed to finetune separated powers to ensure that each can decisively perform its function without domination from any centralising power and without confusion as to who exercises each separated power, and under what norms. None of this is to deny that democracies must at times debate trade-offs between greater accountability and greater efficiency. Separated powers of civil society and the media to speak assertively during those constitutional debates are critical elements of separated powers that get the separation clear and effective.

Yet it is possible for civil society to become an overwhelming source of domination. We saw this during the tyranny of China's Cultural Revolution during the 1960s where judges, artists and intellectuals were pilloried by youth as class enemies. We saw it well into the twentieth century in parts of the US South, where the domination of the Ku Klux Klan meant it was impossible for a court ever to convict a white man for murdering a black citizen. In such contexts, UN and national human rights institutions, the law, the police and the judiciary should flex their muscles decisively to call such dominating civil forces to account.

We believe a healthy republican mobilisation, particularly from the younger generation of Timorese civil society, is under way in Timor-Leste. That is not to deny that it has a long way to travel towards establishing a deeply republican democracy in the new nation. Currents in civil society that support the further pluralisation of power and accountability have attracted financial support from international donors that have also been worried about separated powers. For example, the Government of Portugal provided support for the establishment of the Office of the Provedor (a Portuguese version of the ombudsman function regulating maladministration, human rights and corruption abuses by executive government) on 26 May 2004, with the first Provedor taking office on 16 June 2005. The *Civil Service Act* was also passed by the Parliament in June 2005 to underwrite the independence of the civil service (Report of the Alkatiri Initiative Review 2006:45–7). In 2000 the Office of the Inspector-General was established to monitor all civil service control actions for corruption. In February 2010, Adérito Soares was appointed by the Parliament as the first Anti-Corruption Commissioner. It is beyond the scope of this book to evaluate how well all these new separations of powers are beginning to function; because one of us is hands-on in that endeavour, it is all the more inappropriate for us to attempt it.

Rather we seek to connect an analysis of the error of misplaced realism to a profound new risk: that the networked civil society that defeats realist power can in turn be corrupted. It can be corrupted by the nodal actors of the very networks that allowed the republic to prevail over a former tyranny. We argue that this risk can be defeated by demands for accountability from those same civil society networks and with assistance from independent accountability institutions. We are not pessimistic that there will be an inevitable triumph of oligarchy. On the contrary, we believe the world has become somewhat less oligarchic during our lifetimes (Kenny 2011) and that UN peace processes have made a mixed, but on balance positive, contribution in that direction, including in Timor-Leste. At the same time, the Timor-Leste record is mixed rather than splendid. While new accountability institutions have been established, they have yet to demonstrate their long-run contribution to republican freedom as non-domination (Pettit 1997). Indeed, there is a danger of what Soares (2011) dubs institutional ritualism (see also Wilson 2010). This means creating on paper one accountability institution after another as a ritual of comfort to international society. Yet each in the succession of new institutions fails to deliver accountability substance in the same way as its predecessors. International society derives more comfort from the institutional appearance of accountability in the new democracy than from its substance.

The Analogy to Social-Democratic and Feminist Struggles

Social democrats are people who struggle for a more equal distribution of wealth and power. It is a struggle that never ends. While it is theoretically possible by the lights of social-democratic theory to have too much equality—for example, such that people who work longer hours are not paid proportionately for it—in practice, too much equality is a problem that never occurs. This is because existing privilege in the long run is always so effective in using privilege to extend privilege. This is equally true of networks of male privilege and the imperative for unending feminist struggle.

We argue that the republican struggle for practically effective separations of powers has that quality as well. This is because the executive government (or the military high command at the moment of a coup) seeks to preserve and enhance its power by pushing back other branches of governance that might curtail it. The executive branch has more powerful levers at its disposal—guns, money, the power to hire and fire judges, and to close newspapers—compared with other branches of governance. The genius of republican theory in a long trajectory that comes to us from Greece and Rome to northern Italy and northern

Europe (Pocock 1975; Skinner 1983), to Montesquieu to Madison and Jefferson in the American Revolution, is that it institutionalises some limited resources that enable checks and balances from alternative branches to the executive government. These are never fully successful in securing for the people freedom as non-domination from executive tyranny (Pettit 1997). Hence, vibrant local civil society politics always has work to do in struggling for more practically effective separations of powers. And international civil society always has work to do in supporting local civil society so it can mount that challenge against expansive executive governments.

Moreover, all this is especially true post conflict. Michael Barnett and Christoph Zürcher (2009) argue that peacebuilders tend to deliver the rituals and symbols of a republic rather than its substance. This conclusion is reached by modelling the behaviour of three players: peacebuilders who want peace and democracy, state elites of the target country who want to preserve their power, and sub-national elites who want to maintain their power in the countryside without being pushed around by national elites. In the game of peacebuilding, according to Barnett and Zürcher, each of these three players depends on strategic interaction with the other two to achieve their objectives. Peacebuilders cannot deliver peace and agreement on a democratic constitution without national and sub-national elites signing on. State elites have some interest in playing ball with the peacebuilders because they bring resources that rich democracies supply; yet they also fear curtailment of their power by a republican constitution that actually works. National elites need sub-national elites not to be spoilers of their rule, just as peacebuilders need them not to be spoilers of the peace. Sub-national elites want resources that both the state and the peacebuilders can provide, but not at the price of a national constitution that greatly curtails the domination of local spaces that they were able to win during the war.

Barnett and Zürcher define four possible outcomes of this three-player game. *Conflictive peacebuilding* is the worst outcome, where national or local elites periodically return to violence, or threaten it, to achieve their objectives. *Captured peacebuilding* is the second-worst option, where peacebuilders give national and sub-national elites most of what they want to preserve their domination in order to preserve the peace (as in the case of Northern Alliance warlords in Afghanistan and relatives of President Hamid Karzai even being allowed local opium monopolies as part of the local domination package). *Compromised peacebuilding* is the second-best option, where national and sub-national elites live with a constitution that curtails their power on paper and peacebuilders live with a lot of practical domination of local space by extant elites in order to nail down the peace and a democratic constitution. *Cooperative peacebuilding* sees all three players cooperating to build a peaceful republic.

Going slightly beyond Barnett and Zürcher's analysis, we hypothesise that conflictive peacebuilding is the likely outcome in the common situation where the international community is simply not willing to put in the resources to motivate local elites to play ball with any of the other three outcomes (for example, Somalia, Rwanda in the mid-1990s). Captured peacebuilding is most likely in scenarios like Afghanistan and Iraq in the 2000s where peacebuilders put massive resources in, but where the peacebuilders never secure legitimacy for the peace and therefore also must call on national and sub-national elites to keep fighting off spoilers. Barnett and Zürcher deduce plausibly that, across a wide range of peace processes, a compromised peace will be the equilibrium outcome of their peace and democracy game.[3] What we hypothesise is that compromised peace is the likely equilibrium outcome in a case like Timor-Leste where the international community is willing to invest huge resources and where the intervention has local legitimacy, to complement the international legitimacy that delivers the staying power to keep the resources flowing.

The important point of Barnett and Zürcher's analysis is that cooperative peacebuilding is not the best-case outcome that is possible; compromised peacebuilding is in the wide range of circumstances where cooperative peacebuilding is impossible. A reason that again goes beyond Barnett and Zürcher for why cooperative peacebuilding almost never happens is that if all the players were sufficiently committed to building a peaceful republic to make it work, it would actually be difficult to motivate the international community to pay to make that possible. We agree with Barnett and Zürcher (2009:48) that

> compromised peacebuilding might not be such a terrible result…given the alternatives[4]…Symbols…can matter. They can provide new focal

---

3   This equilibrium is based on the posited ordering of preferences of the three players in this table:

Rank Order of Preferences of Different Actors for Different Outcomes

	Peacebuilders	Target government	Rural elites
4	Cooperative	Captured	Captured
3	Compromised	Compromised	Compromised
2	Confrontational	Confrontational	Confrontational
1	Captured	Cooperative	Cooperative

Source: Barnett and Zürcher (2009:34)

4   The inevitability of compromised peacebuilding is implicit in other work such as that of Eide et al. (2005:3) on dilemmas of integrated missions: 'At least three dilemmas are raised in relation to integration. The *humanitarian* dilemma reflects a tension between the *partiality* involved in supporting a political transition process and the impartiality needed to protect humanitarian space. The *human rights* dilemma relates to the tension that arises when the UN feels compelled to promote peace by working with those who may have

points. They can become public commitments that even hypocritical reformers must take into account. They can be used by local and international reformers to continue to press for change.

This potential resides in changing Barnett and Zürcher's three-player game into a four-player game in which the fourth 'player' is actually a network of civil society activists.[5] This move is also consistent with Michael Barnett's (2006) earlier normative work on the virtues of a 'republican peace' compared with a 'liberal peace' (see also our concluding chapter). The fourth internationally networked civil society player makes it a less realist game in which demands to give real meaning to symbols of peace, democracy and republican separations of powers can be mobilised from below. We see this in Timor-Leste when the Catholic Church organised a huge demonstration against Fretilin corruption and domination of the nation in 2005. This was an important lesson to Fretilin whose members were so inexperienced in democratic politics that they thought a two-thirds majority in elections gave them a mandate to ignore civil society opposition.[6] If there is one thing the recent history of Timor confirms, it is the power of the crowd in history (Rudé 1964), for both good and ill. As in post-revolutionary France, there are weapons of the weak available to the republican crowd that over time might convert a compromised peace into progressively more meaningful republican separations of powers. This can happen when civil society advocates of genuine separations of powers manage to divide and conquer elites during a moment of weakness when one elite faction can be enrolled to deepen republican reform against the resistance of others. As Rudé (1964) points out, the crowd never prevails in history on its own, but it can when it persuades elite factions that directly pull levers of power to defect to its cause (especially the military in Chenoweth and Stephan's 2011 huge comparative study).

At another level, however, our analysis is more pessimistic than that of Barnett and Zürcher because Timor-Leste is a 'most likely case' (Eckstein 1975) of a compromised peace growing into a republican peace. This is because its two

---

unsatisfactory human rights records, while still retaining the role of an "outside critic" of the same process. The *local ownership* dilemma relates to the need to root peace processes in the host country's society without reinforcing the very structures that led to conflict in the first place.'

5 Of course, this is a shabby abstraction as the fourth player is actually a bundle of many players in the network. Our move to what might in reality be a 30 or 40-player game takes us beyond what we are capable of understanding through formal game theoretic logic. Nevertheless, it is an analytically helpful move to explain the limits of the three-player game and the prospect of transforming outcomes when many additional players demand that real meaning be given to symbols of peace and separated powers.

6 'Allied to the Church were anti-Fretilin political groups, including former members of UDT, a significant proportion of the F-FDTL, former Fretilin members around Xanana Gusmão and José Ramos-Horta, and an unpalatable mixture of ex-combatants, ex-militia, quasi-criminals and youth gangs associated with CPD-RDTL, Colimau 2000, Sagrada Familia and various martial arts clubs…The government ignored this powerful if shifting combination of forces, noting that it had been elected to govern with a two-thirds majority and that these groups were ideological opponents rather than representing legitimate civil grievances' (Kingsbury 2009:114).

most respected leaders, the current Prime Minister and President, were not 'hypocritical reformers', as in the Barnett and Zürcher (2009:48) quote above. They were genuine pluralist democrats who dedicated their lives to a networked struggle for a republic with a separation of powers. And they had succeeded in uniting all the sub-national elites behind that project, as manifest in the 82 per cent vote for Gusmão in 2002. We learn from this case that pluralist networked struggle for republican separations of powers is quite likely to lead to those who control the key nodes of that network corrupting separations of powers in important ways.

This just takes us back to the fundamental point about social-democratic, feminist and republican campaigning against concentrated power. It never reaches an end point. Victory never arrives. Activists who think it has invite defeat of the very victory they point to. This insight is an old one that is repeatedly forgotten. Benjamin Rush complained in 1787 of those who confuse the struggles of the '*American revolution* with those of the late *American war*. The American war is over; but this is far from being the case with the American revolution. On the contrary, nothing but the first act of the great drama is closed' (Arendt 1963:300).

Networks can only govern themselves nodally (Drahos 2004; Johnston and Shearing 2003; Shearing et al. 2003). Inherent in that proposition is the fact that even sincere democrats like Gusmão who seize nodal control are at risk of corrupting the separation of powers to preserve their hard-won power. The remedy is never-ending struggle to establish new nodes that reorganise civil society to put checks and balances in the path of the old nodes. Our fieldwork reveals plenty of that among youthful activists on the streets of Timor-Leste. There are therefore grounds for hope for sustained peace in Timor based on rejuvenations of separations of powers. Equally, the next chapter shows how hard that road is when disappointed youth are also enrolled to new projects of violence by one member of the old republican elite against another. We might interpret the events we describe in the next chapter as arising from the fact that the United Nations went beyond compromised peacebuilding, in Barnett and Zürcher's (2009) terms, to being captured by the high command of Falintil on matters of defence policy.

9. Transitional Security

We have seen that INTERFET and its successors quickly, and with the loss of only a few lives, negotiated the complete evacuation of the Indonesian military from Timor-Leste, the disarming of militias and the cantonment of Falintil and secured the tensions across the West Timor border. More importantly for long-term security, Gusmão, Ramos-Horta and Alkatiri led diplomatic initiatives that forged productive, even warm, relationships with the leadership of Indonesia. They were from the day of their independence unfailingly forgiving of Indonesia and Indonesians.

The security problems that were to emerge for Timor-Leste were not from Indonesia. They were internal. And they were not internal divisions based on the 1975–99 divide between Timorese who supported independence and those who did not. They were divisions that opened mainly as a result of mismanaged security sector policy. In 2006 these divisions exploded.

Three Divides

Xanana Gusmão and CNRM[1] had supported the idea of a Timor-Leste without a military from 1998 to early 2000. How could tiny Timor-Leste defend itself against Indonesia again, or Australia? Best, on one view often discussed in the lead-up to independence, to do without the drain on the development budget and the internal security risk provoked by a military. This view did not prevail, however. Falintil was revered in Timor-Leste and so its leadership was able to secure comparatively well-paid jobs for themselves and the fighters who were most loyal to them. This opened up three kinds of divides. In August 2000, the King's College Report (2000) recommended that a national military be formed in accordance with one of three force development options. By then, one of the arguments for a national military was that Falintil had been in cantonment for too long 'without dependable means of support or a clearly-defined role' and this was 'potentially explosive' (King's College Report 2000:3.6). Had reintegration programs with generous terms been offered to Falintil members who left their guns behind in the cantonment as they rejoined their families and villages, this situation might have been averted in a cheaper manner. One reason for thinking this is what happened when the disgruntled majority of Falintil who did not get jobs in Falintil–Timor-Leste Defence Force (F-FDTL) was eventually helped by the International Organisation for Migration (IOM) reintegration program.

---

1 See CNRM ('East Timor peace plan', <www.uc.pt/timor/cnrm>) which advocates a police force with border protection capability but 'no army because Timor-Leste does not want any more war' (ICG 2008:4).

We will see that the overwhelming majority of them were pleased in retrospect to be 'free' from F-FDTL. As in other post-conflict societies, in Timor-Leste, completely decommissioning F-FDTL would have been a rocky transition, but not an impossible one to attempt.

The first divide, therefore, was between the government and the military high command on one side and most Falintil members who missed out on jobs in the new defence force, F-FDTL, on the other. Only 650 members of the old Falintil were selected, embittering more than 1000 fighters who had endured the frustration of 14 months of cantonment. Many responded by destroying every worldly possession they had accumulated during cantonment, spurning the initial IOM offer of reintegration assistance, and heading straight home (McCarthy 2002:33). Older veterans who had struggled through the worst times tended to resent the inclusion of younger recruits who had joined Falintil only after 1997. Some elements excluded from the F-FDTL became powerful political factions in the new nation, and semi-militarised ones, forming the backbone of some of the youth gangs that seized the streets in the political crisis of 2006. These groups undertook drill and other military training in public.

Elle Sette (L-7), who was pushed out of Falintil for a period after 1984, after his brother led a coup attempt against Xanana Gusmão, says none of his 500 Falintil fighters was accepted into the F-FDTL (ICG 2006b:5). Elle Sette formed a cult-like organisation that blended Catholic and animist beliefs called Sagrada Familia. He is today an influential Member of Parliament. Another important paramilitary veterans group was Colimau 2000. Most members of these groups as they grew were not actually veterans; some former militia members joined, and many unemployed youth. But they started as vehicles for the resentments of excluded veterans. There was also resentment at the policy that Clandestinos and widows who did not actually carry weapons, yet who often suffered terrible wounds in events like Santa Cruz, were considered neither for F-FDTL nor for the combatant reintegration program (McCarthy 2002). There are even claims that some pro-Indonesia militia elements exploited the politicised exclusions from F-FDTL to remake themselves 'under the cover of forming a "veterans" association, misrepresenting themselves as former pro-independence fighters' (Shoesmith 2003:233). Rogerio Lobato, who was excluded from the UN transitional government, who was considered as the first Secretary of State for Defence (a position he had held in the Fretilin government in exile) but denied it in the initial Fretilin government when Taur Matan Ruak (TMR) threatened to resign as military commander, built a power base for himself by organising and privately arming disgruntled veterans (ICG 2006b:5).

UNTAET missed opportunities here. One was the opportunity to insist that it (with help from donors) would fund generously the reintegration of *all* Falintil fighters into civilian society, but provide zero funds for establishing a new national army. No level of generosity for Falintil reintegration could have approached the cost to the international community of funding a defence force and then seeing its factionalism nearly destroy the nation again.² Another mistake was to allow Falintil to regard as an 'internal matter' (Rees 2002, 2003:2) who would move from Falintil to the new F-FDTL and who would be supported by the Falintil Reinsertion Assistance Program implemented by the IOM and funded by USAID and the World Bank (Kings College Report 2003:2D.2). Because this process was dominated by Xanana Gusmão and his military commander, Taur Matan Ruak, Fretilin and other key stakeholders were not consulted on the composition of the defence force. Given the tense relationship between Gusmão and Alkatiri, this set in train a cycle of security sector paranoia. If the international community was going to make the mistake of funding a Timor-Leste military, it at least might have insisted on a procedurally fair process for settling its composition that would imbue confidence in it among the major political elements of the new nation. The United Nations failed to protest power plays that ensured '[n]either the police service nor the defence force are adequately supported or managed by East Timorese civilian oversight' (Rees 2003:4).³ This is one of the ways that the United Nations must itself be an important element of the separation of powers in transitional administration.⁴ It must use UN power to prevent any domestic faction from attempting to institutionalise its capture of the monopolisation of force within a new state. If this lesson is not learnt from Timor-Leste, the United Nations could repeat the unfolding of the 2006 scenario that Edward Rees foreshadowed in 2003:

> In response to the establishment of the F-FDTL, there was an increase in paramilitary security groups across the country (involving disaffected former Falintil and Clandestine activists) operating throughout the country. These groups were loosely connected under the umbrella of the Association of Ex-Combatants 1975 (AC75), headed by the now Minister for Internal Administration [Rogerio Lobato], and include among

---

2   The non-universal combatant reintegration program that was put in place was not very expensive (about US$1000 per beneficiary) in providing some resettlement cash and support for mostly 'kiosks and cattle' projects, and some training in skills such as livestock management, and was a moderately successful one by international standards, according to McCarthy (2002). Opinion survey evidence also indicated it reduced the high recipient antipathy towards the F-FDTL high command (McCarthy 2002:53, 67). Most interestingly, in a short time, most former soldiers had come to the view that civilian life was better than the life of a soldier in either the old Falintil or the new F-FDTL, often using the word 'freedom', even though there were new challenges for them (McCarthy 2002:70–1). Important here was a quick 50 per cent reduction in bachelor status among demobilised veterans and a sense that 'marriage is an act of optimism' (McCarthy 2002:73). See Chapter 10 on childbirth as an act of optimism.
3   'Early decisions regarding demobilization and establishing the defence force and police services were made in a spirit of political and practical expediency rather than with a view to the long-term development of East Timor' (Rees 2003:4).
4   One of our panel members said, in sympathy with the UN mission, that defence force development was not in its mandate. While defence force dismantlement and reintegration are not development, the point on the limits of the mandate is well taken. Our argument is that UN mandates must defend against domestic factions attempting to capture a monopolisation of force.

others Sagrada Familia and the Committee for the Popular Defence of the Democratic Republic of Timor-Leste. While most are politically oriented, others have more criminal motivations. Under the patronage of a lead Fretilin Central Committee member and one time Minister for Defence [Rogerio Lobato] from 2001 until 20 May 2002 these groups challenged the legitimacy of the F-FDTL. This process culminated on 20 May 2002 after a series of veteran marches across the country with the appointment of the political patron of these groups to the portfolio of Minister of Internal Administration—the political master of the police service…Old divisions in the anti-Indonesian resistance movement are being institutionalised in the new East Timorese state with one political grouping [President Gusmão's allies] finding a home in the defence force and dissidents (under the patronage of the Minister for Internal Administration) likely finding a home in the police service, and some elements of local government…Given these institutions' burgeoning commercial interests, their political differences are compounded even further. It all looks very much [like] Indonesia. (Rees 2003:2, 4)

Hence, the second key security sector divide was between the police and the F-FDTL. In 2006 this blew up into firefights between the military and the police.[5] Competition between the police and the military was a direct product of competition between different politicians of the 1975 generation that compromised the political independence of the security sector. Fretilin Internal Administration Minister, Rogerio Lobato, supplied militarised elements of his police with superior firepower to the military. This included seven F2000 automatic machine guns and 380 semi-automatic assault rifles (UN Independent Special Commission 2006:19–20). Lobato deliberately favoured westerners and veterans excluded from F-FDTL in his special police units that were more highly paid and better armed than the military. They acted as his personal security force (ICG 2006b:6).[6] Lobato thought like a revolutionary, seeing the military as loyal to his political opponent, Xanana Gusmão, and seeing political power as growing out of the barrel of a gun. Militarising the police as part of a wider strategy of factionalising the security sector was also his play to become an indispensably powerful force within Fretilin. Some say Lobato saw himself as a credible successor to Alkatiri as a Fretilin prime minister. Multiple police sources told us that Lobato enjoyed a variety of criminal enterprises such as smuggling;

---

5   There had been numerous clashes between the military and police for years—for example, in December 2004 when F-FDTL troops ransacked Becora Police Station, injuring seven police, after a traffic fine was imposed on a soldier who was then allegedly beaten. Another in 2004 was a fight between police and soldiers over a football match in Lospalos that left the police station in ruins.

6   In reaction, a Nacionalista movement of 80 eastern PNTL officers was formed in 2004, which became publicly critical of its commander and the PNTL as an institution (UN Special Independent Commission 2006:57).

he was a classic example of a man who moved from being a manipulator of the shadow state (Braithwaite et al. 2010c; Reno 1995) to a position of control over the state security sector that would allow him to criminalise the state.

All this created a bad context for the interpretation of distrustful members of the elite of a decision that had actually been made by Gusmão and UNTAET in early 2000. This was to recruit Timorese with police experience from the former Indonesian police into the new Policia Nacional de Timor-Leste (PNTL: Timor-Leste National Police).[7] In other circumstances, it would have been sound reconciliation policy to include a balance of experienced and capable police professionals from the former regime in the new national police. But in the context of the utter politicisation of the security sector by Gusmão, then Lobato, Falintil veterans in F-FDTL were spoiling for a fight with PNTL 'collaborators' who they said 'had been their torturers' (Veteran interview).

The third important divide that opened up was internal to F-FDTL, between soldiers from the eastern and and those from the western parts of the new nation. When Xanana Gusmão abandoned his earlier policy preference for establishing a nation without a military, he worked to establish a military in which 'Xanana's friends got in and his enemies were left out' (Dodd 2002).[8] The effect of this politicisation of the military strengthened a geographic imbalance in its composition; the senior officers would almost all come from the east of the country (Shoesmith 2003:246–7). Eastern domination of the military already existed before this politicisation because the western leadership had been more vulnerable to Indonesian forces and more depleted than the ranks of eastern officers. The capital, Dili, where Indonesian forces consolidated their limited base of control in 1975, was in the west, and the initial decapitation of Fretilin occurred in the west between Dili and Indonesian-controlled West Timor. The fact that it was mainly surviving eastern remnants which continued the insurgency for the next two decades led to unfair taunts of westerners by easterners within F-FDTL that the easterners were the ones who made the sacrifices to win the war. Then, as we saw earlier in this chapter, the east–west divide was mismanaged by the military and exploited by ambitious politicians.

On 9 January 2006, 159 soldiers petitioned the President as supreme commander alleging discrimination by eastern (*lorosae*) officers against western (*loromonu*)

---

7   A total of 370 of 3000 PNTL recruits by 2006 were former Indonesian police (UN Independent Special Commission 2006:57).

8   When Fretilin came to power, led by Secretary of State—Defence, Roque Rodrigues, it sought to use the levers of power to turn F-FDTL into clients of Fretilin, not totally without success, as Xanana Gusmão said in his speech to Fretilin of 22 June 2006: 'Bigadier Taur came to talk to me and said: "President, I told Dr. Roque Rodrigues, Your [Fretilin's] biggest mistake was trying to bring F-FDTL under the power of Fretilin." At that moment I was very happy, because I had finally met again my Younger Brother whom I had earlier lost.' Unofficial translation posted by John M. Miller to East Timor list, 26 June 2006: <http://etan.org/et2006/may/crisis.htm>

troops. They were by then old grievances,[9] but ones that were 'poisoned by political manipulation' as 'many interested parties saw political opportunity' in these security sector divisions. Hence, the east–west security sector schisms spread to the streets of Dili where westerners attacked easterners (ICG 2006b:i–ii). Political leaders blamed the leadership of F-FDTL for not listening to grievances that were a warning signal of significant problems of discrimination within their organisation, while the military leadership blamed politicians for interfering in the military to create divisions that they saw as in their political interests. Both critiques were right. There was both defective and neglectful dispute resolution and a political interference problem. By the end of February 2006, the dispute had deteriorated to the point where 594 soldiers deserted their posts and then were dismissed on 16 March when they refused to return. Prime Minister Alkatiri supported the military commander's decision to dismiss them; President Gusmão opposed it and responded with an inflammatory speech on 23 March that sympathised with the petitioners and lamented east–west divisions as a threat to the nation. In that and subsequent speeches of that period, Gusmão was reckless with the unique power of his words to parochialise the politics of his country (Silva 2010). Four days later, the first house burnings and violence occurred on the streets of Dili, where sentiment in favour of the petitioners ran high, and the first flight of large numbers of refugees out of Dili occurred. Prime Minister Alkatiri said that he spoke to the President after his 23 March east–west speech:

> When I said that it was a terrible mistake, he said it was no mistake, it was a conscious attempt to divide in which he knew exactly what he was doing. He decided that the only way to defeat Fretilin was to divide it and position it as just a party of the east. He is very Machiavellian. (Interview, September 2009)

A Dili demonstration by the petitioners on 24 April that raged for days became a protest against the Alkatiri Government—something that was likely promoted by Gusmão supporters. PNTL lost control of violence around the central government building, so Alkatiri called in F-FDTL to restore order, which they did with excessive force, worsening the impression among the populace that this was the east–west conflict Xanana had warned of in his 23 March speech.

On 3 May 2006, a political opportunist, Major Alfredo Reinado, head of the military police, deserted with his armed men and was joined by two other westerners, Majors Marcus Tilman and Augusto Tara. Reinado further split

---

9   Perhaps 42 mostly western soldiers were discharged in December 2003. This group included a man with the alias Railos, who became a central player in the events of 2006 when he alleged on the Australian television program *Four Corners* that Prime Minister Alkatiri had authorised arms distribution to civilians. This led to Alkatiri's resignation. The 42 discharged soldiers complained of discrimination against westerners (ICG 2006b:6).

the country by announcing that he had deserted because 'on the 28th, it was easterners who shot westerners. I am witness to that. I do not want to be a part of the [army] that shoots westerners' (ICG 2006b:9). Prime Minister Alkatiri believes Reinado was an agent for Gusmão executing a plan, which Australia supported, to oust him through destabilisation. This was the way the Prime Minister interpreted Reinado's armed deserters firing first in a firefight with F-FDTL on 23 May. Minister Lobato, with the knowledge of Prime Minister Alkatiri, responded to this interpretation by arming at least two civilian groups with police automatic weapons. Different men who led attacks on opposite sides alleged they were following instructions from Gusmão on the one hand (Martinkus 2006) and Alkatiri on the other, though it is impossible to validate the truth of such allegations (ICG 2006b:10–11; UN Independent Special Commission 2006:38). While the UN Independent Special Commission (2006:30) found Reinado was in contact with Gusmão in the days after his desertion, it concluded '[t]here is no evidence that an armed group of men under the command of Major Reinado carried out criminal actions on the orders or with the authority of the President'. Similarly, it concluded that while Alkatiri knew of the illegal distribution of police weapons to civilian militias, 'the Commission does not accept that at the meeting on 8 May the former Prime Minister gave instructions to Rai Los to "eliminate" his political opponents' (UN Independent Special Commission 2006:40). It did find that Internal Security Minister Lobato arrived in a flak jacket at police headquarters, shouting 'Kill them all' (UN Independent Special Commission 2006:26). And it recommended that Defence Minister, Roque Rodrigues, and military commander, Brigadier Taur Matan Ruak, be prosecuted for illegal distribution of F-FDTL weapons. Progressively throughout this period, the petitioners' movement 'tightened their links with the parties opposing Fretilin' such as the PD (Democratic Party) and PSD (Social Democratic Party)' (Silva 2010:108).

Reinado was certainly getting financial support from somewhere in a course of action that profoundly destabilised the country—causing Fretilin leaders who feared him to surround themselves with armed men, which in turn caused anti-Fretilin forces who feared them to surround themselves with armed gangs. In a joint account with his partner, Angelita Pires, Reinado had $1 million in a bank in Darwin, Australia. Damien Kingsbury (2009:190–1) has explored tentatively Reinado's links to elements in the Indonesian military and an allegation from an intelligence source that mobile telephone intercepts indicated that the funding source was a Timor-Leste politician (who was neither Gusmão nor Ramos-Horta) (Kingsbury 2009:190–1).

The International Stabilisation Force Arrives

Figure 9.1: Rampaging youth flee as the International Stabilisation Force arrives in Dili

Photo: Brendan Esposito/ Fairfax Media

By the time the government decided to request international peacekeepers, both Gusmão and Alkatiri were in fear of their lives. On 25 May 2006, F-FDTL assaulted police headquarters. The United Nations negotiated a ceasefire whereby 85 police would surrender unarmed behind a UN flag and be allowed to walk to UN headquarters. Some soldiers opened fire, killing 10 and wounding 30 police. Australian peacekeepers arrived soon after this incident, followed by troops from Malaysia, Portugal and New Zealand. This had a positive effect on the security situation even before they landed, with some truckloads of thugs headed for Dili turning around when they saw Australian naval vessels heading into Dili Harbour. Thanks to the timely peacekeeper intervention, only 38 people were killed in the fighting of April and May 2006 and only 150 000 were displaced into refugee camps after 1650 homes were destroyed. Without the peacekeepers, there could have been a civil war of major proportions. There were five phases of the 2006 peacekeeping operation: 1) a military phase conducted by the International Stabilisation Force (ISF); 2) ISF in joint patrols with Australian police support;[10] 3) UNPOL with ISF backup; 4) UNPOL with PNTL support; 5) PNTL with UNPOL support. A sixth phase—of PNTL completely taking over UNPOL—began in 2011.

---

10 Later with New Zealand, Portuguese and Malaysian police, then later again morphing to a UN policing operation: UNPOL.

9. Transitional Security

Figures 9.2a and b: The scene of the murder of 10 police under a UN flag at the hands of their own military, Dili, 2006

Photos: Manuel de Almeida/epa/Corbis

While major fire fights with guns ended with the arrival of the peacekeepers, warfare between gangs with disparate political affiliations did not. Perhaps 250 people were killed one by one in this lower-intensity violence, according to UN police sources, between 2006 and 2008. The initial perpetrators of violence were not going to desist until Prime Minister Alkatiri was forced to resign, which he did on 27 June 2006 when Ramos-Horta became Prime Minister. Elements who wanted to destabilise the Gusmão–Ramos-Horta control of the security sector were then not going to let up. Competing political groups paid young men to cause mayhem. On balance, the political conspiracy theories on both sides might be seen as neither totally right nor totally wrong. Much of the gang violence developed a momentum of its own. Martial arts groups (MAGs) and other youth gangs attacked one another and attacked refugee camps and other innocent civilians. Rocks and Ambon arrows fired by a slingshot, not guns, were the weapons of choice in this street fighting that terrorised Dili between 2006 and 2008. The Timor-Leste police had now utterly disintegrated in Dili, though not in the rest of the country. So gang violence in the streets of the capital had to be managed by UN police.

UNPOL faced an enforcement-swamping problem when so much violence was occurring during 2006 in particular. Ultimately, gang fighters would disperse when sufficient UN police were deployed with sufficient force, but often that deployment was too slow from stretched and exhausted UNPOL. One international police adviser saw the problem as one of failing to get local police capability with local knowledge on the street more quickly: 'The gangs are playing games of hide and seek with the internationals. It's fun' (Interview, November 2006). At one UNPOL community policing consultation we attended in 2006 on the outskirts of Dili, a message from locals was 'please get PNTL back on the street because "they know who are the troublemakers, who to talk to sort things out".' Another leader explained to the foreign police that if you send someone to jail you must tell the *chefe de suco* (village leader) why and what happened. Otherwise there will be rumours and community policing will not work.

UN dialogues did not defuse the major potential powder keg. The United Nations, President Gusmão and Prime Minister Alkatiri each ran separate and unsuccessful negotiations to persuade the armed group led by Alfredo Reinado to surrender their weapons and submit to justice. He had promised to do so only when Alkatiri resigned; yet when Alkatiri did resign, Reinado strung along the new leadership, preserving his options as an armed spoiler of the new democracy.

Security Sector Divides and Youth Gang Warfare

In mid-2006 all political factions, with good reason, believed their political adversaries had fomented violence on the street to destabilise them or exact revenge against them for alleged wrongs. Some leaders we interviewed also believed that some in their own political network did not have clean hands in this regard, while never admitting to more than indirect personal responsibility for tolerating violence on their own side—though some said 'we all bear responsibility' or words to that effect. It was true that most leaders did bear some responsibility. After the devastation of 1999, the masses of Timor-Leste and a majority of the nation's elite were influenced by a culture of nonviolence that led them to resist the creation of an army. For most of the terrorised population of Dili and some other districts between 2006 and 2008, commitment to nonviolence was all the more confirmed by the events that oppressed them again. At the same time, between 2006 and 2008, a multitude of subcultures of violence festered. There were disparate pre-existing resentments these subcultures played to. 'The children traumatised in 1999 became the rock-throwing youth of the street of 2006' (Interview, September 2009). East versus west was just one resentment that had historical precedents long before east–west divides in the security sector split wide open. There were different variants of east–west conflict over eastern and western language-group control of different sections of markets in Dili, over control of bus routes and gambling, others that had origins in divide-and-rule Portuguese colonialism, others that were probably pre-colonial. None of these seemed to cut so deep as to be a fissure worthy of significant attention in the CAVR report, for example, and east–west was not a clear ethnic divide.

Like all societies, Timorese society had many crosscutting cleavages around which resentment could be mobilised and there was no sense in which east versus west was a great divide. It would be a mistake to see any of Timor-Leste's cleavages as unusually profound in a comparative cultural sense. Indeed, it seems truer to reality to see the forces of national unity as profound for a new society of many language groups—say, compared with our Solomon Islands case (Braithwaite et al. 2010c). What has been unusual about Timorese history is the pressure mundane cleavages have been put under by top-down entrepreneurs of violence, both Indonesian and Timorese. These top-down political entrepreneurs created both security sector cleavages and opportunities for bottom-up entrepreneurs of violence. Put another way, in the history of Timor-Leste, elite subcultures of violence and bottom-up subcultures of violence manifest in militias and youth gangs persistently put harder pressure on the dominant culture of nonviolence than most societies suffer over their mundane divides.

Grievance-Driven and Politicised Youth Gangs

We have already described how the Indonesian military cultivated a variety of militia memberships in its fight against Falintil. This was part of a wider pattern in the politics of Suharto's New Order of the military's party, Golkar, and then other political parties: cultivating youth groups with paramilitary qualities, often uniformed, training in martial arts the predominantly young and male but not totally so, and often groups criminalised into the administration of protection rackets. Most importantly, when push came to shove, where financial inducements failed to persuade *kampung* (village/community) leaders to push all their flock to vote for the machine's local or national candidate, the function of the Indonesian youth group leadership was to threaten violence. If it became clear after the election that votes were not delivered from a particular village in the numbers promised then the youth group might be empowered to indulge in a certain amount of mayhem and looting in that village.

Figure 9.3a: An Australian soldier negotiates with a gang leader, 2006

Photo: Candido Alves/AFP

Figure 9.3b: Australian soldiers detain alleged gang members in Dili

Photo: Candido Alves/AFP

Most of Indonesia continues to grapple with a legacy of politicised youth gang violence, as does Timor-Leste. So the argument here is that within a broad culture of nonviolence, elite traditions of enrolling organised youth group violence endure, as do bottom-up traditions of entrepreneurship with violence. Some of the youth gangs that did a great deal of street fighting with rocks and homemade dart-shooters from 2006 to 2008 were formed in Indonesia decades ago—some still engaging in youth exchanges with their Jakarta forebears. Adérito Soares declares that he was member of Kera Sakti while he was studying in Indonesia. Korka, probably the largest martial arts group, originally Indonesian, officially aligned itself with Fretilin in 2005 and during the gang fighting of 2006. Then a change of leadership cut Korka's ties to Fretilin. In many parts of the country, Korka fought against Persaudaraan Setia Hati Terate (PSHT), prominent members of which had links with two parties in Xanana Gusmão's coalition: the Social Democratic Party (PSD) and the Democratic Party (PD). A security firm, Sereprosetil, was mostly operated by PSHT members (Scambary 2006:15). With 1100 employees in 2006, growing to 1700 later in the decade, Seprosetil was the second-biggest private employer in the country (the biggest was another security firm, Maubere Security);[11] the directors of Seprosetil were the most senior members of PSHT. Fraud against the company by gang members pushed it to the brink of bankruptcy until it was taken over by US and Australian interests and renamed APAC. During the occupation, many of these youth gangs 'protected their communities from Indonesian security forces and the latter's proxies; now they protect their communities from one another' (TLAVA 2009a:1). Several clandestine informants said they joined Indonesian martial arts groups as a cover for clandestine meetings that would not be targeted by the Indonesian military. Like Fretilin, political parties that were formed by leading Clandestinos enrolled violence from youth gangs. The youth groups that fomented non-gun violence on the streets of Dili after peacekeepers made gun violence a dangerous form of revenge against adversaries are often referred to as 'martial arts groups' in the Indonesian tradition. Others were seen as 'ritual arts groups', associated with traditional mystical belief systems of certain Timorese cultures believed to confer secret powers of invulnerability (Myrttinen 2008). Others are based on churches, ethnicity and locality (*barrio*)—often a very small quarter of a suburb of Dili was patrolled by a gang whose pride, identity and turf were that tiny locale.

James Scambary's (2006) work on gangs and youth groups in Dili shows that these groups were not mainly about violence. They were generally spontaneous building blocks of youthful civil society that therefore can and indeed have served as foundations for reconciliation and reconciliation programs (see Chapter 10). Even during those difficult periods when they were put under most pressure from elite conflict, such as 2006, youth groups should be seen as organisations that do more good in providing recreational opportunities and building social solidarity than harm through violence. They are organisations that peacebuilding policy should generally steer and encourage rather than discourage. There are a few exceptions that are mostly organised for criminal purposes. Scambary (2006:5) points out that one should not be preoccupied with the seemingly violent names of some gangs, which are commonly taken from Indonesian rock bands, album covers or Hollywood action films. Examples are 'Beaten Black and Blue', 'Predator' and 'Provoke Me and I'll Smash You'. Scambary points out that one member of the last group was a volunteer staff member of the local branch of the Global Partnership for the Prevention of Armed Conflict.

---

11 Maubere Security was started by Chubb Security, then sold to its Australian CEO, Warren Knight, and other (Timorese) senior managers when reorganised. The first Maubere Security staff were recruited by Warren Knight from the Falintil cantonment. Then they also hired some militia leaders and some gang leaders; the senior managers we interviewed saw getting leaders of violent groups into legitimate, responsible employment as a contribution to peace. In addition: 'You can use them to defuse trouble in their own gang area to improve security for your clients.'

There are 15–20 martial arts groups with about 20 000 registered male members and very few females and perhaps 90 000 non-registered members, which Scambary interprets to mean that 'probably some 70 per cent of young Timorese men are active in martial arts groups' (2006:2, 6, 2009:271). Kera Sakti and Kung Fu Master are groups that claim 30 per cent or more female membership. 'While all groups claim to preach principles of self-discipline and non-violence, much of the district based communal violence is committed by these groups or at least in their name' (Scambary 2006:6). Because of their large scale and martial arts training, these martial arts groups were often the most attractive targets for enrolment by political leaders or security sector faction leaders with cash to fund attacks designed to teach their political opponents a lesson. But most of the fighting was much more chaotic than that. Once anomie and chaos broke out, scores that could not be settled at other times could now be indulged.

Disputes over the justice of easterners moving in to occupy houses formerly owned by Indonesian civil servants who fled in 1999 were often picked up by very local gangs that identified with that locality. Uncertainty over contested property claims under Portuguese, Fretilin, Indonesian, indigenous and UN transitional law became a major cause of conflict that had lain dormant until anomie took hold. Sometimes these local gang members who happened to be members of a martial arts group would mobilise other loyalists of that martial arts group to their local project of eviction, revenge attack or extraction of protection money. Daniel Fitzpatrick (2002) and Andrew Harrington (2007a) both foresaw that the failure of the United Nations to attempt to manage ad-hoc (anomic) occupations of vacant housing in 1999 and 2000 by people who had not previously been residents of Dili would create conditions for conflict down the track. Failure of settlement by either the rule of law or by informal reconciliation of grievance over these occupations meant that the 2006 elite political conflict and the police–military conflict spilled quickly into large-scale evictions and house burnings in Dili (and not elsewhere).[12] Youth gang neighbourhood protection associations also existed in part because there was a rule of law vacuum; uncertainty of tenure was defended by organisation for violence.

There were *barrio*-based ethnically distinct gangs with hundreds of members 'whose main activity seems to be organized crime', such as Commando, an eastern group that spread across the country 'as a sort of organized crime syndicate' (Scambary 2006:6–7). These groups, led by young men with names like Lito Rambo and Ameu Van Damme, were responsible for much of the worst violence of 2006. The gangs that perpetrated much of the 2006–08 violence were often organised around loyalty to such individual leaders.

---

12 We are thankful to Daniel Fitzpatrick for this point.

Figure 9.4: An Australian soldier comforts a Timorese man who has lost his home in the unrest in Dili, 4 June 2006

Photo: Tim Page/Corbis

Many traditional Timorese interpreted the street violence of 2006 through the prism of a traditionalist form of anomie theory:[13]

> When the *Bandu* [ritual prohibitions] is violated, social order is out of balance, and people act and behave improperly in society in the form of lootings, thefts, murders, gang fighting, burning houses and other immoral behaviours. Interviewees also said the Government's lack of acknowledgement of traditional authority and values is one of the key problems behind the crisis facing East Timor. As a result, the ancestors, who set the rules and regulations for the society, are upset and they disturb the spiritual world causing imbalance to the real world... [Other interviewees] suggested that the East Timorese people, through the government, have forgotten the martyrs...who sacrificed their lives during the resistance. These martyrs or fighters are part of the spiritual

---

13 Anomie theory in Western scholarship derives from the work of the French sociologist Emile Durkheim (1897). The Greek etymology of anomie is from '*a*' (without) and '*nomos*' (law). Norms (*nomos*) is a much wider concept than law today: it means customary expectations of behaviour that coordinate interactions with others. Anomie is instability resulting from a breakdown of the regulatory order that secures norms. In conditions of anomie, following violent gang leaders rather than legitimate rulers becomes an option because no-one is clear any longer what the settled rules of the political game are, or who are the authoritative leaders.

world at the moment. When they are upset, the spiritual world is out of order…East Timorese described this phenomenon as *Malisan husi Matebian sira* [curse from the martyrs]. (Trindade and Castro 2007:18)

This *Malisan* (curse) version of anomie theory is more prescriptively helpful than Durkheim's French version of a breakdown of the normative order. It means that if reconciliation rituals are conducted in the right spirit, the ancestors or the martyrs can be relieved and the causes in the spiritual world of breakdown of the normative order of the real world can be lifted, and everyone can have confidence that everyone else will follow the rules of the game again. Most helpful of all for reconciliation that endures is the prospect of dire consequences for anyone who violates a spiritually solemn reconciliation commitment. We discuss this in the next chapter.

Barrio gangs that led violence were unlike the ethnically mixed martial arts groups; they tended to have one leader and to be based in one extended family that dominated one tiny ethnic immigrant enclave of the city. The overwhelming majority of gang violence in Dili was initiated from these rural immigrant enclaves; almost all of 40 Dili gangs in Scambary's study were organised around migrant families (Scambary 2009:281). Some of the rural conflicts they brought into the capital were ancient, and enrolled many from larger multi-ethnic groups. For example, citing the anthropological research of Andrea Molnar (2004), Scambary (2009:278–9) finds Dili gang fighting between PSHT and Colimau 2000 started with fighting in Ermera District, spreading village to village across the western highlands until seven deaths had occurred; however, its origins were in historical antagonisms over rural lands between pre-colonial kingdoms that blew up in Portuguese times. Scambary (2009:281) cites the work of another anthropologist, Janet Gunther (2007), in concluding that gang violence imported into the capital from one subdistrict of Viqueque had its roots in a failed anti-colonial rebellion in 1959 that is still a source of fervent feuding in that subdistrict today. The implication for community policing policy is that it needs to focus on reconciling these very old conflicts at the source in a way Portuguese and Indonesian policing neglected to do. That said, it would be a mistake to see most of the gang fighting as based on very old, politically profound conflict. Much of the rural conflict that came into the city in conditions of national anomie (see also Muggah et al. 2010) was over getting a girl pregnant, breaking a pipe to steal water, stealing agricultural produce from gardens, even 'garbage wars' (James Scambary, Personal communication).

Numerically and politically, martial arts groups have been the most important youth groups that have been most sustained across time. A number of the grievance groups started by disaffected veterans who were not embraced in F-FDTL have fallen away as their grievances were abated by payments to a wider circle of veterans as a post-2007 peacemaking policy. As spoilers like

Rogerio Lobato, who had mobilised them, moved on to other projects, so did they. Most of the *Kakalok* (magic or mystical) or *Isin Kanek* (wound) groups (Twelve-Twelve, Seven-Seven, Five-Five, Three-Three) formed as clandestine organisations of the Indonesian occupation. They became inactive post conflict, except 7-7, which remade itself as a martial arts group and controller of cock-fighting and gambling rackets (Scambary 2006:6, 15).

Beyond these groups/gangs which have been responsible for violence, there are youth groups of various kinds associated with churches, neighbourhoods, NGOs, music and sports that, even if they are much smaller than the martial arts groups, are much more numerous and engage huge numbers of young women. A number of them are determinedly antiviolence groups, such as Dalan Klot (Narrow Path), which has the motto 'Construction, not destruction' in its drive for communal renewal and 'PLUR' (Peace, Love, Unity, Respect) (Scambary 2006:17, 21).

Healing Across the Divides

Luckily for Timor-Leste, at the time of writing the three major security sector divides outlined in this chapter have been substantially, though not completely, healed under a new political contract among the nation's powerbrokers in which they have agreed to compete with one another mostly through the ballot box, and with some help from reconciliation processes discussed in Chapter 10. This healing has been a near-run thing at many points during the first decade of the history of the new nation, and convulsed it with violence on the streets between 2006 and 2008. The excluded Falintil veterans are now stabilised in some cases as minority forces within electoral politics, with their own representatives in the Parliament. Subjectively, 87 per cent of citizens felt safer in 2008 than they did in 2006 (Chinn and Everett 2009:18). From the perspective of republican theory, the subjective element of no longer feeling dominated by violence is even more important than the objective progress in resolving some of the sources of the 2006 violence (Braithwaite and Pettit 1990; Pettit 1997).

The police and military are no longer positioned as fiefdoms of competing politicians, though political independence is far from accomplished. The head of the military, Taur Matan Ruak (TMR), was frequently discussed as a possible future political leader, and the military, which has not let go of an interest in a political role in the state, remains a base from which he might exercise that option. As this manuscript was being finalised, TMR stepped down from the military amid rumours in late 2011 of a run at the presidency. At least the frequent rumours of the 2003–06 period that F-FDTL would step in to resume political authority should the government 'fail' might now, one hopes, be a thing of the past (Kingsbury 2009:111). In our interviews, senior Timorese and Australian military informants told us of approaches that were made to TMR in the early 2000s to lead a coup (see also Cleary 2007:292). Off the record, Mari Alkatiri named the individuals who made an approach to his defence commander when he was Prime Minister. The proposition was that TMR arrive at the Council of Ministers meeting and arrest Alkatiri and his key ministers. Alkatiri's view was that when this failed, with support from conservative funders in Australia and Indonesia, these coup-plotting individuals then sought to divide both the police and the army (in east versus west terms) to destabilise his government. Relationships between the military and the police are greatly improved. East–west tension within the military healed in traumatic circumstances after the shooting of President Ramos-Horta and Reinado in 2008.

Figure 9.5: President Ramos-Horta and Major Reinado to his left at a secret peace negotiation assisted by the Centre for Humanitarian Dialogue weeks before the two were shot

Photo: Fairfax Media

Alfredo Reinado and fellow rebel Leopoldino Exposito seemed, according to forensic evidence (our source is Australian police serving with the United Nations at the time), to be shot by weapons held at their heads (Toohey 2008) after an alleged assassination attempt on both President Ramos-Horta and Prime Minister Gusmão in 2008. President Ramos-Horta almost died from his wounds. Kingsbury's (2009:208) interpretation is that the encounter Reinado launched that fateful day was 'intended as a kidnapping or an attempt to force a final decision in Reinado's favor, but which went wrong'. Kingsbury thinks Reinado believed he was being double-crossed by the government in negotiations in which Ramos-Horta proposed his imprisonment and then release under a general amnesty for all parties convicted over the violence of 2006. Opposition leader Alkatiri claimed in our interview with him that the alleged attack on Prime Minister Gusmão occurred an hour later than the one on President Ramos-Horta and was a 'complete simulation' in which '45 bullets penetrated' the Prime Minister's car and not one struck any of the several occupants inside.

The death of Reinado, who was so popular among western youth, and the near loss of a popular president, was a deep shock to the nation. Just as the street violence of 2006 was a shock that forced a renewed commitment to a democratic contract for the nation and renewed support from the United Nations to that end, so the shock of the 2008 shooting of Reinado and Ramos-Horta renewed the democratic contract, got refugees out of their camps and into new or old homes, and consolidated a national consensus that the military ought to stay out of politics and that politicians must desist from politicising the military and the police.

In this chapter, we will not revisit the considerable literature on the crises of the Timor-Lese security sector during its first decade (for example, Fluri 2003; Goldsmith and Dinnen 2007; Goldsmith and Harris 2009; Hood 2006; King's College Report 2000, 2003; La'o Hamutuk Bulletin 2003; Lowry 2006; McFarlane and Maley 2006; Peake 2008; Rees 2002, 2003, 2004, 2006; Ryan 2000; Sukma 2002; Wilson 2007, 2008, 2010; Wilson and Belo 2009). Rather we seek to transcend the gloom inevitable from engaging with its blow-by-blow accounts of security sector chaos and conflict that started very early after independence and almost unravelled the nation in 2006. Suddenly in 2006 the UN peace operation that had been seen through rose-coloured glasses from New York, and from most of the world's capitals, was thought of as another UN failure after all. There were profound failures of UN security sector policy that the 2006–08 crisis exposed. And 'smoke and mirrors', ritualistic security sector reform did characterise much of the United Nation's work from 2006 to the present (Wilson and Belo 2009; Wilson 2010).

While there is a need to see how weakly institutionalised the separation of powers in the security sector remains, it is now more strongly institutionalised than it was in 1999, 2002 and from 2006 to 2008. While there was a considerable failure of the integrity of the Timor-Leste justice system that prevaricated in the face of the international pressure to prosecute Police Minister Rogerio Lobato, and while there has been 'smoke and mirrors' justice that convicted him yet allowed him to leave the country for health reasons without returning, Lobato seems finished as a political force.

Democratic politics has prevailed in the most fundamental sense of showing that making the police a militarily armed fiefdom of an ambitious, criminal politician is an inferior path to political power to building popular electoral support. Future potential military mutineers saw that mutiny was a failed path to power for Alfredo Reinado and the imprisoned (but now pardoned) Salsina, notwithstanding their renegade popularity. With the shooting of Reinado there is no longer a half-credible spoiler of the peace on the scene. In the aftermath of 2006 and 2008, it is a profound liability for a Timor-Leste leader to be seen as the kind of politician who relies on violent gangs as a path to power. That is seen as a legacy of one of the worst aspects of Indonesian rule. Indeed it is. Suharto's party, Golkar, showed the way by mobilising violent youth groups to intimidate local opponents of the political machine. The Indonesian military organised youth into militias that razed housing and terrorised the people of Timor in 1999. Today, Timor-Leste, with international support, invests in youth programs to reintegrate formerly violent members of martial arts groups into the legitimate opportunity structures of the nation, as discussed in the next chapter. A final learning experience for Fretilin was the further decline in popular support it suffered after the 2007 election when some of its militant elements went on the rampage, in some districts burning houses and returning to some street violence. As Henri Myrttinen (2009:221) put the change: 'Among the political elite, democracy is seen as "the only game in town", but many of the players have at times bent or tweaked the rules of the game for the benefit of their own group.'

The separation of violence from politics is the most important aspect of the separation of powers for any nation. No-one would hold up the contemporary Timor-Leste police, military or youth group culture as exemplifying the best democratic ideals. Yet their powers over violence are much more separated from politics as a result of lessons learnt by the nation from the killing of 2006–08. There is corruption in the police, torture and other abuses (Amnesty International 2003; Human Rights Watch 2006; Wilson 2010), but the police are almost certainly less corrupt and use torture and rape less than the Indonesian police who occupied East Timor until 1999. Indeed, an Asia Foundation survey found on a random sample of Timorese that 59 per cent reported their police to be 'Not corrupt', 17 per cent 'Sometimes' or 'Always Corrupt', with 19 per cent saying they 'Don't Know'—quite encouraging numbers—with corruption not rating among the six most serious challenges facing the police (Chinn and Everett 2009:35–6).

The Timor-Leste military is much more sharply separated from politics today than the Portuguese colonial military, Fretilin's military in 1975 or the Indonesian military in Timor from 1975 to 1999 ever were. That is not to say that there are not some more recently emerging challenges such as the joint operation against the mutineers (of the police effectively working under the command of the military) that we will discuss as a threat to the separation of the functions of the military and the police. The organised forces of violence in Timor-Leste still torture people and still beat them,[14] but much less so than at any time under Indonesian rule. Youth groups still matter in politics in Timor-Leste, but in a less violent way today than in decades past.[15]

While the United Nations badly bungled security sector reform continuously from 1999 to 2011, without pressure from the United Nations and international community networks more broadly to replace rule by threat of violence with rule of law in the security sector, Timor-Leste would almost certainly be back in civil war today. We should not judge a peace process a failure because it suffers even large setbacks like those in Timor-Leste between 2006 and 2008, or because mismanagement, waste and ritualism characterise UN security sector reform efforts. The Timor-Leste peace process has been a success because it has secured continuous improvement in the medium term in the separation of violence from politics. During its first decade, Timor-Leste has secured a greater separation of violence from politics than Australia achieved between colonisation in 1788 and the Eureka Stockade of 1854, at which time police sorties against Aboriginal groups who threatened propertied interests also persisted. Timor-Leste has made more progress in the separation of violence from politics than the Deep South and the wild west achieved in the United States until after the civil war ended in 1865; more progress in a decade than South Africa made in three and a half centuries up to the election of Nelson Mandela.

Those most responsible for politicising the security sector have been large personal losers as a result of it. Rogerio Lobato appears washed up as a political force, his criminal businesses have suffered from his marginalisation, and the house of his in-laws was incinerated on 25 May 2006, killing six (four of them children). He was convicted of manslaughter for his role in the street violence of 2006. His most senior police agents lost their jobs and some of his more junior ones lost their lives. Mari Alkatiri lost his prime ministership and then the 2007 election and also lost his family home to fire. The Defence Minister, Roque Rodrigues, lost his job on 30 May 2006 on suspicion of distributing defence force weapons to civilians. The leader of the original petitioners, Major Salsina, served a prison sentence over the attack on the Prime Minister and President until he received a presidential pardon. The former military police commander Alfredo

---

14 An Asia Foundation (2004:43) survey found that only 41 per cent of citizens believed that the laws that protect accused criminals from beating by the police are followed. Twenty-eight per cent of respondents felt it was a 'bad law' that prohibited the police from beating suspects.

15 One of our anonymous referees issued the reasonable warning that our text might be too upbeat here: 'There is still a worrying undercurrent of violence as illustrated by serious rioting and attacks on local communities in 2011—for example, in Bobanaro and Covalima. The PNTL remain problematic. The 2012 elections will test the security agencies. Given a trigger, wide-scale violence remains a possibility.'

Reinado lost his life. Xanana Gusmão might hardly seem a loser as he regrouped to win the 2007 election. Yet in a way he has fallen further than anyone—from being a Nelson Mandela figure, admired across the globe for creating unity within diversity, to being the leader who gave divisive speeches so incendiary as to fuel the flames that engulfed his nation. From attracting 82 per cent of votes in the first presidential election, he now leads a government in which his coalition enjoys a bare majority of the vote, and truncated legitimacy in the east (Higashi 2009). The new generation of leaders will have the opportunity to enjoy the legitimacy of being unity leaders—something that it is proving difficult for Gusmão and Alkatiri to regain.

Mistakes of Security Sector Reform

The literature on the mistakes made during the process of security sector capacity building is a formidable and impressive one that we will not cover in depth here. Here we seek merely to summarise the main dimensions of those failures.

The Timor-Leste experience confirms Bayley and Perito's (2010:34) conclusion—drawing on the experience of Iraq among other places—that police reform fails if a politicised or criminalised ministry that controls the police is not also reformed. In Iraq, the Ministry of the Interior was politicised to the point where rival militias and organised criminal gangs controlled different floors of its building and where power struggles were settled by assassinations in the parking lot.

> More important than the police and the courts, however, are the institutions that stand behind them. The interior and justice ministries are essential to providing good governance. If the ministries that support the police and judges are instead dysfunctional, corrupt, or politicized, the police and the courts will have little chance of fulfilling their missions. (Bayley and Perito 2010:150)

Minister Lobato's politicisation and militarisation of the Timor-Leste Internal Administration Ministry, and the formation of factions opposed to Lobato therein, fit the Bayley and Perito analysis. As Bob Lowry, who was contracted to mentor the Timor-Leste National Security Adviser, put it: the Timor experience 'raises the question of whether it is worthwhile providing technical assistance for institutions and forces that have doubtful political foundations' (Lowry 2006; see also Goldsmith and Dinnen 2007). While this politicisation caused the total collapse of policing as an institution in Dili in 2006, in the rest of the country police continued to go to work and do their job. District and subdistrict police commanders no longer answered to a commissioner in Dili who, fearing for his life, had deserted his post for the hills. As we will argue in the next section, rural police continued to do their jobs more or less as well or as badly as they had done them before the security sector crisis in Dili. How well or how badly this was varied greatly across different parts of the country, depending on the nature of community policing relationships between local police and *chefe de sucos* and *chefe d'aldeias*. In a village society where the authority of the capital and its institutions was always remote in practical terms, lines of informal community authority from a police commander answering to a *chefe de suco* and a local government head, mostly to both, were alternative lines of command that continued to give legitimacy and direction to rural police when the Police Commissioner was no longer in command.

UNPOL was excessively concentrated in Dili to do the job of capacity building across the nation, with 482 of the 662 members of UNPOL as of March 2003 located in Dili and most of the rest located in regional towns, as opposed to rural communities (La'o Hamutuk Bulletin 2003:3). There is an irony that it was in Dili, where UN and donor policing assistance were concentrated, that the policing crisis was so deep, while in many rural areas where UN presence was thin, there effectively was no policing crisis. Understanding this irony depends on seeing Bob Lowry's point above that UNPOL police training work can be worse than a waste of money if it does not conquer the politicisation and criminalisation of the police ministry; it might just teach the bad guys to shoot straight.

Within Dili, the second King's College Report (2003:101) also found that UNTAET initially focused on personnel recruitment and training while failing to support the development of PNTL as an institution, leaving its inexperienced officers floundering without an administrative and budgeting framework that could get policing capacity flowing out to where people lived, through institutional capacity in complaints handling, logistics and strategic planning. Bu Wilson has also cogently made this point, when she notes that the United Nations believed it was engaged

> in 'training' without appreciating that the building of an institution is a significantly bigger undertaking. The resulting lack of 'architecture' and functioning oversight mechanisms for the PNTL was then one of the structural reasons that it was comparatively easy for the institution to be so thoroughly politicized by Rogerio Lobato. (Wilson 2008:2)

A UN expert police mission to Timor-Leste in 2008 subsequently reached similar conclusions, also noting the weak development of management, command and control and ongoing core capacity deficits (Wilson and Belo 2009:8). The training investment was certainly considerable in personnel and dollars; one international police advisor quipped in 2006: 'PNTL has been one of the most highly trained police forces in the world over the past six years.' Wilson and

Belo (2009:10) link the failure in institution building to a 'national balance' model of deploying 40 or more different nationalities of police to work beside Timorese counterparts that 'does not work'. 'It is a mistake to believe that "cops on the beat" have the capacity to establish a public service organization' (Wilson and Belo 2009:10).[16]

In November 2002, 32 countries were contributing UNPOL officers, the largest contributors being China (76), the Philippines (74) and Ghana (69), with the number of contributors gradually increasing since. Outstanding executive police are not necessarily good trainers or management consultants. Timorese police leaders complain that these deficits were compounded by rotations that were too short to learn local police organisational cultures, by illiteracy in the language in which policing is conducted, and want of sophistication in how village societies work. Timorese police also complained in our interviews that UN police believe that what they learn about the local culture in the capital city translates to the districts where most people live, and of a tendency of newly arriving national contingents to retrain locals in procedures learnt in their home country that contradict the procedures taught by the previous contingent from another nation (Goldsmith and Harris 2009).

The UN screening process to weed out the human rights abusers and criminals within the police failed utterly because PNTL and the police ministers who succeeded Lobato did not have confidence in it and ran a parallel process, which was the process that prevailed (ICG 2009:5–7; Wilson and Belo 2009:6, 9–12). One senior UN official said in 2009 that the Police Commissioner was loyal to the Prime Minister, and the police 'who did terrible things who have been screened back in have been allowed in because they would be loyal to the Commissioner'. The United Nations would have done better to seek to improve, influence and regulate a screening process owned by the local security sector on the principle that something done very well by the United Nations is always inferior to something done tolerably well by locals, particularly so where resentment of outside domination means the local process prevails regardless of which has more merit. This was a bad outcome indeed on the screening issue. Our interviews with leaders of all the screening efforts make it clear that serious criminals remain in PNTL; police who are members of gangs continue to work with them to secure local monopolies of illegal gambling, prostitution, smuggling and drugs. The failure of the screening process shows in the awful human rights record of the police that has persisted since the post-1999 UN

---

16 See also Bayley and Perito (2010:48–9) on the need, when local policing collapses during a crisis, to separate the personnel required for UN executive policing from the management and police academy experts needed to assist with rebuilding a police institution.

screening was overlaid by the post-2006 re-screening after that conflict (Security Sector Reform Monitor 2010). None of this is to deny that some of the worst of the worst have been pushed out of PNTL.

Handover from UN executive policing to PNTL policing has generally been badly managed. The United Nations in Timor has done a worse job than the Regional Assistance Mission to Solomon Islands (RAMSI) in Solomon Islands, for example (Braithwaite et al. 2010c), in not leaving behind the equipment that allowed a local police station to function in the way it did when the internationals were in it. Fieldwork stories abounded of UN police, especially after the first UN exit, leaving little more than a chair and a desk behind when they handed over to their Timorese counterparts. Even in 2009, there were endless stories of telephony that had been part of the UN infrastructure replaced with PNTL having to 'use their own mobile phones for communication and usually buy credit for their phones out of their own funds. There are no mechanisms for this to be refunded' (Wilson and Belo 2009:16). Wilson and Belo (2009:19) found that PNTL officers did not value the 'veneer of mentoring' provided by UNPOL, but did value UNPOL as 'glorified taxi drivers, and a source of generators, fuel, paper, phone cards and computer maintenance'. This value evaporates when there are no longer UN cars to drive.

While the UN model of security sector reform substantially failed in Timor-Leste in the sense of one national police contingent moving into a district and training local police in one way, to be replaced with a different national contingent doing training in a totally different way, in another sense the Timor experience vindicated the UN model. The International Stabilisation Force that returned to Timor in 2006 was much more dominated by the Australian military than the previous UN military peacekeepers. One survey found that more than 80 per cent of respondents considered the UN peacekeepers better, a major reason being 'because the peacekeepers are not serving the interest of one foreign state' and 'UN peacekeepers are neutral to every political group in Timor-Leste' and even 'we appreciated the intervention by Australia and its multinational forces to stop the atrocities, but the peacekeeping operation should be conducted by the UN because people start thinking that the intervening country will colonize us if they stay in our country for too long' (Grenfell et al. 2009:16).

These are similar to survey results in Afghanistan, where citizens reported an overwhelming preference for NATO and US troops to be replaced with UN peacekeepers (Grenfell et al. 2009:17). A Pacific Island peacekeeper referring to the longer-run Australian domination of the military side of regional peacekeeping saw leadership by one country as not a problem so long as it was not the country with the strongest opinions and interests in the political direction the peace took: 'Timor would have been better with New Zealand in the lead. In Bougainville, Australia and the UN came in and followed the New

Zealand template, thankfully. New Zealand was widely admired in Bougainville for the role they played—a sensitive and flexible role. But the UN always has to be there even if it does not lead—if its help is to flow' (Interview, February 2007).

Gendered Violence and Impunity

A survey conducted in 2002 compared victimisation rates for gendered violence in the year before the survey with those from the year before the 1999 ballot. Assault of women by perpetrators outside the family decreased from 24 per cent under Indonesian rule to 6 per cent in 2001–02; for sexual assault, the fall was from 23 per cent to 10 per cent (Hynes et al. 2004). More rights-sensitive policing doubtless had some role in this accomplishment, given that police were involved in 22 per cent of the most serious violence against women before the ballot (Hynes et al. 2004). Militias and Indonesian military were, however, even more important perpetrators. So we might say that peace and the ending of Indonesian occupation, rather than any improvement in policing, were the main reasons for this reduction in gendered violence by non-family members. This interpretation is reinforced by a strong association between displacement to refugee camps in West Timor after the ballot and the experience of these forms of gendered violence (Hynes et al. 2004:306).

There was, however, no statistically significant difference in levels of physical assault perpetrated by an intimate partner between 1999 and 2002, with the incidence rising from 24 to 25 per cent (Hynes et al. 2004). The second-most prevalent legal problem reported in this survey was domestic violence—surprisingly, rating well ahead of theft, household/neighbourhood quarrels and motor accidents (see also TLAVA 2009b). A much larger survey, of 11 463 households, with a superior methodology in 2009 confirmed what a huge problem domestic violence continues to be when 38 per cent of women aged between 15 and 49 reported that they had experienced it since age 15, 29 per cent in the 12 months before the survey (National Statistics Directorate 2010:228). Slapping was by far the most common form of domestic violence—experienced by 28 per cent of women. The hypothesis that ongoing street violence has made it worse was suggested by the result that the incidence was 52 per cent in Dili and 35 per cent in rural areas. There is also a serious problem of physical violence by women against their spouses, with this being reported for 13 per cent of ever-married women, though the rate was eight times as high among women who themselves were victims of domestic violence (National Statistics Directorate 2010:243). As in surveys from many other countries, in Timor-Leste, divorced or separated women experience by far the highest victimisation rates. The incidence of sexual violence is much lower, with 3 per cent of women having experienced it since age 15 (National Statistics Directorate 2010:231–3).

As with domestic violence, among sexual violence victims' perpetrators were overwhelmingly husbands. Of ever-married women who suffered sexual violence, 71 per cent experienced the crime at the hands of their husbands/partners, 9 per cent from a former husband/partner, and 7 per cent from a current or former boyfriend (for all women). Stranger sexual violence is low in Timor-Leste by international standards, with only 4 per cent of the 3 per cent of women who were victims violated by a stranger.[17]

Also on the positive side, in five of six rural police stations we visited in 2009, groups of local police we chatted with said that domestic violence was the biggest crime problem in their subdistrict. This was subsequently more systematically confirmed by Chinn and Everett (2009:18) in a sample of 250 police: domestic violence was by far 'the most serious security problem facing the area in which you currently work', being cited four times as often as 'land grabbing' as the most serious problem (Chinn and Everett 2009:18). Our suspicion is that an awareness accomplishment in police education and police responsiveness to what village women are saying has not been matched by enforcement assertiveness. Bu Wilson has explained the institutional reasons in Oecussi:

> Oecussi police face very real constraints in that the court only comes to Oecussi for two days a month, there is no Prosecutor any more and there is a backlog of cases going back to 2000. There is consequently no capacity to fulfill the legislative requirement for someone who has been arrested to be brought before a judge within 72 hours. This means the very great majority of cases are handed over by PNTL and UNPOL to traditional justice, including cases of sexual assault. (Wilson 2008:11)

Timidity has been a common response in the face of on the one hand a failure of the formal courts to actually hear gendered violence cases and on the other hand criticism by feminist advocates and international NGOs when the police do respond by pushing gendered violence to indigenous justice. And Myrttinen notes that 'even when cases of gender-based violence are brought into the formal system, the male-dominated judiciary often tends to discriminate against the women bringing charges' (Myrttinen 2009:226). State policy and donors alike have shuttled between taking the view that because the justice of the courts is not

---

17 This might seem puzzling given the extraordinary number of rapes documented earlier in this research during the 1975 invasion up to a final surge in 1999. We must bear in mind that most of these rape victims are now over forty-nine years of age or are dead and therefore not in these survey data. Also the extreme youth of the Timor-Leste population means that women in this 2009 survey are disproportionately young. Even so, the fact that there must be many military and militia rapes reported by older women in these data affirms the interpretation that stranger rape is at a low level in Timor today.

effectively available to most Timorese living in villages, and indigenous justice is, the priority is to influence the practice of indigenous justice so that it affords equal rights to women; and making the investment to ensure that the justice of the courts is actually made effectively available at the village level. The result of this policy vacillation has been that the police dither, leading to a consensus view (backed by some data) that intimate partner violence has not been reduced. Outcomes for women might be better if there were a serious policy commitment to continuous improvement in rights sensitivity, and specifically sensitivity to gender equity, within indigenous justice led by indigenous women, at the same time as there was real progress on improved access to the justice of the courts. In such a world of genuine commitment to progress on both fronts, police might do something rather than nothing, deciding, in light of the form of justice most practically available in the most rights-sensitive way in their village, to send cases to either indigenous justice or court.

As we will discuss in the next chapter, justice system capacity constraints have also been an important reason for impunity for war crimes and for the politicised violence of 2006. The UN Independent Special Commission of Inquiry (2006) into the 2006 violence recommended prosecution of 68 individuals, which included very senior people such as the Minister for Defence and the heads of the armed forces and the police, and recommended further investigation of 70 others. The East Timor NGO Forum pointed to the extent of impunity in a 2008 press release after Rogerio Lobato was allowed to leave prison for extended medical treatment in Malaysia: 'not one convicted person [in respect of the 2006 violence] is in a legally recognized prison facility' (Murdoch 2008a). Soldiers convicted of killing the 10 unarmed police surrendering under a UN flag in 2006 served their sentences in a special open facility built for them by the military until they were pardoned by the President in 2008, though UN officers said that when they made surprise visits to them in their prison, they were never there even before they were pardoned. One of them was even present when the President was shot in 2008. This total effective impunity is of course much more than a manifestation of a capacity constraint; it manifests impunity as a political policy.

Impunity started with the United Nations. In a number of our interviews, we were told of credible rape allegations against UN peacekeepers that were not dealt with by a full investigation and law enforcement but by sending the peacekeeper home. Women's NGOs also argued during our interviews that the presence of peacekeepers had greatly increased prostitution and therefore trafficking in women in which both the police and martial arts groups were involved.

Progress and Regress in Security Sector Separations of Powers

While there are many dimensions to the disappointments of policing reform in Timor-Leste, failures to institutionalise separations of powers in the new society are at the root of many of them. The impunity problem is in considerable part a separation-of-powers problem: the security sector, especially F-FDTL, sees itself as the elite of the society and above the law in the same way as the political elite sees itself as above the law (Wilson 2007:54). Timor-Leste had an inspiring young policewoman who we interviewed as a leader of PNTL consciousness raising on gendered violence in 2006. We have seen that the fruit of her unit's work is still evident in rural police stations today. Unfortunately, that inspiring work ground to a halt for a long period after she was badly wounded by an F-FDTL bullet in May 2006. We think Bayley and Perito's (2010) conclusion is right that a first priority is depoliticising and decriminalising the police ministry so it can be a civilian regulator of a separation of powers of the police under a rule of law as opposed to a rule of men. Likewise with civilian control of the ministry of defence over the military, a constitutional separation of the military from politics and from policing is needed, regulated by civilian enforcement of that constitution. The shooting of President Ramos-Horta by deserters from the military in 2008 ushered in a joint operation of the police and the military to arrest those who participated in the attack and got away, and others who supported the attack. This involved police working effectively under the control of the military to arrest armed men. There were countless human rights abuses—for example, in police interrogations of people believed to have knowledge of where deserters might be hiding.

The joint operation had its upside for the nation; the police and military working together to clean up the mess that existed in the aftermath of the shooting of their President contributed greatly to reconciliation between members of these organisations who had been shooting at each other two years earlier. Xanana Gusmão 'dined with Salsina's [the petitioners' leader] family and humanised the dispute. He supported the family. Ruak said to Salsina's men "you rebuilt this nation too. You were part of the struggle that created our country"' (Interview, September 2009). But the joint operation was a travesty of the constitutional separation of the police and the military and a confirmation of the post-revolutionary ethos of the military as an organisation of greater prestige and authority in civilian affairs than the police. Since the formal end of the joint operation in 2008, the police and the military have continued the practice of operating together on major matters across the country (Wilson 2010).

One non-Western kind of separation of powers was resilient and had paradoxical effects from 2006. We found that rural police often had a weak PNTL identity and a stronger identification with their police district or subdistrict. Western police consultants tend to view this as a bad thing, a failure of command and control to work downwards from the authority of the Commissioner in Dili. This reality is mirrored by citizens who often refer to the 'Maliana Police' rather than the 'Policia National (PNTL)' as if the 'Maliana Police' were an independent, locally accountable police force. In a sense, police, especially at the subdistrict as opposed to the district level, are locally accountable. They seek guidance from elected local government leaders to whom they have no formal legal reporting relationship in any local policing crisis. And in day-to-day decisions on routine enforcement matters, they consult with the *chefe d'aldeia*, *chefe de suco* or the *suco* council for that village on what procedure should be followed on that matter. If the village leadership says this is a difficult matter for them to handle or a very serious crime that requires prosecution and likely imprisonment, that is what the local police officer is likely to do. This policing strength is being reinforced by an 'early warning network' initially developed by the NGO Belun (2009a, 2009b, 2010) and now being expanded by the government—as a conflict-prevention network of traditional chiefs across the country that watches for early signs of emerging conflict—and built in collaboration with the police. Belun is a strong NGO, making this an interesting example of an area of state weakness under repair through Timor's NGO strength bridging its village governance competence to state institution building. One of our panel members commented, however, that 'sadly, few people read and reflect on Belun's reports'. Belun's (2009a, 2009b, 2010) early warning reports in 2009–10 suggested a society with a low incidence of public violence—for example, reporting no firearms violence apart from two 'sightings of guns' (see also Rees 2010:15): 'crimes committed with illicit manufactured weapons in Timor-Leste remain very infrequent' and unaccounted-for police/military weapons are now very low.

If the village leadership says a matter can be most effectively dealt with by indigenous justice on the mat in the village (*nahe biti*) then the constable is likely to deliver the alleged offender up to the mat. One response to UNPOL who complain Timorese policing is plagued by weak command and control is to say there is a kind of community policing ideal in play here that makes local sense. Yes, it is a form of community control that tends to be male dominated, which does not take women's rights as seriously as it should, even when all *suco* councils are required to have at least three female members. Then, in a world where the mat processes many more cases than the court, one could argue that the rights-conscious police officer can achieve more for women's equity by seeking to regulate the equality of all the justice on the mat than by trying to take more cases to clogged courts, especially when those courts are not very sensitive to women's rights. Local police officers are a respected influence across Timor-Leste, on civil as well as criminal matters.

Higashi's (2009:19) survey of 319 Timorese in three districts asked them: 'If you have some conflicts with other people on personal issues, such as your land, water, and house, with whom do you meet and discuss to solve these problems?' Only two categories of people were regularly nominated: 87 per cent nominated 'community leaders' and 84 per cent Timorese police (more than one response was possible). UN police, other UN officials, F-FDTL, Members of Parliament, Timorese Government officials and other categories did not rate in comparison with these two. The same survey revealed that an overwhelming majority, especially in the east, do not have confidence in the courts.

We have already seen that this reality of how policing works in practice had the paradoxical effect of preserving the rule of law in most of rural Timor when it collapsed in Dili. This meant that refugees whose houses were razed in Dili could flee the violence there to the safety of communal policing (that was only partly about PNTL) that continued to protect people in most districts outside the capital. Another way of putting this is to say that a separation of powers in Timorese society of indigenous justice authority (that enrolled local police) from the authority of the state created safe havens for refugees all over the country. This would not have happened if top-down politicised factionalism in the Dili police command had spread down to rural policing. The substantive (as opposed to formally legal) separations of powers between state and indigenous authority over policing whereby local police were accountable not only to the justice of the state but also to community leaders and indigenous justice in some senses saved the nation. Another way of putting this is to say that Tanja Hohe's worst fears did not come to fruition in 2006 because the 'international paradigm' had such limited influence beyond Dili where an 'indigenous paradigm' continued to reign, including over policing. Hohe's work assesses

> the clash between the international paradigm of attempting to (re)build the Western liberal-style democratic state under UNTAET and the existing indigenous paradigm of traditional political legitimacy that prevails among the majority of the population at the local level. Without reconciling the two in future UN interventions, such efforts will continue to be either irrelevant to a self-evolving reality or in fact cause local systems to collapse without being able to adequately replace them. (Hohe 2002:569)

In Hohe's terms, what happened could be described as a collapse of policing in Dili thanks in part to UN maladministration of the security sector, and the irrelevance of the United Nations to resilient traditional authority over policing in rural Timor-Leste. One might have hoped for UN policy that started by asking the questions 'what is already working in preserving security?' and 'how might a new separation of powers grow to preserve that power that already protects people from violence?' That is, one might have hoped for a preservation of communal policing efficacy more by design than by default. One reason the 'indigenous paradigm' has been as resilient as it has on questions such as policing is that for decades the clandestine system that ran parallel to the Indonesian Government system was itself based on traditional sociopolitical structures (Hohe 2002) in order to give it the support to resist Indonesian governance projected from military leaders in Dili.

Because the conflicts that migrated into the city were so often rural conflicts transported to the city by rural young men who had migrated to town, the (admittedly mixed) success of rural communal policing in creating islands of civility (Kaldor 1999), or bubbles of security (Shearing 1997), preserved spaces where reconciliation could begin, including reconciliation of the very rural conflicts that started a lot of the gang violence. In the next chapter, we consider how transitional justice and reconciliation spread across Timor-Leste after 1999 and after 2006, and we find in both periods that the justice of the courts largely failed to do its job and that rural justice through community reconciliation largely succeeded in advancing peace.

Figure 9.6: Sister Guilhermina Marcal from the Canossian Sisters Convent attends to a refugee on one of her journeys to bring frightened people who have fled to the mountains back to her convent, 2006

Photo: Brendan Esposito/Fairfax Media

Security Sector Strengths

In the previous section, we argued that PNTL did not collapse in 2006; only its capital-city hierarchy collapsed. Its rural base was preserved. This rural base was actually the overwhelming majority of the police service. This decentralised quality of policing was a positive legacy of Indonesian occupation. Timorese demand was for police that were based where the people live, meaning few of them should be in Dili. Unlike UNPOL, whose officers were concentrated in Dili, PNTL followed the Indonesian pattern of police numbers dispersed across the country pretty much in proportion to the distribution of the population. UNTAET and the post-independence government stuck with the Indonesian decentralisation architecture of dividing Timor-Leste into 13 districts, 65 subdistricts and 448 villages (*sucos*), usually comprised of multiple hamlets (*aldeias*). All subdistricts have a police station and, at the time of our 2009 fieldwork, a program of re-establishing at least one police officer in each village was under way. In this, peacebuilding in Timor-Leste makes a striking contrast with our previous case study, Solomon Islands (Braithwaite et al. 2010c), where almost all police and all police vehicles were concentrated in the capital and other major towns.

Today, affirmative action to move young western officers up through the ranks of F-FDTL is working, with a majority of officers now westerners, and overall the F-FDTL has the 35–65 balance that matches the proportions of easterners to westerners in the nation's population. Most Timorese admire Falintil and therefore F-FDTL for its courageous effort in liberating their land. This delivers it democratic legitimacy. The healthy thing about the nascent democratic politics of Timor-Leste is that this F-FDTL legitimacy is seen as legitimacy for forging a democracy that leaders elected by the people rule, as opposed to leadership by the military itself. This is a different legitimacy than other military-led struggles for independence conferred on the generals of people's armies in China, Burma and Indonesia. Credit for this rests with the fact that Gusmão and the other leaders of the new nation were much more committed to democracy and pluralism than was suggested by Australian and Indonesian spin between 1975 and 1999. Credit also resides with international pro-democracy networks, within which the United Nations was both part of the problem and part of the solution.

Progressive accomplishment of a separation of violence from state power and of a separated independence of police, prosecution, judiciary and of the military from control by political factions was an accomplishment of internationally networked governance. Without UN and donor pressure, when the heat of political conflict between Gusmão and Alkatiri became red hot, both these men might have utterly corrupted the republic they dedicated their lives to creating by dominating the separations of powers it constituted. Without pressure from international civil society networks, working with and supporting domestic mediators that included Ramos-Horta, centralist UN bureaucrats might have strengthened the domination of the very top leaders much more than they did. So a lesson of Timor-Leste's recent history is that separations of powers cannot be entrusted to men of noble ideals such as Gusmão and Alkatiri and institutions of noble ideals such as the United Nations. Democracy will fail without continuous struggle by wide networks of energised democrats to defend and expand separations of powers. Democracy has certainly not yet failed in Timor-Leste precisely because of that civil society activism within Timor supported by activists without.

The mistake of retaining a defence force having been made, a potential future strength of F-FDTL for making the best of this situation is to engage it with UN peacekeeping. Precisely because F-FDTL has experienced its own security sector's role in the nation almost completely unravelling, it can bring rich wisdom to UN peacekeeping. Its officers have experienced not only internal conflict, but also a long international war and a long UN peacekeeping presence in their own country. During this long UN mission, most F-FDTL members have acquired skills in English and Portuguese. They have also learnt a great deal about how UN institutions work (or fail to). The future security of Timor-Leste requires that F-FDTL be given a useful function for the future. UN peacekeeper remissions could diversify Timor's export income in a way that would be most helpful to its impoverished economy. Experience in the military end of humanitarian relief could also enhance F-FDTL preparedness for future disaster relief work inside Timor-Leste.

Understanding Community Policing Strengths

The emerging strengths of the security sector go beyond strengthening separations from politics. There are also emerging strengths of engagement with civil society. While policing substantially failed to prevent rural conflicts from spreading to Dili, it largely succeeded in preventing the Dili violence of 2006 from spreading in a major way to the rest of the country. In the second-largest town, Baucau (population 16 000), in the east, the community policing team went to work in 2006 assuring children (and their parents) in schools and churches with lots of western children that Dili's east–west violence would not spread there. For the most part, it did not, in spite of a huge influx of refugees from that Dili violence. Still, downtown Baucau was what criminologists call a hot spot and UNPOL identified it in this way. Police statistics revealed it to have the highest crime rate in Timor between 1999 and 2003. Much of this was young thugs mobilising martial arts groups to engage in various forms of criminality. There was also an upsurge of political violence in 2007 in Baucau, which was Fretilin's urban heartland, as a result of Fretilin's defeat in the 2007 election. In part, this involved politicians harnessing martial arts groups. We were impressed with aspects of the community policing in Baucau after 2003 and how it had mobilised to defuse gang violence more effectively than in Dili. Six officers of the community policing team had been on a community policing training program in Japan. The community policing team in Baucau was a node of a number of antiviolence networks. They included the Catholic Church, particularly its Commission for Peace and Justice and the Law, Basic Rights and Justice (HAK) Association Peacebuilding Program and other human rights groups.

When fighting broke out between rival martial arts groups, HAK and officers of the State Secretary for Youth would be expected to make the first attempt at mediating peace. If they failed, the community policing team of PNTL would step in with a second attempt at mediation. If the community policing team could not make progress, local police would escalate to making arrests and putting violent offenders before the courts. After convictions were obtained, the community policing team would follow up with dialogue with the protagonist martial arts groups. These were 'lessons learned' sessions about how escalation to trouble with the police might be averted next time.

When we had a meeting with HAK and the leaders of PSHT, a martial arts group with one of the worst records of violence in Timor, the PSHT leaders were tense until the head of PNTL's community policing team, Miguel, walked into the room. Agent Miguel had a sunny demeanour and his warm smile and genuine pleasure at seeing his PSHT friends immediately put them at ease and they broke into relaxed smiles. All the local players said that UNPOL also participated in the larger gang dialogues but was not particularly effective in this area because it was lacking the kind of relationship that Agent Miguel had with PSHT. It was said UNPOL also did not really understand what was going on. *Lisan* leaders, the urban and rural *chefe de sucos*, in contrast, we were told, were also very important in defusing gang violence, and the PNTL community policing team worked effectively with them. They said Baucau civil society wanted to show an example to other districts that gang violence could be ended. In 2002 Baucau had led the country in forming the Martial Arts Federation (today reformed as the Federation of Traditional Self-Defence Arts in Timor-Leste) that subsequently went national. The federation functioned like a trade association self-regulatory body. It took on the challenge of improving the law-abiding image of large martial arts groups. It set up early warning networks within their memberships for emerging violence or conflicts that might be prevented before they came to bloodletting.

The federation also helped mobilise the martial arts groups to make a success of the biggest tourist coup Baucau had seen: the 2009 Tour de Timor cycle race. The martial arts groups provided security for the bicycles and for the area where the cyclists and their support teams would sleep. They helped clean up the town and helped with preparing meals and drinks for the cyclists. In 2007 and 2008 in the aftermath of the post-election violence, this network of peacemakers organised peace marches in which all martial arts groups marched for peace in their uniforms, as did other youth and school groups. Success turned on the two martial arts groups that had been locked in the most violent conflict learning to work together to organise the peace marches.

We asked the community policing team in the presence of the martial arts group members if they ever approached martial arts group leaders to pull into line spoilers who put the peace at risk. Both sides agreed that not only did the police ask the martial arts group leadership to manage spoilers they could not handle, but the martial arts group leaders also asked the police to pull into line spoilers they could not manage. Astute community policing can, and did, enrol even the most violent of gang leaders as agents for peace.

Conclusion

There are not many, or perhaps any, nations in recent history that have had more serious disputes than Timor-Leste with its two most powerful neighbours: Indonesia and Australia. It is a testimony to the diplomacy of the Timor-Leste leadership that in the face of so much spilt blood and spilt oil, neither Indonesia nor Australia poses a security threat to Timor-Leste. Some we interviewed would say that the tense relationship between Australia and former Prime Minister Alkatiri called this into question.[18] The Howard Government certainly had a very strong preference for Gusmão over Alkatiri (Martinkus 2006).

These informants say Australia conspired with Gusmão as he conspired with the petitioners in 2006 to destabilise Alkatiri's government. And this was a play of the street violence card. We do not have the evidence to conclude whether this allegation against Australia is well founded. Nor do we conclude it is wrong. The circumstantial evidence for Australian involvement in destabilisation by politicising the security sector was not only argued to us by Fretilin informants. A senior, well-placed Australian military insider also did so. Even if Howard Government officials were involved in such destabilisation of Alkatiri, they would surely believe today, as Gusmão does, that the violence of 2006–08 spun out of control in a way that almost unravelled everything that had been

---

18   When Hilary Charlesworth and John Braithwaite interviewed Dr Alkatiri, after we said something critical of Australian policy, he warned with a wry smile that we ought to be careful as conversations in his office were almost certainly listened to in the Australian Embassy!

accomplished in Timor-Leste, at great cost to Australia. So even if we are naive in thinking Australia did not threaten Timor-Leste's security in 2006, we still argue that an accomplishment of the moderation of Timor-Leste's leadership, including Alkatiri's in the face of considerable Australian provocation, is security with its powerful neighbours into the future.

The street violence born of a politicised security sector ultimately acquired a life of its own on the streets of Dili, Baucau and other towns. It continued long after, as far as we can tell, all political parties stopped paying gangs to cause death or destruction.[19] Revenge was the biggest reason for the violence continuing after the original causes in security sector policy were no longer in play. A second was that conditions of anomie—normative chaos, breakdown of the rules of the game—created an opportunity for countless new and old (even centuries-old) scores to be settled. A third was that these young men were often playing a game. There were unwritten rules of this game that guns would not be used in the fighting, even though most of the major groups involved in fighting had access to high-quality weapons. One major reason was doubtless that the UN police would not do much to you if you threw rocks or fired a dart with a slingshot, but they would if you brought a gun onto the field of gang battle. Indeed, UNPOL would call in backup from units with machine guns. Another reason was concern that friends would often be in the other gang in circumstances where gang memberships could be widely encompassing (TLAVA 2009a:6).

It was in some ways a highly dangerous sport in which now and then an individual was killed, but not warfare in which many would be shot with weapons. The objective was a spectacle of controlled mayhem manifesting a readiness for extreme violence, as in traditional group warfare, rather than untrammelled violence itself (Myrttinen 2007:15). UN peacekeepers were good at stopping gun violence, but not so good at regulating the gang fighting with rocks (see Braithwaite 2008:97–106). Stopping these deadly dynamics took much more than removing the original causes. It took the reconciliation that we will discuss in the next chapter. A problem that the security sector caused could not be solved by force or by policing in the city. It also required reconciliation in

---

19   One knowledgeable local informant said that gangs were often paid $50 to burn a particular house, $100 to attack a refugee camp and $150 to kill someone. Another said gangs were also being paid $6 for smashing a police car window. In police intelligence interviews, we were told that even though by December 2006 payments of this kind to gangs had stopped, the fighting continued because of the momentum of vengeance over previous attacks. A reason for this, in turn, is the culture of loyalty in most martial arts and ritual arts groups. When you become a *warga*—a member who has graduated through all stages of training—you must take an oath that if there is an attack on another *warga*, this is an attack on you. This negative solidarity makes such groups attractive for enforcement of political control over a locality. Political parties then gave the groups some positive solidarity in return through giving them local contracts for work, such as the distribution of subsidised rice.

Dili. Perhaps more importantly, it required reconciliation in the urban areas that brought their rural district grievances into the anomic environment of 2006–08 Dili to be fought out there by their young men.

There were other formerly dormant root causes of violence activated by the anomie, including land law conflicts that could not be settled by title deeds that had been destroyed in 1975 and 1999, and extremely high youth unemployment—issues we consider in Chapter 11. Yet youth in good jobs were part of the gang game as well. Humanitarian agencies told stories of young men being employed to help in refugee camps by day and stoning them by night (Scambary 2009:277).

The 2006–08 conflict in Dili was like the 1998–2003 conflict in Honiara, the capital of Solomon Islands (Braithwaite et al. 2010c), in that the conflicts that moved into the city were mostly conflicts born in rural areas. Therefore, if there were a policing solution that might have nipped these conflicts in the bud, it would have been rural policing. We have found that a strength of Timor-Leste policing compared with that in Solomon Islands is that it is more decentralised. Rural police add value in the way they support and defer to indigenous reconciliation that can prevent violent conflict on their rural turf before it moves onto proxy turf in the city. Some good examples of rural policing did help prevent rural conflicts from moving to the capital. But until the political and security sector anomie in the city ceased being the great attractor of a battleground to fight out rural animosities (from 2008), this was an uphill battle.

UN security sector reform tends not to see youth gangs as part of the security sector. Yet a martial arts group like PSHT that did much of the fighting between 2006 and 2008 was originally promoted during the occupation by the Indonesian military, enrolled by factions of the Timor-Leste security sector to do its dirty work, and as a result made much money. It was greatly strengthened as a political force with huge memberships that candidates must cultivate if they wished to be elected. PSHT then infiltrated the police, dominating one strategic police unit almost totally with its insider members (Myrttinen 2007:13; James Scambary, Personal communication, 2009). So a martial arts group captured by elements of the security sector then reversed that capture to a degree. PSHT acquired many of the weapons that were lost from security sector armouries in 2006. For this reason, in the next chapter, we consider transitional justice and reconciliation for the security sector and for youth groups and gangs as highly related challenges:

> Many groups still refer to themselves as clandestine groups, nearly 10 years after the last Indonesian soldiers left, indicating that they still

carry their resistance identity and have not yet found a new role. Veterans have been demobilized, and gang and MAG [martial arts group] members need to be too. (Scambary 2009:284).

As there were multiple identities there were also multiple types of conflict: MAG conflict; gang conflict; politically orchestrated conflict; land conflict; communal conflict; and conflict involving all these elements. Because of these overlapping identities and membership, each of these conflicts can spark the other types of conflict. It can therefore sometimes be difficult to distinguish a family dispute from a political or a gang dispute. Most gang violence is therefore really communal violence, but can spark a secondary conflict through the involvement of one or more MAG members, drawing random retaliation by an opposing MAG, in turn igniting unrelated, previously dormant communal or MAG conflicts. With constant population movement between town and country, people often bring news or rumours of conflicts with them sparking reprisals and new conflicts. The practice of payback in which an innocent family member is targeted for reprisals can turn a MAG conflict into a family conflict as non-MAG members are drawn in. (Scambary 2009:283)

Most days during two of the weeks of our 2006 fieldwork, John Braithwaite took a dawn walk with the UN Dili police chief and the national intelligence chief in which we discussed things we were picking up from our interviews on what was making the gang violence that had occurred the previous day tick, and what their intelligence was finding. Scambary's research shows why we were so confused: we were describing to each other 'confusion as to the origin of disputes' and a situation in which 'mediators would sometimes report that they would resolve one issue only for another to take its place' (Scambary 2009:283). Hence, the importance of culturally attuned reconciliation between youth gangs that is one of the themes of the next chapter.

10. Transitional Justice and Reconciliation

In its preamble, the *Constitution of the Democratic Republic of Timor-Leste* recognises the rule of law and the separation of powers, which are themes of this book. It also recognises indigenous justice in Part I, Section 2, which says '4. The State shall recognize and value the norms and customs of Timor-Leste that are not contrary to the Constitution and to any legislation dealing specifically with customary law'. So indigenous justice is not an alternative to the rule of law in Timor-Leste; it is part of the rule of law.

In this chapter, we consider how the United Nations and the first governments of Timor-Leste set about constructing institutions of justice. The first part of this story is a mundane tale of flawed international assistance to re-institutionalise courts, prosecutors, public defenders and a legal profession. We tell this tale briefly. In Chapter 9, we have described the flawed institutionalisation of the police (PNTL). Land law is used in this chapter as a case study of the dilemmas of post-conflict law in a developing economy. Then we describe transitional justice mechanisms, especially the Commission for Reception, Truth and Reconciliation (CAVR), which struggled to comprehend the crimes of Timor-Leste's long war. After considering the contribution of indigenous justice to post-conflict reconciliation, the chapter concludes with a discussion of options for integrating state and non-state justice.

The complexity of the different forms justice has taken makes this our longest chapter. It is important because we see Timor-Leste as being at risk of future violence because justice systems have not provided a satisfactory alternative to violence for resolving festering conflicts. The courts mostly do not work at all in this regard. When traditional reconciliation is used as an alternative, too often there has been a reconciliation that has avoided working through the root causes of the conflict and removing them as threats to future peace. Too often a feel-good ritual of reconciliation has substituted for restorative justice that confronts and resolves the specificities and structural sources of injustice. Too often the courts have been used ritualistically as well, creating the appearance of justice while being captured by a politics of impunity. Many anguished families still wait to be told where their loved ones' bones can be found.

From UN Justice to State Justice

The legal profession in East Timor before 1999 was largely Indonesian, mostly part of a ruling-class apparatus of tyranny, as opposed to a profession that practised a rule of law. Consequently, most of East Timor's lawyers fled to Indonesia after the ballot. The state legal system had to be built from scratch. The first legal problem INTERFET faced was to disarm and arrest marauding militia members encountered by peacekeepers. Under what law should the militias be arrested? Indonesian law was the law the people had just voted out in the referendum. No copies of Portuguese colonial law were on hand and none of the initial peacekeepers and few of the locals could have read them in any case. Some Australian military lawyers suggested Australian law since at least INTERFET would understand how to administer it fairly. Arrests were made in the event under Indonesian law. UNTAET's first regulation in November 1999 affirmed Indonesian law as applicable so long as it did not contradict the Universal Declaration of Human Rights and the six core UN human rights treaties. UNTAET then set about appointing judges to administer this modified Indonesian transitional law. An interesting moment of resistance was an Appeals Court decision in 2003 in which the judges chose to apply Portuguese, rather than Indonesian, law in defiance of UNTAET Regulation 2000/15 (Pascoe 2006:Fn. 185). Timor's transitional experience showed the need for a basic international criminal law that UN-authorised missions could opt to use in appropriate transitional situations. The rule of law got off to a low-legitimacy start.

After most wars, nations survive with some sort of supply of lawyers in-country supplemented with returning exiles and retired lawyers who are prevailed upon to return to practice in the nation's hour of rebuilding. It proved difficult to persuade the children of Timorese refugees in Australia and Portugal to come back in the early years; few had studied law in any case. In 1999, the United Nations estimated there were 70 East Timorese nationals in the country who had legal training, few of whom had practised law and none of whom had worked as a judge or prosecutor (Harris Rimmer 2008:144). The difficulties were palpable five years on when all 22 of the newly trained Timor-Leste judges failed their written examinations on the law in May and September 2004. As a result, they were suspended from hearing cases. In the same year, all the local public defenders and prosecutors (including the Prosecutor-General) likewise failed their examinations.

Up to 2004, internationals had done most of this work. When Timorese failed their exams, internationals took over again, until mid-2007. Since foreign lawyers were so few and so expensive compared with locals, the realities of the justice budget meant that a huge backlog of cases accumulated. The backlog persists at the time of writing,[1] with cases from 2000 still not tried. In 2007 the backlog was still rising at a substantial rate. Nevertheless, in 2007 and 2008, the courts of Dili and Baucau increased threefold the rate at which they completed cases in comparison with the years up to 2005, so at least urban courts were seriously improving their caseload performance (Asia Foundation 2008:10). As with its policies of police development, the United Nations had failed at climbing the mountain of legal capacity development, though things look more promising now. The peacebuilding pathology was the same. Too many of the foreign lawyers found it easier to do the job themselves. They did not consider that legal work done tolerably well by locals was better for the development of justice than work done very well by internationals.[2]

Timor-Leste's legal vacuum attracted idealistic human rights lawyers, particularly from Australia and Portugal, who were touched by the nation's suffering. They tended to regard human rights principles as absolute standards, and saw themselves as duty-bound to remedy all cases of individual rights violations they encountered. Lawyers who are capacity-builders sometimes do better to see rights-development practice as a process: success can be measured by continuous improvement of indigenous capacity to implement rights, as opposed to how completely rights are honoured in the present. This reduces the risk of international domination and a collapse of rights infrastructure once internationals pull out. A practical obstacle beyond the fact that Timor-Leste judges were still struggling with the new legal system was that they were still learning the new language of the law: Portuguese (Marshall with McKenna 2005). The challenges of an early flood of foreign lawyers on short postings (which reduced to a trickle as the backlog they left behind grew) are captured in the following account of a single important case:

> [A] proceeding was heard in Dili where members of the national police service stood accused of rape. At the original 72-hour hearing, there had been a total of five prosecutors and seven private legal aid lawyers, following which a number of the accused were held in pre-trial detention for ten months until the commencement of the trial. At the trial there was only one prosecutor (who had not been present at the 72 hour hearing) and two private legal aid defence lawyers, only one of whom had been present at the 72 hour hearing. The judge only questioned one of the accused before adjourning the trial. When the court recommenced over a week later, two different defence lawyers and a different prosecutor

---

1   A judge in a September 2009 interview told us that the backlog of criminal prosecutions was more than 3000 cases.
2   'In late 2002 the UN administration decided to end the "experiment" with a defense function that relied on inexperienced Timorese public defenders working in uneven mentoring relationships with international counsel. An internationally staffed Defense Lawyers Unit was created…[bringing] about a marked improvement in the defense function' (Cohen 2006b:5).

were present. Unable to contact the defence lawyers who had previously acted for their clients, the new defence lawyers requested the judge to adjourn the remainder of the trial until the other lawyers were available. They then left the court. The judge then appointed an apparently random Portuguese person sitting in the body of the court to represent the accused, before releasing them because of the lack of evidence and because they had been in long term pre-trial detention. (Marshall with McKenna 2005:44)

As with police development, so with development of the courts, the ratio of professional practice competence to expertise in the development and management of institutions was too high. There was insufficient case-management training, staff management and supervision, financial management, computer networking, management of physical files, language translation services, and victim support logistics (JSMP 2005a:18–19, 2005b).

Most Western justice systems fast-track commercially important cases while defendants in prison and victims in rights-sensitive cases are kept waiting. The rights consciousness of post-conflict Timor-Leste created a reverse pathology. Between 1999 and March 2005 in Timor-Leste, the Court of Appeal heard no civil matters, and no international judge had heard a civil matter in the District Court, undermining investor confidence that there was a court system they could turn to if their investment were imperilled (Marshall with McKenna 2005:45). According to our UN police informants, this was a live development issue as there were frequent arbitrary exercises of power by the political leadership against businesspeople. These included shutting people out of businesses and seizing property (see also Federer 2005:111–15).

In the criminal cases that were taken up, a culture of political interference in the decision making of prosecutors and judges quickly set in. UN police and justice officials repeatedly complained of specific instances of this in our interviews. This was particularly demoralising for prosecutors and police who developed cases against alleged offenders with links to the political elite. Consequently, there was corrosion of morale among officers of the legal system—morale that was needed to come to terms with the unmanageable backlog. The leadership failed to see that political activism towards securing the independence of prosecutors and judges was a vital step to consolidating a separation of powers and to giving the aggrieved a genuine alternative to received traditions of dispute resolution through violence (which became politicised). Not only did the political leadership fail to give priority to this aspect of institution building, through their personal political interference they tore down such good work as legal technocrats managed to put in place. Both Prime Ministers Alkatiri and Gusmão in their time responded to pleas for them to interfere in legal decision making, thereby educating citizens to the view that they lived under political party rule, even one-man rule. These leaders thus undermined the ethos that their electors lived under the rule of law of a republic. The frequency of victims of crime taking their case to a Member of Parliament is also a challenge.

Land law was particularly politicised, especially with respect to urban land. In Chapter 8, we have already questioned whether in a new nation where some members of the political elite hailed from the largest landowning families in the country there was actually any political will to settle land law. It is common in developing economies for political elites to decide to keep land law chaotic, maximising their options for land predation for personal/familial use and for political favour (Fitzpatrick 2006). As one Timorese political leader put it: 'Unsettled land law…allows the rule of party to prevail over rule of law' (Interview, December 2006). In a sense, whether one's claim to land were based on customary title, colonial Portuguese title, title granted during Fretilin's brief land-reforming rule of 1975, title recognised by the UN transitional administration, post-conflict Timor-Leste title, or even title claimed as purchased under Japanese administration in the 1940s, it was a claim vulnerable to someone else asserting title under a head of authority dating from a different period.

This uncertainty was a cloak during the 2000s for many evictions from land occupied by people politically out of favour, or by thugs acting in ways that were tacitly accepted by political leaders. We interviewed many people who claimed that they were evicted from their land because of their political affiliations. Police told us stories of having to mop up after what they believed were evictions they could do little about because they were supported by political elites. An Asia Foundation (2004:3) national survey of 1114 citizens found that '[l]and disputes are the most common legal issue faced by citizens and most believe the *adat*[3] process (including the village head) is the best venue to seek remedy if family-to-family discussions fail', though respondents from the capital city were an exception, of whom 52 per cent said they would prefer government courts to rule on land disputes (pp. 46, 62).

Nixon (2008:337–41) found that almost half of legal disputes in Timor-Leste are land disputes. He reports a survey of 717 randomly selected rural and urban Timorese asked 'who should make a compulsory decision (arbitrate) concerning a land dispute or claim, in the event that such a decision must be made?'. A substantial majority of respondents chose *katuas* (elders) in preference to any other authority. Only 10 per cent nominated the courts.

---

3   *Adat* is the Indonesian term for customary village law still widely used in Timor-Leste. It is for Timorese a synonym of the Tetum word for customary village justice: *lisan*.

Separated Powers over Land

Land law in post-conflict economies is a challenge that opens up the possibility of a more hybrid and differentiated vision of the separation of powers than Montesquieu's (1977) classic formulation in *The Spirit of the Laws* (executive, legislature, judiciary). Not only is it richer to see the Provedor, the prosecutor and the police as having powers separated from those of the judiciary and elected leaders of the executive branch, it is also richer, perhaps even vital, with land law to be open to an asymmetric constitutional vision. Symmetric constitutionalism implies separations of powers that operate in the same way in all corners of a country: one law, one separation of powers, for all citizens. Canadian constitutional jurisprudence concerning the Francophone legal enclave of Quebec, which enjoys provincial responsibility over various matters that are national responsibilities elsewhere in Canada, has influenced Western thinking on why asymmetric constitutionalism might be characterised more as a responsive virtue than as a rule of law vice (Kymlicka 1998; Webber 1994).[4]

Here we deploy a separation-of-powers analysis to read the rich veins of policy analysis in Daniel Fitzpatrick's research on land law reform in Timor-Leste and beyond (Fitzpatrick 1997, 2000, 2005, 2006; Fitzpatrick and Barnes 2010; Fitzpatrick and McWilliam 2005; Fitzpatrick et al. 2008). That work does not prescribe a model for post-conflict land law so much as define a typology of policy options that a nation like Timor-Leste can mix and match to its evolving land policy dilemmas. Land law reform is not something that UNTAET alone decided to duck, deferring to the interests of Timor's political elites on the topic. The successive governments of Prime Ministers Alkatiri, Ramos-Horta and Gusmão still have not at the time of writing finalised a private land law of 'who owns what land, where, and under what title' (Fitzpatrick and Barnes 2010).[5] Law No. 1/2003, however, did settle the succession of Portuguese and Indonesian state title to the Timor-Leste state, and Law No. 12/2005 provided for leases over state and private land.

Few root causes of violent conflict are more frequently deferred than land law on reform menus across the globe. Land disputes are root causes of civil war that are already potently recurrent in Peacebuilding Compared. Examples include

---

4 Another interesting Western debate has been around the economic-efficiency virtues of asymmetric constitutionalism in the post-fascist Spanish Republic, particularly in consideration of conflict potential in the Basque country (also Catalonia and Galicia) where tastes for governance and welfare have such a differentiated history (Garcia-Milà and McGuire 2002). Moreover, this literature reveals that constitutional asymmetry is also common in unitary non-federal states, even to the extent of consociationalism being supported for particular regions, but not for most regions (Italy; Northern Ireland in the United Kingdom, with also non-consociational asymmetry for Wales and Scotland) (Conversi 2007).
5 A USAID-funded project in November 2008 tabled a draft framework for a land law that informed a June 2009 draft transitional land law still being debated in Parliament.

conflict over 'transmigration' (Braithwaite et al. 2010a), immigration of refugees from other conflict zones (as in the Great Lakes region of Africa), swallowing of villages by huge mining projects and logging (Bougainville, Solomon Islands, Indonesia [Braithwaite et al. 2010a, 2010b, 2010c]); overpopulation and intense competition for scarce land, including environmental change that floods lands (Rwanda again; Bengali encroachment on indigenous land in the Chittagong Hill Tracts); displacement of people by dam projects for flood mitigation and hydroelectric power (Bangladesh again); land invasions by people fleeing volcanoes (North Maluku again [Braithwaite et al. 2010a]); immigration from rural to urban land vacated after a previous conflict (Timor-Leste); immigration to rural areas for plantation labour (Solomon Islands and Bougainville again). In the second Asia Foundation crime victimisation survey of 1040 Timorese (Chinn and Everett 2009:8), 'land grabbing' was the most commonly reported form of victimisation, with the second most common being domestic violence—both more frequent than all other forms of physical attack that result in injury combined and all other forms of theft combined.

Fitzpatrick's work suggests that it can make sense for large swathes of rural land to be exempted from state land law that otherwise applies outside those rural exceptions. At least this is the case where customary custody shows accepted competence in environmental management, in sharing land for grazing or communal purposes, allocation for family farming, quarantining sacred land, and other land as available for outsiders' commercial use in ways attuned to local resource demands. In some circumstances, it can also make sense, as post-conflict Timor-Leste has done, to accept prior colonial state land appropriations as facts on the ground (in the Timor-Leste case, land acquired by both the Portuguese and the Indonesian states) and formalise these as state land sufficient for future state needs. In other circumstances, prior colonial occupations are contested, and states must tread carefully to avoid conflict. One reason massive carve-outs can enhance welfare is that when they have a status-quo quality, this might render them unlikely to open large conflicts. Moreover, in circumstances where departing Indonesian forces systematically destroyed all land registration records in order to make it hard for the successor government to 'see like a state' (Scott 1998), sacred houses (*uma lulik*) (Fitzpatrick and McWilliam 2005:59) and the state could be allowed to continue existing occupation and land administration without imposing registration and documentation costs on such usage. For the most part, customary systems in Timor-Leste can allow long-term leases for major projects without conflict and provide 'tenure security at relatively low cost' (Fitzpatrick et al. 2008:7). Moreover:

> There is no pressing need to define the boundaries of customary land, at least in relation to the rights of different origin groups. These boundaries may be difficult to determine. Attempts at demarcation may produce inter-

group conflict. In Mozambique, customary authority over rural land has been recognized without the need for demarcation of group boundaries. Uncertainty of group boundaries is not currently a constraint on agricultural productivity [see Tanner 2002:23–4; Toulmin and Quan 2000:223]. Group boundaries may only require demarcation when a land conflict is such that state intervention takes place. (Fitzpatrick et al. 2008:8)

Template agreements might be mandated when customary groups or the state opt to alienate some of their land through long-term leases for mining, tourism or other commerce (Fitzpatrick 2000:159). When a customary group wishes to engage as a group in land dealings with foreign investors, group incorporation is an option for giving both sides the certainty they want with a large investment (Fitzpatrick 2005:472). In the interests of reconciliation with a powerful neighbour, Xanana Gusmão's promise to honour bona fide Indonesian title can also be respected (Fitzpatrick 2000). Where customary group claims were overridden by Indonesian (or Portuguese) titles, there might be a right to compensation (Fitzpatrick 2000:155). Given that state title is considerable and that famine and war vacated formidable tracts of land, Fitzpatrick (2000:155) suggested a state-administered land bank for land reform to assist the mediated movement of the dispossessed as an option. In comments on our draft, he warned that he would be cautious about that today where state land tenure is contested, as it often is post conflict. A land claims commission to hear and mediate disputes that fall between the cracks of such evolving patchworks of tenure was an option for Timor-Leste (Fitzpatrick 2000:155). Where customary authority to settle claims collapses and when mediation fails, Fitzpatrick (2000:158) suggests the District Court could sit as a land court. In other words, asymmetric governance of land could work through customary institutions where they continue to be accepted as legitimate, through executive branch mediation where custom does not apply, and through the judiciary where that fails. This land governance can be nested to minimise uncertainty driven by forum shopping.

Fitzpatrick and his colleagues describe a confusing patchwork of separated powers over land. Here a *uma lulik* allocates; there the *chefe de suco* governs land because traditional land management by the *uma lulik* was forced to retreat long ago by Portuguese or Indonesian colonial governance of land through a *chefe de suco*;[6] there the executive government owns; somewhere else there is alienation to long-term foreign leaseholders where that might be done by the *uma lulik*, the Prime Minister alienating state land, a land claims commission

---

6   Fitzpatrick commented on our draft that in such circumstances, 'either the notion of management of customary land under the authority of the *uma lisan/rai nain* is contested or authority has receded into a generalised notion of spiritual stewardship and day-to-day issues fall more within the purview of the *chefe de suco*. This is not to say that the *uma lisan/rai nain* and *chefe de suco* are necessarily two separate systems that are in conflict. But it is to acknowledge the diversity, plurality and potential difficulties of a peacebuilding approach that emphasises the *lisan* system.'

or a district court. Of these only the District Court would hold sway over all Timor-Leste and really it would have no authority over most of the landmass in the normal circumstances of the jurisdiction of the *uma lulik* being uncontested from within.

Does it matter that all this seems so confusing in its carve-outs? It matters for tidy minds that wish to 'see all the land like a state', and see it symmetrically. But does it seem untidy to Quebecois that they have a different criminal law than Alberta, that their province has control over its criminal law in a way that Alberta does not? Does it matter to villagers in a rural corner of Timor-Leste that authority over land law is separated into totally different hands and according to utterly different principles to urban law in Dili? They do not need to 'see like a state'; they will be less confused when they are allowed to 'see like a village', in continuity with the way their parents saw their village lands and the possibilities for alienating it. They probably do not want some grand synoptic scheme to unsettle the security of their land tenure, bringing them into conflict with neighbours. The following principle, while asymmetric, is clear and could be put into simple language: 'The starting point for legal regulation of rural land could be a default or presumptive position that custom governs land outside city boundaries' (Fitzpatrick et al. 2008:8).

A much more complex principle for village people is the following symmetric principle: 'Any legal space for custom will be subject to the human rights provisions of the Constitution. These provisions will act as a safeguard against potential abuses in the name of "custom", including the denial of women's rights to land' (Fitzpatrick et al. 2008:8).

While a more complex task of education and comprehension is required to grasp the implications of this principle, it is an important one, of much more general import than simply in reform of land law. It can come to ground what we will describe as a set of 'engaged universals' (Tsing 2005).

The work of Fitzpatrick and his colleagues suggests that no unified symmetric legal ordering of land is attractive in a context like Timor-Leste. There is little charm in a synoptic anthropological project of codifying all local land-tenure systems, abstracting general principles from them, putting the principles into national law then allowing those general principles to be implemented locally in the local ways that gave birth to the overarching principles. There would be too much error in the anthropological inference; the flux of disparate local systems would be a deviously moving target; judges might misunderstand custom as settled rather than as fluid and hybrid; codification might do violence to regimes that do not work primarily through code; judge-made law based on the general principles could come to conflict with the specificities that gave birth to the principles. The entire grand project of anthropological codification would be unsettling for a post-conflict situation that needs more settling in the cause of future conflict prevention.

This would be even truer of the other major symmetric option of imposing a nationally uniform land registration system like the Torrens system, used in Australia. It would conflict with the land order of every *uma lulik*. It would impose paperwork costs that a poor nation would strain to administer without creating new forms of corruption. The court backlogs described above would get even longer. The poor would be disadvantaged because of Max Weber's (1954) insight in *Law in Economy and Society* that the more law enshrines formal rationality, the more it favours formally rational organisations—organisations like Indonesian firms that understand the new law and wish to speculate in land. Weber might have added that the more the law enshrines customary rationality, the more it favours those who inhabit the world of custom. Land law that is messy from the perspective of formally rational organisations like state bureaucracies, urban law firms and big business can be harder for them to manipulate to redistribute wealth in their favour. At the same time, the transaction costs of negotiating long-term leases under asymmetric land law need not be high. And big business and big government benefit as much as anyone from a land law that is sufficiently messy to prevent future armed conflict.[7]

Geographically segregated powers over land administration can act as a check on the abuse of power. This is the most general virtue of all separations of powers. A developer wanting to build a tourist lodge or a collaborative coastal fishing venture might be at risk of customary owners demanding a bribe. Still, they have the option of refusing to pay it and moving onto another *uma lulik* with their development proposal. The separated powers over land administration

---

7 Fitzpatrick (2005:453) cites the following comparative literature: 'while systematic land titling programmes may be useful in urban and peri-urban areas, there is substantial evidence that in places subject to customary tenure they commonly fail to achieve their objectives of increased certainty and reduced conflict (Bruce, 1993:50–1; Knetsch and Trebilcock, 1981:32–3). In many cases, for example, titling programmes have allowed wealthier and more powerful groups to acquire rights at the expense of the poor, displaced and/or female occupiers (Binswanger et al., 1993; Lastaria-Cornhiel, 1997:1317–34; Platteau, 1996:40–4; Platteau, 2000:62, 66, 68; Toulmin and Quan, 2000:218–9). In other cases they have increased conflict by applying simplistic legal categories of "owner" and "user" to complex and fluctuating interrelationships (Fitzpatrick, 1997:184; Knetsch and Trebilcock, 1981:40; Lavigne-Delville, 2000:108; Simpson 1976:236; Toulmin and Quan, 2000:219). In yet other cases they have increased uncertainty by overlaying formal institutions on informal arrangements, with the results that (1) disputants are given the opportunity to manipulate overlapping normative orders through "legal institution shopping" (Bruce, 1998; Platteau, 1996:41–6; Toulmin et al., 2002:13), and (2) the register loses value over time as an accurate record of local land relations (McAuslan, 1998:540; Okoth-Ogendo, 2000:125–8). In other words, the fact that individualized State-enforced property rights may be both an ideal source of security for economic investment, and an evolutionary product of increased land scarcity and resource value, does not necessarily mean that regulatory interventions to introduce these rights will be either effective or appropriate (Platteau, 1992:102–3). In some circumstances, customary systems will be providing sufficient tenure security at low cost to encourage available forms of investment.' A more recent literature review with a more econometric perspective, by Easterly (2009:431–3), also finds a failure to establish an association between land-titling interventions and improved development outcomes.

mean that they will not be blocked everywhere from realising the proposal absent a bribe to the Prime Minister, the Tourism Minister or the Fisheries Minister. They will be less likely to confront a reality that only a business crony of the Prime Minister would get such a land permit. Legal pluralism in land governance actually creates incentives for local villagers to cooperate to make consensus building over their *uma lulik* land policy work.

Fitzpatrick's default to customary governance empowers ancestral origin houses to seize a big piece of governance back from a state that appropriated this in Indonesian times. That state corrupted land law in favour of regime cronies. In rural economies where wars can be fought over land reform, where power over land is a more strategic form of power than in industrial or post-industrial societies, a commanding path to power is to be able to see land like a state, to systematise land administration like a state, and then to corrupt it from the top down. Quilted land regimes can frustrate unchecked central state power and the shadowy power of shadow states of business cronies (Reno 1995). This is akin to the messy reality that it is harder to corrupt a jury than to corrupt a single judge. Separated powers corrupt small time, and leave open the option of contracting on a patch where the corruption is less. Absolute power corrupts big time, leaving subjects little choice but to submit to centralised tyranny.

Some patchwork of separated powers over land of the kind opened up by Fitzpatrick and his colleagues might allow dual-economy dynamism. This is the dual-economy idea of gradual opening to investment based on private property rights combined with collaborative sharing of land that traditionally has worked for village economies in appropriate contexts. A patchwork might allow both kinds of economic development to grow together thanks to flexible hybridity in institutions for land. Institutions that simultaneously strengthen village subsistence economies and market economies, as opposed to forcing a choice between traditional production and modernity, is a theme we return to in the next chapter. We do not argue for any particular direction for the evolution of the hybridity of Timor-Leste land law; there is no simple recipe. We argue here only that rejecting the imperatives of any law and economics recipe—any rule-of-law recipe that demands one law for all—is an option. Abandoning standard recipes and opting for democratic experimentalism in a patchwork land law might allow some patches of the law to succeed while the failure of others might foster adaptation (Dorf and Sabel 1998).

Institutionalising Further Checks and Balances in the Justice System

The United Nations established the Judicial Training Centre with an eye to resolving some of the capacity challenges at root in the long run. A Timorese NGO, the Judicial

System Monitoring Programme (JSMP), received international funding from 2001. It was an innovative check for an emerging justice system as an advocate for justice development. JSMP produced critical analyses on the courts and the justice system more widely, including traditional justice and the Commission for Reception, Truth and Reconciliation (CAVR). Its Women's Justice Unit was a leader in evaluating systemic effects of the Timorese justice system on women.

In 2005, the Office of the Provedor for Human Rights and Justice was established. This is a check and balance in the Portuguese tradition of governance (which has many elements in common with the office of the Ombudsman in the Northern European tradition). The Provedor is mandated to investigate complaints of human rights abuses, maladministration and corruption and to advance human rights and justice promotional activities and advocacy. Like other justice institutions, it has tended to be Dili centric, with 70 per cent of 2006 complaints coming from Dili residents (UNMIT 2007:8).

The Anti-Corruption Commission (CAC) opened its doors in 2010, with one of the authors as the first Commissioner. The Asia Foundation (2004:25) found that nine out of 10 Timorese are worried about corruption; 76 per cent are very concerned. In 2010, Transparency International ranked Timor-Leste at 127 out of 186 countries—much better than the ranking of 146 the previous year. There are, however, no hard data on corruption in Timor-Leste. Rumours about corruption and public perceptions of it suggest that something serious might be taking place. The CAC has robust powers in its founding law; however, in order to carry out its mission of preventive action and criminal investigations, it needs people with good skills in an institutional terrain that is new for Timor-Leste.

While Timorese tend to be critical of alleged corruption by high-level government people, they are less critical of petty corruption. Some say: 'We have suffered for many years. It is time for us to enjoy life. Why shouldn't we take some money from the public purse, even if it is corruption?' Others have the attitude that if the boss (*katuas* or *ferik* in Tetum) can dip into the public purse, why can't they? Another justification is that: 'Our salary is too low, we need a bit extra.' These excuses are coupled with other day-to-day expressions from those involved in both petty and grand corruption. These expressions include: 'Don't forget our beer money' (*Keta haluha ami nia serveza*), which a public officer might say to a businessperson bidding for a project. While the specific reference is to beer money, this can mean a cash bribe, giving building materials or a plane ticket to Bali. A businessperson bidding for a project might promise to public servants who have helped him that 'your efforts will not be forgotten' (*Hau la haluha o nian kolen*). More recently, there has been a trend to ask for 'phone money' (*osan pulsa*)—Tetum code ostensibly for money needed to buy the ubiquitous pre-paid mobile phone cards. While discussing the responsibility of public servants to tackle corruption, there can be a tendency in Timor-Leste to justify any misconduct by saying that 'we are still in the process of learning' (*Ita sei iha prosesu aprendizagem*), so mistakes, including corruption, are to be expected. While Timor-Leste is a very new country with an abundance of problems facing it, it is regrettable that some public figures tend to abrogate their responsibilities with such justifications (Soares 2011).

Soares (2011) also notes that there are strong public expectations about the magic of criminal investigations, which are expected to send corruptors to prison. There is little understanding of the preventive side and of the possibilities for responsive regulation of corruption. There is some progress in the work of public prosecutors in trying corruption cases, with an appeal pending from Ruben Braz, the former Dili District Administrator, for a three-year corruption sentence, as we go to press. In general, few corruption cases have been brought to the court. The pros and cons surrounding the case against Vice-Prime Minister, Luis Guterres, remind us, however, that much effort has to be made in order to continue to improve the notion of the separation of powers. In May 2011, there was a huge political debate regarding corruption allegations against Vice-Prime Minister Guterres. Guterres was accused of abuse of power and illicit enrichment by employing his Mozambican wife to work as a political adviser at Timor-Leste's mission in New York. The court decided to dismiss the case because the evidence presented by the public prosecutor was found to be insufficient. Prior to and during the trial, the Parliamentary Alliance Majority (AMP) party, the coalition led by Prime Minister Gusmão, attacked the Prosecutor-General, Ana Pessoa, a former MP and member of the opposition Fretilin party, alleging that the case against Guterres was political revenge. Guterres was a former Fretilin member who challenged Mari Alkatiri's leadership at the 2006 Fretilin congress and formed and led a splinter Fretilin Reform (Fretilin Mudansa) faction. Once the court dismissed the case, Fretilin's Parliamentary leader, Aniceto Gutteres, alleged that the court's ruling had been made under political pressure from the government (*Diario Nacional*, 10 May 2011).

It is interesting to note that AMP's attack on the Prosecutor-General was based on the argument that the Prosecutor-General had politicised the institution. In attacking the Prosecutor-General, however, they were to some extent trespassing on the principle of separation of powers for which they were advocating. Allegations that the Office of the Prosecutor-General has been politicised might have been handled through proper channels, such as the Magistrate's Council, and not through attacks by AMP MPs. The republican view is that efforts to combat corruption require robust institutionalisation of separations of powers and public engagement with that imperative.

In a village society, the most important checks and balances against abuse of power are institutionalised not within remote state institutions in the capital, but within the village. It is important to understand that state and non-state justice systems compete for legitimacy, and people who work within each system care about that legitimacy. So we hypothesise that one reason Western legal systems prioritise fast-tracking of commercially significant cases over matters that involve human rights is that the efficiency, legitimacy and responsiveness to commerce of the courts are under growing competitive challenge from commercial arbitration and private mediation specialists, domestic and international. Timor-Leste is not a sufficiently important market for private arbitration and mediation for this pressure from non-state dispute resolution to be felt. We argue below, however, that Timor-Leste state criminal justice and land justice experience intense competition from non-state justice. Opinion survey research shows it has little legitimacy in the hearts and minds of the overwhelming majority of the population. An Asia Foundation survey of 1114 Timorese found:

> Community leaders, rather than the police, are identified as being primarily responsible for maintaining law and order[8]...Although the formal courts are generally well regarded, they are not rated as positively as the *adat* process.[9] The formal courts are perceived to be less accessible, less fair, less protective of rights, and less reflective of community values.[10] Only a narrow majority (52 percent) would want a judge or official from the formal court system to come to their area to help settle cases. (Asia Foundation 2004:3, 6)[11]

Ninety-four per cent of respondents were comfortable bringing a dispute to the *chefe d'aldeia* or the *chefe de suco*, and 93 per cent to the traditional *adat* process (in many cases, overlapping conflict-resolution options) (Asia Foundation

---

[8] In answer to the question 'Who is responsible for law and order in your community?', 81 per cent gave as their first choice 'Community leaders/elders/*chefe de suco*', 14 per cent gave Timor-Leste Police, and no other category of response attracted more than 1 per cent (Asia Foundation 2004:39). A more recent non-national survey in Dili, Liquica and Lautem found that for 'serious crimes, such as robbery and kidnap', 93–98 per cent nominated the police as the actors to take the problem to, with only 60–80 per cent nominating 'community leaders' (multiple responses allowed) (Grenfell et al. 2009:22). There is variation between areas on this. In Nanu, 90 per cent of respondents agreed that the means exist within the community to resolve local conflicts (only 5 per cent disagreeing). Citizens there defined different roles for the *chefe d'aldeias*, *chefe de sucos*, *liurai*, *adat* leaders and *suco* council members, while '[f]igures such as police and administrators were discussed in a very secondary sense and only in instances where a conflict of some kind was beyond the means of the community to deal with it, especially for serious crimes such as murder' (Grenfell et al. 2009:109). In many other areas of Timor-Leste, people see a much more prominent role for the police than this Nanu leader: 'Rape is also like that, if the community traditional leaders, if the parties feel okay about resolving it through traditional leaders, okay, that's it. If not, one says this can't be done like this, then it has to be resolved through the police' (Grenfell et al. 2009:110).

[9] For additional data to this effect, see Laakso (2007:219).

[10] Another interesting reason ordinary Timorese give for preferring to take conflicts to *adat/lisan* rather than to the police is that 30 per cent said *adat* 'saves face and allows people to avoid embarrassment' (Asia Foundation 2004:66).

[11] By the next Asia Foundation (2008) survey, however, confidence in the formal courts had increased significantly. Even so, the rule of local law remained more important in 2008 than the rule of national law: 'When asked the question, "*Who is responsible for making the rules that govern people's lives?*" respondents say the *aldeia* (21%) and *suco* chiefs (21%) are most responsible for making the rules that govern people's lives, followed by parliament (14%) and government (13%)' (Asia Foundation 2008:14). In 2004, when asked 'who is responsible for law and order in your community?', 81 per cent of respondents' first choice was 'Community leader, elders and *suco* chiefs', compared with 89 per cent who gave the same response in the 2008 survey (Asia Foundation 2008:16).

2004:49).¹² Another survey of administrative officials across the nation in 2003 found 86 per cent of officials considered local systems cheaper and more accessible than the courts, 84 per cent saw them as easier to understand than the courts, three-quarters saw local systems as faster, more efficient and placing greater emphasis on reconciliation between conflicting parties than the courts, and a majority saw local systems as fairer and less corrupt than the courts (Nixon 2006:93).

This can be a puzzle for UN justice workers and for the class of local urban professionals they train and pay. State and UN legal elites tend to believe they offer a more advanced and rights-respecting form of justice. Robert Ellickson (1991) has shown why this should not be a puzzle at all. He concludes that tightly integrated communities (of which many Timor-Leste villages are instances) mostly prefer their own norms to rules and procedures handed down by state law because their traditions have evolved to be collectively cost minimising and welfare maximising in their local context, while state law is invariant to context. Even in Western urban contexts, the criminal law industry fails to grapple with why it is that victims, offenders and communities all report that they feel their rights are more respected in cases randomly assigned to restorative justice conferences compared with court (Braithwaite 2002:Ch. 3). Restorative justice gives people a voice, compared with criminal courts where their grievances are appropriated by lawyers who are expert in state norms that are invariant to context. Because the criminal law so fervently believes its own propaganda, the institution mostly fails to apply the lessons of that evidence to make its own procedures more participatory, restorative and responsive to the rights concerns citizens actually have in specific contexts.

We argue in this chapter that conditions of transitional justice offer superior opportunities for such learning to ossified Western justice systems. Our interviews suggest that rural Timor-Leste men and women want more effective access to a responsive justice of the courts for certain purposes and prefer access to *nahe biti* (traditional justice) on the mat in their village for other purposes. So the challenge in our analysis becomes one of seeking responsively nuanced separations of powers between non-state and state justice—separations where state justice is a check on and balance to the abuse of rights in non-state justice, and vice versa.

For women in Timor-Leste recovering from a long history of widespread sexual violence in war, balanced potency of access to the justice of the police and courts and to indigenous justice is particularly important. On the one hand, women

---

12   These results are not very different from Indonesian surveys by the Asia Foundation, the World Bank and the UNDP, finding 86 per cent or more of respondents believing it is better to resolve disputes by *musyawarah* (deliberation and consensus building) than by going to any formal legal institution (Asia Foundation 2005:38; UNDP 2007; World Bank 2004:37).

want to be able to take serious crimes to the police because male traditional elders sometimes protect their relatives and political colleagues against rape accusations. On the other hand, for spiritual reasons that have real bite over the consciousness of men, women feel custom offers them the strongest sense of safety and freedom:

> Here, well it's our *adat*, we have used *lulik*[13] for everything so women can go anywhere, even young unmarried women are brave enough to walk on their own because our ancestors and fathers have put *lulik* on the people who we meet in the street. So if there is anyone who wants to do something bad to a woman then they won't because they are scared of the *lulik*. Even if we meet someone in the forest we won't be scared because our ancestors have used *lulik*. Even people going to Luro by themselves. (Prominent female leader Teresa de Jesus Fernandes, quoted in Grenfell et al. 2009:74)

There is complexity in the relationship between state and non-state law that can be managed only by the sensitivity of non-state justice actors to state justice imperatives and vice versa. In our interviews, we were told many stories of individuals being punished in village justice institutions for seeking and winning a justice outcome from the police or courts that village elders judged unjust. Grenfell et al. (2009:114) observed this in their research: 'if they report it to the police they're afraid because that doesn't use *adat* rules, but government rules. So then if you come back here the people won't accept the outcome.' Most village-level police and elders have the wisdom to consult with one another and with the parties on whether a particular case is best resolved in the first instance by state or by non-state justice. In this negotiation, leaders are sensitive to the way the backlogs in the state system can cause re-victimisation:

> [G]oing to the courts disadvantages the victim. He has to look for a lawyer, and then every day he has to check on the case, and [is] waiting forever for the police to come and call him. But if it's a case like this then he's already a victim, [he has] already sustained a loss, so rather than burden him further, it's better to burden the perpetrator. (Golgota elder Elisia Araujo, quoted in Grenfell et al. 2009:117)

One reason it is best that this brokering is done at the local level rather than according to centralised rules under state bureaucracies is that while the latter are seen as captive of political forces in the capital, across different communities a maximum of one-third and as few as 10 per cent of citizens either disagree or strongly disagree with the statement that 'I feel that I can influence figures of authority who are relevant to my community' (Grenfell et al. 2009:Appendix

---

13 '*Lulik* is all that is sacred…*lisan* wisdoms and practices…not only sacred objects' (Father Jovito de Jesus Araujo, quoted in CAVR 2006:Part 9, p. 7).

1, question 10). In the practical separation of powers operational in Timor-Leste, the power of village elders enjoys most institutionalised accountability. Even where that power is hereditary, it is required to listen in ways that state bureaucratic power is still learning.

War Crimes

> They [human rights activists] say we don't care about the victims? We care, [Xanana Gusmão] and I have lost relatives, friends and comrades over the years. We know the cost of war, the value of peace and necessity of reconciliation.
>
> — President José Ramos-Horta, 2007 (quoted in Harrington 2007b:23)

UN Secretary-General, Kofi Annan, called a press conference on 10 September 1999 to announce that 'crimes against humanity' in East Timor would be punished. Twelve years on, very few of these crimes have been or are likely to be punished. The grand assurances of international leaders against impunity are rarely met. Since World War II, Rwanda and the former Yugoslavia have been the outlier cases of maximum international investment and commitment to war crimes trials, yet only tiny proportions of the suspected war criminals were tried. Even the prospect of a partial international tribunal modelled on Rwanda and Yugoslavia faded quickly in Timor 'as Western states rushed to normalize ties with Indonesia' (Power 2008:327). In this sense, realism kicked in to quell the momentum towards an international tribunal.

Still there was a need for symbolic measures so that something vaguely approaching the Secretary-General's initial announcement could appear to happen. The compromise was funding the hybrid Serious Crimes Panel of one Timorese and two international judges to focus only on the crimes of 1999. Ultimately, the Serious Crimes Unit of UNMISET was funded with 47 international staff and a five-year time line for investigations until May 2005 before it was de-funded. This was enough staff (though hardly enough time) to support only a few complex murder investigations in the nations from which these investigators came.

War crimes trials are always complex because perpetrators have fled the jurisdiction, witnesses are killed or terrorised and also politically compromised in their testimony if they have been collaborators themselves (which is sometimes true of survivor witnesses)[14] and people speaking different languages

---

14 'We do not have witnesses. We wish we did' (Defence counsel, Los Palos Special Panel case, charging 10 with crimes against humanity [Combs 2007:39]).

are involved on all sides. Only 55 trials were conducted. In the circumstances of such limited time and funding, plea bargains allowed 84 convictions of mostly low-level Timorese militia members and the imposition of mostly lenient sentences. Some of the plea bargains and the trials produced procedurally unjust convictions (Cohen 2006a, 2006b; Combs 2007:114–26). Some had the view that those convicted were young men who were naive enough to return to East Timor—scapegoats used to allow the United Nations to say it had a record of convictions for crimes against humanity. More sophisticated criminals did not return.

Lenient sentences must be balanced against the usual situation with war crimes trials of long periods of detention without trial (up to three years) contemplating an uncertain future. Four-fifths of all suspects indicted under the serious crimes process never went to trial, including almost all the prominent indicted suspects for the most egregious crimes, such as Indonesian Defence Commander General Wiranto (Pascoe 2006). They were safe in an Indonesia that refused to extradite suspects who fled there. More than that, Sergio Vieira de Mello, Gusmão and Ramos-Horta agreed that many potential militia spoilers of the peace across the border in West Timor should be granted de facto immunity to return to their villages in East Timor. These deals were done by Gusmão (against opposition from Serious Crime Unit prosecutors) both in order to defuse them as spoilers and to normalise relationships with Indonesia (Gunn and Huang 2006:148).[15] Kirsty Sword Gusmão, Xanana's wife, was also involved in sensitive negotiations to obtain the release of women and girls as young as fifteen believed to be held against their will by militia leaders in West Timor as 'war trophies' (Harris Rimmer 2007:327). Quite apart from cases of sexual slavery, there were militia members in West Timor who continued to rape refugee women—continuing the war for these women. The practical way to end it in some cases was to bring these young men back under the discipline of their elders and their church in East Timor, or by allowing women to return voluntarily to their homes by enticing back the militia leaders who were forcing them to stay in the West Timor refugee camps.

The geopolitical might of Indonesia loomed over all these realist decisions. Prime Minister Alkatiri supported war crimes trials, but Gusmão and Ramos-Horta

---

15 There was an informal agreement between the Prosecutor-General and the UNTAET Chief of Staff that arrest warrants for key militia leaders who cooperated with reconciliation would not be executed (King's College Report 2003:280). 'Let us not lose sight of the idea of reconciliation in all of this! When I asked the First Transitional Government to initiate the meetings along the border, one of the conditions I demanded was that those persons accused or suspected of having committed crimes in Timor could cross the border without being arrested, so that they could talk and could reconcile with the victims. This was the type of agreement we had with the First Transitional Government and we managed to obtain real results because of it' (Gusmão 2005b:114). Gusmão then went on to explain how this approach was reversed just before the end of the UNTAET mandate with an announcement that war crime suspects thenceforth crossing the border would be arrested.

did not want to rock the boat with Indonesia, prioritising reconciliation with their powerful neighbour. This was in line with some diplomatic advice from Australia and the United States, urging pro-Indonesian gestures upon Timorese political leaders to fast-track normalisation. Ironically, then, within the same year that the pro-Indonesia network sustained a great policy defeat in 1999, it was able to influence the direction of regional diplomacy, supported by Gusmão and Ramos-Horta.

Let us reverse the realist lens, however, in fairness to these two men. In 1999, they had great reason to fear a repeat of their Fretilin civil war victory of 1975, which was undone by armed infiltration across the West Timor border. This was not hypothetical. The armed spoilers were angry, trained and experienced fighters, and already operating minor hit-and-run missions across the border. These militia leaders had no future other than through listening to those Indonesian generals who assured them that the military would succeed in destabilising the new government in Jakarta. Militia leaders in West Timor refugee camps in 1999 were being told that the military would eventually restore order—including in Timor. In those refugee camps they had tens of thousands of fearful East Timorese from whom they could recruit, as well as West Timorese relatives and patriots, and they had weapons suppliers and a cross-border haven.

Everyone in 1999, not just the pro-Indonesia network, feared disintegration and the collapse of democracy in Indonesia. Habibie had mortally wounded himself with his East Timor policy, especially after the Americans humiliated him (and Wiranto), forcing him to accept what the Indonesian right saw as an invasion of Australian troops. Gusmão and Ramos-Horta cared about preserving Indonesia's fragile democracy;[16] for a decade they had seen the clandestine network and the Indonesian democracy movement as fundamentally the same and they felt loyalty towards those struggling against an angry military to preserve Indonesia as a democracy. Moreover, they were concerned that a military coup in Indonesia would lead to a regime that would destabilise their own fragile state. Gusmão specifically feared Timor's nemesis, Suharto's son-in-law Prabowo, becoming a future president (Interview with Gusmão personal staff, September 2009). The most likely successor leadership in Jakarta was that of President Wahid who was a genuine peacemaker and who quickly visited Dili in a spirit of reconciliation and affection for the people of Timor-Leste. Remarkably, the people on the streets of Dili warmly reciprocated. For Gusmão and Ramos-Horta, reconciliation

---

16 Gusmão said: 'We must respect the courage of the Indonesians in accepting our independence and not disrupt their progress towards democratization by demanding formal [criminal] justice' (Pascoe 2006:Fn. 307). Ramos-Horta said: 'Why didn't the UN establish a tribunal here back in 1999…There is not much we can do to bring Indonesians to trial by ourselves. This isn't only pragmatism. I sincerely believe that Indonesia is making progress on democratic reforms and strengthening the rule of law…SBY [Susilo Bambang Yudhoyono]…can't challenge them [the military] in this way without risking that his opponents would gang up on him. It is important that we do not destabilize the slow process of democratization in Indonesia because it is our best guarantee' (quoted in Kingston 2006:283).

was in the air with the democratic forces in Indonesia, and they went with it, because they saw the alternative as militaristic and unfriendly to their long-term survival. Then there was the diplomatic pressure from their new powerful friends whom they were counting on to pour in most of the vast aid their razed nation needed. Diplomats from the United States and Australia, and from the European Union and Japan as well, urged realism upon their relationship with Indonesia, and were telling Jakarta that they were so urging Dili as part of their own projects of normalisation with a democratic Indonesia that they wished to preserve. Sergio Vieira de Mello offered the same counsel. This realist diplomatic pressure would have been hard for such a dependent polity to resist.

Then there were many Falintil comrades who had perpetrated war crimes and signalled to their leaders that they expected them to stand by them. It would not be easy to hold together veterans, who felt aggrieved enough by their oppressive cantonment, as a political faction that would support Gusmão and Ramos-Horta in future elections. Gusmão and his inner military circle were not innocent of killing their own. Ramos-Horta, too, was involved in the deadly factional politics of the long insurgency. As a leader who, like Alkatiri, was safe overseas from direct involvement in spilling Timorese blood, Ramos-Horta acknowledged that 'we all had blood on our hands'. It is unlikely that Gusmão and Ramos-Horta were concerned for themselves, although protecting some in their inner circle might have had some influence on their calculations.

Most fundamentally, Gusmão and Ramos-Horta were genuine in wanting to embrace the people of Indonesia in forgiveness. They brought their people with them in this regard; survey research indicates a high level of inter-group forgiveness in Timor-Leste compared with other post-conflict societies, with more than 80 per cent of people agreeing with forgiving enemies (Neto et al. 2007a, 2007b).[17] From the time of Nelson Mandela's visit to Gusmão in prison during which the advice he gave was 'dialogue…dialogue…let's find a peaceful solution' (Gusmão interview, June 2011), Gusmão embraced Mandela's reconciliatory approach. Mandela's fear in South Africa was that a long line of prosecutions of whites would destabilise internal reunification and prosecutions of African National Congress (ANC) leaders could fracture his own base, and he

---

17 In a 2006 interview with one of Timor-Leste's top civil servants, he did not agree that Timorese forgive after killing. 'They forgive Indonesia and Australia. They are pragmatic in their dealings with Timorese who have killed their own but hold revenge in their hearts waiting for the right opportunity. Unless there is a deeply ritualized commitment to reconciliation [a traditional blood oath]. We deal with it as we move on. Don't forgive but take it easy. But when the time comes you can get revenge.' John B: 'And that time is now [2006]?' Civil servant: 'Yes' (Interview, August 2006). Another UN official said: 'Once lawlessness broke out [in 2006] they were settling all sorts of scores. When the adrenalin is out and there is impunity and no police on the street you take your chance to settle those old scores of which there are many and for which there is much latent revenge. That is why there was so much chaos and so many crosscutting issues on the streets. Maybe you attack someone or burn their house down because they had sex with your wife' (Interview, September 2009). But the official said it was mostly not about killing or defeating militarily another group. This was because it was more about revenge that did not need to go as far as killing. So the death toll was not high.

wanted to concentrate scarce development dollars on fighting black poverty,[18] putting limits on how many of those dollars went to potentially thousands of long criminal trials.

Were Gusmão and Ramos-Horta Realists?

So, there was a mix of considerations, only some of them realist and international, that led Gusmão and Ramos-Horta to a reconciliatory approach to transitional justice. The desire to embrace and stabilise the forces of democratic transition in Indonesia was idealist—part of their anti-realist struggle over 24 years. The realist thinks that the strong prevail over the weak in international affairs, whereas the strong are characterised by military and economic might. With Indonesia in 1999–2001, realist strength still rested with the military and they were using it to destabilise the Habibie and Wahid governments. These two presidents were not strongmen; they were scholars who were passed the parcel of an economy that was suffering one of the worst recessions any nation has suffered in the past century (Krugman 2008). Neither president survived long, due largely to the chaos the military helped foment across their tottering regimes. Fortunately, Indonesian democracy did survive and grow. The Clinton Administration, the Australian Government, their pro-Indonesia network of realist diplomats, Gusmão and Ramos-Horta were arguably among the network of friends of democracy in Indonesia who offered significant support to helping it thrive.

It could be argued, then, that support for Indonesian democracy was a long-run project of a republican politics to support separations of powers within Indonesia and is distinguishable from realist international relations thinking. Our critique is of those who renounce republican ideals of government for the people by the people, of those who renounce struggle to support polities with separations of powers because the weight of mighty nations with mighty armies and mighty economies wants a renunciation of liberation—in other words,

---

18 So did Gusmão: 'But in these meetings, people also talk about reconciliation and justice. And I used to ask about the militias and about what to do with them: "Justice should be done and they should go to prison because they deserve it" would always be the immediate response. But when they learn that, in prison, the state has to feed the prisoners three times a day [post conflict, Timorese were lucky to get two meals a day] and take care of their health, that the prisoners have time allotted for sports and to study, that they have clean water, electricity, mattresses, blankets and clothes and that, for this reason, the state has to cut spending for schools, for medications, for roads, and so forth, the population immediately reacts by saying: "Oh! No! This is unfair!" And they add: "Send them here. They can stay in their houses, but they will have to work for the community for so many days a week. We will not hurt them, but they will have to rebuild what they have destroyed"' (Gusmão 2005b:122). 'All the sacrifices will only be honoured when we reach an equitable level of development, based on a steadfast determination to eradicate poverty in our country. It will be meaningless if we have all the perpetrators in jail, but the people continue to face high infant mortality, endemic and epidemic diseases, without decent housing, without clean water and food. Without a change in the current poor standard of living, the grief of the past will not be healed' (Gusmão 2005b:136).

renouncing republican values for the sake of a realist politics of the national interest, kowtowing to the forces of the mighty in international affairs. Instead, we suggest continuous struggle against the odds for republican values until the right moment when the weak can prevail against the strong. There is a paradox of the weak being able to harness the power of the strong to their republican project at that right moment—such as the US military and US diplomacy finally switching sides to support Ramos-Horta in 1999. Republican politics is about separating powers; it is also about the weak dividing the strong against itself.[19] It is not about renouncing power politics. Republican politics harnesses powers in institutional architectures that check the abuse of power. It plays power politics in the pursuit of a balance of powers that secures freedom as non-domination. That means playing hard at the two-level game of domestic and international politics (Putnam 1988). On a republican analysis, Gusmão, Ramos-Horta and Alkatiri were astute contributors to seizing the moment of economic crisis in Indonesia by supporting rather effectively the democratic forces of domestic Indonesian politics against Suharto and the military. This helped divide the Indonesian polity against itself in the cause of democratic transformation in Indonesia.

They also struggled successfully over 24 long years to divide the Australian people against their political leadership. In 1999 Prime Minister Howard and the Labor Opposition made the smart decisions at their table of domestic politics to switch sides and act in support of domestic public opinion. That decisively divided the Western alliance as other middling powers and Kofi Annan began to sympathise with Howard. Then Bill Clinton, heeding also the counsel of leaders such as Edward Kennedy and Nancy Pelosi at his own domestic table, finally rejected the realist advice of his National Security Advisor. American military power was then made available for the protection of General Cosgrove's imperilled INTERFET troops.

Hence, our narrative is all about the weak pursuing a politics of divide and rule over the strong. It is not about idealist aloofness from power politics. So we cannot at this point in our analysis say that Ramos-Horta and Gusmão were suddenly wrong to consider Indonesian power in prioritising reconciliation over punishment of war criminals. They were harnessing and dividing and balancing Indonesian power all along in pursuit of republican objectives for both Indonesia and Timor-Leste. On this account, we would not view them as freedom fighters of early 1999 who were turncoat realists by late 1999.

---

19   The discussion of anti-monopoly enforcement rejoins this theme in Chapter 11. Divide-and-conquer tactics that allow the weak to enrol the strong to their projects in global politics are theorised more fully in Braithwaite and Drahos (2000).

In weighing the place of criminal trials in a democratic project of transition from war, it is always necessary for freedom fighters to weigh the considerations confronting Mandela in South Africa and Gusmão and Ramos-Horta in Timor. If Mandela insists on prosecuting the incumbent South African leadership, will they refuse to hand over the South African military to his control? If Gusmão insists on prosecuting this militia leader in West Timor, will he succumb to Gusmão's appeals to lead his men back to a peaceful life in their villages in East Timor, and to surrender their arms? What is the balance between spending money on criminal trials that might be divisive if they drag on for too long and on directing money to rebuilding and development work that will help construct peace and unity? In saying these are the right questions to ask, in concluding that Gusmão and Ramos-Horta pondered them in an ethically responsible way, we are not necessarily agreeing with the balance they struck. Indeed, our strong view is that there should have been more criminal trials than there were and in particular that key figures such as General Wiranto should have been tried.[20]

Our conclusion is that it was a return to realism by the United States and other UN members to oppose an international criminal tribunal for Timor-Leste. Our conclusion about the position of Gusmão and Ramos-Horta is quite different. They were not freedom fighters turned realists. They were asking the balancing questions that republican freedom fighters must ask. But they did not get the balance right from a republican normative perspective of securing peace with freedom and justice.

The republican normative view is not that all those guilty of crimes against humanity must be punished. That never has happened after a war and never could happen. On a republican analysis, it is irresponsible for public figures to claim this is possible or wise or say this is what should happen. For this reason, we are critical of UN Secretary-General, Kofi Annan, at his press conference of 10 September 1999. It raised unrealistic expectations about punishment that could only deliver more pain to victims. The extent of criminal punishment, on a republican interpretation, should be decided in terms of what will maximise

---

20 One reason is the evidence that, statistically, credible prosecutions in combination with a truth commission on average seem to reduce human rights abuses, likely through a combination of deterrence and memorialisation (moral education) effects (Sikkink 2011). In Sikkink's (2011:184) study of 100 countries that underwent a transition from authoritarianism to democracy or from civil war to peace between 1980 and 2004, the prosecution effect was modest, with her repression scale 3.8 per cent lower in cases with the maximum possible prosecution score (20) in comparison with countries where the prosecution score was zero. Having a truth commission as well further increased the reduction in repression. Of course it is possible, statistically, that lower repression allows more prosecutions and a truth commission to take place, rather than the reverse. Another study, by Olsen et al. (2010a, 2010b), on a somewhat different data set failed to find a positive effect of transitional justice prosecutions and truth commissions alone in reducing human rights abuses cross-nationally. A combination of prosecutions, a truth commission and amnesties occurring together, however, did reduce human rights abuses. Olsen et al. interpret this as support for a 'justice balance' approach to transition, where credible trials and truth commissions can support accountability and amnesties can support stability.

freedom as non-domination (see Braithwaite and Pettit 1990). That leads to the very cautious diplomacy of modest but serious expectations for criminal trials that Ramos-Horta pursued. Our critique, however, is that the balance of criminal trials accomplished in the wash-up from that diplomacy was sorely insufficient with regard to the most serious perpetrators.

Timor did not build on the international criminal trial momentum of the 1990s, because Indonesia saw the risk that the weight of world opinion posed to them. It responded with a strategy of delayed impunity. The essence of that response was to: a) conduct an Indonesian Human Rights Commission inquiry from September 1999, allowing it to recommend prosecutions of many big fish (Hirst 2008:6); b) establish the Ad Hoc Human Rights Court on East Timor in response to the Human Rights Commission recommendations in March 2001 and lay charges against many higher-profile alleged perpetrators of crimes against humanity; c) prosecute, as time wore on, only 18 individuals of which only one conviction stood (of Timorese militia leader Eurico Guteres, whose sentence was halved on appeal) after appeals were finalised in May 2006 (Cohen 2003; Pascoe 2006:Fn. 189); d) announce in March 2005 and slowly establish the Commission of Truth and Friendship bilaterally with five Timor-Leste and five Indonesian commissioners that did expose some new truth and critical national self-reflection, but brooked no new prosecutions. This approach of the Indonesian leadership did something to keep international momentum for international criminal trials at bay while preventing their military from turning on them.

Ironies of the Commission of Truth and Friendship

There were, however, some ironies in how this impunity strategy unfolded. It was initially proposed by Timor-Leste, but driven by Indonesian civil servants who ran the secretariat. Like non-governmental observers generally, John Braithwaite was shocked at the weakness of the Timor-Leste Truth and Friendship Commissioners in failing to challenge Indonesian military commanders at the Jakarta hearings when they said, for example, that no Indonesian soldiers committed rape—in contradiction of previous evidence the commission had heard and of the overwhelming evidence in the CAVR report.[21] Yet the final

---

21   Megan Hirst (2008:23) likewise concluded: 'The primary complaint [by human rights NGOs] has been that the hearings provided a platform for those accused of bearing responsibility for international crimes in Timor-Leste to defend themselves without being seriously challenged by available evidence contradicting their claims.' When John Braithwaite put the unchallenged denial of rape by Indonesian soldiers to the Timor-Leste Co-Chairman, Dionisio da Costa Babo-Soares, he knew exactly the testimony referred to in the question. He felt it was not necessary for the commission to chastise the general because they had the evidence. They

report surprised. It was in some ways responsive to the deluge of criticism its hearings had received from human rights NGOs, including Indonesian ones. It did push some doors open towards truth about the extent of the human rights abuses that had occurred and how these could not possibly be interpreted as the work of 'rogue elements'. It did speak some truths to the people of Indonesia and the people of Indonesia did listen to some of the most horrible truths about 1999 more openly than before.

The Commission of Truth and Friendship began a process of questioning the once 'near-universal perception within Indonesia that the 1999 violence was a result of a conflict between two opposing East Timorese factions, rather than a military-orchestrated terror campaign' (Nevins 2003:684). Most strikingly, the commission's terms of reference invited it to recommend amnesties (something the Timor-Leste Commission for Reception, Truth and Reconciliation was prohibited from doing) and it recommended none. When the terms of reference were released, its mandate to focus on institutional, not individual, responsibility seemed a disturbing retreat from the approach of previous truth and reconciliation commissions, such as South Africa's. Yet the Peacebuilding Compared project is revealing that quite often reconciliation comes more quickly than truth. And Timor-Leste might be one of those cases where reconciliation slowly nudges peoples towards truth. Even from Bougainville—the case where individual truth and reconciliation about war crimes have been greatest to date in the analyses of the project—we learnt that often an individual admission to murder or rape would start with a military unit as a collective admitting responsibility for the pillage of a village. The individual admission often came much later, after iterated collective negotiations and rituals of reconciliation gave them confidence that they could return the individual bones for which they were responsible without retaliation.

Our colleague Jodie O'Leary is completing a PhD on the idea of 'institutional responsibility' in truth and reconciliation processes, drawing on the history of the Commission of Truth and Friendship. Perhaps we were indeed too harsh and distrustful in our initial reaction to the commission. Adérito Soares was so distrustful that he declined an approach to serve as a Timor-Leste commissioner because there was no consultation at all with civil society groups in Timor-Leste (the Church, victims, and so on) on its establishment, and because he wanted first to discuss changes to certain terms of reference. In the event, the report

---

allowed people to save face in the public hearings. He said there were people who denied everything in the public hearings but in the private hearings told the truth of the situation, what their orders were, who had given them and how the carnage was implemented. That private testimony, he said, convinced the Indonesian commissioners that Indonesian crimes against humanity had occurred, and in turn allowed a report that held the Indonesian military and intelligence services institutionally accountable for them. In turn, he credited that with a huge campaign in Indonesia arguing that the two ex-military presidential candidates in the 2009 election who bore some responsibility for atrocities in Timor should not be elected President or Vice-President.

did promote diagnosis of the problems of the responsibility of institutions such as the Indonesian military and intelligence services.[22] An army and intelligence mentality of a revolutionary people's army was one critical institutional factor identified:

> Another underlying cause of violence arose from the conception of military institutions as based upon the legacy of the revolutionary army of freedom fighters. This legacy created distortions in upholding the principles of democratic rights. Above all, these distortions arose from the conception that the revolutionary army is the embodiment of the people. This conception tends to lead military institutions to believe that they have direct 'ownership' of the state and its national resources, including the people. This conviction of 'ownership' by the military puts them in the position of policymakers, and subordinates civilian authority in the realm of politics. This, in turn, produced very weak democratic control over military and intelligence institutions. (Commission of Truth and Friendship Indonesia–Timor-Leste 2008:302)

An important part of this institutional problem diagnosed in the commission's report was the long history of the use of paramilitaries as auxiliaries of Indonesian security agencies: the 'Total People's Defense and Security System', which was explicitly designed to extend the political reach of the military among the people. A related institutional failure was of the police to disarm civilians when they formed themselves as militias (p. 274), which was a manifestation of the deeper problem of the subservice of the police to the military in matters of domestic security. Among the reforms proposed was the development of 'a human rights training program focused specifically on the role of security forces and intelligence organizations in situations of political conflict' (p. 291), a transformation of security and intelligence doctrine to a professional, democratic ethos under a rule of law, and a special training emphasis on the rights of women and children to protection.

Another commission recommendation was visa-free 'peace zones' that already had a de-facto existence on the border between East and West Timor. The 'peace zones' should accommodate family reunions, cultural events, traditional markets, houses of worship and 'a meeting place for government officials, public and community figures' (p. 293). This was linked to training programs in 'conflict mediation approaches and other mechanisms to promote peaceful resolution of disputes' (p. 292), including establishment of a 'Documentation and Conflict

---

22 Not only did the report find that the intelligence services bore an institutional responsibility for the terrible events of 1999, it also identified specific intelligence officers as leading specific atrocities. For example: 'In the case of an attack and killing of people in Liquica Church compound on 6 April 1999, Emilio Barreto testified that Sargeant Tome Diogo from the Intelligence Unit of Kodim 1638/Liquica was involved in the attack. In addition the witness testified that it was Tome Diogo who gave the order to begin the attack' (Commission of Truth and Friendship Indonesia–Timor-Leste 2008:172).

Resolution Center' in Dili and Jakarta on the grounds that '[h]ealing the wounds of the past and achieving true reconciliation will be the work of a generation' (p. 302). The two governments were urged to develop 'effective programs to equip government, religious and community leaders to identify, prevent and resolve emerging and active social and political conflicts' (p. 296). These should embrace 'traditional forms of resolving conflicts which employ local wisdom and traditions' and 'survivor healing programs' (p. 296). It also proposed a joint 'Commission for Disappeared Persons' to identify the whereabouts of Timorese children separated from their families, dual citizenship for children born of mixed national heritage and joint promotion by the two governments of cooperative historical research to encourage an understanding of their shared history (Commission of Truth and Friendship Indonesia–Timor-Leste 2008:295). While implementation progress is very slow, there is reason for hope that the two governments might implement much or some of this.

The commission was the first time that two nations that had been at war came together in a bilateral truth commission—and this when, as Dionisio Babo-Soares noted, the 'international judicial atmosphere provides little room for "undefeated" countries like Indonesia' to cooperate with its citizens being tried by an international tribunal and to then survive politically (cited in Harrington 2007b:16). Susan Harris Rimmer (2008:58) has said to us that in a better future world, the international community would take the pressure off peacebuilding leaders like Gusmão and Ramos-Horta (vis-a-vis a powerful state like Indonesia) by asserting international authority to prosecute the worst crimes against humanity.[23] Harris Rimmer in her conversations with us also quoted Sergio Vieira de Mello as saying the United Nations has 'the attention span of a three-year-old', implying that it is difficult in any circumstance to get commitment and cash for long investigations and trials. Possibly its attention span has lengthened since his death. In retrospect, we might see the Commission of Truth and Friendship as a flawed journey of bilateral learning to have occurred in such a short space of years after the ending of hostilities. It added significant value. It is also possible that one day the people of an increasingly democratic and open Indonesia might even agree to an international tribunal for the crimes of 1975–99 (see also Walsh 2011). Not likely, but not impossible.

Years before Indonesia took the initiative of establishing the Commission of Truth and Friendship, Timor-Leste had established the Commission for Reception, Truth and Reconciliation (CAVR). In 2009, the CAVR report was published in Jakarta in bahasa Indonesia and attracted some publicity and truth telling in reporting by the now free Indonesian press. This became an additional reason

---

23   Harris Rimmer (2008:58) quotes President Gusmão from 2004: 'I say don't force East Timor to punish. Have an international tribunal. The international community should deal with punishment of crimes, not East Timor.'

for us to rethink our previous cynicism about the truth and justice journey between Timor-Leste and Indonesia and open our minds to what then President, Xanana Gusmão, said in a letter to the UN Secretary-General of 22 June 2005:

> The Commission of Truth and Friendship is not a final phase of justice. Over time, as both [Timor-Leste and Indonesia] mature democratically, people's need for justice will be met. There is, after all, no statute of limitations for such crimes. As nations become more politically mature, past grievances and past wrongs can be righted. (Pascoe 2006:Fn. 331)[24]

The Commission for Reception, Truth and Reconciliation (CAVR)

The CAVR was established by UNTAET Regulation No. 10 of 2001. The 'Reception' part of its title referred to the reception of refugees back from West Timor. After collecting statements from 7669 people, conducting more than 1000 interviews (Rae 2009:180), 217 hearings, six healing workshops for survivors of human rights violations who were deemed unusually vulnerable (Laakso 2007:173–4), extensive data collection, statistical analysis and other research, CAVR produced a beautifully written report of 3500 pages. It is one of the best documentations any nation could have of its recent history. The combination of politically plural Timorese commissioners who were independent of the executive government and dedicated international staff resulted in potent prose that held the United Nations institutionally accountable for its failures, as well as the Governments of the United States, Australia and Portugal, international corporations and of course many different types of actors within both Indonesia and Timor-Leste (CAVR 2006:Part 8). The appointed commissioners were a diverse group including leaders formerly affiliated with the pro-integration party Apodeti and with UDT.

UDT leaders showed wonderful leadership towards reconciliation in the televised CAVR hearings:

> '[A]s Secretary-General of UDT, I ask forgiveness of widows and young children from our action'. [Then] Joao Carrascalão admitted his responsibility as a UDT leader. 'I am here to make reconciliation…In twenty-four years I have been so ashamed.' [Prime Minister] Alkatiri [later] said, 'I wanted to hear what Joao would say before I decided what

---

24 This conclusion is reinforced in the report of the Commission for Truth and Friendship Indonesia–Timor-Leste (2008:303): 'These conclusions do not represent the end of a process of closure and reconciliation, but rather a beginning.'

to say. He spoke truthfully. I congratulate him for his courage. 'UDT killed Fretilin and Fretilin killed UDT', Lu'olo said. 'As President [of Fretilin] I apologise and ask forgiveness.' (Scott 2005:362)

Daly and Sarkin (2007:64) quote remote villagers as saying that national leaders never before came to listen to them, but this happened for the first time with the CAVR process. In addition, because commissioners invited ordinary people to send messages that they thought should be heard by the whole nation and because hearings were broadcast on radio and television and much listened to, the invitation to tell and the commitment to listen and record each story 'transform(s) it from hidden shame to part of the permanent record of the founding of the new nation' (Daly and Sarkin 2007:64).

The Community Reconciliation Process, which we discuss in the next section, also gave voice to a large section of the Timor-Leste population. Most commentators see CAVR as a success in making its contribution to the peace, while seeing the total package of truth, justice and reconciliation as having failed badly because other institutions faltered in making their contributions. So, the Serious Crimes Panel failed to deliver criminal trials for the most culpable, Indonesian justice failed, international justice failed and the Commission of Truth and Friendship conducted insipid hearings in light of these failures. The CAVR report (2006:Part 11) recommended contributions to a reparations trust fund for victims, particularly from Indonesia, but also from members of the Security Council who bore some responsibility for the nation's misfortune, and weapons manufacturers who profited from it. Timor-Leste's political leadership, particularly Xanana Gusmão, but also José Ramos-Horta, rejected this out of hand. Instead of government-to-government approaches for compensation to victims, it was the Commission of Truth and Friendship that emerged from intergovernmental conversations.

Elizabeth Stanley (2009:110) summarises the final outcome as 'offering a participatory and recognition-based justice without a corresponding redistributive justice'. The Gusmão point of view, in contrast, is that payments to victims would be an obstacle to redistributive justice at three levels. First, demanding reparations from Indonesia or Australia would not be in the long-run interests of the security of the nation and therefore would jeopardise all Timor-Leste's justice gains, and would not achieve a result in any case. Second, such demands would not be the best way to sustain the commitment of donor nations to keep aid flowing to Timor-Leste. Third, victim reparation is not the most strategic anti-poverty investment to make with either foreign or domestic funds. Quite a lot of it would go to the elites who were targeted by the Indonesian military, such as Xanana Gusmão's own family. The latter need not have been the case had the government heeded the reparation fund priorities CAVR (2006:Part 11, p. 43) suggested in the conclusion to this part of its report: support for single mothers and scholarships for their children, support for the disabled, widows and survivors of sexual violence and torture, support for severely affected communities (funded from collective applications) and memorialisation.

Both these perspectives have merit and only local politics can sort out the competing merits. In doing so, there are complex questions of detail. Should victims who fled to other countries as refugees receive payments? Should only violence that produces permanent injury attract payment? What about torture? Where does torture begin and police beating of a kind that frequently occurs throughout Indonesia end? Should families who lost children to starvation receive payment? Should destroyed houses attract payment? Destroyed businesses? Destroyed homes that also housed a business? Destroyed crops? Should a person who lost a limb while being coerced by militia to be present during an attack on a pro-independence village receive payment? Most importantly of all, how much in the way of reparations should be put aside for victims so traumatised or ashamed (including many female rape victims) that they will not be ready to share their story for years or decades?

Whether reparation is a good idea or not turns considerably on whether all of these questions of detail could be settled in ways that would not trigger diabolical new conflicts. There actually was an extremely limited program of reparations to victims who participated in the Community Reconciliation Program and were judged to have suffered serious trauma; US$200 was paid to 712 people, of whom 196 were women. Considerable feelings of injustice were reported to us among people who felt they had suffered more than these 712, at the under-funding of women, even that some had lied to get the $200 (see also Stanley 2009:125–6).

Almost all families in Timor-Leste suffered terribly from the occupation and conflict, are poor and would like to receive reparation payments. The peoples of wealthy nations such as Australia might have agreed to fund reparation as a symbol of culpability, recognition and vindication of the suffering of victims. That can still be associated with implementing the recommendation of the CAVR (2006:Part 11, p. 4, para. 1.6) that nations which supported Indonesia with military cooperation programs during its occupation of East Timor should apologise to the people of Timor-Leste for that failure to honour their international human rights obligations.

We would not, however, interpret Xanana Gusmão and José Ramos-Horta ruling reparations to victims out of hand as a failure to listen to the considerable demand among their people for reparations, of them being aloof from the very democratic impulses they struggled to bring about. On the contrary, the process of CAVR debating in public hearings, recommending reparations, political leaders disagreeing, their disagreement being understandably and robustly criticised, but their being elected regardless—all this seems the essence of the kind of democratic debate of complex issues that the people of Timor-Leste fought for.

There is a third position, between one supporting the CAVR recommendations for reparations and one supporting the Gusmão–Ramos-Horta view that this is not in the interests of the people of Timor-Leste. This is to take the view that a grassroots institution such as the CAVR calling for reparation from culpable institutions, especially ones like armaments corporations who would never pay, and the political leadership insisting it was folly to pursue such claims, amounted to a good division of labour between the important business of symbolic politics and the important business of practical politics.

The Community Reconciliation Process (CRP)

Unlike so many of the internationally funded programs of the early 2000s, CAVR employees were 80 per cent local, and commissioners 100 per cent. Regional staff from each district ran the Community Reconciliation Process (CRP) in their district. While we will see that the CRP was a perpetrator-centred process that could have done much more to give voice to female victims (Harris Rimmer 2008), at least in requiring by regulation that 30 per cent of the regional commissioners who chaired the hearings were women (CAVR 2006:Part 9, p. 43), front-stage empowerment of women was higher than among officers of the formal justice system. There were even some cases where all the members of panels (usually with three to five members) were women (CRP interviews, September 2009). Regional commissioners negotiated with local elders the appropriate way of ritualising *nahe biti bo'ot* ('stretching the big mat' on which deponents[25]/ perpetrators, victims and elders would sit) for that locality (Scheeringa 2007). *Adat* (*lisan*) leaders had a reduced role from their traditional role of judge and jury, deferring to the mediation role of a panel of prominent community members and a chair from the CAVR staff from that district (Larke 2009:658), but it was nevertheless an important role. Pre-negotiations before the ceremony often lasted three months. Usually the ceremony itself ran for one day, during which more than one deponent would be heard. There was usually chewing of betel-nut, drinking of wine or blood or both mixed together, cooling conflict by sprinkling coconut water, sacrifice of animals and reintegrative feasting (Babo-Soares 2004; Stanley 2009:114). A storyteller and interpreter of traditional law (*lian nain*) would mediate between victims and perpetrators in pursuit of an

---

25 The use of the term 'deponents' rather than perpetrators was intended to communicate that it would often be the case that people who burnt houses did so under fear of violence from the Indonesian military, so it would be possible for all present at the CRP—deponents, victims, community members—to share an identity as survivors of the occupation (Larke 2009:660).

agreement and restoration of balance between the spiritual and the secular worlds that had been disturbed by the wrongdoing. There was great variation from place to place in how large the spiritual balancing issues loomed. Figure 10.1 reports the typical seating arrangements for CRP hearings because it is a distinctive Timorese contribution to the spatial separation of powers over transitional justice. This was complemented at the opening of the hearing with space for a reconciliatory prayer by a local Catholic priest in the local language. This also represents the genius of the CRP in mobilising a ritually serious engagement of truth and reconciliation by drawing upon the legitimacy of state justice (through reading a letter from the Prosecutor-General authorising the hearing), of *lisan* through ritual calling upon ancestors to join the proceeding and enforce its conclusions (CAVR 2006:Part 9, p. 24) and of the legitimacy of the Church through the priest's prayer.

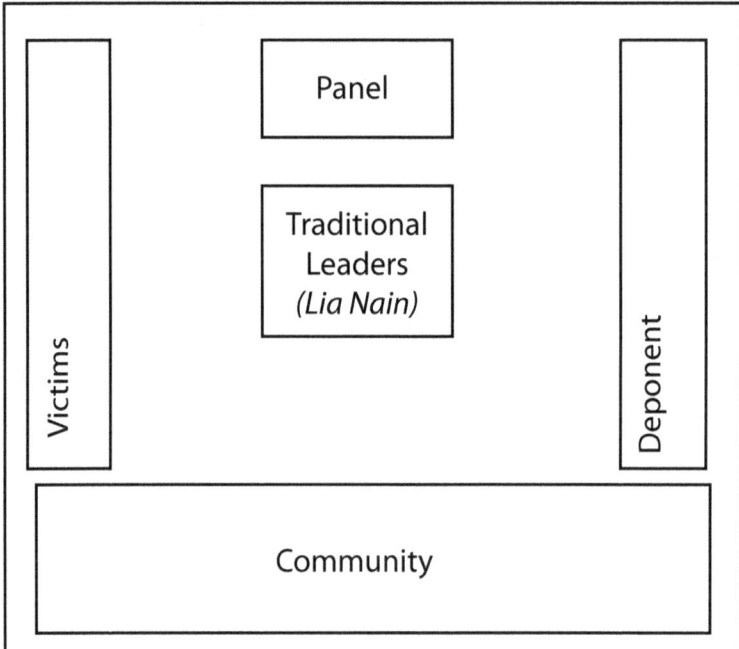

Figure 10.1: Typical seating arrangement in a CRP hearing

Source: CAVR (2006:Part 9, p. 17)

Where agreement on a peaceful way forward was not reached, cases would be referred to the police. Where it was reached, the Community Reconciliation Agreement would be read out and signed by panel members and by deponents, who would apologise to the community. Once perpetrators of crimes had been welcomed back into the community at the end of the process, they could no longer be prosecuted for those crimes. Many of the matters dealt with were not crimes, but the kind of degrading speech that occurs during violent conflict that is crucial to heal, but quite beyond the competence of a criminal court:

> In one of the CAVR reconciliation meetings, the mother-in-law of a former militia member came to reconcile with her son-in-law. In the past, this militia member had deeply offended his mother-in-law by cursing her in public, which was severely aggravated by the fact he used the name of her sexual organs. The mother-in-law said she was willing to reconcile, but she expressed the following: after this meeting, I will go home naked. By stating that she would go home naked, the woman expressed that the offender had undressed her publicly. The community leader present at the meeting had a firm knowledge of customary law and immediately knew the right solution. The son-in-law had to dress her again by providing her with a traditional weaving (*tais*). The offender provided the *tais* and his mother-in-law stated that she accepted him again. (Scheeringa 2007:138)

In Timorese traditional law, cases like this one are extremely serious because a tight connection is drawn between violent speech and violent acts: violent speech is read as part of violence and a precursor to physical assault. Fox's (2007) research among the Roti of West Timor found that resort to physical violence was ridiculed as evidence of a lack of speaking ability.

Most CRP cases would commence with the Chair of the local Community Reconciliation Process Panel explaining the process, followed by remarks by village leaders. Unlike Timorese courts and the Indonesian courts before them, here, the entire proceedings were conducted in the local language. The opening remarks (in common with the closing agreement) would usually include a renunciation of the use of violence to achieve political ends. Then the perpetrator/deponent would read a statement he or she had voluntarily prepared in advance with assistance from CRP staff. Questions were then asked, including from victims, who were also invited to make statements of the impact of crimes on them. Reparations and other measures would then be agreed and registered with the Dili District Court (Zifcak 2005:52–3). In a majority of cases, apology was not accompanied by reparation or community work in the agreement (Combs 2007:221). The final stage of the process usually involved some kind of ritual of readmission of the wrongdoer to the community.

Figure 10.2a: Community Reconciliation poster

10. Transitional Justice and Reconciliation

Figure 10.2b: Community Reconciliation poster

Photos: CAVR

Only 20 per cent of those indicted by the Serious Crimes Panel process went through to a trial (and these were overwhelmingly less serious criminals than the 80 per cent not indicted). In contrast, 90 per cent of deponents who requested that they be called to account under the Community Reconciliation Process—1371 individuals—saw the ordeal through to completed community reconciliation hearings (Scheeringa 2007:138). The incomplete cases were adjourned and then dropped, or were cases where the deponent did not attend. If the CRP was a less punitive justice than that of the Serious Crimes Panel cases, it at least consistently delivered the kind of justice it provided once a case was under way.

Yet it would be a mistake to conclude that the widest impunity gap was where serious crime process indictments were not realised as trials. Numerically, the much more gaping impunity was with alleged serious crimes that were not indicted. In theory, district courts were responsible for serious past crimes that were not crimes against humanity, but in practice they mostly just sat among a backlog that district courts never returned to. Some crimes against humanity were not indicted because they were missed at that time, sufficient evidence had not been accumulated by that time, the perpetrators were informally promised impunity if they returned to East Timor and surrendered their weapons, or the Serious Crimes Unit did not target them as one of their highest priority cases for which they could find the resources to prosecute. There were also many serious crime defendants who were presented to the CRP as potential deponents and rejected there because they were above the seriousness threshold of the crimes the CRP was allowed to deal with. Putting it crudely, the big impunity gap was with cases that were too serious for the CRP and not serious enough given the limited resources of the serious crimes process.

There was also a problem, in the words of Zifcak (2005:53), of the CRP becoming a 'victim of its own success' after 30 000 people had attended its hearings (others say 40 000). His rough estimate is that there were another 3000 deponents interested in coming forward to make admissions and seek reconciliation after the CRP shut down. There were also cases where the CRP visited local towns but not more remote villages where people were waiting and expecting them to come (Stanley 2009:16).

Zifcak's (2005:54) evaluation concluded that reintegration of perpetrators was based more on their level of contrition than on how much truth they spoke, that not much truth was revealed in many CRPs, and in some cases specific victim concerns were not addressed or wounds were reopened (see also Kent 2005:63–4).[26] There was minimal trauma counselling follow-through for victims

---

26 People whom we interviewed also expressed concern that in the CRP, burning down a house and the entire possessions of a family was sometimes not viewed as a serious matter. Zifcak (2003:11) writes: 'In a

(CRP interview, September 2009). On the other hand, Larke (2009:660) pointed out that, backstage, most CRP deponents provided to the Serious Crimes Unit 'details of the individuals and structures that had coordinated and commanded their actions'. Deponents and victims shared a deep sense of injustice that the masterminds of the violence enjoyed impunity in Indonesia. More work went into preparing deponents for the CRP than preparing victims. Female victims were particularly neglected (Kent 2004). Unlike most restorative justice processes, in the CRP, victims were frequently not afforded an opportunity for personal testimony; it was a process centred on deponent reintegration, with the victim role only reactive to the deponent statement (Larke 2009:665).

Victims had no right to object to a deponent being declared reconciled and therefore immune from prosecution. Victims suffering trauma getting little access to professional support was perhaps one reason so many victims, especially female victims, decided against participation (Stanley 2009:116–18). Cases of murder—even participation in the mass murder of 74 people or more (Robinson 2003:234–6), as recorded in the documentary film *Passabe* (Leong and Lee 2004)—were (illegally) reconciled by CRP hearings, and in some of these cases there was dissatisfaction at the leniency of outcomes: 'I saw a case in which people had had their mother killed and it was reconciled by giving a goat. That is not the right process' (quoted in Stanley 2009:121).

Some people complained that CRP staff protected militia relatives from being called to account (Stanley 2009:119). There were also cases where CRP staff oversimplified conflicts as caused by Indonesia when the independence conflict had in fact been used as an opportunity to settle older inter-village scores (Stanley 2009:124).

Closing the Impunity Gap

The basic design idea of taking an impossible weight of cases off the serious crimes process by establishing the CRP was prudent. But the impunity gap could have been further closed by: a) allowing the serious crimes process at least a modicum of extra time and resources;[27] b) leaving more discretion to the CRP to confront serious cases that the courts did not have the resources or time to

---

hearing I observed, for example, one perpetrator accepted responsibility for burning down 19 houses in tandem with militia colleagues. This was a lot. Yet, the final agreement was that the matter should be resolved by the issue of a public apology alone.' Victim dissatisfaction, particularly with failure to locate missing persons, was also a big issue with the serious crimes process (Reiger and Wierda 2006:32).

27 Implementing CAVR (2006:Ch. 7, p. 24) recommendation 7.1.1 is something the international community really should have seen itself having an obligation to fund: '7.1.1 The Serious Crimes Unit and Special Panels in Timor-Leste have their respective mandates renewed by the United Nations and their resources increased in order to be able to continue and try cases from throughout the period 1975–1999.'

process; c) keeping the doors of the CRP open indefinitely via a low-cost model of continuing state–police support for post-conflict indigenous justice;[28] and d) UN-endorsed smart sanctions such as visa refusals and freezing bank accounts of culpable leaders of the Indonesian military and state from the 1974–99 period.[29] In other words, the impunity gap could have been closed at a few of its widest points without a hugely costly succession of thousands of criminal trials and a large prison construction program. Bread-and-butter case management investments for the District Courts discussed earlier would also have helped.

The impunity gap was mostly a result of good rule-of-law intentions. Consider sexual violence: CAVR documented 853 cases—a number generally agreed to be a huge undercount because of victims who suffered secretly and then just disappeared, and because so many survivors were not emotionally ready to reveal their story by the time the CAVR finished taking statements. The CRP provided no justice for any of these 853 identified victims because the intent was that such cases would go before the Serious Crimes Panel. The tragedy was that in the upshot Larke (2009:670) found that only five cases that included charges of sexual violence had been tried. Harris Rimmer (2008:154) concluded there were only three that were decided under the serious crimes process[30]— one of them a case where the judges found that they had no jurisdiction over an abduction to West Timor and rape alleged to have occurred in West Timor. That case in effect institutionalised impunity for cross-border abduction and rape. The second case was a conviction for aiding and abetting a rape for which the alleged principal perpetrators were hiding in Indonesia, and the third a four-year jail sentence for a militia commander convicted of rape.

Political leaders stepping back from interfering in the judicial branch would also have helped build some confidence in Timor-Leste's flawed transitional justice. In August 2009, a former militiaman, Maternus Bere, was arrested on an outstanding warrant for crimes against humanity after he crossed from West to East Timor. He had been indicted years earlier for his alleged role in the Suai Church massacre of at least 40 unarmed people including children and priests in 1999 (Robinson 2003:225–8). Militia responsible for the massacre raped considerable numbers of women in the vicinity afterwards (Wandita 2007:1–12). One of Bere's associates was alleged to have abducted and forced into sexual slavery in West Timor a girl known in Timor-Leste as Alola. Bere was alleged to be complicit in Alola's abduction (Daley 2009:29). Kirsty Sword Gusmão established the Alola Foundation for the support of women and children in 2001 in the girl's memory. On 10 September in a nationally televised address,

---

28 The CAVR report (2006:Part II, p. 30, paras 8.1–8.2) recommended more or less to this effect.
29 See CAVR (2006:Section 11:4, para. 1.9).
30 We presume the other two cases referred to by Larke (2009) were run by line prosecutors in the district courts after the serious crimes process shut its doors.

Prime Minister, Xanana Gusmão, announced Bere was released from custody and handed to the custody of the Indonesian Embassy without judicial sanction of his order to lift the indictment. This was an abuse of the separation of powers, transacted in a shocking way, for which the Prime Minister openly accepted personal responsibility. We return to lessons from this case in the final chapter.

Figure 10.3: Refugees seeking safety in a Suai church to avoid attacks before the Suai massacre. Many of these refugees perished

Photo: John Stanmeyer/VII/Corbis

Another worrying aspect of this history is that it has left open to people the interpretation that the only justice that worked was mob justice. We interviewed one INTERFET peacekeeper still suffering in 2009 from post-traumatic stress disorder. He had the job of picking up a militia member arrested for his alleged involvement in the Suai massacre to take him to Dili where he would be tried. A crowd stepped in front of his truck as he was leaving Suai and demanded that he hand over the man. The soldier was concerned for the safety of the people if he tried to get away by driving through the crowd. He was concerned for the safety of a private who was with him if he simply refused to use his keys to hand the man over. So he agreed to do so if the crowd cleared a path for his truck, created a circle where everyone stood back from the man, and agreed that nothing should be done to him until the truck departed. When the peacekeeper took the handcuffs off the man and pulled him out of the back of the truck he was screaming and clinging onto the seat to stay in the truck. He told the man to kneel in the centre of the circle as the crowd moved back from him as agreed. The elder with whom he negotiated this arrangement kissed the peacekeeper's hand as a sign of respect. As the peacekeeper safely drove away, he saw in the rear-vision mirror the crowd surge in on the man accused of the atrocity. The peacekeeper felt the man deserved what happened to him as he had admitted to his participation in the Suai massacre. In Dili, the peacekeeper truthfully told a military police superior what he had done and offered to take full responsibility for it after initially saying the suspect must be coming on a later vehicle. The officer said that as far as he was concerned 'nothing had happened'.

A number of simple things could have been done to ameliorate the problem that 'those who did submit to the CRP felt resentful because perpetrators of more serious crimes remained outside the scope of either process' (Reiger and Wierda 2006:35).

Zifcak (2005:54) speaks for most of the qualitative researchers of transitional justice in Timor-Leste when he concludes: 'Most people I interviewed regarded the CRP as a qualified but significant success. At the same time, most regarded the continuing de facto immunity of serious and middle-level perpetrators from any criminal or civil prosecution as an unqualified failure.'

The UNDP (2004:11) evaluation of the CRP concluded that it had helped reduce tensions in many communities and that victims and deponents mostly reported high levels of satisfaction with the justice and reconciliation obtained, as did CAVR's (2006:Part 9, pp. 33–40) own two evaluations based on 40 and 116 interviews with participants. The CRP was probably also useful in preventing violence against individuals returning from West Timor by communities suspicious of what they had and had not done (Kent 2005:62). Some who were herded across the border during the chaos of 1999 were afraid to return for fear of guilt by association with the militia who herded them. 'Reception' of militia leaders of such herding was one of a variety of contexts where, in practice, for the safety of communities, the CRP dealt with more serious crimes than were allowed under its guidelines (Combs 2007:222).

Deponents interviewed by Lia Kent (2005) had been worried about people 'speaking behind their backs' and reported feeling 'freer' or 'lighter' after clearing the air and felt their children would be more accepted. The CRP was also successful in restoring the authority of community leaders over violent young men—a ritual that signified that 'the base of power lay once again in the community and with its leaders' (Larke 2009:667). This is one of the neglected ways in which we would regard the CRP as a considerable, if qualified, contribution of the Timor-Leste peace process to international thinking about how to graft hybridity into a transitional separation of powers (Brown and Gusmão 2009). The CRP created a distinctive new separated power in civil society that actually reinforced the power of *lisan* (the authority of traditional elders) and also reinforced the power of the state justice system. Through our lens of evaluating the Timor-Leste peace in republican terms, we see the CRP as an innovation that mattered because it enriched separations of powers in both state and society.

Without stepping back from the need for more trials for crimes against humanity, the modest cost of the CRP shows that it might not be impossible—if a program of this kind were extended to very serious crimes, over a period of many years— to deny impunity to most war crimes, large and small. Nancy Combs (2007) discusses this as the option for large numbers of restorative guilty pleas and reparation agreements combined with an opportunity for victims to have a say on what should happen in particular cases. People might be more satisfied with this justice than most criminal lawyers would predict. Or at least they might if the United Nations and other political leaders desisted from pronouncements that all crimes against humanity should be prosecuted, when the United Nations and its members never go even slightly close to providing the justice budgets required to realise such an objective[31]—and when the Security Council is always opposed to the very long transitional justice windows required to lend integrity to such a policy.

Addressing the Timor-Leste Parliament when the CAVR report finally was presented, President Gusmão, consistent with his positions outlined above, strongly opposed the recommendation that reparations be sought from other nations complicit in the crimes of the Indonesian military. And he excoriated the recommendation to re-establish the Special Panel for Serious Crimes to further pursue those alleged major criminals who had escaped justice. The great surprise, however, was that he opposed making the report public. Fortunately, he did not have the power to withhold it. It was a sad moment to witness such a great democrat advocating a course so distrustful of open debate with the people of so many of the people's truths in the report.

---

31   A problem is that the UN system encourages loose rhetoric on the role of punishment in regulation of undesirable things, such as the report of the Commission of Experts (2005:125) on human rights in Timor-Leste: 'No violation of human rights, no invasion of human dignity and no infliction of pain and suffering on fellow human beings should be allowed to go unpunished.' Lying to loved ones inflicts great pain quite frequently. Should it always be punished?

The Place of Non-State Justice

There is a tendency for some of the literature to interpret post-conflict justice and reconciliation as occurring through either the CRP or criminal trials. Grassroots reconciliation that had no or limited connection to the CAVR, the state or the United Nations was widespread. For example, from 2000 through to the present, returning refugees from West Timor have been greeted at the border by the receiving community, where a grassroots ceremonial handover occurs. In this ceremony, refugees

> are expected to face their own communities and confess their offences… An elected representative of the refugees or an elder makes a confession on behalf of the group. After receiving that confession, the community members present can address complaints to particular individuals, and a discussion typically ensues. Upon arriving home, refugees participate in a welcoming ceremony, which also features confessions and apologies. The ceremony will culminate in an exchange of betel nut or an 'oath of blood', in which both sides drink each other's blood. (Combs 2007:219, drawing heavily on the work of Babo-Soares 2004)

Breach of these oaths (*juramento*) may result in 'punitive acts by the ancestors, such as loss of crops or the death of a family member' (Graydon 2005:34; Hohe 2003; Hohe and Nixon 2003). In a society like Timor-Leste where the promises of state punitive enforcement of the law are rarely delivered, the promise of punishment from above when oaths to renounce violence are breached is probably of considerable value in violence prevention. People certainly believe it is. Dionisio Babo-Soares concludes that with family and wider community mediation of post-conflict reintegration and reconciliation, 'welcoming ceremonies were held in a way that allowed the representative of the refugees to address the public, usually in a public square, confessing their actions and offering apologies and their acceptance of being brought before the court should they be found guilty' (Babo-Soares 2004:20).

So, in a sense this non-state justice was couched to reinforce the limited enforcement power of state justice while calling on both the clout of the ancestors and the informal power of the disapproval of friends and family listening in the public square should undertakings be breached. '[P]ressure normally takes the form of shaming and acquiring a disgraced name in case of non-compliance' (Trindade and Castro 2007:25).

Elders are sometimes called upon by civil society groups to support contestation of their authority from state justice because that contestation is part of the meaning of the Democratic Republic of Timor-Leste they struggled for. Police and courts in turn are sometimes urged to support *lisan* or *adat* justice because that represents part of the survival of a Maubere identity they resisted Indonesian oppression in order to salvage. Jennifer Laakso (2007:238) makes the importance of traditional justice to identity clear by quoting a number of *chefe de sucos* and *chefe d'aldeias*:

> If the traditional model is lost, it means the culture is lost, and where do the people of Timor-Leste go? Then we will have no identity to show to the world. Timor is strong now because of this identity that it has. (Maliana *chefe*)

> If we lose our traditional model everyone in society will have no morals or culture and will not be living like civilized people anymore. (Suai *chefe*)

> It should not be lost. Resolving problems through *adat* is part of our culture, and if we lose this, it means we will lose our culture. Loss of culture for us is like another war. (Suai *chefe*)

Case-management and justice system administration failings combined with a long history of rural distrust of state justice caused most people to persist with customary justice in their search for a venue that would give them an authoritative result in resolving their disputes. McWilliam (2007a, 2007b) describes Timorese village dispute resolution as providing a form of 'restorative custom' that delivers more widespread satisfaction than the courts. In the earlier part of this chapter, we saw the overwhelming evidence that most citizens and even most state administrative officials for most purposes prefer non-state justice in the village to state justice in the courts. Indonesian occupation strengthened *lisan* justice as the only viable alternative to the justice of the Indonesian state (Hohe and Nixon 2003). While international legal advisers and educated urban elites alike agreed that a modern state legal system was what mattered, and agreed that customary non-state justice was something to be sceptical about, an eternity of delay and backlogs of state justice vindicated non-state justice as the kind most citizens preferred during the first 12 years of Timor-Leste's transition.

Non-state justice can be better equipped to deal with contextually specific lived injustice that sits beneath violence. For example, Fataluku society in Lautem is caste based, and 'there was a tendency for militia members to be from the *akanu* (slave) caste' (Kammen 2003:82). *Alcolhimento* (reception–welcome–reintegration) of such militia back to the new Democratic Republic of Timor-Leste required empathy for that caste injustice. The traditional justice of reception came under pressure to graft onto itself the sensibility of the liberation of the new Timor-Leste as a society in which no-one would be welcomed as a slave. Across Timor-Leste in various ways state law proved less capable of grafting into its legal culture a capability of responding to such complex local social injustices. We have already seen in the discussion of the CRP that it was *lisan* that was able to reframe both the killer and the killed, the arsonist and the homeless, as victims of an unjust war and an oppressive military occupation.

On the other hand, on the crucial legal issues of rape and domestic violence, state policing, UN–NGO–state human rights and feminist advocacy, and even to some degree the backlogged courts have been a check on and balance to oppressive traditions in *lisan* for accommodating gendered violence, such as requiring marriage to their rapist for unmarried victims (Hohe 2003). While most men and women might continue to prefer the justice of *lisan* to the justice of the courts for gendered violence, police and human rights advocates have succeeded in persuading them that victims have a right to state justice and that the norms of state justice with respect to rape and domestic violence can always trump *lisan*. Therefore elders today must be more responsive to demands from victims, to feminist and rights sensibilities within their village, when young women resist forced marriage to the very man who oppressed them, when men insist that they have a right to beat their wife and children. Carolyn Graydon (2005:37) reached the preliminary conclusion from her field research that

> local justice leaders are surprisingly open to engagement in debate and training around human rights issues in the local justice domain. They crave the opportunity to talk to each other and to engage with the government on how they can best fulfill their roles. Early indications are that many view positively suggestions that local justice mechanisms could over time be reformed to mitigate human rights concerns. There was also support for an approach of identifying human rights values already entrenched in East Timorese culture as the basis for running education campaigns concerning sensitive human rights issues such as domestic violence.

We return to this theme in Chapter 12 when we discuss Sally Engle Merry's (2006) work on the 'vernacularisation' of rights consciousness. In a sense, we see a state of play where *lisan* is a check on the inability of state law to grapple with contextual injustices in a local language in which citizens can understand the proceedings, and state justice is a check on the failure of traditional justice to guarantee the rights of women, the right of investors to secure leases to land on which they build their business, and certain other rights of modernity. This is quite a progressive aspect of transition from a republican point of view. It might be read as reflecting the tensions consciously drafted into the law by the Constituent Assembly. Article 31 of the Constitution entrenched a primacy of state criminal law, though Article 2.4 required the state to 'recognise and value norms and customs of East Timor and any legislation dealing specifically with customary law'. This constitutional compromise can be read as a continuation of the primacy of state law that had been applied by the United Nations. In entrenching this primacy of state law, the East Timor Constituent Assembly, which drafted the Constitution, can be seen as acting in opposition to the views that were 'expressed in a grassroots consultation process on the content of the Constitution, indicating that communities wanted local systems of justice to acquire substantive formal recognition and usage' (Graydon 2005:68).

Yet the reality of constitutional interpretation on the ground has become one where *lisan* normally prevails, but where state justice trumps it when someone succeeds in making an issue of the injustice of a decision emanating from *lisan*. *Lisan* has the power of default justice; state rights law has the power of reform justice. Grappling with the non-justice realities of backlogs, international judges (JSMP 2005a) as well as local judges were soon interpreting this tension in the Constitution to decide that serious cases did not need to be tried under state law when non-state justice in the village had deliberated the case and the parties had agreed on compensation and other remedies. Yet it is inconceivable that a rape victim who was being forced to marry her rapist would not have this struck down in favour of punishment of the rapist if she could manage to have her case heard in a district court. Because elders know this, they serve their authority poorly if they refuse to back down when a young woman says she will take her rape case to court should they insist on her marrying the man. Local police commanders can be quick to assure elders that the case will be taken away from their jurisdiction unless there is accommodation of such victim demands.

This is the sense in which feminist and human rights networks—partly through their own direct agency, partly through the agency of the police—have become significant checks on and balances to rights abuse in traditional justice. The hybridity we describe might be the beginnings of a productive separation of powers between traditional justice, state justice and human rights advocacy from civil society and international society. It happened in spite of the failure of UNTAET to 'appreciate the resilience of local structures' (Hohe 2003:35) and take non-state justice seriously through any conscious policy settings to reconcile state and non-state justice.[32] The weak link of this separation of powers is that in practice it is difficult for a woman to push her way through court backlogs to get a rape trial or a domestic violence trial into the District Court.[33] The reform priorities by our republican lights are to improve practical access of rape and domestic justice survivors to the justice of the courts and to continue to ratchet

---

32 See Grenfell (2006), Laakso (2007) and Nixon (2006) on why this path is still open. 'The central argument of this thesis is that during times of political transition, a hybrid legal system, which combines local and introduced justice systems; utilizes indigenous language; and is sensitive to cultural tradition and context is more likely to promote sustainable peace than imported systems…If local justice mechanisms continue to be ignored, and artificial and non-organic justice mechanisms remain the sole focus in the future, it could adversely impact communities across Timor-Leste by increasing division and atomization, and potentially lead to serious conflict' (Laakso 2007:242, 246).
33 Laura Grenfell (2006:312) reports Judicial System Monitoring Programme tracking of 148 domestic violence cases in the Dili District Court in which 104 of the complaints were withdrawn, with lengthy delays mentioned as an important reason.

up the pressure on police and traditional elders through relentless human rights education so that when the inevitability of *lisan* justice as default justice kicks in, it does so in a fashion that is increasingly respectful of rights. By relentless, we mean human rights education that never accepts that the job is complete, but that persists from decade to decade, generation to generation, rejecting the folly that programs that last only a few years can secure transformation.

De-legitimating *lisan* justice is not the priority on this analysis. To the extent that non-state justice shuts down, the state justice backlog will become more intractable and injustice will spiral downwards. Contestation between state and non-state justice where the access to justice that each provides is improved by the contest seems the more productive path of continuous improvement in rights to non-domination.[34] The flaws of Timor-Leste's justice system are very visible, regularly revealing cases of shocking abuse of rights. Nevertheless, a separation-of-powers analysis helps us see that its dynamic is much more clearly one of continuous improvement than is evident in societies where international intervention has caused the collapse of non-state justice, leaving state justice swamped and unchallenged by contestation from traditional justice.[35]

Contestation seems a more productive model than what in our interviews was often described as a philosophy of minor disputes being settled on the mat and the most serious matters going to the police and courts. First, this does not seem an accurate description of what happens. We have seen that in the two domains survey research shows to be the most common forms of serious legal conflicts—land and domestic violence disputes—resolution is mostly by non-state justice. And rape and murder are also frequently negotiated on the mat. Second, in circumstances where almost none of the rape and violence of 1974–99 and 2006–08 resulted in punishment by courts, where tens of thousands of deaths and the rape of a large proportion of the female population resulted in an aggregate of fewer than 100 years of prison sentences (even then reduced by pardons), the hope for some level of justice for serious crimes was found in the CRP and in non-CRP *lisan* justice. *Nahe biti* (justice on the mat) in future will continue to be the hope for much of the justice after serious violence.

---

34   In one of our UNMIT interviews, a senior justice support official said that their approach was 'a progressive realization approach to human rights' (Interview, September 2009).
35   David Mearns (2001:4) actually used separation-of-powers discourse in reaching a similar policy conclusion: 'The formal system should embrace the principles of victim compensation (restorative justice), transparent and public deliberation, *and consultation with village elders and the families of victim and perpetrator* in the determination of punishment. This will produce culturally appropriate and socially acceptable outcomes that are likely to be adhered to. Magistrates and judges must act as *independent* monitors and courts of appeal for the decisions of local leaders regarding disputes arising in their area. They must over-rule decisions that are against natural justice, corrupt, politically motivated, or breech the international standards of human rights. They should be trained to understand the social and cultural values of the people they judge. While local cultural understandings and practices should be taken into account, local political and administrative authority must be separated from judicial powers. The confidence of all citizens in the legal and justice systems of the new state will depend on this.'

State–non-state justice contestation is the more productive model than tracking less serious matters to the mat and more serious matters to the police, because sometimes it is a grave mistake for the police to slough off pleas for help from the community with matters they regard as 'less serious'. Hohe and Nixon (2003:50) make this point by reference to an incident from the research of Mearns (2001:20) where a man arrived at a police station in an agitated state, suggesting that the police had better come quickly to his village:

> When asked what the problem was the man reported that another man in the village was harassing his daughter. Persuaded to elaborate, he went on to say that the man was accusing his daughter of being a witch and practicing magic against the man and his family. The international policeman stopped the man immediately and said there was no law dealing with this and the police could not become involved in such matters. He advised the man to return to the village and try to sort the problem out by 'traditional' means. A couple of days later, the man returned to the police and told them that he had taken their advice and resolved the issue by traditional means—he had killed the accuser. Needless to say, he was arrested for murder.

The Mearns (2001) example should not be read as peacekeeping exotica.[36] In societies where sorcery is feared, sorcery allegations often cause violence, even to the point of conflict over sorcery allegations sustaining civil war in parts of Bougainville, including Siwai (Braithwaite et al. 2010b:31) and Selau (Braithwaite et al. 2010b:67). 'Witches' have been murdered from time to time in Timor-Leste (for example, Mearns 2001:21), including recently (Wright 2009). The wise approach for a police officer is to listen when culturally knowledgeable locals suggest that a dispute is a situation they should be concerned to defuse. State–non-state justice contestation means the police listening to traditional elders and disputants when they believe non-state justice should handle it and also listening when they believe the police should get involved. And it means traditional elders listening to the police when the police argue that this is a matter that would be better settled before a judge. The state–non-state sovereignty contest should not simply track the seriousness of the alleged offence. Elders often ask the police in Timor-Leste to intervene with comparatively minor offences by young men they cannot manage on the mat or to help out when young men are armed with machetes even if they have committed no offence yet. Threats of domestic violence where no-one has actually been hit can be cases where joint mobilisation of the authority of both the police and the elders is justified. Swaine (2003:4) argues '[a] combination of the two systems were

---

36 'Matters such as witchcraft and sorcery and belief in the power of ancestors and other spirits to apply sanctions remain a real force in social life in East Timor. Conflict arising from such issues has to be dealt with in order for social life to continue but the formal justice system cannot deal with it' (Mearns 2001:3).

seen [by victims] to be most forceful…Police were seen to have more force and capacity to scare husbands into stopping their actions' while follow-up *lisan* justice could result in greater acceptance of and compliance with agreements (see also Grenfell 2006:327).

Our interviews revealed that *lisan* justice is layered (see also Grenfell 2006:317). When an alleged injustice is of a member of one family against another, elders of the two families will first meet to try to resolve it to everyone's satisfaction, sometimes under the oversight of the *lian nain* or traditional judicial authority. If a sense of injustice persists, it goes to the *chefe d'aldeia* and then on appeal to the *chefe de suco* who may involve some or all of the *suco* council in hearing the case. If that fails, the police are called in or it may go to the *chefe de posto* (subdistrict head). As Deborah Cummins (2010:1) puts it, the *suco* council acts as a 'bridge between modern and traditional institutional structures' that permits a politics of mutual recognition. The *suco* council is a check and balance not only on state structures, but also on the local authority of a *chefe de suco*. There is a hybridity where the traditional penetrates the modern and vice versa. A subsidiarity principle rather than a separation of powers is in play in this layering. Yet there is no doubt that higher layers can be quite independent of lower layers and act as a check and balance against abuse of powers at lower levels. Josh Trindade (2008) has argued that Timorese ancestors had an understanding of institutional design similar to the separation of powers where the *liurai* (ruler) is bound (acts under the spiritual authority of) the *dato* (the spiritual authority) and the *dato* is bound by *lulik* (all that is sacred) including norms inherited from and overseen by deceased ancestors. James Fox also detects checks and balances in Timorese traditional governance:

> At the heart of this governance is a critical distinction between power and authority. Ideas of authority are paramount in the Timorese conception of governance. Authority is represented as an inner unity: symbolically 'feminised', immobile and silent. By contrast power can be multiple: symbolically masculine, active and invariably clamorous. Whoever or whatever attains power can only act in relation to, and in recognition of, authority. Power can speak on behalf of authority, but is not that authority nor can it assume authority without relinquishing its recourse to force. Without deference to authority, even the most powerful of forces loses all allegiance. But with authority, there can be a balance—an array of different powers—in recurrent complementarity. Thus there existed in Timor a variety of levels of delegated power with 'checks and balances' that maintained coherence and militated against excesses. (Fox 2008:121)

Xanana Gusmão (2005a) has interpreted *lia nain* (literally, 'keepers of the word') as 'men of law' who have a role separated from the different layers of community–

village–district governance. One of the consequences of transition from a government more dominated by Mari Alkatiri until 2006 to one more dominated by Xanana Gusmão has been recognition of the resilience of non-state justice, and acknowledgment of the limits of state justice and of the impossibility that it could simply sweep away non-state justice:

> As the world moves towards restorative justice as a way to solve the problem of overcrowded prisons, to save money from the tax payers because prisons and the death penalty no longer are acceptable as the best form of deterrence, customary laws in various countries may gain new vigour and respect, because they contribute towards real harmony and reconciliation of communities and, above all, they provide a reasonable degree of sense of security for the local communities, which no amount of police force can do. (Xanana Gusmão quoted in Laakso 2007:242)

The traction of traditional powers varies greatly from place to place and is hybridised with colonial and state forms of authority in different ways in different places. We should not think of peacebuilding as coopting these different layers of traditional governance into some kind of vision of how separations of powers should work in a particular place. Rather, the point is for a constitutional separation of powers and for donor interventions to leave space for whatever residual separations of powers of non-state origin continue to be effective checks that humble power in that particular place. And to be careful about crushing them through the way modernist reforms are implemented.

Impunity Again, Payouts to Buy Peace, Reconciliation Fatigue

The near-fatal wounding of President Ramos-Horta in February 2008 and the killing of rebel leader Reinado jolted all levels of civil society and the state into resolve to put a mostly permanent stop to mob fighting and get refugees to move from the camps that continued to destabilise the country. It also ushered in another bout of impunity. On 20 August 2010, President Ramos-Horta commuted the sentences of 23 individuals involved in the attacks in which he was shot and of the only three F-FDTL members sentenced to prison over the attacks on the police in May 2006 that killed 10 and wounded 30 of those who had been surrendering under the UN flag. The three F-FDTL members were not to be found in prison when UN officials checked. In fact, the United Nations has a photograph of one of them standing over President Ramos-Horta in full uniform carrying a gun just after the President was shot. UNMIT officials believed three and a half years after the killings that these men had not paid any compensation to the victims' families as ordered by the court. The only senior leader to go to prison over the violence of 2006, former minister responsible for the police Lobato, had already been freed within months of his conviction in 2007. Other senior figures recommended for prosecution over the violence of 2006 by the United Nations were not touched. Here is Kingsbury's (2009:170) account of Lobato's remarkable release:

> Having a sometimes-strained relationship with Alkatiri...there was a real possibility that Lobato could discuss more freely what he knew about the events of 2006. To this end, it appeared that there was an arrangement that if Lobato went to prison and stayed quiet during the election period, his associates would help him manufacture an excuse to leave prison, whereafter he could be allowed to escape. Within weeks of being jailed, Lobato began a campaign to be assessed as having a heart problem that needed urgent attention overseas. [After some doctors refused to sign a medical certificate, Lobato obtained one and headed straight from the doctor's surgery to the airport]...and boarded a Lear jet with his wife and two children bound for Malaysia. There was a stand-off at the airport for twenty-four hours when prison guards refused to allow the plane to leave. However, under pressure from Fretilin to allow Lobato to have medical treatment or else it would boycott parliament, and with him promising to return, the then just sworn in Justice Minister, Lucio Lobato (Rogerio's cousin), approved his departure and the plane left. He did not have medical treatment, did not stay in Malaysia and did not return to East Timor.

So again the courts were allowed to play no significant role in the justice transition from the nation's violent convulsions of 2006–08. Various reconciliation bodies played much more important roles. There were in some cases high-profile ritual reconciliations within the police, within the military and between the police and the military.[37] The petitioners were each paid US$9000 and returned to civilian life in July 2008. This generous dollop of cash ended their era of collective grievance, dispersing them to new lives across the country.

From 2006 a number of NGO and government bodies organised reconciliations between fighting gangs and reintegration of refugees back into communities to which they had previously been afraid to return. By 2008 this work appeared to have been successful, with 95 per cent of a random sample of citizens, 95 per cent of a police sample and 96 per cent of a community leaders sample reporting 'No' to the question: 'After the return of IDPs to your community/area, has there

---

37   At these reconciliations, PNTL and F-FDTL were 'maturely compromising for their country. They were re-stabilising the country. They were honest with each other. There was a lot of emotion. These were guerillas acknowledging their mistakes, but doing it in a way that protected their sense of pride' (Interview, Senior civil servant, September 2009). They hugged one another at the end.

been an increase in conflict' (Chinn and Everett 2009:20). UNMIT established the Gang Task Force with the Timor-Leste Police. Some reconciliations were led by the President or the Prime Minister. Various peace agreements were signed between gangs that had been fighting each other. Organisations involved in this work included the government's Simu Malu (meaning 'welcome one another') process for refugee reintegration, the Peace and Democracy Foundation, Ba Futuru, Comição Justiça and Paz, HAK Association Peacebuilding Programme, Belun, the Catholic Commission for Peace and Justice and the National Committee for Dialogue (an initiative of President Gusmão) (Kingsbury 2008). The last also organised high-level dialogues and national reconciliation, including among the President, Prime Minister and others at the top. Many of the reconciliations drew upon *lisan* traditions. Others used gang youth work techniques from elsewhere such as identifying moderate gang leaders and working with them to steer the group to nonviolent projects. There were also many pro-peace marches during 2006, and a women and peace conference that helped create an environment for reconciliation to begin.

When we interviewed the leadership of President Gusmão's National Dialogue in November 2006, it was chaired by Maria Domingas Alves, founder of the women's rights organisation Fokupers and now a senior cabinet minister. National Dialogue meetings were moderated by prominent church leaders such as Norwegian Bishop Gunnar Stålsett and Bishop Belo. We were told that the dialogue had reached a consensus that the ancestors had been asked to help ritually during the conflict against Indonesia. The ceremony to close this off with the ancestors and express appreciation to them had not been held. 'As a result leaders have spoken without consideration because they were lacking the wisdom of the ancestors.' Loch and Pruella (2011:315) comment on the total disconnect between internationals' analyses and the predominant indigenous analysis that the fighting of 2006–08 was 'caused by disharmony between the world of the living and the dead'.

On 6 December 2006, a large traditional reconciliation ceremony was held in the square in front of the main national government buildings. During that period, our research team attended various reconciliation meetings and *lisan* rituals for peace that were poorly attended. By late 2006 people were suffering 'reconciliation fatigue'; they were jaded and cynical about the sincerity of their leaders in wanting peace after an change of leadership seemed only to change which side was working to create chaos on the streets that might destabilise the incumbent Prime Minister. The 6 December 2006 event was not as well attended as one might have expected given what a dramatic occasion it was, though there were thousands of ordinary people present and everyone who was anyone nationally and in the diplomatic community. There were prayers and speeches by church and political leaders as Gusmão, Ramos-Horta, Alkatiri and the first Fretilin President, Francisco Xavier do Amaral, sat side-by-side in the centre of the front row. At a later stage of the proceedings they moved to sit together on the big *lisan* mat. Here are some of John Braithwaite's fieldwork notes from the four-hour event:

> I sat at first among the section of seats allocated jointly to PNTL and F-FDTL officers. The GNR (Portuguese UNPOL) patrolled this part of the audience with automatic weapons. I spoke to Captain Barales of the GNR. He said 'Individual places were marked carefully for them [with an eye to avoiding conflict or tension]. Details', smiled Barales, who indeed was an impressive details man. National symbols such as the singing of the national anthem were combined with *lisan* symbols throughout. In their speeches, the leaders admitted mistakes and said they would not make them again. In the oath they said that for he who breaks the national peace there would be no mercy. That person would bring awful afflictions from the ancestors upon the land. Norwegian Bishop Gunnar Stålett [who had nominated Belo and Ramos-Horta for the Nobel Prize] quoted at length from the Belo and Horta Nobel acceptance speeches. That was the most moving part of the proceedings for me when he read Horta's words that it was the imprisoned Gusmão who should be there, not he. I heard others around me say they were moved. Yet it was not as moving as it could have been because there was reconciliation fatigue here. And there is more than a bit of impunity-induced cynicism. So many people feel the leaders want to forget the injustices and use traditional reconciliation as a cover for doing that. Also the Xanana-inspired gestures at reconciliation get discredited by Fretilin and vice versa. Yet they seem genuine about engaging with the reconciliation. The commitment of the leaders to reconciliation and tradition is sincere; it is their commitment to justice that is not…There was a great rush forward when it was announced that something would be done between Mari Alkatiri and Xanana Gusmão. I imagine that they either hugged or shook hands but I could not see with hundreds of people pushing in front of me. There was dancing and sharing of betel nut by traditional leaders from across the island. At one key moment in the long oath to 'peace, love and wisdom' I was near Alkatiri [I could not see the others through the crowd] and saw him hug at least 30 other leaders. He seemed emotionally engaged with it most of the time [interesting, as the leader who seemed most dismissive of both *lisan* and the Catholic Church]. A squealing pig was brought out. An Australian official with whom I shared an interest in Bougainville peacemaking reminded me of a kindred Bougainville reconciliation at which Australian Foreign Minister Downer sat uncomfortably for four hours with a squealing trussed pig under his chair. She said with kindness in her voice that the pig is going

to have a bad day. Indeed the pig was ritually carved up in an adapted ritual of national unity. As I recall the eyes were given to Alkatiri and the first Fretilin President Francisco Xavier do Amaral because they had the vision to see the path that would take the nation to independence. The ears went to the leaders of the Parliament because they must listen to each other and to what the people are saying. The tongue went to the traditional elders present because they are the true speakers for the people. Lawyers will be pleased to know that the President of the Court of Appeals got the brain. Standing next to a lawyer who thought this was a good choice, I smiled with a worried shake of my head. Xanana got the remaining body as the embodiment of the people [this reminded me of Mario Carrascalão saying to me that 'every Timorese has Xanana running in their veins']. At the end Xanana and (I think) TMR [Taur Matan Ruak] danced with the dancers waving a sword. A Timorese UN police interpreter who was at the ceremony wandered off for a moment and was found stabbed to death in a nearby alley. Later there was a riot at the site with people injured and half a dozen cars smashed up. But the press coverage the next morning was all positive and reintegrative.

The most interesting part of the ritual was that it involved political leaders going as far as one might reasonably expect them to go in admitting their personal responsibility for the violence as they prepared to face one another in a 2007 election. Yet agreement on blaming the nation's calamities on their failure to close the peacebuilding loop with the ancestors on the mat took pressure off them. Now things would be better because the ancestors were in the loop. It was not necessary to delve any deeper into the root causes now that the nation understood and had put right this factor that was external to elite machinations. Their reckless actions in inflaming gang violence could be forgiven. Now we were asked to understand that, for example, Xanana was a lesser man when he was making those inflammatory speeches only because the ancestors had abandoned him at that time.

Figure 10.4a: Mari Alkatiri (left), José Ramos-Horta (centre) and Xanana Gusmão (right) with other dignitaries awaiting the ceremony described in John Braithwaite's 2006 fieldwork notes

Figure 10.4b: Xanana Gusmão on the mat with traditional elders

Figure 10.4c: Elders dance around Xanana Gusmão (centre) after the ceremony

Photos: John Braithwaite

While these reconciliations doubtless did contribute to the successful reintegration of refugees and the ending of gang fighting, the decisive contribution was generous payouts after the shooting of President Ramos-Horta to those living in the refugee camps that were the focus of so much of the gang fighting. Refugee families were paid up to $4500—a lot of money in Timor-Leste—in compensation to return to their place of origin and rebuild (Kingsbury 2009:207), and 150 000 refugees benefited, which was 14 per cent of the population. Much of this was funded by the European Union. Many national and international staff involved in administering this program said there was a great deal of fraudulent claiming, even cases of four different families claiming that a particular house that was torched in 2006 was theirs. In the short term, it was probably highly cost effective in freeing up donor funds tied up in expensive UNPOL commitments. The masses held when camps were closed were attended by all factions who had fought over those camps; they were beautifully conducted by the bishops as rituals of reintegration among those factions. Of course, resettlement was not universally accepted: Muggah et al. (2010:55) reported at that time that 3000 of the 150 000 refugees were still awaiting resettlement and many of those who were resettled went into transitional arrangements like burnt shells of houses.

In the long term, the whole package involves a moral hazard. At some future time of unrest will troublemakers calculate that the lesson of Timor-Leste history is that no-one is punished for violence and that those who lose their house in the violence are given enough money to build a rather good new house? In a society where the justice system is prevented from working, will elites draw the lesson that violence as a political tool can get leaders their way, and even be reputation enhancing? A senior Australian military officer put it colourfully in 2006:

> Xanana and TMR would never kill each other, which is saying something because there are a lot of people they would kill…TMR's offsiders would kill Alfredo if they had a chance…It's not a bad thing in Timor to have on your CV that you have killed a few people.

While the moral hazard concern should be pondered seriously, in this context we have probably overstated it. Leaders also learnt lessons from 2006–08 about the limits of what they could get away with, how they could be burnt by fires of their own lighting. The social capital of the dialogue teams that did so much good work in crafting the peace of 2008 has been consolidated for the future through a UNDP program that rolls them into the new Department of Peace Building and Social Cohesion, established in 2010. The strategy of the new department has four components

1. institutionalising peacebuilding mechanisms and procedures in the National Government
2. strengthening conflict-resolution capacity and mechanisms at the community level
3. enhancing women's participation and role in peacebuilding
4. conflict-sensitive development (Scambary 2010:34).

Everyday Rituals of Rebirth

Peacebuilding scholars have a tendency to focus, as we have in this chapter, on the contribution to peace and reconciliation of formal rituals such as war crimes trials, truth commissions and *lisan* justice rituals on the mat in villages (*nahe biti*). One of the things we learnt about how reconciliation actually proceeded following the seven other Indonesian conflicts we studied was the importance of rituals of everyday life (Braithwaite et al. 2010a). Following Muslim–Christian conflicts, these included a Muslim leader shepherding a group of his flock to the church to attend the funeral of a respected Christian leader soon after the bloodshed, Christians helping to rebuild the mosque they had burnt down, Muslims bringing gifts on Christmas Day to Christian neighbours, Christians reciprocating by attending the celebrations for Mohammad's birthday, folk of one faith welcoming with music, affection and piles of food returning refugees of the other, Muslim children helping Christian refugee children to catch up on the lessons at school they had missed, Christians returning to purchase goods from a Muslim trader and exchanging smiles for the first time, common kindnesses of everyday life where a Muslim religious leader picks up in his car a weary, old Christian man struggling to get to the market.

At the village level, we have also seen countless and diverse local kindnesses across UDT–Fretilin, militia–victim and other divides. Annette Field (2004) documented the importance to healing in rural Bidau of rituals, particularly weddings and funerals, which brought people together in feasts, sociability and shared emotion. Repair of 'wounded' landscapes and damaged selves fed off each other as citizens transcended trauma in remaking landscapes and remaking themselves (Field 2004:352). Field found sharing of housing as the homeless were helped to rebuild their lost dwellings was also important as the gradual erection of new buildings signalled rebirth. Loch and Prueller's description of the central importance of families in conflict rebuilding the *uma lulik* (shared sacred house) together has much in common with the importance of *gotong royong* (joint bearing of burdens through shared work) that we found in our six Indonesian cases of peacebuilding where churches, mosques and other symbolic structures were rebuilt (Braithwaite et al. 2010a):

> These reconstruction efforts bring together men and women, materials, rituals, leaders, and—most remarkably—community members who are in conflict with each other. The restoration of ancestors' houses is too important an issue to be hampered by ordinary human quarrels. Reconciliation of the conflicting parties is a prerequisite for the reconstruction of an *uma lulik*. The process of rebuilding East Timorese sacred houses has a psychohygienic or even group therapeutic function. People carry materials together, dance, sing, sweat, and laugh and thereby reconcile the family networks of 'wife-givers' and 'wife-takers' connecting the houses…East Timorese intellectuals have even suggested the construction of a national *uma lulik* in Dili as this might foster national unity and peace following the latest crises (Trindade and Castro 2007). (Loch and Prueller 2011:324)

Hundreds of *uma lulik* have been built across Timor-Leste since 1999, constituting local reconciliation through rebirth of cultural attachments. Susan Harris Rimmer (2007) draws our attention to quite a different ritual of everyday life that can heal—the birth of a child and the coming together of families and friends at a christening.

Census data from 2004 revealed a baby boom, perhaps in response to the emotional losses of the occupation. The fertility rate was found to be the highest in the world, at 8.3 babies per woman.[38] The baby as the symbol of both wound and healing is clearly at play in Timor at the present time (Harris Rimmer 2007:323).

Harris Rimmer's interpretation of this striking statistic is speculative, yet could be a profound peacebuilding insight. In the West, we speak of the baby-boomer surge after World War II as purely a statistical artefact of large numbers of young people serving overseas, unable to create children with their partner at home, then a wave of doing so when they return. Yet when those of us who are baby boomers talk with mothers of our parents' generation they sometimes speak of their children symbolising the birth of a new life, of healing after the sorrow, anxieties and privations of their war. And, of course, Falintil fighters in the 1980s and 1990s were few in number, were not overseas and were hiding among the people producing their share of babies. Tragically, so were many of the wives of Falintil men whom the Indonesian military targeted to compromise them as unfaithful, in order to alienate them from their communities and their husbands. This included the first wife of the Commander-in-Chief, Emilia Baptista Gusmão, who 'bore a child by an Indonesian army officer after one of the many interrogations she was put through to influence him [Xanana] to surrender' (Harris Rimmer 2007:329). The child later died. The aftermath of the razing of all the infrastructure of the country, houses burnt to the ground, every person employed in a waged job now unemployed, hunger because of crops unattended by fleeing villagers, livestock stolen and trucked to West Timor—this is a quintessentially irrational time to deliver new mouths to be fed. So we find Harris Rimmer's speculation about the fertility spl urge immediately after 1999 compelling. And we think it might have a practical peacebuilding implication. Harris Rimmer's (2007:323) paper focuses upon mother–child policies as a post-conflict welfare priority, especially discrimination against children born of rape by the enemy and the absence of 'official policies to deal with the needs of these children and their mothers'.

We see another implication that directs our attention to the fact that organising formal rituals of reconciliation is costly and sometimes can disappoint by opening up as much conflict as it heals. An alternative path for peacebuilders is to be alert to the naturally occurring opportunities for harnessing rituals of everyday life to the project of peace. So, for example, priests might be trained to reframe the christening of a postwar babe as an opportunity to embrace people who were formerly killing one another—in the church within this ritual of

---

38 This amazingly high statistic of 8.3 births per woman is estimated for women's lifetimes in UN comparative statistics. For World Bank data on Timor-Leste having the highest fertility in the world during the first half of the 2000s, see: <http://siteresources.worldbank.org/INTTIMORLESTE/Data%20and%20Reference/21988255/PopulationGrowth2008English.pdf> (viewed 26 April 2011). By 2007–09, the post-conflict baby boom had fallen back to 5.7—still one of the highest in the world (National Statistics Directorate 2010:53).

rebirth of the village and the nation. Where this is a baby born of rape, there are things that can be said in the church that might help bind the community to non-discrimination and to affirmative offers of support in the church for mother and child. Likewise with christening and communal commitment to the perhaps 40 000 war orphans (Harris Rimmer 2007:326), some of whom might never have been christened in this widely Christian country. Healing through the renewal of birth is just one instance of opportunity for reconciliation through rituals of everyday life. Our point is simply that peacebuilders can ponder projects of sensitisation to the possibilities offered by rituals of everyday life because they might be more potent and more cost-effective than set-piece contrived reconciliations at the local level, and even at more aggregated levels of the polity.

The Big Picture of the Transition to Justice

When a formal justice system is built from scratch, there is much to do. A legal profession must be trained and imbued with professional norms, professional experience and a work ethic. A rights culture needs to be planted and nourished. A multitude of institutions is constructed: layers of courts, from appellate down to district; an independent prosecution service; a victims' support service; police; prisons; a probation and parole service for reintegrating offenders; a forensic service, and so on. Laws themselves must be written, requiring a legislative drafting service. We have sought to give a sense of how fraught and protracted drafting a land law is bound to be. In the next chapter, we argue that an anti-monopoly law is a fundamental of separating powers. Timor-Leste's lawmakers have not begun to think about this yet.

As all this is being built there is a danger of legal formalism crowding out customary justice. The worst outcome is where the modernist legal project crushes custom before formal law acquires anything approaching the justice-processing capability that customary justice surrenders to it. A rule-of-law vacuum attracts the most oppressive of forces. This is a bigger problem than semi-organised gangs of young men resolving grievances through violence instead of through legitimate dispute-resolution channels. Anomie in which no legitimate institutions can authoritatively assert and enforce the rules of the game invites in totalitarian forces who insist that only their authoritarian revolution can install law and order. This is the history of groups like the Taliban getting a foothold in rural areas where disorder makes life unsafe in post-conflict contexts like Afghanistan. David Kilcullen has described the Taliban as an 'armed rule of law movement'.[39] The justice services Taliban courts offer are not just about regulating violence but also about settling destabilising civil disputes such as land claims.

The approach to this problem we have advanced is to aspire simultaneously to expand access to the justice of the courts and to the justice of customary dispute resolution. In the next chapter, we take this normative analysis further with the idea of vernacularising state justice (particularly rights jurisprudence) into customary justice and vernacularising customary justice into the justice services of state police and courts (Merry 2006).

War crimes trials can overwhelm a country by sapping the limited justice capacities of a people into processing the past so that justice is neglected in the present; this, we argue, can increase risks of future violence. More than that, prioritisation of formal justice can leave poor people feeling that the state does not spend enough on training the nurses and teachers that are their priority, because the state spends too much on training lawyers. Timor-Leste is a rich and instructive case study in how those dilemmas were debated. One reason, we conclude, is that much of the work of truth, justice, reconciliation and memory was done neither on the mat nor in courts, but within rituals of everyday life.

---

39 Comments at the launch of Mason (2011), The Australian National University, Canberra, 21 April 2011.

11. Transitional Social and Economic Development

The previous chapter dealt with transitional justice; this one deals with transitional social and economic structures after the conflict. Again we engage a networked governance and separations-of-powers lens upon the topic. We do not consider all the key economic development challenges—only those that illuminate the relationship between networked separations of powers and development.

Timor-Leste is very poor, though much less poor than it was when it was part of Indonesia, when the gap between it and the rest of Indonesia in per-capita GDP was cavernous (and where its meagre income was disproportionately captured by immigrants from Java and other parts of Indonesia). Since 2006, Timor-Leste has enjoyed exceptionally strong economic growth (with official estimates ranging from 5 to 12 per cent in 2009—the height of the global recession [UNDP 2011:17]). It moved past 22 developing countries that had been ahead of it on the UNDP's Human Development Index, grinding from a ranking of 142 in 2004—one above Sudan and two above Democratic Republic of Congo—to a ranking of 120 among the world's nations. This occurred in spite of a huge, 5.8 per cent contraction in the non-oil economy in 2006 as a result of the violence that took over the streets in that year (UNDP 2011:4).

Timor-Leste remains a subsistence agricultural economy that is forced to import large amounts of food, where the overwhelming majority of the population goes hungry every year in the months before and after Christmas (Grenfell et al. 2009; UNDP 2006:20). The argument of this chapter is, first, that the steady, impressive improvement on the Human Development Index is a result of some progress in dispersing monopolies of control over economic power, though much monopoly remains and monopoly power is proving a resilient adversary to a fundamentally social-democratic polity. Then the chapter considers separations of powers between the Central Government and the governance of villages, formal power and customary power. Oil is central to Timor's story and therefore must be central to well-crafted separations of powers in Timor. We find the Petroleum Fund has interesting design features in republican terms. Finally, the chapter considers donors and other international influences, using Cuban influence over Timor's health institutions as a positive exemplar. Outsiders can contribute to more richly separated domestic powers over human development, or they can diminish republican freedom as non-domination.

We argue in the early sections of this chapter that the mentality of most leaders of Indonesian East Timor was one of exploitation, of using the province to build personal wealth in the process of being a loyal part of Suharto's crony capitalism. Whatever their flaws, this has not been the mentality of the front-line leaders of the independence movement—Gusmão, Ramos-Horta and Alkatiri—or of the former student leaders of the clandestine network so dominant in NGO networks today; or of the many individuals in Timor's international support network. While the members of the international support network live wealthy lives in places like Australia, working for East Timor's development was not a strategic way for people to maximise their wealth. Timor-Leste's first three prime ministers all worked long days and nights while they served in that office, driven by a deep desire to reduce poverty in their long-suffering country. Their disagreements with one another—including disagreements over the politics of pluralism, and the old disagreements over Maoism versus social democracy—were and are disagreements underwritten by different visions of how to conquer poverty, which for all of them continues to be the imperative that matters most. Even at the conservative end of Timor-Leste politics, Mario Carrascalão, businessman and a governor during the Indonesian occupation, is a social democrat driven by a politics of poverty reduction. That political consensus—like the growing consensus for political pluralism, constitutionalism with a separation of powers and the consensus for more *suco*-centred governance—is a source of hope. In a way, the elite consensus is not only a social democratic one, but a civic republican one as well. As Douglas Kammen (2003:81) argued, Xanana Gusmão's ideological leadership buried the revolutionary socialist discourse that was prominent in the 1970s and built unity around an older master–slave metaphor: a vision of the Maubere people throwing off the shackles of foreign and feudal dominations forever.

While corruption is a huge obstacle to social and economic development in Timor-Leste, it would be inaccurate to put Timor-Leste in the same category as certain post-conflict African states that have been characterised as suffering from a criminalisation of the state. These are leaders who disagree on the past more than on the future. There is considerable disagreement between Fretilin and the Gusmão Government on whether more than 3 per cent of the Petroleum Fund should be used each year for infrastructure development in the present. In one of our interviews with him, Mari Alkatiri saw great importance in a separation of powers between the meddling and sometimes corrupt hands of this generation of politicians and the Petroleum Fund. He believed there was not yet the capacity to manage these funds well at the national or local levels. This is a big contest, but a healthy one. Western economists also cannot agree upon how to get the balance right between investing in the social and economic development of the current generation and savings for their grandchildren's development projects. It is a good contest of ideas for development that occurs within the context of all Timor factions agreeing on the desirability of having a Petroleum Fund that is constitutionally proofed against looting by any oligarch of the present generation.

Colonialism and Monopolisation of Economic Power

Many senior Indonesian military officers considered a period posted to East Timor as their opportunity to make a little pot of gold. They monopolised the coffee trade, retailing and other business; they stripped the sandalwood trees that became harder to find, though more valuable as they became rare. The mentality was one of exploitation, of using the province to build personal wealth as a cog of Suharto's crony capitalism.

Obviously, this was a failure to separate the powers of the military from self-interested influence over commercial affairs. So we see this as an interesting further dimension of the separation of powers problem that is a theme of this book. It has two aspects. One is military power that overreaches to dominate the commercial life of a province. The other is monopoly power, whether imposed by a military or by other means. Monopoly concentrates economic powers that should be separated and put in competitive tension. Dispersed, competitive economic power is the most important check and balance on exploitation of consumers. Any kind of highly concentrated economic power—whether in the hands of the state, the military or mega-corporations—risks domination of citizens and of states.

In the aftermath of the 1975 invasion, the Indonesian military seized central control of agricultural policy in Timor, shifting production sharply away from traditional subsistence agriculture and towards cash crops, particularly coffee but also rice and other niche crops. The military could extract most of the profit from cash crops in a way they could not from subsistence agriculture. This had a doubly negative impact on Timor's poverty. First, hunger increased because fertile land previously dedicated to diversified subsistence agriculture was converted to cash monoculture. Second, exploitation by the military meant that farmers lost most of the benefits of their labour. After the invasion, P. T. Denok Hernandes International was established under the nominal control of two Indonesian Chinese in Dili, but actually under the control of General Murdani and other leading generals (Taylor 1999:125). It took over the coffee plantations formerly owned by a Portuguese state company. A coffee export monopoly was then constructed step by step by confiscating the land of other plantations and the smallholders who comprised the rest of the coffee industry. The military enforced rules requiring all coffee trading to occur through Denok's regional agents. Other military rules punished possession of more than 10 kg of coffee and any transportation of coffee other than by Denok. Before petroleum, coffee was by far Timor's most important export; post conflict, one-quarter of Timor-Leste households continue to be involved in coffee production (Nevins 2003:687).

Then Denok moved to take control of the sandalwood trade[1] in similar fashion and other smaller export commodities like cumin, copra and cloves. Monopoly power allowed Denok to reduce catastrophically the prices paid to farmers; in West Timor in the 1980s, farmers were receiving six times the price for coffee that East Timor farmers received (CAVR 2006:Ch. 7.9, p. 14). When the Suharto family, especially the President's wife and his son-in-law Prabowo, noticed the profitability of Murdani's Denok monopoly, they claimed a stake in the systemic control of the commerce of the province, sometimes allowing Denok to run local collection while they controlled export marketing. The monopoly system shut down industrial as well as agricultural diversification. Prior to the invasion, Portuguese Timor produced some basic tools for agriculture, manufactured clothing (in addition to handwoven *tais*), household goods, building materials and food processing (Taylor 1999:127). Apart from traditional *tais*, these all disappeared, with the purchase of such goods integrated into Indonesian trading chains controlled by Suharto cronies/family.

The demise of Indonesian occupation ended military-orchestrated commercial monopoly. Understandably, therefore, neither the UN transitional administration nor the parliaments of Timor-Leste's first decade prioritised an anti-monopoly law and a competition regulator. There was precious little commercial activity to monopolise during the first decade. During its second or third decade, however, Timor-Leste will need to attend to this risk to its future. Case by case, the government started this process with the telecommunications sector in 2010. In 2002 the government granted a medium-term licence for Portuguese Telecom to launch Timor Telecom as a monopoly provider. The government decided in 2010 to undo this monopoly in light of evidence of much cheaper telephony in West than East Timor. Fewer than one Timor-Leste citizen in five ever uses a telephone (Grenfell et al. 2009). The irony could be that Indonesian telcos that are providing those cheaper prices to West Timor could in future be the firms that break the Timor Telecom monopoly and improve the quality and reach of its service to consumers.

Electricity is another service fundamental to improving investment in other sectors that is also cheaper in West Timor (one-quarter of the East Timor price [Moxham 2008:14]) and much more prone to blackout in the East. Electricity reached only 10 per cent of rural households in 2006 (UNDP 2006:2). Most people in Timor-Leste believe that their electricity supply is getting worse rather than better (Grenfell et al. 2009:20). In this case, it was UNTAET as the monopoly public provider of electricity that grossly mismanaged and under-invested in electricity infrastructure that would by now have paid for itself many times over (King's College Report 2003:205). This was investment that would have

---

1 Forestry generally seems to have been virtually unregulated in East Timor during the Suharto years, with a number of areas experiencing declines in woodland of up to 96 per cent (CAVR 2006:Ch. 7.9, pp. 17–18).

been made in any contestable private market for electricity. There remains considerable potential for poverty alleviation by tackling the inefficiencies of the electricity monopoly. Investment in Timor's considerable potential for hydroelectric power sits as a great opportunity for the future.

Other revivals of Indonesian and Chinese commerce in Timor-Leste are proving less welcome, generating some localised resistance, resentment and even violence. One small-time Indonesian retailer of pots and pans was murdered after he returned to a rural area to restart his business during our fieldwork. Of more general political concern was the secret approval of a US$150 million shopping centre and hotel on prime Dili real estate formerly used by the United Nations and Timor-Leste's security forces (Murdoch and Hyland 2009). This is the largest non-petroleum private project the new nation has seen. Jakarta tycoon Tommy Winata is the beneficiary of this approval, which was granted without a tendering process for the public land. Winata is widely viewed as the 'banker' for the Indonesian military and a large donor to Indonesian political parties. His Artha Graha Group is a huge Indonesian player in gambling, nightclubs, logging and plywood, hotels, real estate, information technology, insurance and banking. We interviewed one prominent general who was indicted for crimes against humanity in Timor who retired to Winata's payroll; it is alleged he is not the only one (Murdoch and Hyland 2009).

One associate of Tommy Winata is an East Timor-born organised crime boss in Jakarta, Hercules Rozario Marcal. These two men also share in common past links to Kopassus and to Suharto's son-in-law Prabowo Subianto. Before Winata's hotel approval, Hercules received government approval to build a mini-mart and swimming pool on the site of the former refugee camp opposite Dili's main wharf (Murdoch 2008b; Murdoch and Hyland 2008). This approval does not seem to have been implemented to date. Approval of this 2008 development proposal raised a storm, particularly when Hercules announced that he was interested in other investment opportunities in Timor-Leste (Wilson 2010). Bu Wilson (2010:153) has quoted a UN security source that Timor-Leste's Chief of Police, 'Longuinhos Monteiro has close links with Hercules who organizes his hotels and other arrangements when Monteiro is in Jakarta'. The reason this blew up as such a controversial business approval in 2008 was not only that Hercules was a notorious Jakarta gangster, virtuoso of protection rackets and enforcer of the Suharto regime whose thugs terrorised East Timor independence activists in Jakarta in the 1990s. It was also that Hercules had contact with and might have met rebel leader Alfredo Reinado days before he was accused of shooting President Ramos-Horta. Reinado's telephone had a listing for 'Hercul'. Two of Reinado's men who got away after involvement in the attack on the President and Prime Minister were later arrested by the Indonesian Government in Hercules' home in Jakarta (Murdoch 2008b).

While all economic monopoly is bad by the light of republican political theory, some monopolists are worse than others. In Chapter 9, we saw that a depressing statistic of the Timor-Leste economy is that the two largest private sector employers are both private security firms. We also saw that one of these firms was controlled by leaders of one of the most violent and politically powerful of the martial arts groups that terrorised the streets of Dili from 2006 to 2008, PSHT, and mostly employed PSHT members. There was also local concern at the political implications of Seprosetil Security's purchase by an ex-Federal Bureau of Investigation (FBI) officer to become APAC (Myrttinen 2008:12). At least this sector is a duopoly rather than a monopoly. The concerns, whether well placed or misplaced, over the political agendas of their owners highlight the risks of any kind of excessive concentration of economic power in sensitive or strategic industries.

A more positive piece of the competitive landscape is banking. While commercial banking is restricted to Dili, there are three banks competing there: one Australian, one Indonesian and one Portuguese. Three is as many as such a small market could reasonably be expected to support. These licensing decisions brought in from the outset the Indonesian competition so lacking in the public and Portuguese monopolies granted to electricity and telcos respectively. The three banking licences have also gone one each to the countries most likely to be sources of private sector investment in Timor-Leste. Prospects for nurturing from scratch indigenous Timorese banking know-how could come from the bottom up in future from the micro-finance sector. The World Bank supported village micro-finance as part of the Community Empowerment Project (CEP) and a Small Enterprise Project (SEP) for business loans in regional towns. CEP and SEP, however, experienced poor repayment rates of approximately 40 and 60 per cent respectively (Marino 2006:117). The most successful micro-finance initiative in terms of membership, and a repayment rate of 98 per cent, seems to have been Moris Rasik ('independent life' in Tetum) (Marino 2006:118). It used the Grameen Bank model of lending only to poor rural women, reaching 7000 clients through 10 western branches by 2004 and more than 100 000 in 2008 (UNDP 2011:36). It was supported by HIVOS (Netherlands), Grameen Foundation USA, AusAID, NZAID, USAID and several Singapore-based organisations as part of CASHPOR, the network of Grameen Bank replications in Asia (Marino 2006:118).

Micro-finance in developing economies should be seen as a crucial plank, in republican political theory terms, of a separation of financial powers for securing freedom as non-domination (Pettit 1997). Small economies need big banks to link them to fruitful forms of foreign investment. Big banks with networks of ATMs are also one of the elements that nurture tourism from their home countries.[2] Our

---

2   The ANZ Bank manager explained how promoting Australian tourism was good for his bank as well as for the economy of Timor-Leste. He took pride in the increase in Australian tourist arrivals from 3000 in 2006 to 6000 in 2007 and 12 000 in 2008.

interviews with managers of these big banks indicated that this was where their interest resided and where they had a sense of corporate social responsibility to contribute to peacebuilding.[3] They saw lending to the micro-businesses of the rural poor as a market where they lacked expertise.[4] In this way micro-credit is a check and balance on the bias of big banks to only take care of the big end of town, including bigger NGOs.[5] Micro-finance is republican finance because it is a dispersal of financial power and a corrective to arbitrary exclusions of access of the poor to finance.

This section highlights an error in Gough Whitlam's analysis of why poverty reduction in East Timor would be better served by integration with Indonesia. Yes, electricity and telecommunications are much cheaper for West Timor's poor than for those of Timor-Leste. Just as Timor-Leste has benefited from competition from Indonesian banking, however, likewise it can choose a competition policy that allows electricity and telephone consumers to benefit from Indonesian contestation into these markets. All things considered, and notwithstanding the challenges of economic recovery from the ravages of war, today there is less poverty in Timor-Leste than in Indonesian West Timor,[6] and economic growth has been faster in Timor-Leste in recent years. If small economies get their economic policy settings right, whether they are in Europe, Asia or Africa, they can draw in the benefits that big economies in their neighbourhood generate, without themselves being absorbed by those big economies.

Media policy is another example of this. Many Timorese still listen to Indonesian radio and some even continue to read quality Indonesian newspapers, drawing on the considerable diversity of the contemporary Indonesian media. Timor-Leste itself has avoided the worst excesses of monopoly that afflict the media in many other countries. There are competing newspapers and electronic broadcasters. There is also an Internet community of conversation over news across the border into democratic Indonesia and into the many countries where the solidarity movement has left rich residues of engagement with Timor's democracy. Information monopoly is not one of the burdens on the development of Timor-Leste.

---

3   One Dili bank manager we interviewed saw the three banks doing a good job of compliance with money-laundering rules as another important corporate social responsibility to anti-corruption and peacebuilding in Timor.
4   One banker said they nevertheless had an important role when micro-finance organisations came to them with loans by their clients that were so big they could risk the future of a tiny bank. The big bank could then negotiate to take over those lumpy loans.
5   In a crisis of violence on the streets, serving NGOs by taking risks to keep cash flowing from ATMs to NGOs who need to pay men with trucks to transport refugees to safety can be a crucial contribution to peacebuilding. The ANZ Bank manager told of braving the violent streets of Dili in 2006 with a suitcase filled with $1 million he carried from Australia to refill his empty ATMs.
6   Poverty is much less in Indonesia as a whole (thanks to the prosperity of industrial centres like Jakarta) than in Timor-Leste. But in terms of the Whitlam analysis, the West versus East Timor comparison seems the more relevant one of like with like.

New Separations of Local Economic Power

Chapter 8 discussed the World Bank and Asian Development Bank Community Empowerment Project (CEP)[7] as an effort to disperse economic power over development that was resisted by centralists of UNTAET. It was at least an early effort of the people of Timor-Leste learning to become democratic. Village Development Councils with equal numbers of men and women were established across the country based on 3000 hamlet-level elections of some kind (Ospina and Hohe 2002:78). Each subdistrict received US$25 000–75 000 to decide their own local development projects at the village level, with a requirement that half of them had to come from women's groups. Traditional leaders were not eligible for election—a policy not intended to undermine their leadership, though it was often criticised for that reason, but rather intended to disperse power through a new institution. The CEP was an impressively Timorised program that did not draw internationals away from the comforts of Dili. A majority of those elected were young, at least in comparison with the older traditional leaders. In observation of meetings, however, it was apparent that older traditional decision makers dominated and elected women were marginalised (Ospina and Hohe 2002:96, 110–14).

Ospina and Hohe (2002:88–9) undertook the most systematic research on the CEP and found it mostly popular at the local level because it was more participatory and inclusive than past development planning and supported projects villagers mostly felt were worthwhile (see Box 11.1). There were, however, many examples of waste, embezzlement and poor management of the program at the local level that were seized upon by UN and international NGO leaders who sought to discredit it. The CEP had to contend with top-down opposition from internationals and bottom-up opposition from traditional leaders—and sometimes former resistance leaders—who felt their exclusion de-legitimised the decision making (Hohe 2004). Perhaps a more sustainable path might have been a CEP that significantly improved the dispersal of local power without turning it upside down, but with a clause that made continuing funding conditional upon continuous improvement in inclusiveness and broadened participation of women, youth and lower-class citizens. It was a mistake of the World Bank to think there was a local governance 'vacuum' that it could fill with a visionary bottom-up form of governance. It might have done better to

---

7   The CEP was a successor to the Kecamatan Development Program (KDP) in Indonesia, but much more ambitious because it occurred in a context where there was no local level of government to support it. Indeed, part of the overreaching ambition of the project was to constitute a new post-conflict, local level of governance. The KDP has been transplanted, in modified form, to the reconstruction program in Afghanistan and the Philippines, to a KDP extension into Aceh post conflict, to Bangladesh and beyond. World Bank evaluation research suggests that poverty reduction has been greater in KDP areas than in control areas and that it has achieved some limited success in creating bottom-up demand for good governance and to stop corruption (Davis 2007).

start by providing resources to extant traditional and resistance power-holders on condition of future elections that would broaden participation and secure that continuous improvement of inclusion.

From a civic-republican perspective, the ambitions of the CEP were important. People not previously empowered to lead decision making were elected at hamlet and village levels to come up with local development plans that would be more than just decisions to build a bridge or plant a plantation. The idea (that has been more or less realised in Indonesia and elsewhere) was that village plans would be building blocks for subdistrict development plans, then district plans, until ultimately planning meetings at each of the lower levels would feed into national plans.

Example of a Community Empowerment Project in Afaloikai, Baguia Subdistrict, Baucau

Afaloikai (*afa* = stone, *lokai* = herdsmen), the most remote village in Baguia Subdistrict, is located on the slopes of Matebean Mountain (*Matebean Mane*). Its 1048 inhabitants live in four hamlets: Oquilari, Waimata, Buibela and Lena'a, the last two high in the mountains, a three-hour walk from Afaloikai town. The majority of the population speaks Naueti, an Austronesian language. The population of Afaloikai was exiled to Baguia and Watecarbau (Viqueque) for more than 10 years during the Indonesian occupation; in two hamlets, resettlement was not allowed until 1994. During these years, only guerilla fighters and the Indonesia army were in the area.

The people of Afaloikai have a very positive perception of CEP. They are unanimous about its positive impact and about the fact that the community participated actively in it for the development of their village. The village chief confirmed that community members expressed satisfaction with the program's achievements during both cycles.

The program has been very inclusive without distinction to gender or religion: men and women, Catholics, Protestants and animists worked together for the welfare of the village. Although those who worked received a modest stipend, this was not their prime motivation, as stated by a Catholic catechist:

> The community is involved in this process, people come to work on a self-supporting basis but at the end we receive a

small honorarium but it is not so much. For us the important thing is that we must do something for our village, especially as development is already a commitment for Afaloikai people.

The grant for the Emergency Cycle (R20 million) was used mainly to rehabilitate 4.5 km of road from Disoe to Afaloikai. The four hamlets agreed to use the funds in the reconstruction of the village road, and people from all four hamlets worked on the project, receiving R23 000 per day.

> In the first cycle the money from the World Bank was finished and we did self-supporting to finish our program. We had to do that because the program is for the community, not something else that only makes one person rich, but we do it for all the people. (OJT leader, Afaloikai)

According to the villagers, CEP would have a major impact if the authorities at the subdistrict level, such as the CNRT subdistrict chief and the ETTA/UNTAET administrator (DFO), made a serious effort to rehabilitate the road between Osso Huna and Haikoni.

In the second cycle of CEP, the people chose another infrastructure project: water supply. Again, the four hamlets agreed to work together, using half of the R40 million grant to the village. The money was controlled by the Village Development Council and each person working received R20 000 per day (about US$2). Local leaders and the hamlet chiefs supervised the work and the CEP Village Facilitator kept a daily checklist of the workers. The CEP noticeboard displayed all expenditures on materials and wages.

The project had been finished for three days before the visit of the research team and was changing the daily life of the people, particularly women and children who previously carried water more than 1 km at least. Now each hamlet has a tank and each compound its own tap. With the other half of the grant it was proposed that the OMT would buy a sewing machine or, if there was enough money, one for each hamlet.

Village Development Council members are proud of their position and believe the program makes a difference in people's lives. Their major motivation and satisfaction are working for their people and seeing progress in the area. The community trusts the program and supports it, even if the work is hard and they have to go to each hamlet on foot, sometimes returning very late.

The relationship between the Village Development Council and the other major actors in the village is outstanding. Council members discuss and consult with the *chefe do suco*, the *chefes d'aldeia* and the elders about their projects. This good relationship is in part the result of the election process to select council members. All the population from the four hamlets came to the *suco* and elected the members by a show of hands. Village facilitators (one female and one male) were also selected through a public meeting attended by the people of all hamlets.

In Afaloikai, gender balance is not an issue for the people. Men and women on the Village Development Council participate equally in providing ideas and, with equal numbers and pay, in project implementation. The was underlined by the OMT leader:

> In our village no-one has come to say, why just men come to work or why just men get paid because we have a good coordination amongst each other: if men come to work women also come to help, this is the reality of Afaloikai.

And confirmed by the village chief:

> In other areas women do not work as carpenters, only men. Here women know how to build houses and make other things. For instance to build houses: men have their one concept but women also have their own ideas and contribute to it...Women are working side by side with men for the development of their village.

Men and women have the same right to participate in meetings:

> Because now the situation is changing so women and men have the same right to be involved in the decision-making process.

The consultation and decision-making processes take place through public meetings organised by the Village Development Council. Everyone participates and gives their opinion. Ideas are noted during the public meeting and, on the grounds of these notes, the council writes proposals to the Subdistrict Development Council, where the final decision is taken.

> Decision-making power is with the people. The community decides what to do in the hamlet. Afterward the decisions are passed to the Village Development Council and then to the Subdistrict Development Council. (Village chief)

> Decision making by discussing at the village level provides the opportunity for all community members to be involved in the activity and strengthens the moral responsibility to participate and to help decide. (OMT representative). Ospina and Hohe (2002:91–2).

In the years after the CEP was sunk, all major political parties came around to the view that development planning had been too top down and Dili centric since 1999. Xanana Gusmão led the way in this policy shift. He saw a need to 'widen opportunities for the poor to organize themselves' especially at the hamlet and village levels (Gusmão 2006:i). Central to his rationale for this were checks and balances from below: local participation and 'empowerment of the poor...would also contribute to higher accountability and transparency of the use of public resources that are spent in their name' (Gusmão 2006:i). It is possible that in learning to be democratic, the development of rural infrastructure and agricultural development, where most of the poverty is to be found, would have been better served by developing local governance institutions before a national parliament, rather than after. Two elections at the village (*suco*) level have been held, in 2004 and July 2009. Under the rules for these elections, 27 per cent of those elected must be women and, in practice, in 2008, 28 per cent of the 4877 *suco* council members elected were women. Adding reserved seats for women, the UNDP (2011:38) reports 45 per cent of council members were women in the latest data. The 2004 and 2009 laws that enabled *suco* council elections embraced a hybridity of traditional and modern legitimation (Cummins 2011:91): traditional authority was both legitimated and coopted by guaranteeing a place for *chefe de sucos*, *chefe d'aldeias* and *lia nain* (animist ritual leaders and interpreters of indigenous law) in the *suco* council, while grafting the 'modern' elements of women and youth representatives. At this stage, the modernist graftings have not taken deep root: 'viewed from the inside, the *suco* council represents a very thin layer of "modernity" over what are essentially traditional governance relationships that the state has recognized and co-opted' (Cummins 2011:93), and women council members are mostly mute, though not always (Cummins 2010). *Suco* governance has no budget to speak of. Many among Dili elites continue to believe that *suco* leaders are too primitive and unsophisticated to be capable of good governance. So leadership ideals to devolve governance are being frustrated by urban elites; their ideals to modernise traditional governance by grafting gender and age equality are being frustrated by local elites for now.

Three-quarters of the population is engaged in agriculture, but agricultural productivity is low because of under-investment by development programs in remote rural areas. This policy error is now being slowly reversed and prospects for poverty reduction as a result are considerable. Fishing is also undercapitalised and under-regulated for sustainability. Decentralised development assistance to target the productivity of fishing could enhance sustainability and considerably reduce rural poverty and hunger. As with farming, investment in fishing skill development as well as in cheap technologies is needed.

Separating Powers Over Oil

Chapter 1 referred to Australia's aggressive negotiation with Indonesia and then Timor-Leste for a share of the petroleum resources offshore between Australia and Timor as an Australian betrayal of Timor. The Treaty on Certain Maritime Arrangements in the Timor Sea was finally signed by Australia and Timor-Leste in January 2006. Many have written on the many stages of those negotiations and whether they were an abuse of the spirit of the international law principles at issue—at the hands of a more powerful state negotiating with a fragile one desperate for cash flow (Cleary 2007; Drysdale 2007a, 2007b; Munton 2006; Neves et al. 2008; Nicolau and Scheiner 2005).[8] It is not the purpose of this book to add to or evaluate that debate. What is of central interest for our purposes is the way the Government of Timor-Leste led by Prime Minister Alkatiri established the Petroleum Fund with the royalties that are now flowing from the petroleum exploration in the Timor Sea.

We construe the Petroleum Fund Law as a distinctively important separation of power. In effect, it checks and balances the timing of oil profit spending. It makes it difficult for contemporary politicians to squander a proportion of the largesse from oil and gas sales that exceeds the absorptive capacity of their fledgling economy. The Government of Timor-Leste constrained itself initially to spend each year only 3 per cent of the value of the petroleum wealth in the ground that has been licensed for development plus 3 per cent of interest and other assets. Amendments in 2010 to the Petroleum Fund Law increased this to 5 per cent after arguments had been canvassed in an election campaign that somewhat more investment in education and infrastructure today would be a better investment for the future—a position that American development economist Jeffrey Sachs has argued in Dili in recent times. Whether it should be 3 or 5 per cent, why is this constraint important? Contrast the behaviour of Colonel Gaddafi of Libya in 2011, who used Libya's oil revenue to pay mercenaries from Chad and elsewhere to kill his own people, to pay members of the Libyan diaspora to show up at pro-Gaddafi demonstrations in cities like London, to hire terrorists to launch

---

8 Cleary (2007:xxx) put the allegation against Australia this way: 'The Australian government believed it could grind down its opponent by dragging out the negotiations for decades. Over the course of these negotiations, which spanned six years, the Australian government's tactics even involved threatening to block development that would provide vital revenue for the mammoth task of post-war reconstruction.'

revenge attacks on civilians on the soil of his enemies—all this after decades of waste of public monies to support his dictatorship. Fortna's (2008:63) data from 95 civil wars show that the effect of possession of oil on prospects for freedom and democracy post conflict is hugely negative. She interprets this result in the same terms as Ross (2001): oil riches allow governments to fund patronage that thwarts pressures for reform, to fund repression of reformers and to benefit from economic growth that does not depend on education and entrepreneurship (that can energise demand for reform). Putting most of the oil loot aside for future generations averts such tendencies to tyranny.

Figure 11.1: Toasting series: Australian Foreign Minister, Alexander Downer, toasts Timor-Leste Prime Minister Alkatiri after signing the Timor Sea Treaty, July 2001

Photo: Kerry Weaving/AFP

So how does it work? Timor-Leste's Petroleum Fund Law of 2005 mandates that all public revenue from petroleum exploitation flows directly from the oil firms to the Petroleum Fund. Then the law mandates the Central Bank of Timor-Leste, which enjoys legal independence from the executive government, to manage the fund conservatively, which means mainly government bonds. Only 10 per cent of the pool was available for higher-risk investments in the early years while the Central Bank was learning to be a prudent fund manager. Amendments in 2010 allowed 50 per cent of investments in equities. The executive government cannot withdraw monies from the fund without the approval of a vote of Parliament for that specific withdrawal. Before the vote in the Parliament, input must be received from the Petroleum Fund Consultative Council, which includes technocratic, church and civil society expertise. This report includes an estimate of the sustainable income from the fund at that time and whether the proposed withdrawal would exceed it. There are also rules about where and how these monies can be deposited. In combination, this regime creates considerable transparency and checks and balances that make it politically difficult—though not impossible—in a democracy for the government to overspend the estimated sustainable income. The IMF is also an important external regulator that produces reports on compliance by the Timor-Leste Government with its Petroleum Fund rules.[9] In 2008 the Fretilin opposition, with support from civil society and transparency groups, petitioned the Timor-Leste Court of Appeal, which ruled in its favour that the government's US$400 million mid-year budget was illegal in that it was greater than the sustainable income (ABC 2008). Oversight of use of the fund, as the key development strategic issue for the nation, has continued to be active by both the courts and the Parliament.

Jenny Drysdale (2007a, 2007b) has used the Petroleum Fund for a productive analytical engagement with the idea of the 'resource curse' in the peacebuilding literature. This is the idea that exploitable natural resource riches increase risks of civil war as a result of political factions seeking to use armed force to secure control of the exploitable resource. Drysdale's contribution is to argue that whether resources are a curse or a development blessing depends on the quality of the institutions of a polity. Our particular focus in this work is on institutions of separations of powers. Like Drysdale, we also see the Ombudsman, the Inspector-General, the Special Purpose Auditor, the Anti-Corruption Commissioner and the courts as checks and balances on Petroleum Fund misuse. Joining Drysdale in a specific way, our hypothesis is that if separations of powers work well in a polity, resource riches will deliver fiscal balance and sustainable growth that create legitimacy for the democratic governance that separates those powers. On the foundation of that legitimacy, militaries are likely to stay loyal to elected governments and eschew coups to exploit the resource fund.

---

9   See IMF (2010): 'TLS [Timor-Leste] has made significant progress on fiscal transparency over the last few years, as a result of a wide range of reforms in line with international good practice. These include: (1) a transparent and sustainable framework for the governance of the petroleum sector, with a well-managed, supervised, and regularly audited Petroleum Fund; (2) a relatively, well-structured, basic budget process; (3) adequate reporting of annual donor-funded commitments and expenditures in the budget; (4) use of a modern integrated financial management information system; and (5) an efficient treasury single account (TSA) that executes almost all budgetary transactions. Budget documentation is comprehensive, and quarterly and annual fiscal reports on general government (GG) and the Petroleum Fund are available to both executive and parliament in a timely fashion. New legislation on budget and financial management, procurement, civil service, and the petroleum sector has supported these reforms, while on the institutional side, restructuring of the ministry of finance (MOF) and, recently, the establishment of a new Public Service Commission and an Anti-Corruption Commission have been important developments.' On the other hand, this report is also critical that 'an independent State Auditor, while required by the constitution, is still lacking and internal audit is very weak'.

Aid and the Powers of Donors

From the beginning of the UN transitional administration, Australia lobbied for recognition of the exploration rights that had only just begun to produce oil under the agreement for sharing the Timor Sea bed Australia had negotiated with Indonesia. Australia complained to the Secretary-General about the obstinacy of UN staff in Dili (Cleary 2007). The UN Department of Political Affairs quickly realised that there could be no automatic transfer of this agreement to Timor-Leste. Oil was as big an issue as there was in the triangular diplomacy of Australia–Timor-Leste–Indonesia. Timorese leaders resented the way Australia recognised an illegal invasion as a step towards sharing sovereignty with Indonesia over a seabed that was not Indonesia's to share. When the UN Department of Political Affairs stood up to Australia, the latter backed off and Foreign Minister Downer agreed to the negotiations described in the previous section.

In terms of our analysis, we can understand this as the United Nations being a crucial part of a separation of powers within Timor, securing the Timorese from domination by a more powerful country. In times of transitional administration the United Nations has a special importance in domestic separations of powers. Moreover, the United Nations has an important place in all nations' separations of powers at all times. This might seem a peculiar conception of separations of powers: surely, readers might think, the idea of the separation of powers is about the partition of domestic sovereignty in a democracy where the people of that place are ultimately sovereign. International interference is an infringement of that sovereignty of that people, not a partitioning of it. This marks a clear distinction between liberal-democratic theory and civic republicanism. For the civic republican, democracy and sovereignty are not good in themselves. They are only virtues insofar as they contribute to people's freedom as non-domination (Pettit 1997). For the same reason, a rush to a democratic election months after a civil war to supplant a UN transitional administration is a good thing in liberal terms because it replaces international paternalism with the sovereignty of the people. It is usually a bad thing according to republican theory because a rush to elections before separations of powers are in place, particularly institutions like independent election commissions, political parties with platforms they have had time to hammer out and courts, runs great risks of an election outcome that will be discredited and recontested through violence (see also Paris 2004). On the republican analysis, such premature elections are good if what one values is liberal democracy for its own sake, bad if one's yardstick is republican freedom as non-domination. National elections are important to securing separations of powers that work in guaranteeing republican freedom. But elections are only one of many separations of powers that help secure liberty.

In 2000, UNTAET was more important than elections to securing freedom from domination by Australia for Timor's poor. For a republican, the test of the normative value of a separation of power is how much it contributes to protecting people from domination by arbitrary imposition. Republicans can therefore accept the United Nations exercising its power to stand up to Australia, even when that power had no democratic grounding in the sovereignty of the people being protected. Those people also did not belong to a state that was a UN member at that time.

More controversially perhaps, interference by the World Bank (an agency controlled by the major economic powers) can be beneficial on a republican analysis. Hence, in our discussion of the Community Empowerment Project, consider World Bank funding conditions that half the elected members of village councils be women and half the projects funded from women's groups. These conditions can be viewed as positive if the marginalisation of women is so bad that such bold steps are needed to begin to unlock the domination of women by men. In terms of liberal-democratic theory, it is more difficult to justify such foreign interference in local democratic processes and choices.

In developing countries, donors like the World Bank are an important part of the separated powers on the ground. Because outside donors are funding so much of the poverty-reduction work, their role is vital in enhancing freedom as non-domination. Again, there is a key difference between liberal and republican theory here. According to liberal theory, a person can be poor but politically free; by republican lights a poor person can never be free from domination by those with wealth and power to whom they must submit to survive (Pettit 1997). Of course, there are countless examples in the history of development assistance, including in Timor, of donors dominating more than helping to reduce domination. The republican remedy to this risk is contestation of donor power. Donors like the World Bank must have constitutions that render their power transparent and contestable from multiple quarters, but particularly from the people who are being served by its poverty-reduction initiatives. This is one of the senses in which the CEP was virtuous; it shifted power over project selection from World Bank offices in Washington and Dili to village councils in rural areas. Indeed, we must go further and say that donors *only* become a useful part of domestic separations of powers when donors render their power non-arbitrary by constituting its own contestability.

Donors frequently fail this republican test. In Timor-Leste, Australia failed it consistently throughout the 1970s, the 1980s, the 1990s and the 2000s. Australia threatened to withdraw its foreign aid in retaliation for Prime Minister Alkatiri not acceding to Australia's terms for Timor Sea exploitation. AusAID also cut off funding to Timorese NGOs because they publicly criticised Australia's oil politics of the 2000s (Cleary 2007). Alkatiri rightly responded that Timor-Leste would rather do without Australian aid if the condition for getting it were Australian domination. This was Alkatiri's finest moment. This is not to suggest that everything Alkatiri did in the negotiations was right and everything Australia did was wrong. Our point is that Alkatiri led the kind of contestable republican politics that is vital if donors are to be accepted as contributing to developing-country separations of powers in ways that are not arbitrary external impositions that actually reduce freedom as non-domination.

Useful contrasts for understanding the republican politics of donors with a place in developing-country separations of powers are health and education policies in Timor-Leste. If courts, prosecution, police and justice are the domains where Timor-Leste has put in a worse performance than many other post-conflict states, health is where it has put in a comparatively better performance. Improved health outcomes are one reason Timor-Leste is moving up the Human Development Index (UNDP 2011). In the short space of nine years, between 2001 and 2010, life expectancy in Timor-Leste improved from 57.6 to 62.1 years, infant mortality fell from 68 to 44 per 1000 births and the incidence of malaria and tuberculosis halved (UNDP 2011:21–2, 30), and this occurred on top of the structural improvement in life expectancy created by the ending of the long civil war in 1999. Much of the credit for this must go to the good governance performance of the health ministers and the senior Timor-Leste health bureaucrats of the past decade. One donor might also be singled out: Cuba. Cuba exercised considerable influence in shaping the steady progress of the Timor-Leste health system. Why was Cuba a more civic-republican donor than Australia? One reason is it was not a regional player and had no interest in Timor-Leste's oil, or in getting anything much from Timor-Leste. This leads to perhaps a general principle of republican aid: the most non-dominating donors tend to be faraway countries that have no regional axes to grind. As one senior Australian military officer with wide experience of many peacekeeping operations put it: Australia has done the worst job 'where we wanted to shape an outcome'. Small countries also tend to be less dominating than major powers that have interests in constituting a new state as a compliant member of the world order they dominate.

The history of Cuba's engagement with health system improvement in Timor-Leste is particularly paradoxical. In interviews, we were told that when Fidel Castro met with the leadership of CNRT after 1999, he said he felt bad that he had given so much support to so many unsuccessful or corrupted revolutionary movements while giving none to a Timor-Leste that actually had a successful revolution. Castro said he wanted to make up for this with support Timor-Leste's leaders thought would be useful. In the short term, that support became 300 Cuban doctors to take the places of the Indonesian doctors who had fled, followed by scholarships for 600 Timorese to study medicine and other health sciences in

Cuba. Cuba also helped Timor-Leste institutionalise the training of its own new generation of doctors, nurses, and hospital and health centre administrators for its 65 Community Health Centres and 175 health posts (Anderson 2007:73). Cuba thus supported the right of Timorese to health; it exerted benign influence over health policy; it did so by serving the legitimate leaders of Timor-Leste; it did not seek to take over.

Ninety per cent of East Timor's schools were burnt in 1999; 88 per cent of the teachers who taught in them were non-Timorese and comparatively privileged employees of the Indonesian state who mostly fled to West Timor. Collier and Hoeffler (2000:23) found that increasing secondary school enrolment for males by 10 per cent above the global median reduces the risk of the onset of war by 30 per cent from the median risk of war. Previous generations of children had missed education in the decades of fighting before 1999. Yet education never shut down and Timor-Leste did not have to build educational institutions from scratch because of the role of one non-state institution in its separation of powers over education policy and practice: the Church. The Catholic Church made a great contribution to the education of the 1975 generation of Timorese leaders (Hill 2002). The quality of that education reverberates in the formidable intellects and the breadth of sophistication of these leaders.

While the Catholic Church in Timor-Leste is highly indigenised, a considerable part of its educational excellence can be attributed to the fact that it is a global institution that draws teachers and donor funds from around the world to support education in an impoverished Catholic enclave like Timor-Leste. In a number of countries in the South-West Pacific, and in other Indonesian provinces like West Papua, state education systems are corrupt and teachers often take their pay packet without turning up to school—as happened a lot in Indonesian East Timor. Yet operating in parallel with them across the region are church and Islamic education systems where teachers do turn up for classes and where the dedication and quality of education are high. This situation gives donors who wish to support the education of a future leadership for a poor country an alternative to pouring funds into a leaking, corrupt state system. In a place of utter educational failure like West Papua, this can be done by supporting educationally excellent Islamic schools, Protestant schools and Catholic schools. Among the educationally disadvantaged indigenous minority children of the Chittagong Hills Tracts of Bangladesh, where the Peacebuilding Compared project is currently in the field, one of the best ways—almost certainly, the best way—of donors supporting improved educational outcomes is to support Buddhist schools (that accept non-Buddhist indigenous children).

Put another way, our point is that the separation of powers between the state and religious institutions opens a path for donor power to compensate for state failure. There is a more general point about the virtues of opening up more separations of powers so there are choices for donors between more and less corrupt and efficient conduits for service delivery. The same can be said of the rich development of an NGO culture in Timor-Leste (Patrick 2001) with some 400 local NGOs. NGOs becoming stronger in itself contributes to separations of powers and opens alternatives to state funding paths for getting services to recipients. Rebecca Engel (2007:23) reports the number of NGOs increasing from 34 between 1975 and 1999 to more than 300 by 2003. She also reports, however, a mixed record of coordination among NGOs and donors to make their impact effective and a tendency for internationals on postings too short to acquire an understanding of the country to often call the shots over the heads of local NGO leaders. It was part of the philosophy of the Community Empowerment Project that village councils would become focal points for donors to directly connect funds to a locale without necessarily going through dysfunctional state delivery (Cliffe et al. 2003:4).

Catholic Church education is a good example of why a separation of powers within the state is an impoverished way of viewing the requirements of contemporary republican theory. Republican thought will be more relevant to the conquest of poverty and other sources of domination when it becomes more open to state and non-state separations of many powers, where civil society powers such as those of the Church, and foreign powers such as those of donors or the IMF, can also be constitutive of freedom as non-domination (or destructive of it).

Of course, a counter-argument is that when donors abandon the state education system hope fades for the majority of children who have no choice but to attend state schools. It need not if donors commit to continue to direct their support to non-state schools until corruption is reduced in the state system and until there is evidence of regular attendance of teachers at schools and step-by-step improvement in educational quality. Donor power can be used this way as a lever to improve the prospects of state schoolchildren being lifted out of poverty. Meanwhile, investment in the religious education system can constitute benchmarks of excellence the state system can aspire to when it commits to liberation from corruption. Meanwhile, a future elite like Timor's 1975 generation of politicians can be trained and generations of teachers experience what an outstanding school should look like. The members of the 1975 elite and teachers who enjoyed the benefits of a good-quality Catholic education are indeed now on the way to transforming Timor-Leste's state education system.[10] In 2001 the UNDP's (2011) measure of gross enrolment in primary, secondary and tertiary education institutions stood at 56 per cent. By 2009, it had leaped to 71 per cent. For primary education only it has increased from 65 per cent to

---

10   Helen Hill commented to us that 'under the Portuguese there were two types of Catholic education system: one good quality for the middle class; another designed to take away ambition for the poor' (see also Hill 2002:34–9).

83 per cent (UNDP 2011:111). Adult literacy had increased from 36 per cent in 2000 to 58 per cent in just seven years to 2007 and for 15–24 year olds even more sharply, from 50 per cent in 2001 to 81 per cent in 2007 (UNDP 2011:47). Health and education together have been domains of comparative progress (Sakabe 2008).

Vernacularising Separations of Powers

Sally Engle Merry's (2006) *Human Rights and Gender Violence* introduces an interesting way of thinking about how separations of powers can be brought to life in the interaction between the local and the international. In this chapter, we seek to turn its insights away from the soil of human rights and feminist politics where they germinated. We seek to use Merry's theory to understand how indigenous Timorese resource development can inform national environmental and economic polices and then the interaction between local economic development policies and those of global institutions such as the IMF.

Merry's (2006) book is a study of how local actors creatively adopt human rights ideas and find a way of channelling them through indigenous discourses to reshape social relationships. One of Merry's case studies is the reaction of the international human rights and feminist communities to the Fijian reconciliation tradition of *bulubulu*. The concern at the Committee on the Elimination of Discrimination against Women (CEDAW) hearings at the United Nations has been that *bulubulu*—enacted as a person apologises for wrongdoing, offers a whale tooth and a gift and asks for forgiveness—has been widely used for rape. After Fiji's 1987 coup, the indigenous coup leaders declared use of *bulubulu* for rape legal. Western human rights and feminist resistance to this fuelled ethnic nationalist defiance, even from Fijian feminists. Use of *bulubulu* for rape increased rather than decreased.[11] The upshot was that discourses of indigenous justice, human rights and feminism were all discredited.

Merry also describes a number of much more positive encounters between local tradition and global discourses of women's rights where rights discourse was translated into the local vernacular ('vernacularised'). The key actors in these accomplishments were local intermediaries who had a 'double consciousness' that combined logics of global human rights and local ways of thinking about grievances. 'They move between them, translating local problems into human rights terms and human rights concepts into approaches to local problems'

---

11 In conversation, Sally Engle Merry interpreted the tension as one of *bulubulu* working rather effectively, rather restoratively and in accord with custom in rural areas of Fiji. In urban areas, in contrast, it was captured by a politics of legal convenience that sometimes made *bulubulu* an easy way out that protected men in urban rape cases. These urban rape cases of convenience were what the international NGO activists saw and, reasonably enough, reacted to.

(Merry 2006:229). Another lesson of Merry's work is her empirical finding that global discourses (of rights) were translated 'down' more than grassroots perspectives were translated 'up'.

Lisa Palmer and Demetrio do Amaral de Carvalho (2008) provide a Timorese counter-example of vernacularisation upwards. They found that rural Timorese did not wait for the UN transitional administration, donors and their state to write land and resource management laws and policies.

> [Rather,] local people in Timor-Leste are making and remaking their own laws, mobilizing their customary practices and increasingly, 'performing' their traditions in public demonstrations of their extant capacities. In part, this process can be read as a way of enticing in outsiders, making them a party to the law making process, a witness to its legitimacy. Often critical to such processes, is the ability of local level leaders to draw in outsiders through their engagements with the idea of 'nature'—a concept which allows diverse interests to come together in conversation and build relationships despite what is often a dissonance in the meanings and priorities attributed to the concept. (Palmer and de Carvalho 2008:1321)

Palmer and de Carvalho (2008) show how rural people in one region of Timor-Leste held firmly to their ritual world of resource management. They then performed their rituals, as illustrated by the customary resource management practice of an annual harvest of the culinary delicacy of sea worms. UN officials, Western tourists and the urban educated class of Timorese state leaders were invited to witness the harvest ritual and other resource management rituals. One year it was filmed for television. Vernacularisation was accomplished through the 'power of spectacle'. Then locals invited the outsiders to interpret what locals were doing in their local ritual world in terms of outsiders' more global discourses of resource management and nature conservation.

Through the public staging of the annual *mechi* harvest, local community leaders sought to engage their guests in conversations about 'nature' and its protection, recognising the use-value of the concept of nature. Here the concept of nature acts as a bridge, an 'engaged universal' (Tsing 2005),[12] which allows local leaders to converse with both other Timorese people and the international community over local environmental protection challenges (Palmer and de Carvalho 2008:1323).

---

12 'Universals are effective within particular historical conjunctures that give them content and force. We might specify this conjunctural feature of universals in practice by speaking of engagement. Engaged universals travel across difference and are charged and changed by their travels. Through friction, universals become practically effective. Yet they can never fulfill their promises of universality. Even in transcending localities, they don't take over the world. They are limited by the practical necessity of mobilizing adherents. Engaged universals must convince us to pay attention to them…To study engagement requires turning away from formal abstractions to see how universals are used' (Tsing 2005:8–9).

In other words, their self-limiting resource consumption rituals were vernacularised up into global environmental management discourse. This is not translation of environmental treaties and national law down into local custom. It is a reverse process of locals asserting 'here is our custom; please appropriate it into your policy understanding of what will make for effectiveness in implementing the environmental sensibility and the conservation laws to which you are attached. Please incorporate our resource farming rituals into your national development plans.' They are saying to outsiders that they know outsiders value 'natural' and 'cultural' 'heritage'. So the plea is to allow them to show cosmopolitans how to integrate their local life world into global values. A practical part of this was engaging a Dili NGO, the Haburas Foundation, in a participatory-action research project with local people to document their cultural traditions and rituals that animated environmental management practices.

This seems a splendid documentation of the ritual and political power of the local to enrol national power and the global power of environmental donors. 'Rather than a romantic return to a bygone or even feudal era, this is about local peoples embracing change and opportunity on terms in which they themselves can have an active decision making role' (Palmer and de Carvalho 2008:1334). While Merry's work is about the global idea of human rights as a context for conversations that can build relationships between locals and cosmopolitans who might have rather different agendas, Palmer and de Carvalho's work is about the global idea of nature conservation as a conversational bridge.

Such productive conversations across such conceptual bridges constitute the local as a separated power and the national/global human rights or conservation movement as another separated power. On this view, Merry's vernacularisation of mutual respect actually constitutes or reinforces both these radically different kinds of separated powers. Conversely, a disrespectful contest where the two sides stigmatise each other, sticking within the terms of their own discourse as they do so, as with the *bulubulu* contest, de-legitimates and weakens the contribution both feminism and UNIFEM can make to the separation of powers on one side, and the contribution of indigenous voices and customary institutions on the other. Vernacularisation is constitutive of a republic of respectful conversation because it is constitutive of richly plural separated powers. The art of acquiring a double consciousness of indigenous discourses and global discourses of human rights, environmental protection, transparency and good governance, and so on, is something that can be learnt and taught. The getting of such wisdom counts among the more nuanced skills of the republican craft. Ideologues of global discourses often have globally powerful institutions like the United Nations, the United States, the European Union, the World Bank and the IMF on their side. This means in the long run of globalisation they have reasonable prospects of prevailing over peripheral indigenous discourses.

Prevailing through coercive Western imposition might be pyrrhic, however, delivering a form of compliance but a substance of defiance to domination and a politics that is neither republican nor respectfully conversational. At worst, as we argued in the conclusion to the previous chapter, it might lead to the people inviting in the Taliban.

Dani Rodrik's (2011) wonderful book, *The Globalization Paradox: Democracy and the future of the world economy*, makes a similar case for attuning development policy to the warp and woof of unique national economic traditions, discourses, institutions and histories. Rodrik struggles to understand why so many of the poor countries that have performed best during the past few decades are those which have rejected both the Washington Consensus and the Washington Consensus Plus, as well as good governance templates. Nobel Laureate Joséph Stiglitz (2002) reached a similar conclusion that the Asian societies that had bounced back best from the Asian financial crisis of 1997–98 were those that crafted unique solutions attuned to their own strengths and weaknesses. The success stories of recovery from crisis were the Asian states that most firmly rejected the disciplines of the IMF templates of that time. Instead, they diagnosed the specificities of the bottlenecks in their own economies that had to be opened up if development were to flow again. As the boom economies around it faltered in 1998, China never even entered the Asian financial crisis, just as it continued to grow at a stupendous rate by Western standards during the global financial crisis of 2008–09.

Rodrik sees a key to China's success in growing from near-universal poverty to overtake Japan, becoming the number two economy in the world, as being that it embraced globalisation in its own way, refusing for most of its long boom to join the World Trade Organisation (WTO) because it did not see WTO rules as sensible for China, just as it rejected many of the neo-liberal disciplines of the World Bank and the IMF. Rodrik (2011:150) points out that in the early to mid-1980s, half of all Chinese national regulations had an explicitly experimental status, targeted at dealing with specifically Chinese constraints. China embraced smart globalisation rather than maximum globalisation. Deng Xiaoping and other post-Mao leaders saw opportunities in globalisation and placed great emphasis on markets to drive development: 'But their real genius lay in their recognition that the market-supporting institutions they built, most of which were sorely lacking at the time, would have to possess distinctly Chinese characteristics' (Rodrik 2011:149).

We could say that, among other things, the institutions were vernacularised into a socialist discourse. Today, in recognition of Mao's failure to purge Confucianism from Chinese culture, Confucius is back in Chinese schools. The regime is seeking to help build social capital by vernacularising Chinese institutions in Confucian terms.[13] Notwithstanding this importance of vernacularisation to astute economic development, the more important part of the Rodrik prescription is to attune policies to the institutional specificities, and particularly the bottlenecks, that prevent particular projects from taking off in single economies at single historical moments:

> Economic growth requires a pragmatic government willing to do whatever it takes to energize the private sector. It requires using markets and globalization strategically to diversify the domestic economy away from natural resources. The specific tools and instruments needed to achieve this can vary and will depend heavily on the context. Specific recipes for success do not travel well. It is the broad vision behind them that needs emulation. (Rodrik 2011:148–9)

A way of putting the lessons of Rodrik's and Stiglitz's work into separation-of-powers terms for nations like Timor-Leste is that, though they are weak players in the world economy, they should not allow themselves to be dominated by the templates of the IMF or the World Bank in the diagnosis of their own economic future. They can of course learn from listening to advice from institutions if they wish to be able to call upon grants and loans from them. The IMF and World Bank have a healthy role in balanced separations of powers that shape development policy in a country like Timor-Leste, but one that Timorese should never allow to be a new form of post-colonial domination. The IMF and the World Bank sometimes operate in a republican fashion to separate powers; at other times, they have operated as dominating powers. Nor for that matter should Timor's leaders allow themselves to be dominated by China as the new regional hegemon.

Timor-Leste can draw inspiration from nearby Singapore, which once was as tiny and weak as itself and which now enjoys higher GDP per capita and better universities than regional powers like Australia and New Zealand, which were once thought of as role models of development wisdom. Singapore was far from a republican democracy during its journey to become a tiny regional powerhouse. Yet the World Bank's (1993) revisionist *East Asian Miracle* report concluded that Singapore enjoyed vigorous contestation where it counted for economic development. Separated powers of the Singaporean state, constituted from different fractions of its bureaucracy, engaged in rich and sometimes ferocious debates over the direction of economic policy. The political system might have been dominated from the centre, freedom of speech for political critics of the regime might have been crushed, but the economic system was contestatory (Pettit 1997)—open to contested Singaporean unorthodoxy from separated Singaporean economic powers.

---

13 Note here that in neither Chinese Confucianism nor Maoism is capitalism, and therefore social capital, affirmed in the discourse. So the vernacularisation moves both ways here: Confucianism vernacularises social capital into Chinese discourses and social capital vernacularises Confucianism into capitalist discourse.

Conclusion

This chapter has not offered a comprehensive treatment of the successes and failures of Timor-Leste across the range of policies necessary to secure the economic development of a poor country. It has only touched on key domains from agricultural policy to education, health, competition and trade policy, natural resource development and the environment, arguing that continuous struggle to separate powers is not an impediment to economic development, even though accountability costs can be considerable. On the contrary, a disparate variety of separations of powers is fundamental to economic development, as manifested in Timor-Leste. First, we conceived monopoly as a concentration of power (whether in the private or public sector) that threatens freedom and keeps people in poverty. We argued that some kinds of monopoly are worse than others. Particularly dangerous are commercial monopolies controlled by the military. These were dismantled in Timor-Leste but continue in places like Burma, parts of Bangladesh and many African economies. Commercial monopoly controlled by organised crime—which was part of the tragedy of privatisation of public monopolies in Russia and elsewhere—is particularly dangerous for the similar reason of combining power over violence and domination of commerce. Yet our argument is that all economic monopolies are a threat to freedom as non-domination. The poor of Timor-Leste have been much more disadvantaged than they should have been by private and public monopolies for telecommunications and electricity. In contrast, finance and the media have been less monopolised.

The Community Empowerment Project is widely regarded as a failed program by international commentators on Timor-Leste. We have argued, in contrast, that its ambitions were good ones in terms of creating new separated powers at the village level as a check and balance on Dili power, Washington power and Canberra power. It disappointed because Dili and UN power, as well as feudal power structures at the local level, defeated its republican ambitions. We suspect the current attempts to reconstitute village-level deliberation over development planning, which are seeking to draw upon the recent experiences of democratic Indonesia and Brazil, will be an important journey and a source of hope for realising the Democratic Republic of Timor-Leste.

This chapter considered the virtues of UN power, the Washington power of the World Bank and IMF, and donor power generally as having a noble place in an apt separation of powers. The nobility of such power depends on its transparency and contestability, particularly by local voices and local institutions—a feature often lacking in Timor-Leste's short history. Vernacularised power from the global to the local and vice versa (Merry 2006) was construed as a modality of respectful global–local contestation that has republican virtue.

The Petroleum Fund has been construed here as a distinctively important kind of separation of power. We saw in the previous chapter that powers do not have to be corporeal to be a check and balance that counts against the power of a prime minister. This refers to the discussion of ancestors as non-corporeal agents (whether real or not) that are granted power that in practice constrains in matters of justice and reconciliation. This chapter considers a different kind of radical rethink of the conceptualisation of separations of powers as occurring between generations. It sees the preservation each year of 95 per cent of the value of the Petroleum Fund for the control of future generations as a separation of powers between generations that constrains present leaders to spend only on those projects that have the best return for economic development, leaving comparable choices in the hands of many future generations of political leaders. Optimising that balance of power between the living, the dead and the unborn can be phenomenologically, epistemologically and technocratically tricky! Deliberative governance that embraces illiterate villagers and Washington economists in conversations in which each bridges into the vernacular of the other is the essence of governance wisdom for navigating these challenges.

12. Women in Networked Governance

We have argued that a theory of networked governance is a more useful lens through which to understand the independence of Timor-Leste than a realist one. Realism is based on assessments of national interest from the vantage point of those with political and military power; it discards the more diffuse evidence of what the weak are up to. A realist account of the creation of Timor-Leste is limited because it misses the significance of hope for freedom and the struggle for justice and the complex connections between local, regional and international people and groups working for Timor-Leste's independence. The idea of networked governance in contrast emphasises the need for attention to the way that those with little political or military power can create networks, often slowly and tentatively, enrolling disparate groups to work towards an inspiring ideal of freedom. In other words, networked governance provides a means of regulating tyranny. Timor-Leste illustrates the complex array of connections that came together to allow a tiny country to reach independence and also the fragility of these connections since independence.

Networked governance is organised from nodes of activity or interest; of course, not all the nodes in a network will have identical concerns or strategies and there might be deep tensions between them. The strength and success of a network depend on how dissonance between nodes is managed. Readers will have noted how few women appear in the network narrative of Timor-Leste so far; indeed, men have dominated the systems of networked governance we have described. But this is not the full picture. In this chapter, we explore one of the major nodes in the networked struggle for independence, women, and how they have fared since independence in 2002. We suggest that East Timorese women's networking provides a model of creative and persistent engagement. Women, however, continue to work in the shade of the more volatile charismatic male leaders of the country.

In this book, we propose a civic-republican account of peacebuilding in Timor-Leste, based on an understanding of freedom as non-domination. The greatest risk to human freedom, on this analysis, is being subject to the arbitrary power of others; the notion of checks and balances created through separation of powers provides a critical antidote to this risk. As we have explored in other chapters, a civic-republican conception of the separation of powers is much broader than the traditional focus on the tripartite separation of governmental roles into executive, legislative and judicial. In this chapter, we consider how the separation of powers has contributed to the sustenance of women's networks and influence in Timor.

The elements of a feminist civic republicanism can be found in the work of the eighteenth-century writer and campaigner Mary Wollstonecraft, although there is lively debate about her philosophical and political legacy (see, for example, Curthoys 2010; Mackenzie 1993; Maoulidi 2007; Pateman 2009; Phillips 2000). Wollstonecraft was concerned with women's self-governance, or autonomy, and highlighted the parallels between the arbitrary power of the sovereign over the people and the arbitrary power of men over women. The way for women to escape this domination and think and act independently was for them to be able to control the public aspects of their lives (for example, through economic independence and educational achievement) and also their private, emotional lives, instead of living as passive dependants of men. Some aspects of Wollstonecraft's advocacy reflect the confined social context in which she was writing, but many of her prescriptions to encourage women's self-governance and resist the domination of women by men remain relevant today. She argued for reform of marriage and property laws that treated women as inferior to men and for public coeducation; she also supported women being able to claim the rights of citizenship, for example (albeit tentatively), through representation in government. Implicit in Wollstonecraft's writings is the idea that resistance to domination and arbitrary action requires the separation of male powers at multiple levels—from that of the formal system of government to systems of control such as tradition and religion to those of family and affective structures.

This feminist civic republicanism has resonance in Timor where women's lives have been highly susceptible to domination. The social fabric of East Timor before the 1975 Indonesian invasion was staunchly patriarchal, woven from strands of indigenous culture, Portuguese colonialism and Catholic beliefs, all of which prioritised the masculine over the feminine (Hicks 2004; Niner 2011). Women were largely confined to limited, domestic spheres of life, complementary rather than equal to men. Women worked alongside men in farming activities, but they also were solely responsible for looking after homes and families. Customary law placed many restrictions on women, including their rights to inherit land and property. The traditional East Timorese practice of *barlaque*, or bride price, acknowledges the cost to a family of bringing up a girl and the economic loss created by her departure to her husband's family. Although it is sometimes said to represent the respect in which women are held and to provide women with some security, the *barlaque* system has operated more often as an economic transaction between two families that undermines women's rights (Wandita et al. 2006:289). In rural areas of Timor-Leste, this picture has not greatly changed today.

We noted in the previous chapter that overall health and life expectancy have markedly improved in Timor-Leste since independence. Women's capacity for autonomy has, however, been affected by their low rates of literacy, low representation in higher education (one in three university students are women, and of these only 20 per cent graduate), their extraordinarily high fertility rate (the average number of children for each woman peaked at 8.3 in 2004) and a very high infant mortality (44 per 1000 live births) and maternal mortality rate (440 per 100 000 live births) (UNDP 2009). Women in Timor-Leste receive one-eighth the income of men (Niner 2011:422). In this unpromising context, Timorese women have nevertheless managed to establish some checks and balances on male power.

Women in the Resistance Movement

Despite a history of entrenched patriarchy in East Timor, women became critical actors in the resistance movement. As many men were imprisoned or killed, or caught up in the fighting, women took on new roles. They maintained links between Falintil and the population and liaised with the Clandestinos. Women also performed more traditional activities such as cooking and sewing clothes and uniforms for the guerillas. They cared for the ill and wounded using traditional medical knowledge, and established childcare centres for children orphaned in the conflict, camps for the displaced, and literacy, health and welfare programs (Franks 1996:158, 162). It has been estimated that women made up one-third of those in both armed and non-armed resistance as members of both Fretilin and Falintil (Fernandes Alves et al. 2002); some place the proportion of women among the Clandestinos at 60 per cent (Cristalis and Scott 2005). Young women were active in the major demonstrations during the occupation—for example, at the time of Pope John Paul II's visit to Dili in October 1989 and the Santa Cruz Cemetery massacre in November 1991 (Franks 1996:166; Mason 2005:742–3).

Fretilin had made a commitment to work against the oppression of women early in 1975 and condemned polygamy and *barlaque* in its political manual published before the invasion (Wandita et al. 2006:290). Women set up the Organização Popular de Mulher Timor (OPMT: the Popular Organisation of East Timorese Women) in 1975 within Fretilin. The founding Secretary of OPMT was Rosa Muki Bonaparte, who had returned to East Timor in early 1975 from her studies in Portugal. She said: 'The creation of OPMT has a double objective; firstly, to participate directly in the struggle against colonialism and second, to fight in every way the violent discrimination that Timorese women have suffered in colonial society' (quoted in Franks 1996:158).

Bonaparte was killed by Indonesian soldiers on the wharf in Dili in January 1976 after refusing to leave East Timor. Despite this loss, OPMT provided a powerful network for resistance activities during the Indonesian occupation, coordinating physical support for the guerilla fighters as well as being a major conduit for communication between the fighters and the Clandestinos.

Falintil's commitment to women's equality diminished as the fighting against Indonesian forces intensified. Women had to straddle the uneasy divide between their right to equality and their central role in maintaining Timorese culture and traditions in the wake of the Indonesian invasion. One woman former Falintil fighter told Yvonne Corcoran-Nantes in 2006:

> Women never had the same rights as men. For that reason we created the OPMT but difficulties still existed…In the past there was support for change with respect to culture—radical change. In the guerrilla forces we had the culture of the *aldeia* and we were realistic not idealistic fighters. It wasn't that we didn't have our culture anymore, we had change but with certain limitations, that is, women have [family and cultural] responsibilities as well as rights. (Corcoran-Nantes 2009: 170).

As Corcoran-Nantes observes, this resulted in 'women [being] essentially complicit in supporting the very cultural mores which would impede the implementation of changes to address gender equality in Timorese society in the post-independence period' (Corcoran-Nantes 2009:170).

Women's bodies became a significant site of violence at the time of the Indonesian invasion in 1975, with a systematic campaign of rape and sexual attacks designed to humiliate and undermine East Timorese culture. George Aditjondro explained the sexual violence as a method for an insecure occupation force to prove its ascendancy over highly skilled guerilla forces (cited in Carey 2001:258).

Throughout the occupation, East Timorese women were tortured, detained, imprisoned and killed. The island of Ataúro was used as a prison mainly for women.

Women also suffered great sexual violence. The Indonesian army set up camps in various areas, particularly in the east, where women were herded together and raped over long periods (Carey 2001:259). Women who were active in the resistance—whether as fighters, Clandestinos or members of OPMT—were singled out for sexual violence, as were those whose father, husband, brothers or sons were in Falintil. Many women were kidnapped and forced to live with Indonesian soldiers, giving birth to children to 'Indonesianise' East Timor (Mason 2005:744). Women who were involved even in non-consensual sexual relationships with Indonesian security forces were generally ostracised by their families and communities (Campbell-Nelson 2003). The Indonesian occupiers also used other forms of humiliation against women. For example, in 1976 the

Timor Information Service reported that, after a skirmish between Fretilin forces and the TNI near Liquica, the TNI forced the female population of Liquica to work naked in the rice fields (Taylor 1999:81).

Sexual violence was again a feature of the post-election period in 1999. Systematic rape of East Timorese women in the West Timor camps has been widely documented, including mass rapes where Indonesian soldiers and the pro-Jakarta militias jointly abducted women and then divided them up as spoils (Harris Rimmer 2010:38). After a fact-finding mission in November 1999, three UN Special Rapporteurs reported on a sustained campaign of violence against women:

> Rape was used by the military as a form of revenge, or to force the relatives out of hiding. Much of the violence against women in East Timor was perpetrated in the context of these areas being treated as military zones…[as] rape by soldiers in these areas is tried in military tribunals, and not before an ordinary court of law. Under Indonesian law, for a rape to be prosecuted it required corroboration—including the testimony of two witnesses. Women lived in a realm of private terror, for any victims or witnesses who dared to take action were intimidated with death threats. (UN 1999, quoted in Harris Rimmer 2010:38)

There also were allegations of sexual assaults on East Timorese women in remote areas by UN peacekeeping forces (Charlesworth and Wood 2002:331).

The CAVR managed to document 853 cases of sexual violence during the Indonesian occupation, 142 of which occurred during the 1999 upheaval after the referendum. This included 393 cases of rape (46 per cent), 229 cases of sexual slavery (27 per cent) and 231 cases of other forms of sexual violence (27 per cent). Almost all (93 per cent) were committed by the Indonesian military and police and the Timorese militias backed by them, with 3 per cent by members of the East Timorese resistance. The commission observed that sexual violence was likely to be under-reported not only because of the deaths of victims and witnesses, but also because of the personal trauma of and social stigma attached to victims of sexual violence and their fear of being abandoned by families and communities. The CAVR estimated that the 'number of women who were subjected to serious sexual violations by members of the Indonesian security forces numbers in the thousands, rather than hundreds' (CAVR 2006:Ch. 7.7).

Another form of violence against women during the occupation was through the Indonesian national population control program, Keluarga Berencana Nasional. This became a method not only to control East Timorese women's fertility but also to punish those who opposed Indonesian rule (Carey 2001:265). Covert sterilisation and coercive contraception schemes were deployed to limit the number of children born to East Timorese women, particularly those in the resistance (Franks 1996:164–5; Mason 2005:744–5). It is unclear, however, how widespread this practice was as few cases of forced sterilisation were presented to the CAVR (Wandita et al. 2006:291–2).

Women and Independence

The terms of Security Council Resolution 1272 (25 October 1999) broke new ground in peacebuilding practice by emphasising the need to include persons in the UN mission in East Timor with training in 'international humanitarian, human rights and refugee law, including child and gender-related provisions…' (para. 15). The first regulation adopted by UNTAET in November 1999 also provided that 'all persons undertaking public duties or holding public office in East Timor shall observe internationally recognized human rights standards… [including] The Convention on the Elimination of All Forms of Discrimination against Women' (section 2). A year later, the Security Council adopted Resolution 1325, which called more broadly for a 'gender perspective' in all peace negotiations, including giving attention to the special needs of women and girls during repatriation, supporting local women's peace initiatives and protecting the rights of women and girls in post-conflict legal orders.

The original structure of UNTAET included a Gender Affairs Unit in the office of the Special Representative of the UN Secretary-General (Whittington 2003). The plan was abandoned because of budgetary considerations, but intensive lobbying by women's organisations, donor countries and aid agencies such as Oxfam led to its re-establishment in 2000, albeit without a designated budget line. Two high-level women UN officials, Mary Robinson and Angela King, also played an important role in the re-establishment of the Gender Affairs Unit after a visit to Dili (Charlesworth and Wood 2002:340–1). The unit established 'Gender Focal Point' officers in some districts and collected valuable data on women. It also secured some changes in UNTAET regulations to respond to the concerns of women. There were, however, some tensions between women's organisations and the Gender Unit over priorities for action (Charlesworth and Wood 2002:342–4).

Women's engagement in the fight for freedom gave them a sense of equality with men and they were reluctant to return to their traditional roles at the end of the occupation.

Planning for independence gave East Timorese women hope that their role in the resistance would be acknowledged in both formal and practical structures of equality. East Timorese women who returned from overseas after the occupation also brought with them strong views on sex equality (see interviews recorded in Carey 2001). The hope of recognition of women's rights was, however, in tension with the goal of 'normalisation' after the lengthy conflict, which often meant, especially in rural areas, the strengthening of patriarchal traditions and customary systems (Corcoran-Nantes 2009:168). There were also UNTAET decisions that inadvertently disadvantaged women—for example, the decision to designate Portuguese as the official language of Timor-Leste affected women more than men as five times the number of men than women spoke Portuguese (Corcoran-Nantes 2009:168).

A range of women's organisations has emerged in Timor-Leste, with some tensions between those focusing on the protection of women and promotion of traditional female skills such as weaving and those more explicitly demanding recognition of women's rights. For example, OPMT had been forced to project an apolitical image in order to survive the Indonesian occupation, emphasising the promotion of traditional women's occupations. In 1998 the Organização de Mulher Timor (OMT: Organisation of East Timorese Women) was formed at the same time as the CNRT, and was open to women from all political camps, with an explicitly feminist agenda for equality. Another leading organisation, Fokupers, was established in 1997 and focused on women's health, support for victims of domestic violence and education against violence. The Alola Foundation was set up in 2001 by Kirsty Sword Gusmão, the Australian wife of Xanana, named after the young woman held by militias in West Timor referred to in Chapter 10.

Fifteen women's organisations came together to form Rede Feto Timor Lorosae (the East Timorese Women's Network) in 2000. In June of that year, Rede organised the first Congress of Women of Timor Lorosae, in Dili, attracting 400 women from all parts of Timor-Leste. One aim of this meeting was to influence the CNRT to support women's rights. The congress adopted a National Plan for Action, which called for greater openness and accountability in government, broad consultation on a constitution, resources for women's training for public life, greater representation of women in the National Consultative Council that had been created by UNTAET (reconstituted as the National Council in July 2000), a minimum of 30 per cent women in all parts of the transitional government, and an education campaign on domestic violence. Special Representative Sergio Vieira de Mello took the congress's program seriously and circulated it widely throughout UNTAET (Whittington 2003:1285).

Late in 2000, the UN Gender Affairs Unit and Rede proposed to the National Council that the electoral law require all political parties to nominate a woman in every third position on their electoral lists. The idea had some supporters within the council, but was eventually rejected after advice from UNTAET officials that it was not consistent with international standards for free and fair elections (Morrow and White 2002:38–9; Whittington 2003:1287). UNTAET's Political Affairs Office made a further argument that a quota for women candidates would be unacceptable to the UN headquarters on the basis that it was a violation of the right to self-determination. These were weak grounds, given the support for affirmative measures to achieve equality enshrined in Article 4 of the Convention on the Elimination of All Forms of Discrimination against Women, whose implementation had been made an explicit aspect of UNTAET's work. Moreover, by this time UNTAET had already sanctioned quotas for women in the context of the civil service and in the Community Empowerment Project's plans for council elections (Corcoran-Nantes 2009:172). After the CNRT's rejection of the proposal, Rede and other women's groups petitioned the Transitional Administrator, Sergio Vieira de Mello, to reinsert a quota provision at the time he promulgated the electoral law. Despite his personal support for the quota, Vieira de Mello allowed the views of the National Council to stand (Morrow and White 2002:39).

In the lead-up to the election, Rede began a campaign to ensure that women were placed high enough on the lists of political parties to be elected to the Constituent Assembly, supported by a package of UN assistance organised by Vieira de Mello. The campaign succeeded, with 23 of the 88 seats won by women in the 2001 elections (27 per cent). Women headed up two of the 11 ministries: Justice and Finance. During the constitutional consultations, women's groups drafted a Women's Charter of Rights and obtained 10 000 signatories to it.

The engagement of the United Nations in East Timor and its commitment to human rights, however, prompted some sharp reactions particularly in the context of women's rights. In a New Year's speech in 2001, Xanana Gusmão attacked the 'obsessive acculturation to standards that hundreds of international experts try to convey to the East Timorese, who are hungry for values'. He used as examples the UN promotion of the concept of democracy although 'many of those who teach us never practised it in their own countries before they became UN staff members'; and the notion of gender, although 'many of the women who attend the workshops know that in their countries this issue is no example for others'. Gusmão continued:

> It might sound as though I am speaking against these noble values of participation. I do not mind if it happens in the democratic minds of the people. What seems to be absurd is that we absorb standards just to pretend we look like a democratic society and please our masters of independence. What concerns me is the non-critical absorption of [universal] standards…[and] that the East Timorese may become detached from their reality and, above all, try to copy something which is not yet clearly understood by them. (Quoted in Charlesworth and Wood 2002:335)

Although he acknowledged the value of some international human rights standards in Timor-Leste, Gusmão's speech implied that East Timorese culture did not have an affinity with international standards on women's rights, particularly the right of women to determine their own lives.

Activism by women's organisations nevertheless had a direct effect on the text of the Constitution, adopted in 2002. It provides that one of the fundamental objectives of Timor-Leste is 'to create, promote and guarantee the effective equality of opportunities between women and men' (Article 6). Article 16 contains a general guarantee of equality and prohibits discrimination on a number of grounds, including marital status and gender. Article 17 then declares that: 'Women and men shall have the same rights and duties in all areas of family life and political, economic, social and cultural life.' And Article 39(3) states that: 'Marriage shall be based upon free consent by the parties and on terms of full equality of rights between spouses, in accordance with the law.'

Also significant for women is that the Constitution gives international law considerable status: Article 9 provides that general or customary principles of international law are part of the East Timorese legal system; and that once treaties are ratified, their provisions become part of the domestic law, invalidating any contrary domestic laws. This means that Timor-Leste's accession to the Convention on the Elimination of All Forms of Discrimination against Women (CEDAW) in December 2002 in theory brings its broad prohibitions of discrimination directly into the national legal system. An unclear jurisprudence has, however, developed over the past decade in Timorese courts about the relationship of international human rights instruments to domestic law, making CEDAW's legal status uncertain.[1] Its provisions have not yet been invoked in Timorese courts.

The CAVR's mandate, set out in UN Regulation 2001/10, called for a gender perspective to be integrated into all aspects of CAVR's work. One requirement was that 30 per cent of national and regional commissioners be women and that community-based panels that mediated reconciliation hearings have an 'appropriate gender representation'. Two of the seven CAVR commissioners were women, Olandina Caeiro and Isabel Guterres, and 10 of 28 regional commissioners (Wandita et al. 2006:294). CAVR formed a research team devoted to women and held a national public hearing on women in the conflict over two days in April 2003; it also formed partnerships with a range of East Timorese women's groups—for example, to deliver services as part of CAVR's collective reparations project. Women were under-represented in CAVR's process of taking statements (21 per cent), but the CAVR made considerable efforts to

---

[1] This point was made by the UN Committee on the Elimination of Discrimination against Women in its concluding observations on Timor-Leste's first report (CEDAW 2009:paras 15–16).

include women's lives in other aspects of its work. It invited more women than men to attend healing workshops at which cash grants were distributed (Wandita et al. 2006). CAVR's final report in 2006 listed gender as one of the five guiding principles of its proposed reparations program (the others were feasibility, accessibility, empowerment and prioritisation based on need). It also recommended that at least 50 per cent of the resources for reparations be devoted to female beneficiaries (CAVR 2006:Ch. 11).

Women and the Struggle for Equality

As we have seen, Timor-Leste's post-independence legal system provides strong support for the equality of women. As in most societies, however, this has been only partially translated into women's lives. At both the public and the private levels, women have a sense of being treated unequally to men. This has in turn generated a lively and effective women's civil society that provides an inspiring model for women's activism worldwide.

Quotas for women were in place in the local *suco* elections in 2005, and women were able to stand for the position of *chefe de suco*. This was a direct intervention in customary law and caused considerable tension at the time but now has been accepted. Yvonne Corcoran-Nantes reports that in the subdistrict of Lospalos, although some women were persuaded to run for election as *chefe de suco*, most eventually withdrew. One woman was elected as *chefe de suco* but stood down after community pressure. These events led to mixed emotions among women; some were resentful that their role in the fight for independence had not delivered any political gains, indeed that there had been a 'roll-back' in women's rights, and some were hopeful that the mere fact of women's candidature for *chefe de suco* signalled a change in their status (Corcoran-Nantes 2009:173–4). One woman, a former resistance member, said:

> Women who were in the resistance in the mountains fighting continue to struggle unto now [2006]. Women were in everything then, it depended on your abilities. Then we were all equal, now we are supposed to accept the idea that only men can make the decisions and give orders. The women left the mountains with a different mentality. It seems that the men did not. (Corcoran-Nantes 2009:175)

Elections in 2009 saw 11 women elected as *chefe de sucos* (out of 442 *sucos* in East Timor) and 37 women as *chefe d'aldeias* (out of 2225 *aldeias*).

The 2006 Electoral Law requires that, as a minimum, one-quarter of the list of candidates fielded by political parties for election to the National Parliament must be women. This resulted in women being elected to almost 30 per cent of the seats in the Timor-Leste Parliament in 2007 (19 of 65 seats). Women hold three important ministries: Justice, Finance and Social Solidarity. In the 2007 elections, for the first time a woman, Lúcia Lobato, ran as a candidate for the presidency. Although women in Timor-Leste's Parliament were initially constrained by party platforms, there are some signs of solidarity developing among women politicians. For example, the Grupo das Mulheres Parlamentares de Timor-Leste (GMPTL: Women's Parliamentary Group of Timor-Leste), a women's caucus, has been formed among politicians from all parties forming a network across political divides. GMPTL formed the Gender Resource Centre in 2009, funded by UNIFEM and UNDP. At the same time, observers have noted tensions between the leading women's NGOs, the OPMT and the OMT, because of their alignment with competing political factions, illustrating the influence of the male political realm on the women's movement (Niner 2011:427).

Despite the vexed history of the Gender Affairs Unit in UNTAET, described above, it provided an influential precedent for the newly independent government, which set up the Office for the Promotion of Equality within the Office of the Prime Minister in 2002 (Corcoran-Nantes 2009:167). In 2008 the Office of the Secretary of State for the Promotion of Equality was established and has encouraged implementation of Timor-Leste's commitments under CEDAW, although with minimal resources. Timor-Leste presented its first report to the UN Committee on the Elimination of Discrimination against Women in 2008 and met with the committee in 2009. While acknowledging the hurdles faced by the newly independent state, the committee criticised a number of aspects of Timor-Leste's performance in implementing the treaty. It was concerned, for example, that 'the promotion of women's human rights and gender equality has not been considered as a priority' by the government (CEDAW 2009:paras 13–14), that Timorese law did not go as far as international law in prohibiting discrimination against women (paras 17–18) and that women's practical access to justice was limited (paras 21–2).

Ideas of women's equality have met apparent acceptance at the national level in Dili-centric politics, but there has been much greater resistance in remote rural areas. Here, local politics of culture have limited women's struggle for equality. Domestic division of labour has changed little, with women, even if working outside the home, taking on most of the domestic tasks. In rural communities, such as Lospalos, women's work often sustains their families, with men playing little role economically (Corcoran-Nantes 2009:180–1).

The concept of gender—promoted by many international donors and agencies—is often regarded as incongruous in Timor-Leste. A Timorese member of Oxfam's staff observed:

> Traditionally in Timor, gender is seen as a male [sic] concept that foreigners are imposing on people as a trade off for support in terms of funding and technical assistance. Along with terms such as 'human rights' and 'democracy' the term gender sits on a bookshelf with a donor logo plastered on the front. (Quoted in Corcoran-Nantes 2009: 169)

We were told in interviews in Timor-Leste that women often experienced an increase in abuse after they had attended gender workshops. Corcoran-Nantes's study of the district of Lospalos shows the complexities of changing traditional practices: 'in a difficult period of political, social and economic reconstruction, the reinstitution of cultural conservatism and traditional cultural attitudes led to the prioritisation of a system of gender relations which had persisted for generations' (p. 176). A 2004 survey of knowledge of law and justice in Timor-Leste recorded that a majority supported women's rights to land, although there was opposition to this among younger men and those in rural areas, on the basis that traditional law requires that men make decisions about property (USAID and Asia Foundation 2004:75).

We have seen that violence against women was a major feature of the Indonesian occupation of East Timor and of the post-election violence in 1999. The upheavals since independence have increased women's vulnerability to sexual abuse, especially through being confined in temporary camps in West Timor (Harris Rimmer 2010). But, above all, domestic violence has become a major concern for women, exacerbated by unemployment and economic difficulties. Domestic violence is often associated with the practice of *barlaque*, as paying a bride price to a woman's family is often regarded by men as giving them control over a woman. Indeed, a man's violence against his wife is sometimes referred to as 'beating his *barlaque*' (Corcoran-Nantes 2009:178–9).

The Judicial System Monitoring Programme (JSMP) has documented the obstacles facing women who report domestic violence to the police. These include pressure from families and husbands to withdraw complaints; and the sense of police and prosecutors that domestic violence is a private matter best handled within the family. At the same time, programs to train the police in dealing with gender violence have increased their sensitivity to these issues. The JSMP noted that almost half the criminal hearings in the Dili District Court in a two-month period of close observation in 2003 concerned sexual violence. Most of these were delayed or postponed, however, and only a small number went to trial. No domestic violence cases proceeded to trial. This situation has since improved, but violence against women is still regarded as less serious than other forms of violence (Bere 2005).

A 2004 survey of knowledge of law and justice in Timor-Leste reported that, while three-quarters of the respondents regarded domestic violence as unacceptable, a majority viewed domestic violence as a 'family matter', most appropriately dealt with through the *adat* process, rather than the formal court system. Most respondents, however, thought that rape should be dealt with in a court (USAID and Asia Foundation 2004:75). In 2009 the Parliament adopted a law against domestic violence, and amendments to the Penal Code criminalised most sexual crimes. The efficacy of these legal reforms has been challenged, however, because of entrenched attitudes by the courts. For example, JSMP's 2010 report on the justice sector includes an analysis of a case of severe domestic violence in the Oecussi District Court in which a judge simply fined a man for his long-term beating of his wife, rather than using the more serious penalty of imprisonment allowed for in the Penal Code (JSMP 2010:17–18).

Corcoran-Nantes's work in Lospalos shows that traditional culture in some parts of Timor-Leste accepts a husband's right to chastise his wife for failing in her domestic duties, and the line between chastisement and domestic violence is often blurred. She observed that *chefe de sucos* in Lospalos resented the criminalisation of domestic violence. They argued that *adat* was a superior way of dealing with such matters because it allowed the situation to be dealt with privately and encouraged the possibility of reconciliation and the payment of compensation by the man to his wife's family. At the same time, there is some evidence that the criminalisation of domestic violence encouraged more serious treatment under *adat* law. It has also been a valuable safety net for women who were dissatisfied by their treatment under the customary system (Corcoran-Nantes 2009:182–3).

Conclusion

One legacy of the lengthy Indonesian occupation of Timor-Leste is a deeply militarised society which has accepted violence as a tool to resolve political disputes, as in the 2006 crisis (Niner 2011:428–30; Siapno 2008). This in turn has whittled away the space for women in the public realm. Although the Timorese social context has traditionally accorded little autonomy or capacity for self-governance to women, we observe in Timor-Leste a feisty feminist politics working to counter patriarchal domination, consistent with Mary Wollstonecraft's account of civic republicanism. Timorese women formed significant and effective networks during the Indonesian occupation. In the UN era and after independence, these networks have changed character, strengthening their connections with the international community. The focus of women's organisations varies, but the concerns expressed have been consistent since independence: they have argued for security within their communities and homes and for equality with men in the political system. The work of women's organisations has supported a series of checks and balances on governmental and male power. One result of this activism was the 2006 Electoral Law mandating that political parties must nominate women for at least 25 per cent of the slots on their electoral lists. This has led to a significant presence of women in the national legislature—far exceeding that of most of the major international donors to Timor-Leste, including Australia. Another potentially important check on and balance to male political power has been the creation of the parliamentary women's caucus, encouraging women to become more assertive in policymaking. The cross-party linkages formed in the GMPTL might allow issues of women and gender to be supported across the legislature.

At the same time, the centralisation of national politics in Dili has left local political structures more powerful, allowing claims of culture to trump those of women's rights in rural areas, where the majority of the population lives (Corcoran-Nantes 2009:183). The situation of women in modern Timor-Leste is affected by local traditions and customs. *Barlaque* remains particularly significant in rural areas. Although change is slow, ideas about women's rights are trickling into rural communities, gradually changing the agenda and the vision of what is possible.

Women's groups have also been at the forefront of campaigns to deal with accountability and reparations for the violence during the occupation. There have been two major women's congresses held since independence: in July 2004 and June 2008. The 2004 congress sought the creation of a special international tribunal to deal with the sexual violence that occurred during the occupation, indicating that women are more interested than the Timor-Leste political leadership in accountability. Certainly, women's concerns for reparations for the harms of the occupation have so far been left unmet (Wandita et al. 2006). Both congresses called for better access for women to the court system, the elimination of violence against women through proper implementation of laws and justice for women who were involved in the resistance struggle. The question of reparations on the parliamentary agenda has, however, been overshadowed by the recognition and rights of veterans and ex-combatants. Political leaders confine these categories to the men in the resistance movement and women have been left out of all formal disarmament, demobilisation and reintegration programs (Niner 2011:424–5). This blindness to the involvement of Timorese women in the struggle against Indonesian occupation is pervasive. For example, an International Crisis Group report in November 2011 on the political role of veterans in Timor assumed that all veterans were men (ICG 2011).

Timorese women have been adept at marshalling the support of the international community for their campaigns against male domination, creating global networks that assist in checking and balancing male power. The criticism of Timor-Leste's implementation of the CEDAW by the UN Committee on the Elimination of Discrimination against Women in 2009 provides a useful agenda for action and activism before the second periodic report is due in 2012. Proposals made by the UN Committee include the clarification of the status of international human rights treaties within the Timorese legal system (CEDAW 2009:para. 16), the use of quotas for women in the judiciary and the civil service, particularly the foreign service (CEDAW 2009:para. 26), and the strengthening of domestic violence laws (CEDAW 2009:para. 30). The election of a Timorese woman, Maria Helena Pires, a founding member of Rede, to the UN Committee in 2010 will increase the prominence of international standards of equality.

Mary Wollstonecraft's vision of a society where both women and men are equally self-governing and able to resist arbitrary power has still not been realised anywhere. Feminist struggles across the world demonstrate that concentrations of male power are remarkably resilient, regrouping to resist change and making it difficult to consolidate advances for women. The case of Timor-Leste, however, suggests that it is possible for committed networks to devise checks and balances on patriarchal power that, while fragile, can increase the chance of securing women's autonomy.

13. Republican Networked Governance of Transition

The concept of realpolitik [is] the denial of the individual conscience, the death of the conscience of a people.

— Xanana Gusmão, Defence Plea, 17 May 1993 (Jardine 1995:65)

Australian strategic planners initially named the peacekeeping force IFET: International Force East Timor. They were soon told that IFET already existed; it was the International Federation for East Timor, a global coalition of activists who had campaigned for East Timorese self-determination for years. Even at the very end, strategists were unaware of the powerful forces that had propelled them into a policy reversal. They renamed their force INTERFET (Fernandes 2008:95).

Learning about Nonviolence from Timor-Leste

This book has explored how realism was defeated by a politics of hope for Timor-Leste. It shows how sinews were given to that hope by demonstrating a credible capability for armed resistance. Yet real progress flowed from opting for a politics of nonviolence as the principal axis of struggle that utterly rejected terrorism and racial or religious stigmatisation of the enemy and embraced that enemy reintegratively in victory. Its internal history of greater success when it relied more heavily on networked nonviolence contributes to the growing literature showing that nonviolence has a better success rate than armed conflict. Chenoweth and Stephan's (2011; Stephan and Chenoweth 2008:8) study of 323 violent and nonviolent resistance campaigns from 1900 to 2006 found that 'major nonviolent campaigns have achieved success 53 percent of the time, compared with 26 percent for violent resistance campaigns', while Abrahms (2006) found terrorism enjoyed an even lower success rate, achieving its policy objectives in only 7 per cent of its campaigns (see also Cronin 2009). The history of Timor-Leste confirms their reasons for this result:

> First, a campaign's commitment to nonviolent methods enhances its domestic and international legitimacy and encourages more broad-based participation in the resistance,[1] which translates into increased pressure

---

[1] A key moment here was Gusmão's enrolment of the Catholic Church locally and then globally as a crucial supporter of the campaign by pluralising the Maubere movement (embracing UDT), abandoning most aspects of Maoism and negotiating for the 1983 ceasefire.

being brought to bear on the target. Recognition of the challenge group's grievances can translate into greater internal[2] and external support for that group and alienation of the target regime, undermining the regime's main sources of political, economic, and even military power. Second, whereas governments easily justify violent counterattacks against armed insurgents, regime violence against nonviolent movements is more likely to backfire against the regime.[3] Potentially sympathetic publics perceive violent militants as having maximalist or extremist goals beyond accommodation, but they perceive nonviolent groups as less extreme, thereby enhancing their appeal and facilitating the extraction of concessions through bargaining. (Stephan and Chenoweth 2008:8–9)[4]

Note that in Timor nonviolent struggle and a reintegrative shaming of realists (Chapter 3) that ultimately turned democratic publics against realists formed the principal axis and the most effective axis of transformation towards a just peace, not the only axis. There was plenty of violence as well in both the independence fight and the peace enforcement against militias in 1999–2001 and gangs in 2006. One senior New Zealand peacekeeping veteran, who had also served in other war zones, reported that he was asked at a conference why we do not do away with armed peacekeepers and instead send peace-loving people (like the questioner) who are willing to go in wearing T-shirts saying 'I am prepared to die for peace'? He replied: 'Well, that's nice because I know quite a few warlords who would be happy to kill you' (Interview, February 2008).

Other practical elements of Timor's principled struggle for democracy were a clandestine network that supported the wider democracy and human rights movement in Indonesia, an international solidarity movement and international refugee diaspora that was once divided but then unified under Xanana Gusmão and a diplomatic front in New York, Washington, DC, and other Western capitals led by José Ramos-Horta and in Africa by Mari Alkatiri. The Timorese leadership in exile was a fine exemplar of a patient politics of hope supported by these ever-strengthening sinews of nonviolent resistance. After Nelson Mandela was released from prison in South Africa, Xanana's messages to the

---

2   The key masterstroke of levering internal support was enrolling the Indonesian democracy movement as a supporter by offering the Clandestinos as its front-line troops in challenging Suharto on the streets of Jakarta. Xanana's imprisonment paradoxically increased his capacity, and the capacity of Renetil (Timorese students) leader, Fernando 'La'Sama' Aroujo, who was also imprisoned for years in Jakarta, to accomplish this in conversations with imprisoned democracy movement leaders.
3   Santa Cruz is the key moment here. Almost as important is Gusmão's, Ramos-Horta's and TMR's difficult pushes to hold their fighters in cantonment when their families were being slaughtered in 1999. Unlike 1975, in 1999, Indonesian intelligence was unable to contrive and concoct a media perception that this was a civil war. The American people turned against Indonesia for the first time in 1999 because they saw the slaughter through the lens of a potential genocide rather than the civil war lens.
4   Ramos-Horta's and Alkatiri's long campaigns through the diplomatic front fit this point, the front's rejection of terrorism, rejection of racist vilification and revenge against Javanese, rejection of positioning the war as a fight for survival of Christianity against Islam.

Timorese diaspora from his prison cell (for example, his Christmas message in 1995 [Wise 2006:78]) communicated hope from the remarkable revolution in South Africa. There was a sophisticated subtlety to this politics of hope that could be reinforced when Mandela visited Gusmão in prison in 1997,[5] when Bishop Belo's Nobel Prize seemed to have some parallels with Bishop Desmond Tutu's. Xanana's secreted messages also drew on hopeful developments in places with histories as terrible as Timor's, such as the former Yugoslavia, and even the Middle East, to suggest that this kind of step forward was also possible for them. A Polish Pope who came to pray with the Timorese for alleviation of their suffering nourished that politics of hope in the hearts of young people who attended the papal mass and later lost their lives at Santa Cruz Cemetery.

The organisation of events at Santa Cruz in 1991 was morally flawed, but much less so than insurgency or networked terrorism. Santa Cruz had Gandhian overtones in the sense that people resisted the enemy not with force but by sacrificing their blood to show the sincerity of their cause and the integrity of their nonviolence. The assassin's bullets that ripped into Gandhi's body in 1948 instantly induced a shocked calming of the inter-communal violence that took perhaps two million South Asian lives from 1946, just as the bullets that ripped into Ramos-Horta's body in 2008 ended the 2006–08 period of violence.

Santa Cruz was particularly poignant because many of its martyrs were very young. So much of the international struggle for Timor drew sustenance from human rights discourse and the global movement for human rights and indigenous peoples' rights. Yet in the planning for Santa Cruz, there was undoubtedly abuse of children's rights by the youth leaders, and probably by elite adults of the struggle as well. Our research reveals blemishes in Timor-Leste's most inspiring patriots—Gusmão and Ramos-Horta—and in that other bulwark of competence and persistence in the struggle, Alkatiri. Post conflict, their reputations tarnished more quickly than Mandela's even though they eschewed terrorism more firmly than Mandela. This is because they were less generous than Mandela in sharing power, embracing all elements of civil society and strengthening the separation of powers. Xanana Gusmão's biographer, Sara Niner, put it more sympathetically:

> Xanana believed the unity required for the independence movement to succeed could only be achieved by leading alone, above the internal factions, continually brokering political compromise both internally and externally. While some may protest, history has proved him right. He became the man at the centre, often solitary, searching for allies,

---

5   Our interviews with Indonesian diplomats and former foreign ministers suggest that Suharto agreed to Mandela's unusual request because he wanted Mandela's influential support for his leadership of the Non-Aligned Movement.

and soothing grievances and grief: a middle-way leader to use Little's expression. However, this independent leadership style also fostered a propensity toward unilateral and undemocratic decision-making fitting to a military commander during a time of war but harder to maintain in the confines of a modern constitutional democracy that Timor-Leste now struggles to foster. (Niner 2005:40)

Adérito Soares's interview with Prime Minister Gusmão in June 2011 indicated a change of heart on this question. He said that a lesson he had learned was that young leaders for the future should have been embraced and blooded at the centre of political institutions much earlier. And he indicated a determination to put this right now.

Lessons about Resisting Tyrannies of Transitional Administration

The political histories of Timor's leaders are still being written. There is still time for them to become more effective in strengthening separations of powers and in bringing on a younger generation of leaders who will strengthen them further. There is some quantitative evidence that countries that disperse power more widely (mainly through a proportional political system and the 'inclusiveness' of the representation delivered by the voting system) enjoy a lower risk of civil war (Reynal-Querol 2002). When Xanana returned to the embrace of his people after the 1999 devastation, he seemed to be another Mandela (Wise 2006:80). For a period after that, the United Nations held up East Timor as a peacekeeping operation that had succeeded in creating democracy and justice on the ashes of mass murder. The Timor operation's image is tarnished now, but it is retrievable. The next chapters of Timor-Leste's history could be written as one from which future democrats will derive inspiration for sustained struggle against the forces of repressive realism.

Jaret Chopra (2002) was a distinguished, disenchanted critic from within UNTAET who showed that the failure to work at the separation of powers began with the failure of UNTAET to cultivate separations of powers. The most important blind spot was weakness in UN security sector policy that acquiesced in the police and the military becoming political power bases that were in danger of being captured by one or another dominant political faction. This allowed Minister Lobato in time to constitute the police as the best-armed, best-paid part of the security sector, functioning as his private army.

There were structural drivers of this UN failure to secure a separation of powers. UN peacebuilding faces a massive social selection problem. It attracts many idealistic people who seek a better world, but others who enjoy exercising power, who savour a level of sovereignty few of them could ever exercise at home. UN peacebuilding also faces a problem of being overwhelmed by the number and vast scope of the problems it has to solve. The best way for a UN official to perform credibly in fixing as many of them as can be managed during a posting of six months can be to fix them autocratically, as a UN autocrat who consults as needed with a small clique of local autocrats.[6] The trouble with autocratic problem fixing is that autocratic method makes it less likely that the problem will stay fixed in the long run. UN postings are not for the long run; it is natural for human beings to fix as much as they can for their own period at the helm, as opposed to being focused on fewer fixes that can be sustained in the long term. Pride resides in what is accomplished during our own time in the job. When that unravels later, we tend to blame our successors. These are tricky structural realities for UN peacebuilders to transcend. The Timor-Leste case shows the tragedy of failing to rise to this challenge:

> [S]uch missions can contribute to outcomes more negative than if they had not intervened at all. They may undermine indigenous forms of political legitimacy without establishing a reliable alternative and functioning administrative structure. They have often facilitated the strongest player in taking the capital city. It was a habit of UN deployments in the past to follow on the ground the line of least resistance, unable therefore to challenge recalcitrant warlords, or to prevent the largest factions from dictating terms of a peace process. This is why Hun Sen's State of Cambodia, that lost the 1993 elections, never gave up power. This is also why the Northern Alliance dominated the Bonn conference on Afghanistan in November 2001. (Chopra 2002:995; see also Barnett and Zürcher 2009)

One remedy is to triage performance evaluation of UN officials. First, we should continue to evaluate them on how many big problems they fix. Second, we should assess them on how much they have contributed to building local strengths in problem solving in the process of fixing them. That means evaluating UN officials in terms of the degree of collaboration with locals to solve problems jointly. Third, it means evaluating their work in terms of the contribution it makes to building separations of powers.

---

6   Chopra (2002:997–8) argues that this might be a problem of the diplomacy 'culture' of the United Nations as well: 'Not only was the Transitional Administrator not expecting to stay long, and therefore did not invest in engagement of complicated matters, but his background as an international bureaucrat was rooted in a diplomatic context. It is the diplomatic habit to remain removed from local politics and not to participate in the social process behind it. The problem was precisely that the head of the government and the preconstitutional king of the state, or the proconsul of the territory, was not functioning like a politician in contact with the population and their various interests. He was speaking almost exclusively, in an asocial and diplomatic fashion, to a single individual. As important a figure as Gusmão was, the requirements of leadership were far more complex and demanding than a single relationship could provide.'

These evaluation criteria are often in conflict. In contexts where levels of education are low, it is often quicker to fix something oneself than to train someone to fix it. In other cases, when a UN transitional administrator empowers a court to overrule their decision to lock up a troublemaker, this can make it harder to fix problems of disorder and violence in the short term. But fixes forged with local capacity, through processes that constitute separated powers to fix, are more likely to be sustainable fixes. Longer-run time frames for evaluation would be assisted by duration of UN peacekeeping/peacebuilding leadership appointments more akin to the diplomatic postings that states make for periods of years rather than months.

The United Nations in Timor-Leste has been a success in ending violence on the streets and in conducting a referendum on independence and elections in which people mostly cast non-coerced votes in circumstances where many were plotting to coerce those votes. That could have been accomplished with a simple, short peacekeeping and election monitoring operation. It did not require a transitional administration and the most expensive UN multidimensional peacekeeping operation that had been held until that point in history. The United Nations in Timor-Leste failed to institutionalise credible separations of powers that could lay a good governance foundation for an economically flourishing democracy, especially in the security and justice sectors. UN autocracy is unlikely to lay a foundation for post-conflict democracy. It is likely to collaborate with received patriarchs to bequeath a successor autocracy. Even when the UN autocrats are benevolent like Vieira de Mello and the received patriarchs are committed to pluralism (as were Gusmão and Ramos-Horta, and eventually Alkatiri), the Timor-Leste case shows that this risk remains profound. It must be resisted by concrete tactics of pluralisation. It must be regulated by a transparent discipline of democratic audit that affects the future careers of those who are evaluated.

Indiscipline of leaders is a problem in transitions to democracy of societies like Timor-Leste with hierarchical, aristocratic traditions. In our interviews, ordinary people frequently blamed 'democracy' for the nation's problems, for leaders focused on 'stealing each others' chairs' rather than on serving the unity of the society; political parties were institutions that only caused division. Leaders like Xanana Gusmão and institutions such as Fretilin and Falintil are no longer seen as the moral exemplars of virtuous governance that they were in 1999. A particular problem for the fragile democracy is that they are seen as exemplars of impunity. The culture of impunity is now widely entrenched in the consciousness of elites and angry young men on the street alike. *Lisan* justice has contributed greatly at the local level in compensating for the failings of formal justice and also contributed at the national level from late 2006. But at that national level, leaders are seen—more than ever in the aftermath of the impunity for 2006–08—as above both *lisan* justice and the justice of the courts.

One of the ways a future new democratic government must renew the republic is by instituting an end to the culture of impunity. It can be one that leans more heavily on *lisan* justice than on the justice of state courts, but courts must be given a more credible role in the future than in the past. Impunity will continue to be a dire moral hazard for Timor-Leste unless ordinary people see a fresh start in which the independence of the judiciary and prosecutors seems more secure and leaders are seen to put themselves below the law.

The impunity problem is inextricably linked to the learning about language and legitimacy from Timor-Leste that policing does not work when the police are not fluent in the language of those being policed,[7] and that the courts do not work if trials are conducted in a language most people do not understand. Fretilin in opposition became critical of the government and the United Nations for failing to respect the independence of the judiciary. In one of his interviews with us in 2009, Mari Alkatiri emphasised that the state requires strong central power. This had always been Fretilin's ideology, but now they give more emphasis to a rule of law under a separation of powers. It was only with experience of government that Alkatiri and Fretilin realised how important this was. There is in this hope for a democratic politics that resists the culture of impunity. For example, Mari Alkatiri was critical of then President Gusmão for 'sending notes to the judge who had issued a warrant for [Reinado's] arrest saying he should be free to travel' and critical of the UN security sector leadership for feeling bound to follow the President's wishes in relation to Reinado rather than executing the arrest warrant. 'A "madman" was left armed and at large contrary to the order of the court' (Alkatiri interview, September 2009).

Before we get too gloomy about the failures of the United Nations in institutionalising separations of powers in Timor, we must remember that the United Nations is itself part of the separation of powers that protects citizens from domination during a transition. The fact that ordinary Timorese continued to see it that way is well captured by a result in Higashi's (2009:28) survey looking forward to the 2007 election. When citizens were asked 'Who should mainly conduct the next election in Timor-Leste?', most opted for 'The Timor-Leste government and the UN', with a much smaller proportion opting for 'Only the Timor-Leste government'.[8]

Finally, the United Nations, working with international donors, did a creditable job of sustaining the networks abandoned by the political leadership that had been the lifeblood of CNRT until 1999: the human rights networks, women's networks, youth networks, development networks, and the accountability

---

7   'Yelling at a person to get down does not help when they don't speak English. Yelling louder does not help either' (Interview with New Zealand Maori military peacekeeper who learnt Tetum, August 2007).
8   A still smaller group opted for 'Timor-Leste government and the International Stabilization Forces'.

NGOs that watched over the Petroleum Fund negotiations and critiqued the underperformance of the justice system and the security sector. One might say that the Judicial System Monitoring Programme (JSMP) was a more impressive institution than the judiciary, that human rights and women's rights NGOs were more impressive than state rights enforcement and rights implementation, that the United Nations performed better in nurturing the watchdog networks that critiqued the institutions UNTAET built than it performed at building the institutions. One reason was that the strength of the movement for the liberation of East Timor was networked strength, not institutional strength.

Great social capital was created in Timor as a result of talented young Timorese working with talented and experienced internationals like Pat Walsh[9] at the interface between the clandestine network and the international solidarity movement. That social capital formation continued to grow in Timor-Leste after 1999 in NGOs in which young Timorese worked side by side with internationals who had more education and experience of democratic institutions, but less knowledge of Timor, though trust in civil society was badly set back by the violence of 2006 (Curtain 2006; Kehi 2007). Over time, Timorese became the dominant players in most of the civil society organisations in which internationals had once been more in charge. Most of the younger people moving into senior positions in politics and the civil service today carry with them social capital formed in that fashion.

As the NGOs became more dominated by Timorese, they became more integrated with rural areas, which internationals who valued hot showers and airconditioning had tended to shy away from. Then the NGOs began to draw in new leaders who had developed their social capital in *suco* governance. Village governance experience was thus deployed through NGOs into the wider challenges of the governance of the state. As in all rural societies, such as the Western democracies of the nineteenth century, in Timor-Leste, competence in governance is mainly constituted in towns and villages; less of it is constituted in the capital city. Republican virtue grows most strongly in the capital when it grows organically from republican virtue learnt in the districts and when national governance enjoys the luxury of choosing the brightest and best from those who learnt from mistakes they were allowed to make in the practice of rural and small-town governance. The United Nations did not set out to pump-prime that virtuous dynamic.

---

9   Pat Walsh has worked for decades in Timorese human rights networks, initially through the Australian Council for Overseas Aid. He became a driving force behind and within CAVR.

Rethinking Diplomacy

This book can be read as a case study that exposes two large pathologies of contemporary Western diplomacy: it leans too heavily on realist international relations theory and it implements 'national interests' in negotiation with cliques of national elites. Diplomacy must adapt to a world where so much of its peacebuilding work is not with pre-given nations and states. It is nation building where who the state elites will be and what the key institutions will become are unknown in advance of the consolidation of institutions. Timor-Leste is a 'most likely case' (Eckstein 1975) of the United Nations being able to constitute democracy peacefully through elite statist politics because in Vieira de Mello, Gusmão and Ramos-Horta the United Nations had three individuals to work with who were outstanding diplomats, and were as committed to democratic pluralism as any leaders one could hope to find amongst the ashes of a war. The failures of this 'most likely case' of success suggest that realist, top-down elite diplomacy might not be the way to succeed in building a resilient, peaceful democracy.

In a world of such challenges, diplomacy becomes more like a politics of networked governance. Diplomats become people who get mud on their boots in civil society far from the cocktail parties of the capital. The profession of diplomacy is reformable by being weaned off realism, ruling cliques and cocktail parties and weaned onto the mat in the village. We are confident that diplomacy can become a profession as oriented to differentiating power as to deferring to it. Law might be the profession of guardianship over the separation of powers but diplomacy has increasing responsibility for constituting separations of powers. It is often the midwife to sovereignties that are far from pre-given.

Diplomats will protest the unreality of advocacy like Barnett's (2006) and ours for republican peacebuilding based on deliberative processes that valorize networked governance through unelected bodies that pass two tests: 'inclusivity, or incorporating diverse groups; and publicity, or making transparent their decisions and the reasons behind them' (Barnett 2006:102). That protest sees a development like Wikileaks as a crisis for diplomacy—which must be transacted with maximum secrecy—rather than a prod to republican engagement with it. The republican certainly worries about reckless Wikileaks work that puts lives at risk or breaches the rights to privacy of non-public players. Yet the republican regards Wikileaks as a case of the separated powers of the new media doing its job.

Traditional diplomacy understandably sees it as impossible to hammer out a peace agreement with a thousand participants in front of television cameras. The Peacebuilding Compared research on another Indonesian peace process, Aceh, indeed concluded that it can be necessary to cut a core deal by narrowing the parties to a small number of moderate players each of whom can speak for wider networks. This might involve excluding from the room in the first instance certain powerful players who are determined spoilers. The Indonesian military and intelligence leadership formed one such example in the Aceh peace (Braithwaite et al. 2010a:Ch. 6). Yet our Aceh case study concluded that a weakness of the Aceh process was a failure to expand the peace negotiation table as soon as that core agreement was signed. The insurgent-dominated successor government in the autonomous Indonesian province of Aceh might have been less corrupt and enjoyed more separated powers had wider civil society networks been quickly brought to the table to put flesh on the bones of the framework peace agreement. We also argued that less of the peace agreement might have been dismantled by the militarist factions of the Indonesian Parliament had the Indonesian military leadership also been sitting at that second-stage table.

But we need more than the reform of diplomacy as a profession. The best diplomacy in the history of building architectures of separated powers has been done by loose networks of amateurs. This is true even in Aceh where the diplomatic establishment conferred the Nobel Peace Prize on the quintessential diplomat, former Finnish President Martti Ahtisaari.[10]

If Timor-Leste's leaders today can network into the project of redesign of the architecture of governance new generations of women and men of diverse political persuasions then there is hope. If it can network in separations of powers that are attuned to Timorese politics, if it can continue its progress towards reconciliation with itself and with its more powerful neighbours in Indonesia and Australia, there is contextually grounded hope. Timor-Leste's leaders might then lead a state with a uniquely inspiring story of how to build a republic where fears of domination by a terrible war and a man-made famine, by east or west, by men over women, by cosmopolitans over traditional villagers, by dual colonialisms, especially by poverty, become dominations that are defeated one by one during the next century.

---

10   See Braithwaite et al. (2010a:Ch. 6) for an account of the wide network of amateurs who contributed to the peace in Aceh in combination with a network of professionals like Ahtisaari.

Learning from Timor How to do Better at Separating Powers

We must learn that democracy is the art of disagreeing.

— Agio Pereira (2009:6), Xanana Gusmão's longstanding Chief of Staff

The United Nations should have pushed harder to separate powers. By insisting that CNRT implement its own policy of completely demobilising Falintil, doing without a defence force that consumed 8 per cent of the national budget in 2006 (Kingsbury 2009:135), subsequently increasing to 9 per cent (UNDP 2011), and funding generous reintegration payments to all Falintil members to manage the politics of their resistance to total demobilisation, the United Nations could have saved donors much money later in the decade and freed up substantial resources to fight poverty. Just as important, this could have allowed the nascent Timor-Leste police space to develop their important role in the transitional separation of powers, instead of indulging a politicised arms race with the military. It is interesting to note that this might not have been unpopular with the electorate. In Drysdale's (2007b:81) research, 'Defence' was by far the least popular choice of Timorese for expenditure of monies from the Petroleum Fund, with health, education, water, agriculture, forestry and fisheries the highest priorities.

The idea of the Serious Crimes Unit and the Serious Crimes Panel as hybrid international–domestic institutions was not a bad one in the aftermath of the expensive disappointments of the Rwanda and Yugoslavia international tribunals, the looming disappointments of Cambodia, and in the face of the clever politics of Indonesian resistance to an international tribunal. A hybrid had potential to leave a better legacy of local legal capacity than was left in Rwanda. But the serious crimes process was limply implemented, with funding for it cut off far too soon. Important elements of transitional separations of powers are the responsibility of transitional administrations. One of UNTAET's best decisions in this regard was the 2001 regulation establishing, after consultation with civil society groups, the Commission for Reception, Truth and Reconciliation with a totally Timorese complement of commissioners who served on both sides of the 1975 civil war, and with a contextually distinctive focus on 'reception' (welcome and reintegration: *alcolhimento*) of those who fled to West Timor.

Readers might find it strange to interpret that decision as a great one in terms of establishing a transitional separation of powers, rather than a great decision in terms of justice and reconciliation. During a critical period of the birth of the Democratic Republic of Timor-Leste, CAVR became an important voice independent of the executive government. It defended the Constitution, human rights and other separations of powers during the fragile process of transition.

It was a profoundly participatory institution at a time when civil society participation was being thinned within the new polity. It offered much sage advice in its final report that elites at the commanding heights of the executive government were foolish enough to ignore. How prescient it was, for example, to recommend that '[a]ll political parties make a public commitment that they will never mobilize youth groups for political purposes other than in peaceful and lawful ways' (CAVR 2006:Part 11, p. 31, para. 9.4).

The UN leadership in New York was reckless to distance itself from the CAVR final report when President Gusmão attacked it and initially refused to release it or allow it to be tabled and debated in the Parliament. Influential UN members such as Australia, Indonesia, the United Kingdom and the United States acquiesced in the President's approach to a report that so exposed their realist follies between 1975 and 2006. The job of separated powers in a republic is to contest dominations of executive governments; the job of UN transitional administration is to give transitional separations of powers backbone in that fraught endeavour.

Timor-Leste is not only an inspiring case study of the power of nonviolence and principled engagement in comparison with the bankruptcy of misplaced realism. It is also a depressing case study of corrupted separations of powers. It took 16 years (until 1991) for the greater power of nonviolence compared with armed struggle to become clear in this case. Perhaps it will take more than 16 years before the superiority of separated powers over autocracy realises its potential.

The challenge is not in terms of the Democratic Republic of Timor-Leste catching up to mature republics such as the United States in the separation of powers. The United States does not have a national anti-corruption commission with the powers of that of Timor-Leste. Nor does it have an institution like the Petroleum Fund, which empowers future generations with independent authority over the nation's largest resource so that the current generation of political and business leaders cannot pillage it wantonly. The 2008 global financial crisis laid bare how US political leaders, captured by the leaders of Wall Street, opted for short-sighted profit maximisation, laying waste their economy for the next generation. US internal colonialism crushed the wisdom of the ancestors of its indigenous justice. So the hope is that Timor-Leste can break new ground in the separations of powers over such matters, and much more.

Timor-Leste has a parallel with Nelson Mandela's and Desmond Tutu's education of the world to the virtues of *ubuntu* as a restorative justice value and Gandhi's vision for strengthening *panchayat* justice. There is also greatness in Xanana Gusmão's vision for strengthening the role of *lisan* in Timor-Leste's justice system and holding it accountable to the human rights standards of a republican constitution. There is a possibility that Timor-Leste will realise richer post-colonial separations of powers than South Africa or India have so far managed. We only put it as a possibility.

Our argument has been that Montesquieu's conception of the separation of powers as between executive, legislature and judiciary is impoverished in comparison with pluralised public–private separations of powers. The global financial crisis of 2008 did not occur because the US executive government crushed a legislature that wanted to implement the regulatory reforms needed to prevent the crisis. It did not occur because the courts were insufficiently independent of the President and the legislature. One reason it did occur was that ratings agencies, which hold the solvency of banks and hedge funds to account, were insufficiently independent of the private interests they were rating. Boards of directors of great banks insufficiently exercised independence of judgment over leveraging, over the hedge fund traders and the housing loan brokers who were making them rich in the short term. Board audit committees failed. Major accounting firms failed to blow the whistle in countless cases—a lesson that should have been learned from the previous, more minor collapse when Arthur Andersen failed to do its job of auditing with independence Enron, Worldcom and other companies that collapsed in 2001 (Braithwaite 2009). So the 2008 financial crisis was not caused by a failure of a tripartite separation of powers in the public sector, but by a failure of powers to be sufficiently separated within the private sector. More profoundly, there was a failure of public powers to be sufficiently separated from Wall Street power in enforcing regulations that required these culpable private powers to be separated. Financial regulators were insufficiently independent of a president and of a legislature captured by a Wall Street that funded their election campaigns. And there was a failure of the IMF to call US monetary imbalance to account in the way the IMF would have if this had been the recklessness of a less powerful economy.

Timor-Leste is not the sophisticated economy that would be able to show the rest of the world how to better separate powers over financial domination, though it did manage to keep its banks out of the crisis of 2008–09 and record double-digit growth in 2009, and there are lessons the world could learn from its Petroleum Fund in how a 'resource curse' that is lootable by the present generation can be entrusted to future generations. Timor-Leste did this at the same time that many European economies bequeathed national insolvency to the next generation. The more interesting leadership Timor-Leste is showing is in securing independent authority of past generations over the present. In Chapter 11, we saw that following a *juramento* (blood oath) to refrain from future violence and fear of causing disrespect to the ancestors and their values of communal harmony are significant motivators of nonviolence and respect for the human rights of other citizens. Readers will doubtless find it even stranger for us to frame the *juramento* as a separation of powers than our framing of the CAVR and the Community Reconciliation Process as effective separations of powers. The key idea of a separated power is that it be a check and balance that is independent of the power with the greatest capacity to dominate citizens (normally an executive government, a dictator, a monarch, but sometimes Wall Street). Functionally, why does it matter that the separated power that checks abuse of power is ancient and spiritual rather than modern and institutional?[11] More fundamentally, it is a flawed justice practice to have foreign lawyers design a 'modern' justice system to displace custom that locals shun in droves because it has less legitimacy than the *lisan* legitimated by the ancestors. The more productive role for Western-style courts is as a check and balance on the more dominant justice of *lisan*.[12] We have used the work of Daniel Fitzpatrick and his colleagues on land law (Chapter 10) as a case study of Timor-Leste's potential to deliver rural agricultural efficiency through traditional justice in most land disputes, while empowering state courts to carve out contractual exceptions and state land exceptions that allow private market investment and state provision to flourish. Within that framework, space is institutionalised for the justice of *lisan* to percolate up into the land law justice of the courts and for the justice of state law (such as that which guarantees women's rights) to percolate down into land disputes settled on the mat.

At the traditional national reconciliation of 6 December 2006 described in Chapter 10, the only power above President Gusmão that was able to call the President to account that day for his hubris was the ancestors, their spirit embodied through rural men who were traditional spiritual leaders sitting on the mat. How interesting that he was redeemed by confessing that hubris in their presence and taking a solemn oath to them not to repeat those errors, to listen on the mat in future in deliberative processes that the spirits and the laws of the ancestors oversee. We see this as a fit with the republican principle of commitment to deliberative processes that are agreed to be legitimate in a particular society, which, because they are perceived as legitimate, can work in calling power to account (Barnett 2006). This is not to deny the importance of more modern institutional accountabilities such as elections. Gusmão faced the people in an election in the next year and won. It is to say that an extra check

---

11   One referee answered: 'I guess the question could be posed, it might matter because it may not be sustainable as the country modernises further and the salience of traditional values etc. diminishes. What would replace it?' Our reply would be that it might be replaced with separated powers that have meaning to people with the values prevalent under that new 'modern' circumstance. At every point in history, as beliefs change, the separations of powers that attract legitimacy will also change, and republics must be nimble at adapting to this. There is also a conservative element to republican thought in this regard. If a separation of power is working in humbling power, we should be cautious about dispensing with it (see Krygier 2002).

12   Deliberative balance is needed here of course. One Timorese Catholic leader strongly made the point that the government should be learning from functioning democracies. 'We should not be inventing any wheels here. We do not have people with enough experience. We do not have our own experts. We should be doing an external not an internal review of the government. The justice process should not be excluded. Traditional reconciliation is good, but justice is needed' (Interview, December 2006).

and balance on power that enjoys popular legitimacy, so long as it is not such a dead weight on efficient governance as to cause poverty, enhances freedom as non-domination (Pettit 1997).

With respect to freedom as non-domination for women, as argued in Chapters 10 and 12, this means relenting to *lisan* as the 80 per cent default justice that soaks up the impossible backlog of land disputes, male-on-male violence and petty crime so that it is logistically possible for much greater numbers of rape and domestic violence cases to be accommodated in the courts. The agenda suggested in these chapters was not the impossible one of persuading all or most Timorese women to abandon village justice for dealing with gendered violence, but to persuade a greatly increased number to do so in those cases where village justice crushes women's rights; and to persuade them on the basis that state justice can perform in the future in ways that redeem the failures of its past. It has been a past of women continuing to suffer violence while their case sits in a prosecutor's in-tray, and then not being able to understand the proceedings (the language of justice) if the case did go to court. Dominant village justice that is checked and balanced in this way by the justice of state courts might then better serve those women who view *lisan* as the justice that affirms their Maubere identity, which they fought for against Indonesian justice.

The separated powers of state and non-state justice might then compete with each other to better serve the interests of women in justice. As we argued in Chapter 12, however, both must be checked by feminist and human rights NGOs when they dismiss women. And we have seen that a feminist and rights-conscious civil society has flourished in Timor-Leste on the foundations of the student underground of the long war. While the power of women as a balance on the power of men has a long way to go in Timor-Leste, accomplishments such as a police force that is 20 per cent female, that has a gender violence unit in every police district in the country, traditional justice through *suco* councils with growing and mandated female participation and a national parliament that is 29 per cent female (IPU 2011) are impressive beginnings in any internationally comparative frame. They are also impressive beginnings to separations of powers between institutions dominated by males and institutions where women's voices are more heard.

No institution has failed the Timor-Leste republican revolution more than the police. Instead of functioning as a bulwark of the separation of powers, it surrendered its independence to a criminal politician; it crushed political diversity in civil society. It has barely begun to learn that in policing 'the power of the tongue is greater than the power of the fist' (UNPOL interview, September 2009). On the positive side, we have argued that many rural Timor-Leste police today are enriched by a dual accountability to their Police Commissioner in Dili and local luminaries of *suco* governance and *lisan* justice. They consult *chefe d'aldeias*, *chefe de sucos*, *suco* councils, victims and offenders to reach consensus on which cases should follow the dominant track of *lisan* justice and which should be diverted to state justice. In this and the previous volume of Peacebuilding Compared, on Solomon Islands (Braithwaite et al. 2010c), we have concluded that in village societies many of the conflicts that overwhelm the capital start as rural conflicts. Then they migrate to the city, especially through the agency of gangs of migrant unemployed rural youth in the capital. The newly self-confident rural justice that is checked by growing accountability to state justice and human rights institutions working collaboratively with local constables seems a set of institutional settings with promise. There is hope that it might manage the future conflicts that will inevitably erupt across rural landscapes so traumatised by past atrocities at one another's hands.

Contemporary Western societies such as the United States and Australia have weak alternatives to state justice in comparison with *lisan* justice. These are societies with once rich indigenous justice alternatives that have been largely destroyed, causing despair and alienation among those who suffered that loss of identity. Our argument here is that more than preservation of identity is at stake in nurturing *lisan* in the way Xanana Gusmão advocates. Preservation of more functional and continuously improving separations of powers is also at stake. Most of the UN, foreign lawyer and Fretilin elite in the early 2000s saw the justice agenda as one of building a modern state legal system in which justice would be enacted in courtrooms. Corruption was one area where the United Nations, the Inspector-General, the Provedor, the police and other institutions referred many dozens of corruption investigations to the Prosecutor-General during the first decade of the new nation's existence only to have no cases proceed, because of either the overwhelming weight of court backlogs or political pressure for nothing to happen, or both.

Prime Minister Gusmão always had a more legal-pluralist agenda and this is the agenda that has become more ascendant as UN legal hegemony has faded. The new Anti-Corruption Commission that Adérito Soares now heads is part of that institutional pluralisation. Towards the end of their period in government, Fretilin leaders also learned that they were expecting too much of the courts and had excessively politicised the justice system. Fretilin too became more sympathetic to legal-pluralist policies. The work of Daniel Fitzpatrick and his colleagues shows why it is not impossible for a more vibrant separation of powers for state and non-state land law to emerge from the early years of chaotic and patrimonial Timor-Leste land disputation. A hybrid separation of powers over land could sustain both productive village economies and productive market economies driven by business investment. We have also argued that it could help tackle one of the biggest root causes of corruption.

Gandhi plus Nehru

In India, Jawaharlal Nehru's centralist socialist ideology of an industrialised economy (not so different from that of the younger Mari Alkatiri) prevailed over Gandhi's vision of village agricultural economies with rural justice. Today, India is prone to Maoist insurgencies that appeal to some of the rural majority of the nation which has been cast aside by the Indian urban middle class. Gusmão is a leader who seems to understand that it is not necessary to choose between Nehru and Gandhi in this regard. A dual legal system that simultaneously nurtures vibrant growth in rural agriculture and a vibrant market economy (in the difficult circumstances of limited opportunities) is not impossible (as we saw in Chapter 11). The Community Empowerment Project disappointed because it was both prematurely sequenced (in advance of even minimal local governance infrastructure to support it) and sabotaged by UN bureaucratic centralists who vandalised the attempt at more devolved separations of powers over development. We argued in Chapter 11 that efforts are being made to retrieve village-based empowerment by shifting control over development decisions out of Dili with support from the UNDP and bottom-up leadership from *suco* councils.

So, we conclude that UN transitional administration sometimes attracts oligarchs who overconfidently impose their view of what is best for another country. Guerilla war leaders who assume state power tend to be seduced by oligarchy—unaccustomed to accommodation with civil society, unwilling to be called to account—and pass blame to the United Nations and other internationals when things go wrong. Even so, there is no Iron Law of Oligarchy (Michels 1966) in peacebuilding. Just as international analysis of prospects for Timor-Leste in the early 2000s tended to be excessively rosy, after 2006, they became excessively gloomy. After a decades-long civil war, we should not expect a transition to peace and democracy to be free of violent and oligarchic setbacks. Networked struggle of the younger generation of Timorese to demand greater accountability from their institutions and their oligarchs remains vibrant. Leaders such as Gusmão, Ramos-Horta and Alkatiri have manifested complex mixes of pluralist virtues punctuated with periods of descent into oligarchy. The 1975 generation and UN leaders supported barely enough of the basics of a separation of powers for it to be struggling to strengthen rather than weaken. More importantly, it is leavening with ingredients of a diversity that many Western societies cannot boast. Separations of powers that are not regularly tested by episodes of oligarchy are never likely to learn to become resilient. No-one can doubt that Timor-Leste has been sorely tested by tussles with many tyrants and by being on a civil war footing in 1974–99 and 2006–08. So we should not fail to hope that it might emerge one day from these tests with separations of powers as strongly networked as any republic.

The violence and burning of 6000 homes in 2006 seemed to make such hope forlorn among what one observer described as a culture that is

> strongly opinionated, impulsively antagonistic…[with a] high rate of posttraumatic disorder syndrome, a poor notion of citizenship and the good citizen…[lacking] plurality of perspectives and critical analysis, severe practices of corruption and nepotism, dependency syndrome, emerging potentially conflicting ideas of political identity and a high illiteracy rate. (Boavida 2001)

Yet 2006 can be seen as a moment ripe with anomie in which leaders learnt from their irresponsibility in failing to abide by the rules of the game. They had followed the rules only up to the point that they worked for them, only far enough to keep the Constitution they fought for intact. Beyond that point they resorted to mob rule (Kingsbury 2009:168). Kingsbury argues that in the transition between autocracy and republican democracy 'there is a moment at which leaders are politically exposed, having to let go of one system but not quite being established in the other. Very few of East Timor's political leaders were prepared to face this vulnerability, especially if their competitors did not do the same' (p. 168). All their reputations suffered from their decisions to deploy gangs on the streets to defend their political interests. After that near return to civil war, leaders and the common people today have a better quality of national conversation about the separations of powers needed to secure their belief in nonviolence as the better part of their legacy.

In this book, we have frequently used the expression 'separations of powers' to reflect the pluralised form of the concept we have advanced as supportive of peace with justice. At different points, we have made a case for the importance of the following separations of powers.

- The classic tripartite separation of the legislature, judiciary and executive.
- The power of the people in elections conducted by an electoral commission independent of the legislature, judiciary and executive.
- The legitimate role of the crowd in history to protest in streets secured by a rule of law.
- Separation of control over the means of violence from politics (even if it is a non-state military as in Gusmão's genius in separating Falintil from Fretilin)—a military and police regulated and authorised by democratically appointed civilians, by a constitution that separates the military and the police from politics and regulates them under a rule of law enforced by civilian powers.

- In transitional administration, a United Nations that uses the military force at its disposal to prevent domination of a post-conflict military and police by any one political faction.
- A police separated from the control of the military; community policing as a civilian function that imposes higher thresholds on coercion upon the citizens of the republic than those allowed by military rules.
- Separation of the office of the prosecutor from the offices of the constable and the judge.
- Separated powers over justice that in combination guarantee that no member of any elite may believe that they enjoy impunity from the rule of law.
- Separations of powers within the judicial and legislative branches among lower courts and layers of appellate courts, perhaps different houses of parliaments, parliamentary committees, and legislative drafting services with responsibilities to detect and publicly report breaches of rights in draft laws.
- Separated powers for survivor advocacy institutions (up to truth commissions and the UNHCR for refugees).
- Separated powers for human rights, gender equity and complaints-handling units within key institutions such as the police.
- Accountability to international institutions such as international law, the regulatory enforcement of UN human rights institutions, the International Criminal Court, the IMF, the Basel Committee with bank reserves, the International Civil Aviation Organisation for rights to safe air travel. These international institutions must each in turn institutionalise their own separations of powers.
- UN peace operations must be constituted to avoid the loss of legitimacy that comes with domination by any one regional state power or one great global power.
- Separation of public accountability institutions—the ombudsman (provedor), auditor-general, inspector-general, anti-corruption commissioner, civil service board—from the state institutions they hold to account.
- Comparable separations of private accountability institutions: company auditors, board audit committees, corporate compliance and corporate integrity units, ratings agencies, stock market self-regulators, public regulators of markets, the Forest Stewardship Council, the UN Global Compact.
- Separated powers of anti-monopoly regulators with the authority to prevent commercial monopolies from exercising such unfettered power that they are above the legislature, the judiciary and other powers; ensuring the media is

not monopolised, that there are micro banks that lend competitively to the poor and not just monopoly banks lending only to the rich.
- Where private monopolisation thwarts anti-monopoly law in a domain where freedom as non-domination is at risk, such as micro-finance or broadcasting, the state should support public provision of these services in competition with private monopolies.
- Where public monopolisation of services vital to freedom as non-domination, such as education, becomes corrupt, separated private provision in competition with public providers (of, say, education) is needed so that donors have the alternative of channelling support for this institution through private or charitable providers.
- Separating the power of the military and the police from the power of commerce; rigorous anti-corruption commission enforcement against police or military protection rackets in commerce.
- Separated powers of professions such as law, medicine, architecture, diplomacy and accounting to self-regulate professional integrity standards, including the functioning of such professionals at the commanding heights of the state and commerce.
- Separated powers of the mass media that are not dominated by the state or big business, and of the profession of journalism.
- Separated powers for universities and artistic institutions that build new knowledge and new art with independence of thought.
- Separated powers of telecommunications: independent telecommunications regulators that cannot be dominated by the executive government to deny that free exchange of words and images on the Internet that has emerged as a new accountability of the concentrated power of militaries, police, ministers and corporations.
- Separated powers of future generations over the present generation: a petroleum fund and a central bank independent of the elected government of the moment that have charters to protect future generations from excessive burdens of indebtedness, monetary imbalance and inflation.
- Separated powers in national and international civil society that become progressively more plural—the power of the clandestine movement, the international solidarity movement and churches that created the Democratic Republic of Timor-Leste; women's empowerment groups, trade unions, environmental groups, civil liberties groups, anti-poverty campaigns, and, yes, authoritarian anti-republican civil society voices as well.
- Separated powers of elected village councils to control village development budgets that are not under the control of the national executive government.

- And, most poignantly and importantly, in learning from founding the Democratic Republic of Timor-Leste, ancient ancestral separations of powers that grant a large sphere of power to customary land law, traditional justice on the mat (*nahe biti*), reconciliations that provide an account of making right and making just to ancestors. Within the sphere of *lisan*, there resides a whole set of new layers of separations of powers—for example, among the *lia nain*, the *chefe d'aldeia*, the *chefe de suco* and the *suco* council.

While republican separations of powers have a universal quality, their meanings are constantly transformed in conversation with citizens; their content is recurrently vernacularised by new, disparate voices. The power to vernacularise is itself an important separated power and a fountain for dynamism in all separated powers.[13]

Vernacularisation can be spatially asymmetric, as can formal separations of powers. We have seen that different separated powers over land, for example, can be applied in a modern city from separations that apply under traditional rural governance—different separations in one province (for example, Quebec) compared with all other provinces. While spatial asymmetry adds complexity as it balances power, it can add legitimacy and therefore decisiveness, clarity and certainty to the exercise of authority.

While there are many facets of the variegated separations of powers that constitute a republican ideal, it is an ideal that lends itself to incrementalism (Barnett 2006:112). No republic has fully realised it and none has ever approached the attainment of all its variegated virtue during the first century of its history. Republics, we have argued, should be continuous improvement architectures, with every generation seeking to strengthen the republican architecture bequeathed by its forebears. That continuous improvement across separation-of-powers virtues should be regularly measured and discursively evaluated by UN transitional administrations, by the UNDP Human Development Report, UN human rights institutions, Transparency International, the Freedom House Index, by Human Rights Watch and Amnesty International, by discursive books like this one, and most of all by a republic's own national conversation in newspapers, blogs, universities, parliamentary debates and *suco* council deliberations. Republics require the humility to take stock and seek counsel from other nations that have continued to purge domination and expand freedom at

---

13 Dynamism is a neglected topic in discussion of the separation of powers. One of the things republican revolutions have done throughout history is dis-entrench separated powers, such as the powers of kings and dictators. 'Destabilization rights' (Sabel and Simon 2004; Unger 1986, 1987) and 'democratic experimentalism' unsettle and open up state institutions that persistently fail to fulfil their functions. Destabilisation rights are dynamic checks on failures of institutionalised checks to do their job. Rights to public law litigation to destabilise defunct structures and to appeal to the United Nations under its Responsibility to Protect doctrine by destabilising the Libyan military are examples, as is a common law that adapts and evolves novel doctrines over time. Networks are needed to deliver experimental innovation in the invigoration of separations of powers because of state propensities to rigidity.

a more rapid pace. The United Nations has a legitimate role in brokering that exchange of learning from democratic experience. One reason, given the UN mission of promoting peace, is the evidence from Goldstone and Ulfelder's (2005) multi-year, multi-author study that peace and stability are strongly promoted by fair and open political competition and constrained chief executive power (at least when the executive is not an unelected dictatorship). This is part of the context in which we look forward to the time of F-FDTL and PNTL not just as learners, but also as teachers on future UN peace missions.

Inefficiency

It might be said that such a long list of separations of powers would be a drag on economic efficiency. In Chapter 8, we made the case that a well-crafted separation of powers actually increases decisiveness in decision making. The judge, the police officer, the prosecutor, the general, the auditor, the central banker, the anti-corruption commissioner get on with their job without fear of interference from a president or a business powerbroker who is a 'master of the universe'. This is the idea that the separated powers of a polity can secure together an independent sphere of action for each power that cannot be dominated by any one power calling the shots above all others. Of course there are situations where a dictator who calls the shots can increase economic efficiency by overruling a court, a competition regulator or an environmental authority that is needlessly slowing an investment that would benefit the nation. The experience of history, however, is that autocrats more often exercise their domination for corrupt and patrimonial purposes that reduce the efficiency of national resource allocation. So in the long run many separations of powers that seem inefficient to the politically naive are in practice economically efficient.

Part of the efficiency dividend from separations of powers that are attuned to local realities is from a more efficient division of labour. Because central bank board members focus their intelligence and training on the large and intricate challenge of securing monetary balance for an economy, they are likely to make better decisions of this specialist kind than are the generalist politicians of the cabinet. Because police training is in community policing that enrols the community to do most of the serious business of crime control, they can become much better at it than the military with their training and experience in the use of maximum force. Our Timor-Leste narrative has well illustrated the provocation and inefficiency that can arise when the military takes over public order policing. It also revealed that even when the police (PNTL) were better equipped with modern weaponry than the military (F-FDTL), the specialised training and experience of the military meant that the police were outmatched in the project of taking over a country.

Our interviews exposed how the interference of the Prime Minister in the business-licensing decisions of regulators who should be at arm's length from him has undermined investment confidence. We have seen that one reason for the shocking backlog in prosecutors' in-trays is that legislators persistently interfere in the work of prosecutors. This when legislators are not getting on with their own job of settling land law, competition law, telecommunications law and other facets of the rule of law vital for economic development. The result when one branch of governance devotes energy to seeking to dominate another branch for which they have no training or experience is that the business of law making and law enforcement becomes less efficient, sapping business confidence that their investments and their employees will be protected by a rule of law.

The sheer inefficiency of prime ministers seeking to dominate other separated powers was well illustrated by the moment when indicted criminal of the Suai massacre Maternus Bere was released on the occasion of the tenth anniversary of the independence referendum. Our understanding of what happened on the official dais that day was that the Prime Minister received a call from the Indonesian Foreign Minister to say he would not attend unless Bere were released. The Prime Minister then requested the President of the Appellate Court to overrule the indictment—a request that was declined because the President of the Appellate Court had no power to overrule another judge in this way. The Prime Minister then instructed his Justice Minister to order the release of Bere from prison to the care of the Indonesian Embassy, which the Justice Minister did even though she also had no legal authority to do so. What happened was objectionable to most Timorese because it put on stage the fact that their sovereignty was still hostage to the domination of their powerful neighbour. It showed that impunity prevailed for even the most shocking of crimes against humanity. The point under discussion here in response to critics of the inefficiency of separations of powers is that not only was it objectionable, it was also inefficient to keep the entire Timor business elite, the government, diplomatic, UN donor and NGO elites, all of whom have important work to get on with for the development of Timor-Leste, waiting endlessly in the sun while the Prime Minister sorted out a problem that was not his business with other leaders whose business it also was not. The inefficiency is of course a trivial part of what was wrong with that conduct. Our bigger point is that the most outrageous breaches of the separation of powers are so often among the most inefficient processes a society can witness.

A more economically consequential separation of powers allows the kind of asymmetric separations of authority over land law discussed in the scholarship of Daniel Fitzpatrick and his collaborators. As complex and inefficient as it might seem to have a patchwork of rural carve-outs from urban land law, our argument in Chapter 10 was that this can fuel duel-economy development where both urban capitalist investment and traditional subsistence agricultural economies can become more efficient, each under rather different rules of law. Hence, there is no simple template for highly attuned, highly separated powers. In the course of economic development, they must be retuned as societies change to respond to inefficiencies that emerge.

Nevertheless, in the aggregate, the path to more pluralised separations of powers is a path to greater, not lesser, economic development. A final reason for this is our classic republican argument that separating powers is conducive to non-domination and therefore to a subjective experience of justice and legitimacy of governance among citizens. In turn, our theory is that such experience of non-domination reduces the prospects of civil war. And few things set back economic development as much as a civil war (Collier 2007). Indeed, as Timor-Leste's sharp economic contraction of 2006 shows, even civil disorder that induces fear of civil war is economically catastrophic. In the years ahead, the Peacebuilding Compared project will code diverse separations of powers on more and more post-conflict polities so that ultimately we will be able to examine quantitatively whether post-conflict societies with more variegated separations of powers of different kinds have lower odds of another war and higher economic development. Case by case, we will also continue to diagnose this theme qualitatively in the way we have attempted in this volume.

Gridlock

Our argument has been that, for most tasks of modern governance, networks get things done better than hierarchies. Well-designed networks of power are not only mutually checking upon bad uses of power; they are also mutually enabling of good capacities for power. Networks must be coordinated and sometimes—not always—the state is the best candidate to supply a key node of coordination. For most problems, strengthening state hierarchy to solve problems is not as effective as strengthening checks and balances on hierarchy as we also strengthen private–public partnerships, professions with technocratic expertise on that problem, civil society engagement and vigilance, and other networks of governance, while at the same time strengthening coordination of networked governance. The most effective governance is rarely centrally monopolised; it is usually messily attentive to multiple accountabilities.

This is not to deny that there must be agreement on who will make the final call on matters that have not reached resolution after deep contestation under a separation of powers. Elections are one such state institution with this usefully ultimate capacity to break a logjam (without violence). So are state courts. On legal matters, as valuable as it is to have a rich tapestry of legal pluralism where the national rugby judiciary regulates most violence on rugby fields, it is also valuable to have state appellate courts that have the legitimacy to make ultimate decisions on the basis of a synoptic view of all the adjudication that has occurred across that tapestry.

There is a widespread myth, grounded in the scholarship of Max Weber, that the state can be defined as an institution that enjoys a monopoly of force. In all societies today there are huge armed cadres of private security organisations; in many there are foreign military bases, UN peacekeepers, armed criminal gangs that are immune from state military or police power, terrorist training camps awaiting deployment into the lands of an enemy or private armies of warlords or of political parties. In the most advanced economies, the military machine is as powerful as it is because of the way it is networked with an innovative, technologically sophisticated private defence contracting industry (Dorf and Sabel 1998). Indeed, for great powers, and even for minor powers that can deliver weapons of mass destruction, networked private defence industries constitute the military power of the society much more than the state military organisation.

It is not that the state has, or should have, a monopoly of force. What most states have, and should have, is a capacity to lawfully subdue private controllers of the means of violence. The executive government should have an ultimate authority over the use of force and the state legislature over writing laws on use of force and the state judiciary on implementation of those laws. It is an overarching oversight and regulatory role that the state must have on really big questions like national security. These must allow generals to act decisively within their sphere of competence without interference from politicians who think of themselves as generals, but with budgetary oversight, monitoring for compliance with the laws of war, rules of engagement and so on.

Gridlock is a risk of separated powers. Often it is more important that things are settled than settled right. Paralysis and disengagement in the face of great problems are profound risks, not only in times of war. Executive government has an oversight responsibility for ensuring that really big problems do not fall between the cracks. This is not the same as saying the government should fix them. It is to say that the state has a responsibility to take a synoptic view of a society, and to catalyse action when lesser actors are paralysed by the enormity of the challenge. We see this need most acutely at times of great natural disasters when so many leaders of civil society are busy bailing out their house or looking for lost families. One of the great examples of a chief executive with synoptic vision in the twentieth century was China's Deng Xiaoping when he saw in 1978 that the institutions of state production were bogged down. He opened up the Chinese economy to private institutions that broke through many of the production bottlenecks and bureaucratic gridlocks that were grinding the economy to a halt.

We might even say that the most important role of state political leaders is to be gridlock breakers: to get that budget through the legislative contestation process, to issue an ultimatum to an enemy state of a kind that has less meaning when only a general issues it. Yet the ultimate power to break gridlock resides with the people when they take to the streets in a revolutionary moment in which they persuade the media or the military to side with the revolution. Republicans hope these will be revolutionary moments that dis-entrench bad power and entrench new separations of powers that secure freedom from domination.

Learning to Resist Domination

Accomplishing a republic is not a deadly simple mechanics of getting the separation of powers right. It is an interplay between cultural commitment and ethical education in republican values of freedom as non-domination and governance structures that create an enabling environment for further education in which new citizens learn to be democratic. It is what Anthony Giddens (1984) called a process of 'structuration' whereby agents are enabled and constrained to act by social structures, yet through action create and change structures. In this context, structuration means that cultural commitments to non-domination motivate political struggle to institutionalise structures of non-domination; those structures can nurture enhanced political and cultural commitment to non-domination, which in turn can push forward a new cycle of structuration of non-domination, continuing recursively. That is the ideal republicans strive for. The reality they deal with is more punctuated by crisis and regress, as Timor-Leste's history has illustrated.

Republicanism is of course not just about continuous improvement in separations of powers. It is also about continuous improvement in the struggle against poverty, and in equality for women and people of all races, classes and castes. We have argued that separations of powers are not enough to secure that; tax administration, land law, welfare policy and many other institutions have central parts to play. Republicanism is about forging a society that depends less and less on coercion to achieve its aspirations and more and more on dialogue. And when it reluctantly must resort to coercion, a republic refuses to exercise it arbitrarily; coercion must be sanctioned by the rule of laws written under democratic consent.

Republican coercion also comes with the promise of future commitment to reconciliation and reintegration. While justice must sometimes be coercive, because injustice hurts, justice must heal. It does best when it takes the restorative dimension of justice seriously (Braithwaite and Parker 1999). Democratic conversation can be nuanced and creative under the republican ideal when it is not dominated in accordance with that ideal. Most of all, republics continuously improve in how they flourish with fruits of freedom that are less about material things and more about creative and spiritual diversity born of rich conversation. The *tais* women weave in remote villages are for Timor-Leste one of the highest forms of that creativity, valorizing survival and identity in a republic of many colours and patterns

Just peace is never approached in a direct line from blood and injustice. It emerges in contests with tyrannies and twists and turns of a nation's history. People without realist power who network nonviolently for justice and peace often appear to be losers. They seem like history's losers because most of the time they are losing. Timor teaches us again that all tyrannies end, but not all republics end—at least not until a nuclear conflagration or environmental catastrophe. Autocracies end so long as we refuse to be realists in cowering under them. One reason that not all separations of powers end, not all democracies disintegrate, is that resilient democracies have powers that are separated, checking and balancing the dominations that disintegrate. Global anti-domination networks attuned to local civil society networks that reach from the capital down to the villages are drivers for dividing powers. We hope the contribution of this book has been in helping us see republican politics, feminist politics and nonviolence through the wider-angled lens of Timor's journey.

Appendix: Methodology for Peacebuilding Compared

The methodology for this research consisted mostly of digesting a vast literature on peacebuilding in Timor-Leste. In addition, John Braithwaite and Adérito Soares shared two periods in the field in Timor-Leste together in August–September 2006 and September–October 2009. Hilary Charlesworth participated in the 2009 fieldwork and Leah Dunn and Andrew Goldsmith in a number of the 2006 interviews. Adérito Soares has lived most of his life in Timor-Leste and does today as a senior civil servant. He was also a member of the nation's first Parliament that drafted the Constitution. Before that he was active in the clandestine movement. Adérito was able to do some crucial updating interviews in Timor-Leste during 2011 and has done many interviews and much participant observation for his own PhD research on the right to development, beyond the interviews listed in Table A1. In all of our cases, we have sought to engage participants in the research who have superior local knowledge and superior local language skills, as with Adérito Soares in this case, to compensate for the limited local sensibilities that John Braithwaite brings as the comparativist who leads all the case studies. John Braithwaite also travelled several times to Jakarta, twice to New York, to New Zealand, Fiji, Vanuatu, the United Kingdom, Sweden, the Netherlands, Bangladesh, China, India and across Australia for UN interviews. Kate Macfarlane and Leah Dunn assisted with UN peacekeeper interviews in some of these countries and also in Malaysia.

As in prior Peacebuilding Compared cases, we enjoyed access to very senior UN officials, to a number of former and current foreign ministers of Indonesia, Australia and Timor-Leste, two of Timor-Leste's prime ministers, Prime Minister John Howard of Australia and top commanders of the militaries engaged in the fighting. Table A1 indicates that while we have worked hard at interviews over the past six years, the distribution of the interviews is not as well attuned to the research focus of this volume as we would have liked. Almost one-third of the interviews have been with UN peacekeepers. When the study began in 2005, the focus of the wider Peacebuilding Compared project was more on peacekeeping. That remains just one important focus of Peacebuilding Compared overall and also for this book.

Table A1: Numbers and Types of Peacebuilding Compared Interviews, Timor-Leste Case

Timor-Leste minister or elected official	16
Timor-Leste civil servant/judge	28
Political leader of oppositional group	2
Indonesian military	10
Other Indonesian leader	9
Falintil ex-combatant	4
Timor-Leste military (F-FDTL), petitioners	11
Timor-Leste Police (PNTL)	13
UN Police (UNPOL)	54
UN and international military peacekeepers (INTERFET)	45
Other UN officials	34
Lisan/village leader	7
Church leader	6
Women's NGO	4
Environmental NGO	0
Development NGO	12
Human rights/peacebuilding NGO	16
Other NGO	0
Journalist	2
Business leader	5
Clandestine network leader	5
Martial arts group leader	4
Other student/youth leader	1
Foreign government (ambassador, foreign minister of another country, USAID, and so on)	26
Other international organisations (for example, World Bank)	6
Researcher/university academic	2
Victim/refugees	1
Other	0
Total interviews	297
Total people interviewed	323

In Table A1, as in previous such Peacebuilding Compared tables, interviews are assigned to one category that captures the role on which the interview was most focused. So while only one person is coded as a victim/refugee, many dozens of the people we interviewed could also fit that code. We also visited refugee camps and enjoyed casual conversations with many refugees that were not coded as interviews and witnessed victim testimony at reconciliation processes. Many of the interviews coded as Members of Parliament, civil servants, PNTL and F-FDTL officers were also once members of Falintil, of the clandestine movement, of women's NGOs, or were *lisan* leaders in their village. President Ramos-Horta was coded as a 'minister', though he started out as an activist journalist and might have been so coded. We interviewed Minister Maria Domingas Alves twice and coded her as a minister, though we spoke as much with her about her pre-eminence as a women's movement leader and a leader of peace dialogues. So the data in Table A1 should be read only as a rough guide to the limitations of our data, which are nevertheless considerable. We should have interviewed more *lisan* leaders in more remote parts of the country than the half-dozen districts where we did limited travel. Only a few of those we interviewed were willing to confess any role in militias, though we suspect more of them played such a role. We should have travelled to West Timor to interview militia leaders in exile there. We failed to do any environmental NGO interviews and should have done more women's NGO interviews and interviews with more leaders of martial arts groups.

This book is part of a longer, 20-year project that started in 2005. In this period, we aim to code more than 600 variables—a number we continue to add to, concerning at least 50 post-1990 armed conflicts, including all the major UN and international peacekeeping operations since 1990. For the moment, the project is concentrated in Asia and the Pacific; then it will move to Africa. In the—we hope—unlikely event that we run out of steam before 2030, it could become just a study of peacebuilding in Asia and Africa. But we do then aspire to move on to the Middle East, Europe and finally the Americas. New cases where we are currently in the field are Bangladesh, India, Pakistan and Afghanistan.

There are multiple aims with Peacebuilding Compared. A very important one is books that explore a particular theme in the way that this one explores the error of misplaced realism and the struggle for republican separations of powers after a war. We hope to build inductively a theory of effectiveness in peacebuilding as we lay one thematic case study on top of those that have gone before it, in just the way we have sought to lay another brick with this book towards a more ambitious theoretical structure in the future. As we develop the theory, we also code the variables that allow us to test it more quantitatively by 2025. Hence, in the course of this study, we refined a number of new codes of separations-of-powers variables. Not only will these be coded for all future cases, we also returned to conflicts we have already coded and written up and have coded these new separations-of-powers variables motivated by the Timor-Leste analysis.

To qualify as an armed conflict for inclusion in Peacebuilding Compared, it must be a case where fighting started or continued after 1990. Military coups that do not result in large loss of life, such as those that occurred in Fiji during the period of our study, do not qualify for inclusion. It must be an armed conflict in which one armed group with a command structure is engaged in group attacks with weapons on another armed group with a command structure. Unlike some quantitative studies of 'civil wars', here there is no requirement that one of the protagonists be a state (for example, Goldstone and Ulfelder 2005; Sambanis 2002). We see such a restriction as an analytic error that is well illustrated by the disparate militarised groups that were responsible for killing in our Timor-Leste coding: militias backed by the Indonesian military, PNTL and F-FDTL engaging in fire fights, different factions of F-FDTL doing so, even martial arts groups in a small way. We are open to revising this condition when we move on one day to consider whether cases such as Northern Ireland should or should not be included in the study, but for the moment minimum conditions for inclusion are that two of the following three conditions are met: at least 200 people were killed in the fighting within three years; at least 30 000 people were driven from their homes by the fighting between the armed groups; and an internationally sanctioned peacekeeping mission was sent to make peace in the war-torn region.

Including the last condition prevents us from excluding armed conflicts from consideration that started but were prevented from escalating into mass slaughter by peacekeepers. The analytic purchase of not excluding such peacekeeping 'success' cases is well illustrated by the understanding contributed by our analysis of the impact of the arrival of peacekeepers in Timor-Leste from 2006. In 2006–07, peacekeepers were the most crucial element of the separation of powers that prevented civil war. Timor is actually coded as two different conflicts: one from 1975 to 1999 in which the Indonesian military was a central combatant; and a different outbreak of armed conflict from 2006 to 2008 in which it was not. Across our 600 variables, these two conflicts are coded in radically different ways. The 2006–08 conflict, with 150 000 people fleeing their homes as a result of the fighting, meets the second as well as the third peacekeeping condition. It might even meet the killing threshold of 200 between 2006 and 2008; it is hard to be sure. So we include it on the basis that it meets two of our three conditions—in addition to the foundational threshold of involving organised combatant groups in battles with arms.

In the introductory chapter to each of the three previous books we have already published on the project, we have rather repetitively described in more detail the overall methodological rationale for the Peacebuilding Compared project and the conduct of its coding. Like this one, these books can be downloaded free from the Peacebuilding Compared web site, which also provides much additional information on the totality of the project and its methods: <http://peacebuilding.anu.edu.au>

References

Abrahms, Max 2006 'Why terrorism does not work', *International Security* 31, 42–78.

Aditjondro, George J. 1994 'East Timor: an Indonesian intellectual speaks out', in Herb Feith, Emma Baulch and Pat Walsh (eds), *Development Dossier No. 33*, Canberra: Australian Council for Overseas Aid.

Ahmed, Eliza, Nathan Harris, John Braithwaite and Valerie Braithwaite 2001 *Shame Management through Reintegration*, Cambridge: Cambridge University Press.

Alatas, Ali 2006 *The Pebble in the Shoe: The diplomatic struggle for East Timor*, Jakarta: Aksara Karunia.

Amnesty International 2003 *The Democratic Republic of Timor-Leste: A new police service—a new beginning*, London: Amnesty International.

Anderson, Benedict R. O.'G. 1996 'Scholarship on Indonesia and raison d'etat: personal experience', *Indonesia* 62(October), 1–18.

Anderson, Tim 2007 'Timor-Leste: the second Australian intervention', *Journal of Australian Political Economy* 58, 62–93.

Arendt, Hannah 1963 *On Revolution*, New York: Viking Press.

Arnold, Matthew B. 2009 'Challenges too strong for the nascent state of Timor-Leste: petitioners and mutineers', *Asian Survey* 49(3), 429–49.

Asia Foundation 2004 *Law and Justice in East Timor: A survey of citizen awareness and attitudes regarding law and justice in East Timor*, Dili: Asia Foundation.

Asia Foundation 2005 *Survey Report: Citizen's perceptions of the Indonesian justice sector: findings and recommendations*, Jakarta: Asia Foundation.

Asia Foundation 2008 *Law and Justice in East Timor: A survey of citizen awareness and attitudes regarding law and justice 2008*, Jakarta: Asia Foundation.

Asia Watch 1991 *East Timor: The November 12 massacre and its aftermath*, Washington, DC: Asia Watch.

Aspinall, Edward 2005 *Opposing Suharto: Compromise, resistance, and regime change in Indonesia*, Stanford, Calif.: Stanford University Press.

Aspinall, Edward and Mark T. Berger 2001 'The break up of Indonesia? Nationalisms after decolonization and the limits of the nation-state in post-cold war Southeast Asia', *Third World Quarterly* 22(60), 1003–24.

Aubrey, Jim (ed.) 1998 *Free East Timor: Australia's culpability in East Timor's genocide*, Sydney: Vintage.

Australian Broadcasting Corporation (ABC) 2006 'East Timorese mark 15th anniversary of Santa Cruz massacre', *ABC News*, 12 November 2006.

Australian Broadcasting Corporation (ABC) 2008 'East Timor budget ruled unconstitutional', *Radio Australia*, 14 November 2008.

Australian Broadcasting Corporation (ABC) 2009 'East Timor massacre mystery may have been solved', *ABC News*, 2 April 2009.

Ayres, Ian and John Braithwaite 1992 *Responsive Regulation: Transcending the deregulation debate*, New York: Oxford University Press.

Babo-Soares, D. 2004 '*Nahe Biti*: the philosophy and process of grassroots reconciliation (and justice) in East Timor', *The Asia Pacific Journal of Anthropology* 5(1), 15–33.

Ball, Desmond 2002 'Silent witness: Australian intelligence and East Timor', in Hamish McDonald (ed.), *Masters of Terror: Indonesia's military and violence in East Timor in 1999*, Canberra: Strategic and Defence Studies Centre, The Australian National University.

Ball, Desmond and Hamish McDonald 2000 *Death in Balibo, Lies in Canberra*, Sydney: Allen & Unwin.

Barnett, Michael 2006 'Building a republican peace: stabilizing states after war', *International Security* 30(4), 87–112.

Barnett, Michael and Christoph Zürcher 2009 'The peacebuilder's compact: how external statebuilding reinforces weak statehood', in Roland Paris and Timothy D. Sisk (eds), *The Dilemmas of Statebuilding: Confronting the contradictions of postwar peace operations*, London: Routledge.

Bayley, David H. and Robert M. Perito 2010 *The Police in War: Fighting insurgency, terrorism, and violent crime*, Boulder, Colo.: Lynne Rienner.

Beauvais, Joel C. 2001 'Benevolent despotism: a critique of the U.N. state-building in East Timor', *New York University Journal of International Law and Politics* 33(4), 1101–77.

Bell, Daniel 2000 *East Meets West: Human rights and democracy in East Asia*, Princeton, NJ: Princeton University Press.

Belun 2009a *Early warning and response system in Timor-Leste*, Trimester Report (May), Belun, Dili.

Belun 2009b *Early warning and response system in Timor-Leste*, Trimester Report (September), Belun, Dili.

Belun 2010 *Early warning and response system in Timor-Leste*, Trimester Report (January), Belun, Dili.

Bere, Maria Agnes 2005 'Women and justice in East Timor', *Development Bulletin* (October), 55–7.

Bertrand, Jacques 2004 *Nationalism and Ethnic Conflict in Indonesia*, New York: Cambridge University Press.

Bevir, M. and R. Rhodes 2003 *Interpreting British Governance*, London: Routledge.

Binswanger, H. P., K. Deininger and G. Feder 1993 *Power, distortions, revolt, and reform in agricultural land relations*, Policy Research WPS Working Paper Series 1164, The World Bank, Washington, DC.

Boavida, J. 2001 *Internal report for civil society organizations, sector activities and external liaison section*, July, United Nations Transitional Administration in East Timor.

Boege, Volker, Anne Brown, Kevin Clements and Anna Nolan 2008 'On hybrid political orders and emerging states: state formation in the context of "fragility"', *Berghof Handbook Dialogue No. 8*, Berlin: Berghof Research Center.

Boll, Edward 2001 'The Asian values debate and its relevance to international humanitarian law', *International Review of the Red Cross No. 841*, viewed August 2010, <http://www.icrc.org/eng/resources/documents/misc/57jqzl.htm>

Braithwaite, John 1989 *Crime, Shame and Reintegration*, Cambridge: Cambridge University Press.

Braithwaite, John 1997 'On speaking softly and carrying big sticks: neglected dimensions of a republication separation of powers', *University of Toronto Law Journal* 47, 305–61.

Braithwaite, John 2002 *Restorative Justice and Responsive Regulation*, New York: Oxford University Press.

Braithwaite, John 2008 *Regulatory Capitalism: How it works, ideas for making it work better*, Cheltenham, UK: Edward Elgar.

Braithwaite, John 2009 'Restorative justice for banks through negative licensing', *The British Journal of Criminology* 49(2), 439–50.

Braithwaite, John and K. Daly 1994 'Masculinities, violence and communitarian control', in T. Newburn and B. Stanko (eds), *Just Boys Doing Business*, London: Routledge.

Braithwaite, John and Peter Drahos 2000 *Global Business Regulation*, Cambridge: Cambridge University Press.

Braithwaite, John and Christine Parker 1999 'Restorative justice is republican justice', in G. Bazemore and L. Walgrave (eds), *Restorative Juvenile Justice*, Palisades, NY: Criminal Justice Press.

Braithwaite, John and Philip Pettit 1990 *Not Just Deserts: A republican theory of criminal justice*, Oxford: Oxford University Press.

Braithwaite, John, Valerie Braithwaite, Michael Cookson and Leah Dunn 2010a *Anomie and Violence: Non-truth and reconciliation in Indonesian peacebuilding*, Canberra: ANU E Press.

Braithwaite, John, Hilary Charlesworth, Peter Reddy and Leah Dunn 2010b *Reconciliation and Architectures of Commitment: Sequencing peace in Bougainville*, Canberra: ANU E Press.

Braithwaite, John, Sinclair Dinnen, Matthew Allen, Valerie Braithwaite and Hilary Charlesworth 2010c *Pillars and Shadows: Statebuilding as peacebuilding in Solomon Islands*, Canberra: ANU E Press.

Braithwaite, John, Toni Makkai and Valerie Braithwaite 2007 *Regulating Aged Care: Regulatory ritualism and the new pyramid*, Cheltenham, UK: Edward Elgar.

Brown, M. Anne and Alex Freitas Gusmão 2009 'Peacebuilding and political hybridity in East Timor', *Peace Review* 21(1), 61–9.

Bruce, J. W. 1993 'Do indigenous tenure systems constrain agricultural development?' in T. W. Bassett and D. E. Crummey (eds), *Land in African Agrarian Systems*, Madison: University of Wisconsin Press.

Bruce, J. W. 1998 Learning from comparative experience with agrarian reform, Paper presented to the International Conference on Land Tenure in the Developing World, University of Capetown, South Africa, 27–29 January 1998.

Budiardjo, Carmel 2002 The international solidarity movement for East Timor: a weapon more powerful than guns, TAPOL web site, 17 May, viewed 28 October 2011, <http://tapol.gn.apc.org/reports/r020520etsolidarity.html>

Bueno de Mesquita, Bruce and George W. Downes 2006 'Intervention and democracy', *International Organization* 60(3), 627–50.

Burr, William and Michael L. Evans (eds) 2001 'East Timor revisited: Ford, Kissinger and the Indonesian invasion, 1975–76', *National Security Archive Electronic Briefing Book No. 62*, Washington, DC: National Security Archive.

Campbell-Nelson, Karen 2003 'East Timor women must tell of atrocities by Indonesians', *Jakarta Post*, 9–10 June.

Caplan, Richard 2005 *International Governance of War-Torn Territories: Rule and reconstruction*, Oxford: Oxford University Press.

Carey, Peter 2001 'Challenging tradition, changing society: the role of women in East Timor's transition to independence', *Lusotopie* (2001), 255–67.

Castells, Manuel 1996 *The Rise of the Network Society*, The Information Age Series, *The Information Age: Economy, Society and Culture. Volume 1*, Oxford: Blackwell.

Charlesworth, Hilary 2010, 'The woman question in international law', *Asian Journal of International Law* 1, 1–6.

Charlesworth, Hilary and Christine Chinkin 2000 *The Boundaries of International Law*, Manchester: Manchester University Press.

Charlesworth, Hilary, Christine Chinkin and S. Wright 1991, 'Feminist approaches to international law', *American Journal of International Law* 85, 613–45.

Charlesworth, Hilary and Mary Wood 2002 'Women and human rights in the rebuilding of East Timor', *Nordic Journal of International Law* 71, 325–48.

Chenoweth, Erica and Maria J. Stephan 2011 *Why Civil Resistance Works: The strategic logic of non-violent conflict*, New York: Columbia University Press.

Chesterman, Simon 2002 'East Timor in transition: self-determination, state-building and the United Nations', *International Peacekeeping* 9(1), 45–76.

Chinn, Liam and Silas Everett 2009 *A Survey of Community–Police Perceptions: Timor-Leste in 2008*, Dili: Asia Foundation.

Chopra, Jarat 2000 'The UN's kingdom of East Timor', *Survival* 42(3), 27–39.

Chopra, Jarat 2002 'Building state failure in East Timor', *Development and Change* 33(5), 979–1000.

Chopra, Jarat and Tanja Hohe 2004 'Participatory intervention', *Global Governance* 10, 289–305.

Cleary, Paul 2007 *Shakedown: Australia's grab for Timor oil*, Sydney: Allen & Unwin.

Cliffe, Sarah, Scott Guggenheim and Markus Kostner 2003 *Community-driven reconstruction as an instrument of war-to-peace transitions*, CPR Working Paper Series, Social Development Department, The World Bank, Washington, DC.

Cohen, David 2003 *Intended to Fail: The trials before the ad hoc human rights court in Jakarta*, New York: International Center for Transitional Justice.

Cohen, David 2006a *Indifference and accountability: the United Nations and the politics of international justice in East Timor*, East–West Center Special Reports No. 9, East–West Center, Hawai'i.

Cohen, David 2006b *'Justice on the Cheap' Revisited: The failure of the serious crimes trials in East Timor*, Hawai'i: East–West Center.

Collier, Paul 2007 *The Bottom Billion: Why the poorest countries are failing and what can be done about it*, New York: Oxford University Press.

Collier, Paul and A. Hoeffler 2000 *Greed and grievance in civil war*, World Bank Policy Research Paper 2355, The World Bank, Washington, DC.

Combs, Nancy Amoury 2007 *Guilty Pleas in International Criminal Law: Constructing a restorative justice approach*, Stanford, Calif.: Stanford University Press.

Commission for Reception, Truth and Reconciliation in East Timor (CAVR) 2006 *Chega! The report of the Commission for Reception, Truth and Reconciliation in East Timor*, Dili: Commission for Reception, Truth and Reconciliation in East Timor.

Commission of Experts 2005 *Report to the Secretary-General of the Commission of Experts to Review the Prosecution of Serious Violations of Human Rights in Timor-Leste (the then East Timor) in 1999*, 26 May 2005, United Nations, New York.

Commission of Truth and Friendship Indonesia–Timor-Leste 2008 *Final report*, Commission of Truth and Friendship Indonesia–Timor-Leste, Jakarta and Dili.

Committee on the Elimination of Discrimination against Women (CEDAW) 2009 *Concluding observations on Timor Leste CEDAW/C/TLS/CO1*, 7 August, UN Women, New York.

Conboy, Ken J. 2003, *Kopassus: Inside Indonesia's special forces*, Jakarta: Equinox.

Conversi, Danielle 2007 Asymmetrical federalism and consociational practice: Spain, Italy and beyond, ECPR Conference Paper, Pisa, September 2007.

Corcoran-Nantes, Yvonne 2009 'The politics of culture and the culture of politics—a case study of gender and politics in Lospalos, Timor-Leste', *Conflict, Security & Development* 9(2), 165–87.

Cosgrove, Peter 2006 *General Peter Cosgrove: My story*, Sydney: HarperCollins.

Cribb, Robert 2001 'How many deaths? Problems in the statistics of massacre in Indonesia (1965–1966) and East Timor (1975–1980)', in Ingrid Wessel and Georgia Wimhöfer (eds), *Violence in Indonesia*, Hamburg: Abera-Verlag.

Cristalis, Irena and Catherine Scott 2005 *Independent Women: The story of women's activism in East Timor*, London: CIIR.

Cronin, Audrey Kurth 2009 *How Terrorism Ends: Understanding the decline and demise of terrorist campaigns*, Princeton, NJ: Princeton University Press.

Cummins, Deborah 2010 Local governance in Timor-Leste: the politics of mutual recognition, PhD dissertation, University of New South Wales, Sydney.

Cummins, Deborah 2011 'The problem of gender quotas: women's representatives on Timor-Leste's *suku* councils', *Development in Practice* 21, 85–95.

Curtain, Richard 2006 *Crisis in Timor-Leste: looking beyond the surface reality for causes and solutions*, State, Society and Governance in Melanesia Working Papers No. 2006/1, The Australian National University, Canberra.

Curthoys, Ann 2010 'Mary Wollstonecraft revisited', *Humanities Research* XVI(2), 29–48.

Cusack, Agnes 1999 'Clinton says Indonesia must allow peacekeepers', *The World Today*, ABC Local Radio, 10 September 1999, viewed 2 May 2011, <http://www.abc.net.au/worldtoday/stories/s50881.htm>

Daley, Paul 2008 'Howard the reluctant liberator', *Sunday Canberra Times*, 23 November 2008.

Daley Paul 2009 'Idealism turns into pragmatism,' *Sunday Canberra Times*, 25 October 2009.

Daly, Erin and Jeremy Sarkin 2007 *Reconciliation in Divided Societies: Finding common ground*, Philadelphia: University of Pennsylvania Press.

Davis, Thomas W. 2007 The real world of 'community empowerment' in international development, Paper presented to Australian Political Science Association Conference, School of Political Science, Criminology and Sociology, University of Melbourne.

Department of Defence 2004 *Winning in Peace, Winning in War: The Australian defence force's contribution to the global security environment*, Canberra: Department of Defence.

Documents on Australian Foreign Policy 2000 *Australia and the Indonesian Incorporation of Portuguese Timor, 1974–1976*, Wendy Way, Damien Browne and Vivianne Johnson (eds), Melbourne: Melbourne University Press.

Dodd, Mark 2002 'East Timor's new government faces a challenge from rebels', *Far Eastern Economic Review*, 4 July 2002.

Dorf, Michael and Charles Sabel 1998 'A constitution of democratic experimentalism', *Columbia Law Review* 98, 267–473.

Doyle, Michael W. and Nicholas Sambanis 2000 'International peacebuilding: a theoretical and quantitative analysis', *American Political Science Review* 94(4).

Doyle, Michael W. and Nicholas Sambanis 2006 *Making War and Building Peace: United Nations peace operations*, Princeton, NJ: Princeton University Press.

Drahos, Peter 2004 'Intellectual property and pharmaceutical markets: a nodal governance approach', *Temple Law Review* 77, 401–24.

Drysdale, Jennifer 2007a Sustainable development or resource cursed? An exploration of Timor-Leste's institutional choices, PhD dissertation, The Australian National University, Canberra.

Drysdale, Jennifer 2007b 'The institutional challenges of managing Timor-Leste's petroleum revenue', in Dennis Shoesmith (ed.), *The Crisis in Timor-Leste: Understanding the past, imagining the future*, Darwin: Charles Darwin University Press.

Dunn, James 2003 *East Timor: A rough passage to independence*, [Third edn], Double Bay, NSW: Longueville Books.

Durkheim, Émile [1897] 1952 *Suicide: A study in sociology*, London: Routledge & Kegan Paul.

Easterly, William 2009 'Can the west save Africa?' *Journal of Economic Literature* 47(2), 373–447.

Eckstein, Harry 1975 'Case study and theory in political science', in F. Greenstein and N. Polsby (eds), *Handbook of Political Science. Volume 7: Strategies of inquiry*, Reading, Mass.: Addison-Wesley.

Eide, Espen Barth, Anja Therese Kaspersen, Randolph Kent and Karen von Hippel 2005 *Report on Integrated Missions: Practical perspectives and recommendations*, New York: UNECHA Core Group.

Ellickson, Robert 1991 *Order without Law: How neighbors settle disputes*, Cambridge, Mass.: Harvard University Press.

Engel, Rebecca 2007 *The Building of Timor-Leste: International contributions to a fragile state*, New York: Centre for International Conflict Resolution, Columbia University.

Evans, Gareth 1993 *Cooperating for Peace: The global agenda for the 1990s and beyond*, Sydney: Allen & Unwin.

Farram, Steve 1999 'The two Timors: the partitioning of Timor by the Portuguese and the Dutch', *Studies in Languages and Cultures of East Timor. Volume 2*, Macarthur, NSW: Academy of East Timor Studies, University of Western Sydney.

Federer, Juan 2005 *The UN in East Timor: Building Timor-Leste, a fragile state*, Darwin: Charles Darwin University Press.

Fernandes Alves, Maria Domingas, Laura Soares Abrantes and Filomena B. Reis 2002 *Written with Blood*, Noeno Anuno Sarmento and Lucsendar R. Fernandes Alves (trans), Dili: Office for Promotion of Equality, Prime Minister's Office.

Fernandes, Clinton 2005 'East Timor in transition: an Australian policy challenge', in Damien Kingsbury (ed.), *Violence in Between: Conflict and security in archipelagic Southeast Asia*, Singapore: Institute for Southeast Asian Studies.

Fernandes, Clinton 2008 'The road to INTERFET: bringing the politics back in', *Security Challenges* 4(3), 83–98.

Fernandes, Clinton 2011 *The Independence of East Timor: Multi-dimensional perspectives—occupation, resistance and international political activism*, Brighton, UK: Sussex Academic Press.

Field, Annette 2004 Places of suffering and pathways to healing: post-conflict life in Bidau, East Timor, PhD thesis, James Cook University, Townsville, Qld.

Fitzpatrick, Daniel 1997 'Disputes and pluralism in modern Indonesian land law', *Yale Journal of International Law* 22(1), 171–212.

Fitzpatrick, Daniel 2000 'Re-establishing land titles and administration in East Timor', *Pacific Economic Bulletin* 15(2), 152–60.

Fitzpatrick, Daniel 2002 *Land Claims in East Timor*, Canberra: Asia Pacific Press.

Fitzpatrick, Daniel 2005 '"Best practice" options for the legal recognition of customary tenure', *Development and Change* 36(3), 449–75.

Fitzpatrick, Daniel 2006 'Evolution and chaos in property rights systems: the Third World tragedy of contested access', *Yale Law Journal* 115, 996–1048.

Fitzpatrick, Daniel and Susanna Barnes 2010 'The relative resilience of property: first possession and order without law in East Timor', *Law and Society Review* 44(2), 205–38.

Fitzpatrick, Daniel and Andrew McWilliam 2005 'Waiting for law: land custom and legal regulation in Timor-Leste', *Development Bulletin* 68(October), 58–61.

Fitzpatrick, Daniel, Andrew McWilliam and Susanna Barnes 2008 *Policy Notes on Customary Land in Timor-Leste*, Canberra: The Australian National University.

Fluri, Philipp H. 2003 *DCAF security sector governance status report and needs assessment on Timor-Leste*, Working Paper No. 133, Geneva Centre for the Democratic Control of Armed Forces, Geneva.

Fortna, Virginia Page 2008 'Dilemmas of war-to-democracy transitions: theories and concepts', in A. Jarstad and T. Sisk (eds), *From War to Democracy: Dilemmas of peacebuilding*, Cambridge: Cambridge University Press.

Fox, James J. 2004 The paradox of powerlessness: Timor in historical perspective, The Nobel Peace Prize Symposium, The Australian National University, Canberra, viewed 4 March 2010, <http://dspace-prod1.anu.edu.au/handle/1885/41370>

Fox, James J. 2007 'Traditional justice and the "court system" of the island of Roti', *The Asia Pacific Journal of Anthropology* 8(1), 59–73.

Fox, James J. 2008 'Repaying the debt to *mau kiak*: reflections on Timor's cultural traditions and the obligations of citizenship in an independent East Timor', in David Mearns (ed.), *Democratic Governance in Timor-Leste: Reconciling the local and the national*, Darwin: Charles Darwin University Press.

Franks, Emma 1996 'Women and resistance in East Timor: "The centre, as they say, knows itself by the margins"', *Women's Studies International Forum* 19(1–2), 155–68.

Fukuyama, Francis 2007 Observations on state-building in the western Pacific, Unpublished paper.

Garcia-Milà, Teresa and Therese J. McGuire 2002 *Fiscal Decentralization in Spain: An asymmetric transition to democracy*, Barcelona: Universitat Pompeu Fabra, viewed 3 January 2010, <www.recercat.net/bitstream/2072/1010/1/866.pdf>

Ghai, Yashi 1994 'Human rights and governance: the Asia debate', *Australian Year Book of International Law* 1(15), 1–34.

Giddens, Anthony 1984 *The Constitution of Society: Outline of the theory of structuration*, Berkeley: University of California Press.

Goldsmith, Andrew and Sinclair Dinnen 2007 'Transnational police building: critical lessons from Timor-Leste and Solomon Islands', *Third World Quarterly* 28(6), 1091–109.

Goldsmith, Andrew and Vandra Harris 2009 'Out of step: multilateral police missions, culture and nation-building in Timor-Leste', *Conflict, Security and Development* 9(2), 189–211.

Goldstone, Jack A. and Jay Ulfelder 2005 'How to construct stable democracies', *The Washington Quarterly* 28(1), 9–20.

Graydon, Carolyn 2005 'Local justice systems in Timor-Leste: washed up, or watch this space?', *Development Bulletin* 68, 66–70.

Greenlees, Don and Robert Garran 2002 *Deliverance: The inside story of East Timor's fight for freedom*, Sydney: Allen & Unwin.

Grenfell, Damian, Mayra Walsh, Anna Trembath, Carmenesa Moniz Noronha and Kym Holthouse 2009 *Understanding Community: Security and sustainability in four aldeia in Timor-Leste*, Melbourne: Globalism Research Centre, RMIT University.

Grenfell, Laura 2006 'Legal pluralism and the rule of law in Timor-Leste', *Leiden Journal of International Law* 19, 305–37.

Gunn, Geoffrey C. and Reyko Huang 2006 *New Nation: United Nations peacebuilding in East Timor*, Macau: Geoffrey Gunn.

Gusmão, Xanana 2000 *To Resist is to Win! The Autobiography of Xanana Gusmão with selected letters and speeches*, Sarah Niner (ed.), Melbourne: Aurora Books.

Gusmão, Xanana 2005a 'Address to the International Conference on Traditional Conflict Resolution and Traditional Justice in Timor-Leste', *East Timor Law Journal* 3, 1–4.

Gusmão, Xanana 2005b *Timor Lives! Speeches of freedom and independence*, Alexandria, NSW: Longueville Books.

Gusmão, Xanana 2006 'Message from the President', *Timor-Leste Human Development Report 2006*, Dili: United Nations Development Programme.

Hallett, Brien and Ralph Summy 2000 'Introduction: past, present, and future of the East Timor struggle', *Pacifica Review* 12(1), 9–16.

Hanreich, Herbert 2009 'Asian values assist in repression', *Taipei Times*, 10 December 2009, viewed 30 April 2011, <http://www.taipeitimes.com/News/editorials/archives/2009/12/10/2003460602>

Harland, David 2005 *UN Peacekeeping Operations in Post-Conflict Timor-Leste: Accomplishments and lessons learned*, New York: Department of Peacekeeping Operations, United Nations.

Harris Rimmer, Susan 2007 '"Orphans" or veterans? Justice for children born of war in East Timor', *Texas International Law Journal* 42(2) (Spring), 323–44.

Harris Rimmer, Susan 2008 Transitional justice and East Timorese women, PhD dissertation, The Australian National University, Canberra.

Harris Rimmer, Susan 2010 *Gender and Transitional Justice: The women of East Timor*, Routledge Contemporary Southeast Asia Series.

Harrington, Andrew 2007a 'Ethnicity, violence and land and property disputes in Timor-Leste', *East Timor Law Journal* 2(1), 35.

Harrington, Andrew 2007b The Commission of Truth and Friendship Indonesia–Timor-Leste: competing concepts of justice, MA thesis, University of Ottawa, Ontario.

Hicks, David 2004 *Tetum Ghosts and Kin: Fertility and gender in East Timor*, [Second edn], Long Grove, Ill.: Waveland Press.

Higashi, Daisaku 2009 *Challenge of Constructing Legitimacy in Peacebuiding: Case of Timor-Leste*, Vancouver: University of British Columbia.

Hill, Helen 2002 *Stirrings of Nationalism in East Timor: Fretilin 1974–1978*, Sydney: Oxford University Press.

Hirst, Megan 2008 *Too Much Friendship, Too Little Truth: Monitoring report on the Commission of Truth and Friendship in Indonesia and Timor-Leste*, New York: International Center for Transitional Justice.

Hohe, Tanja 2002 'The clash of paradigms: international administration and local political legitimacy in East Timor', *Contemporary Southeast Asia* 24(3), 569–89.

Hohe, Tanja 2003 'Justice without judiciary in East Timor', *Conflict, Security and Development* 3(3), 335–57.

Hohe, Tanja 2004 'Local governance after conflict: community empowerment in East Timor', *Journal of Peacebuilding and Development* 1(3), 45–56.

Hohe, Tanja and Rod Nixon 2003 *Reconciling justice: 'traditional' law and state judiciary in East Timor*, Final report prepared for the United States Institute of Peace, Washington, DC.

Holliday, Ian 2005 'The Yadana syndrome? Big oil and principles of corporate engagement in Myanmar', *Asian Journal of Political Science* 13(2), 29–51.

Hood, Ludovic 2006 'Security sector reform in East Timor, 1999–2004', *International Peacekeeping* 13(1), 60–77.

Human Rights Watch 2006 *Tortured Beginnings: Violence and the beginning of impunity in East Timor*, 19 April 2006, New York: Human Rights Watch.

Hynes, Michelle, Jeanne Ward, Kathryn Robertson and Chadd Crouse 2004 'A determination of the prevalence of gender-based violence among conflict-affected populations in East Timor', *Disasters* 28(3), 294–321.

International Crisis Group (ICG) 2002 *Liberia: The key to ending regional instability, 24 April 2002*, Africa Report No. 43, International Crisis Group, Jakarta/Brussels.

International Crisis Group (ICG) 2006a *Managing Tensions of the Timor-Leste/ Indonesia Border*, 4 May 2006, Jakarta/Brussels: International Crisis Group.

International Crisis Group (ICG) 2006b *Resolving Timor-Leste's crisis*, Asia Report No. 120, 10 October 2006, International Crisis Group, Brussels.

International Crisis Group (ICG) 2008 *Timor-Leste: security sector reform*, Asia Report No. 143, 17 January 2008, International Crisis Group, Brussels.

International Crisis Group (ICG) 2009 *Handing back responsibility to Timor-Leste's police*, Asia Report No. 180, 3 December 2009, International Crisis Group, Brussels.

International Crisis Group (ICG) 2011 'Timor-Leste's veterans: an unfinished struggle?' *Asia Briefing*, 18 November 2011, viewed 27 November 2011, <http://www.crisisgroup.org/en/regions/asia/south-east-asia/timor-leste/B129-timor-lestes-veterans-an-unfinished-struggle.aspx>

International Monetary Fund (IMF) 2010 *Report on the observance of standards and codes (ROSC), Fiscal Transparency Module*, 9 November 2010, Prepared by the Fiscal Affairs Department, Approved by Anoop Singh and Carlo Cottarelli, Washington, DC: International Monetary Fund.

Inter-Parliamentary Union (IPU) 2011 'Women in national parliaments', *IPU*, 31 March, viewed 28 April 2011, <http://www.ipu.org/wmn-e/classif.htm>

Jardine, Matthew 1995 *East Timor: Genocide in paradise*, Tuscon, Ariz.: Odonian Press.

Jardine, Matthew 2000 'East Timor, the United Nations, and the international community: force feeding human rights into the institutionalized jaws of failure', *Pacifica Review* 12(1), 47–62.

Johnston, Les and Clifford Shearing 2003 *Governing Security: Explorations in policing and justice*, London: Routledge.

Jolliffe, Jill 2001 'Ten years later, Santa Cruz still leaves a scar', *Sydney Morning Herald*, 21 November 2001.

Judicial System Monitoring Programme (JSMP) 2005a Difficulties encountered in finalizing long running cases, Press release, 6 June 2005, Judicial System Monitoring Programme, Dili.

Judicial System Monitoring Programme (JSMP) 2005b *Overview of the Justice Sector*, Dili: Judicial System Monitoring Programme.

Judicial System Monitoring Programme (JSMP) 2010 *Overview of the Justice Sector in Timor Leste 2010*, Dili: Judicial System Monitoring Programme.

Kaldor, Mary 1999 *New and Old Wars: Organized violence in a global era*, Cambridge: Polity Press.

Kammen, Douglas 2003 'Master–slave, traitor–nationalist, opportunist–oppressed: political metaphors in East Timor', *Indonesia* 76(October), 69–85.

Karstedt, S. 2005 'Terrorism and "new wars"', in B. Gokai and R. J. B. Walker (eds), *11 September 2001: War, terror and judgement*, London: Frank Cass.

Kehi, Balthasar 2007 *Overcoming the 2006 crisis in Timor-Leste: more dialogue and social solidarity*, SSEE Research Papers, in L. Palmer, S. Ninr and L. Kent (eds), *Exploring the Tensions of National Building in Timor-Leste*, Melbourne: University of Melbourne.

Kelly, Paul 2009 *The March of Patriots: The struggle for modern Australia*, Melbourne: Melbourne University Press.

Kenny, Charles 2011 *Getting Better: Why global development is succeeding—and how we can improve the world even more*, New York: Basic Books.

Kent, Lia 2004 *Unfulfilled Expectations: Community views on CAVR's Community Reconciliation Process*, Dili: Judicial System Monitoring Program.

Kent, Lia 2005 'Community views of justice and reconciliation in Timor-Leste', *Development Bulletin* 68, 62–5.

King's College Report 2000 *Independent Study on Security Force Options and Security Sector Reform for East Timor*, London: Centre for Defence Studies, King's College.

King's College Report 2003 *A Review of Peace Operations: A case for change—East Timor*, London: Centre for Defence Studies, King's College.

Kingsbury, Damien 2005 'East Timor border security', in Damien Kingsbury (ed.), *Violence in Between: Conflict and security in archipelagic Southeast Asia*, Singapore: Institute for Southeast Asian Studies.

Kingsbury, Damien 2008 'East Timor's political crisis: origins and resolution', in David Mearns (ed.), *Democratic Governance in Timor-Leste: Reconciling the local and the national*, Darwin: Charles Darwin University Press.

Kingsbury, Damien 2009 *East Timor: The price of liberty*, New York: Palgrave Macmillan.

Kingsbury, Damien and Lesley McCulloch 2006, 'Military business in Aceh', in Anthony Reid (ed.), *Verandah of Violence: The background to the Aceh problem*, Singapore: Singapore University Press.

Kingston, Jeffrey 2006 'Balancing justice and reconciliation in East Timor', *Critical Asian Studies* 38(3), 271–302.

Kivimäki, Timo 2003 'Post-hegemonic bargaining', in T. Kivimäki, *Indonesian Hegemonic Bargaining: Strength and weakness*, Aldershot, UK, and Burlington, Vt: Ashgate.

Knetsch, J. and M. Trebilcock 1981 *Land policy and economic development in Papua New Guinea*, Institute of National Affairs Discussion Paper No. 6, Institute of National Affairs, Port Moresby.

Koh, Harold 2010 The Obama Administration and international law, Address to American Society of International Law, Washington DC, viewed 9 May 2011, <http://www.state.gov/s/l/releases/remarks/139119.htm>

Kohen, Arnold and John Taylor 1979 *An Act of Genocide: Indonesia's invasion of East Timor*, London: A TAPOL (UK) Publication.

Krugman, Paul 2008 *The Return of Depression Economics and the Crisis of 2008*, London: Penguin Books.

Krygier, Martin 2002 'Conservative-liberal-socialism revisited', *The Good Society* 11(1), 6–15.

Kymlicka, Will 1998 *Finding Our Way*, Oxford: Oxford University Press.

Laakso, Jennifer 2007 Justice, order and peace: transitional justice and peacebuilding in Timor-Leste, PhD dissertation, University of Queensland, Brisbane.

La'o Hamutuk 2008 *Sunrise LNG in Timor-Leste: Dreams, realities and challenges*, Dili: La'o Hamutuk.

La'o Hamutuk Bulletin 2003 *UNMISET and Internal Security in East Timor*, May 2003, Dili: La'o Hamutuk.

Larke, Ben 2009 '"…And the truth shall set you free": confessional trade-offs and community reconciliation in East Timor', *Asian Journal of Social Science* 37, 646–76.

Lastaria-Cornhiel, S. 1997 'Impact of privatization on gender and property rights in Africa', *World Development* 35(8), 1317–41.

Latour, Bruno 1986 'The powers of association', in J. Law (ed.), *Power, Action, and Belief: A new sociology of knowledge?* Sociological Review Monograph 32, London, Boston and Henley: Routledge & Kegan Paul.

Latour, Bruno 1987 *Science in Action: How to follow engineers and scientists through society*, Milton Keynes, UK: Open University Press.

Lavigne-Delville, P. 2000 'Harmonising formal law and customary land rights in French-speaking West Africa', in C. Toulmin and J. Quan (eds), *Evolving Land Rights, Policy and Tenure in Africa*, London: International Institute for Environment and Development, Natural Resources Institute.

Leadbeater, Maire 2006 *Negligent Neighbour: New Zealand's complicity in the invasion and occupation of Timor-Leste*, Wellington: Craig Potton Publishing.

Lederach, John Paul 2008 Justpeace: The challenge of the 21st century, European Platform for Conflict Prevention and Transformation, viewed 4 December 2008, <http://www.gppac.net/documents/pbp/part1/1_justpe.htm>

Leong, James and Lynn Lee 2004 *Passabe*, [DVD], Singapore: Lianain Films.

Lennox, Rowena 2000 *Fighting Spirit of East Timor: The life of Martinho da Costa Lopes*, Sydney: Pluto Press, and London: Zed Press.

Loch, Alexander and Vanessa Prueller 2011 'Dealing with conflicts after the conflict: European and indigenous approaches to conflict transformation in East Timor', *Conflict Resolution Quarterly* 28(3), 315–29.

Lowry, Bob 2006 Defence and security in Timor-Leste, Paper presented to Beyond the Crisis in Timor-Leste: Options for future stability and development seminar, Development Studies Network, Canberra, 9 June 2006.

MacAskill, Ewen 2009 'US signals major policy shift towards Burma', *The Guardian*, 24 September 2009, viewed December 2010, <http://www.guardian.co.uk/world/2009/sep/24/burma-obama-foreign-policy>

McAuslan P. 1998 'Making law work: restructuring land relations in Africa', *Development and Change* 29(3), 525–52.

McCarthy, John 2002 *Falintil Reinsertion Assistant Program Final Evaluation Report*, Dili: International Organisation for Migration.

McCosker, Anthony 2004 'East Timor and the politics of bodily pain: a problematic complicity', *Continuum: Journal of Media and Cultural Studies* 18(1), 63–79.

McDonald, Hamish 2002 'Masters of terror: Indonesia's findings', in Hamish McDonald (ed.), *Masters of Terror: Indonesia's military and violence in East Timor in 1999*, Canberra: Strategic and Defence Studies Centre, The Australian National University.

McFarlane, John and William Maley 2006 'Civilian police in UN peace operations: some lessons from recent Australian experience', in Ramesh Thakur and Albrecht Schnabel (eds), *United Nations Peacekeeping Operations: Ad hoc missions, permanent engagement*, Tokyo and New York: United Nations University Press.

Mackenzie, Catriona 1993 'Reason and sensibility: the ideal of women's self-governance in the writings of Mary Wollstonecraft', *Hypatia* 8(4).

McLeod, Jason 2008 'Free at last: the struggle for independence in East Timor', *Change Agency Newsletter*, viewed January 2011, <http://www.thechangeagency.org/03_enews/newsletter.asp?ID=198>

McWilliam, Andrew 2005 'Houses of resistance in East Timor: structuring sociality in the new nation', *Anthropological Forum* 15(1), 27–44.

McWilliam, Andrew 2007a 'Introduction; restorative custom: ethnographic perspective on conflict and local justice in Timor', *The Asia Pacific Journal of Anthropology* 8(1), 1–8.

McWilliam, Andrew 2007b 'Meto disputes and peacemaking: cultural notes on conflict and its resolution in West Timor', *The Asia Pacific Journal of Anthropology* 8(1), 75–91.

Makkai, T. and J. Braithwaite 1994 'Reintegrative shaming and regulatory compliance', *Criminology* 32(3), 361–85.

Maley, William 2000 'The UN and East Timor', *Pacifica Review* 12(1), 63–71.

Malik, Mohan 2000 'Burma's role in regional security', in Morton B. Pedersen, Emily Rudland and Ronald J. May (eds), *Burma/Myanmar: Strong Regime, Weak State?* Adelaide: Crawford House.

Maoulidi, Salma 2007 'Mary Wollstonecraft: challenges of race and class in feminist discourse', *Women's Studies Quarterly* 35(3–4), 280–6.

Marino, Pascal 2006 'Beyond economic benefits: the contribution of microfinance to post-conflict recovery in Asia and the Pacific', in Matthew Clarke (ed.), *Aid in Conflict*, New York: Nova Science Publishers.

Martin, Ian and Alexander Mayer-Rieckh 2005 'The United Nations and East Timor: from self-determination to state-building', *International Peacekeeping* 12(1), 125–45.

Martinkus, John 2006 'Evidence mounts against Gusmão', *New Matilda*, 20 September 2006.

Marshall, Shane with James McKenna 2005 'At the threshold of self-sufficiency? The East Timorese judiciary', *Development Bulletin* 68, 43–7.

Mason, Christine 2005 'Women, violence and nonviolent resistance in East Timor', *Journal of Peace Research* 42(6), 737–49.

Mason, Whit (ed.) 2011 *The Rule of Law in Afghanistan: Missing in inaction*, Cambridge: Cambridge University Press.

Mearns, David 2001 *Variations on a theme: coalitions of authority in East Timor—a report on the local and national justice systems as a basis for dispute resolution*, Report prepared for Australian Legal Resources International.

Merry, Sally Engle 2006 *Human Rights and Gender Violence: Translating international law into local justice*, Chicago: University of Chicago Press.

Michels, Robert [1911] 1966 *Political Parties: A sociological study of the oligarchical tendencies of modern democracies*, New York: The Free Press.

Milner, Anthony 1999 'What happened to Asian values', in David Goodman and Gerald Segal (eds), *Beyond the Asia Crisis*, Melbourne: Routledge.

Molnar, Andrea 2004 'An anthropological study of Atsabe perceptions of Colimau 2000', *Anthropos* 99(2), 365–80.

Montesquieu, Baron Charles de Secondat 1977 *The Spirit of the Laws*, D. W. Carrithers (abr. and ed.), Berkeley: University of California Press.

Morrow, Jonathan and Rachel White 2002 'The United Nations in transitional East Timor: international standards and the reality of governance', *The Australian Year Book of International Law* 22, 1–46.

Moxham, Ben 2008 *State-making and the post-conflict city: integration in Dili, disintegration in Timor-Leste*, Working Paper 32, Crisis Research Centre, London School of Economics, London.

Moynihan, Daniel Patrick with S. Weaver 1978 *A Dangerous Place*, Boston: Little Brown.

Muggah, Robert, Oliver Jütersonke, Robin Murray, Edward Rees and James Scambary 2010 *Urban violence in an urban village: a case study of Dili, Timor-Leste*, Geneva Declaration Working Paper, Geneva Declaration Secretariat, Geneva.

Munton, Alexander J. 2006 A study of the offshore petroleum negotiations between Australia, the UN and East Timor, PhD dissertation, The Australian National University, Canberra.

Murdoch, Lindsay 2008a 'Aid groups suggest Timor enforces law', *Sydney Morning Herald*, 31 March 2008.

Murdoch, Lindsay 2008b 'Gangster nets key Dili project', *The Age*, 5 August 2008.

Murdoch, Lindsay and Tom Hyland 2008 'Gangster's role queried in Timor attacks', *The Age*, 16 March 2008.

Murdoch, Lindsay and Tom Hyland 2009 'Dili tycoon deal triggers alarm', *The Age*, 3 May 2009.

Myrttinen, Henri 2007 *Up in smoke: impoverishment and instability in post-independence Timor-Leste*, Kepa Working Paper No. 11, Kepa, Helsinki.

Myrttinen, Henri 2008 *Timor-Leste: A kaleidoscope of conflicts—notes from a visit to Timor-Leste and West Timor, October–December 2007*, Canberra: The Australian National University.

Myrttinen, Henri 2009 'Timor-Leste: a relapsing "success" story', *Taiwan Journal of Democracy* 5(1), 219–39.

Nairn, Allan 1992 *Excerpts from the Testimony of Allan Nairn before the United States Senate Committee on Foreign Relations, February 27, 1992*, Brooklyn, NY: East Timor Action Network.

National Statistics Directorate 2010 *Timor-Leste Demographic and Health Survey 2009–10*, Dili: National Statistics Directorate, Timor-Leste.

Neto, Felix, Maria da Conceição Pinto and Etienne Mullet 2007a 'Intergroup forgiveness: East Timorese and Angolan perspectives', *Journal of Peace Research* 44, 711–28.

Neto, Felix, Maria da Conceição Pinto and Etienne Mullet 2007b 'Seeking forgiveness in intergroup context: Angolan, Guinean, Mozambican, and East Timorese perspectives', *Regulation & Governance* 1(4), 329–46.

Neves, Guteriano, Charles Scheiner and Santina Soares 2008 *Sunrise LNG in Timor-Leste: Dreams, realities and challenges*, Dili: La'o Hamutuk.

Nevins, Joséph 2002 'The making of "ground zero" in East Timor in 1999: an analysis of international complicity in Indonesia's crimes', *Asian Survey* 42(2), 623–41.

Nevins, Joséph 2003 'Restitution over coffee: truth, reconciliation, and environmental violence in East Timor', *Political Geography* 22(6), 677–701.

Nicol, Bill 2002 *Timor: A nation reborn*, Jakarta: Equinox.

Nicolau, Guteriano and Charles Scheiner 2005 *Oil in Timor-Leste*, Dili: La'o Hamutuk.

Niner, Sara 2005 'President Xanana Gusmão: a transforming leadership', *Development Bulletin* 68, 39–42.

Niner, Sara 2009 *Xanana: Leader of the struggle for independent Timor-Leste*, Melbourne: Australian Scholarly Publishing.

Niner, Sara 2011 '*Hakat klot*, narrow steps', *International Feminist Journal of Politics* 13(3), 413–35.

Nixon, Rod 2006 'The crisis of governance in new subsistence states', *Journal of Contemporary Asia* 36, 75–101.

Nixon, Rod 2008 Integrating indigenous approaches into a 'new subsistence state': the case of justice and conflict resolution in East Timor, PhD dissertation, Charles Darwin University, Darwin.

Oenarto, Joséph 2000 *Can East Timor survive independence?* Discussion Paper No. 17/2000, North Australia Research Unit, The Australian National University, Canberra.

Okoth-Ogendo, H. 2000 'Legislative approaches to customary tenure and tenure reform in East Africa', in C. Toulmin and J. Quan (eds), *Evolving Land Rights, Policy and Tenure in Africa*, London: International Institute for Environment and Development, Natural Resources Institute.

Olsen, Tricia D., Leigh A. Payne and Andrew G. Reiter 2010a 'The justice balance: when transitional justice improves human rights and democracy', *Human Rights Quarterly* 32(4), 980–1007.

Olsen, Tricia D., Leigh A. Payne and Andrew G. Reiter 2010b *Transitional Justice in the Balance: Comparing processes, weighing efficacy*, Washington, DC: USIP Press.

Ospina, Sofi and Tanja Hohe 2002 *Traditional Power Structures and Local Governance in East Timor: A case study of the Community Empowerment Project*, Geneva: Graduate Institute for Development Studies.

Palmer, Lisa and Dementrio do Amaral de Carvalho 2008 'National building and resource management: the politics of "nature" in Timor-Leste', *Geoforum* 39, 1321–32.

Paris, Roland 2004 *At War's End: Building peace after conflict*, Cambridge: Cambridge University Press.

Pascoe, Daniel 2006 Justice for serious crimes committed during 1999 in Timor-Leste: where to from here? Bachelor of Asian Studies (Hons) thesis, The Australian National University, Canberra.

Pateman, Carole 2009 'Mary Wollstonecraft', in D. Boucher and P. Kelly (eds), *Political Thinkers: From Socrates to the present day*, Oxford: Oxford University Press.

Patrick, Ian 2001 'East Timor emerging from conflict: the role of local NGOs and international assistance', *Disasters* 25(1), 48–66.

Patterson, Gerard R. 1982 *Coercive Family Process*, Eugene, Ore.: Castalia Publishing.

Peake, Gordon 2008 'Police reform and reconstruction in Timor-Leste: a difficult do-over', in M. Hinton and T. Newburn (eds), *Policing Developing Democracies*, Newburn, UK: Routledge.

Pedersen, Morten B. 2008 *Promoting Human Rights in Burma: A critique of Western sanctions policy*, Denver: Rowman & Littlefield.

Pereira, Agio 2009 'The form of my liberation', *Semanario* (August), 5–8.

Pettit, Philip 1997 *Republicanism*, Oxford: Clarendon Press.

Phillips, Anne 2000 'Feminism and republicanism: is this a plausible alliance?' *The Journal of Political Philosophy* 8(2), 279–93.

Pickering, Jeffrey and Mark Peceny 2006 'Forging democracy at gunpoint', *International Studies Quarterly* 50(3), 539–60.

Pilger, John 1994 *Distant Voices*, London: Vintage Books.

Pinto, Constâncio 2009 Interview with Constâncio Pinto, *Suara Timor-Lorosae*, 12 November 2009.

Pinto, Constâncio and Matthew Jardine 1997 *East Timor's Unfinished Struggle: Inside the Timorese resistance*, Boston: South End Press.

Platteau, J. P. 1992 *Land reform and structural adjustment in sub-Saharan Africa: controversies and guidelines*, Economic and Social Development Paper 107, Food and Agriculture Organisation, Rome.

Platteau, J. P. 1996 'The evolutionary theory of land rights as applied to sub-Saharan Africa: a critical assessment', *Development and Change* 27(1), 29–86.

Platteau, J. P. 2000 'Does Africa need land reform?' in C. Toulmin and J. Quan (eds), *Evolving Land Rights, Policy and Tenure in Africa*, London: International Institute for Environment and Development, Natural Resources Institute.

Pocock, J. G. A. 1975 *The Machiavellian Moment*, Princeton, NJ: Princeton University Press.

Power, Samantha 2008 *Chasing the Flame: One man's fight to save the world*, New York: Penguin.

Purdey, Jemma 2006 *Anti-Chinese Violence in Indonesia 1996–1999*, Singapore: Singapore University Press.

Putnam, Robert D. 1988 'Diplomacy and domestic politics: the logic of two-level games', *International Organization* 42, 425–60.

Putnam, Robert D. 1993 *Making Democracy Work: Civic traditions in modern Italy*, Princeton, NJ: Princeton University Press.

Rae, James DeShaw 2009 *Peacebuilding and Transitional Justice in East Timor*, Boulder, Colo.: First Forum Press.

Ramos-Horta, José 1987 *Funu: The unfinished saga of East Timor*, Trenton, NJ: Red Sea Press.

Rees, Edward 2002 'Security-sector reform and transitional administrations', *Journal of Conflict, Security and Development* 2(1), 151–6.

Rees, Edward 2003 'UN's failure to integrate Falintil veterans may cause East Timor to fail', *On Line Opinion*, 2 September 2003, viewed 20 May 2011, <http://onlineopinion.com.au/view.asp?article=666>

Rees, Edward 2004 *Under pressure: Falintil–forcas de defesa de Timor-Leste—three decades of defence force development in Timor-Leste 1975–2004*, Working Paper No. 139, Geneva Centre for the Democratic Control of Armed Forces, Geneva.

Rees, Edward 2006 *Security sector reform (SSR) and peace operations: 'improvisation and confusion' from the field*, United Nations Peacekeeping Best Practices Paper, United Nations, New York.

Rees, Edward 2010 'Small arms proliferation and control', in E. LeBrun and R. Muggah (eds), *Timor-Leste Armed Violence Final Report*, Geneva: Small Arms Survey.

Rei, Naldo 2007 *Resistance: A childhood fighting for East Timor*, St Lucia: University of Queensland Press.

Reiger, Caitlin and Marieke Wierda 2006 *The Serious Crimes Process in Timor-Leste: In retrospect*, New York: International Center for Transitional Justice.

Reno, William 1995 *Corruption and State Politics in Sierra Leone*, Cambridge: Cambridge University Press.

Report of the Alkatiri Initiative Review 2006 *Strengthening Accountability and Transparency in Timor-Leste*, Dili: United Nations Office in Timor-Leste.

Reynal-Querol, M. 2002 'Political systems, stability and civil wars', *Defence and Peace Economics* 13(6), 465–83.

Rhodes, Rod 1997 *Understanding Governance*, Buckingham and Philadelphia: Open University Press.

Rinakit, Sukardi 2005 *The Indonesian Military after the New Order*, Copenhagen: NIAS Press, and Singapore: Institute of Southeast Asian Studies.

Robinson, Geoffrey 2003 *East Timor 1999 crimes against humanity: a report commissioned by the United Nations Office of the High Commissioner for Human Rights*, Commission for Reception, Truth and Reconciliation, Dili.

Robinson, Geoffrey 2008 'People power: a comparative history of forced displacement in East Timor', in E. Hedman (ed.), *Conflict, Violence and Displacement in Indonesia*, Ithaca, NY: South East Asia Program Publications.

Rodrik, Dani 2011 *The Globalization Paradox: Democracy and the future of the world economy*, New York: Norton.

Roosa, John 1999 'Against all odds: the victory of a lost cause', *Estafeta* 5(3), 1–5.

Ross, Michael L. 2001 'Does oil hinder democracy?' *World Politics* 53(3), 325–61.

Rudé, George F. E. 1964, *The Crowd in History: A study of popular disturbances in France and England, 1730–1848*, London: Lawrence & Wishart.

Ryan, Alan 2000 *Primary responsibilities and primary risks: Australian defence force participation in the international force in East Timor*, Study Paper No. 304, Land Warfare Studies Centre, Canberra.

Ryan, Alan 2002 'The strong lead-nation model in an ad-hoc coalition of the willing: Operation Stabilize in East Timor', *International Peacekeeping* 9(1), 23–42.

Sabel, Charles F. and William H. Simon 2004 'Destabilization rights: how public law litigation succeeds', *Harvard Law Review* 117(4), 1015–101.

Sakabe, Yukako 2008 'International assistance to the nation-building efforts of Timor-Leste', in David Mearns (ed.), *Democratic Governance in Timor-Leste: Reconciling the local and the national*, Darwin: Charles Darwin University Press.

Salla, Michael 1997a 'Creating the "ripe moment" in the East Timor conflict', *Journal of Peace Research* 34(4), 449–66.

Salla, Michael 1997b 'East Timor, regional security and the Labor tradition', in D. Lee and C. Waters (eds), *Evatt to Evans: The Labor tradition in Australian foreign policy*, Sydney: Allen & Unwin.

Sambanis, Nicholas 2002 'A review of recent advances and future directions in the literature on civil war', *Defence and Peace Economics* 14(3), 215–43.

Scambary, James 2006 *A survey of gangs and youth groups in Dili, Timor-Leste*, A report commissioned by the Australian Agency for International Development (AusAID), Canberra.

Scambary, James 2009 'Anatomy of a conflict: the 2006–2007 communal violence in East Timor', *Conflict, Security & Development* 9, 265–88.

Scambury, James 2010 'Groups and gang violence', in E. LeBrun and R. Muggah (eds), *Timor-Leste Armed Violence Final Report*, Geneva: Small Arms Survey.

Scheeringa, Sandra 2007 'Enhancing the local legitimacy of transitional justice institutions: local embeddedness and customary law in CAVR', in D. Kingsbury and M. Leach (eds), *East Timor: Beyond independence*, Clayton, Vic.: Monash University Press.

Schwartz, Adam 1999 *A Nation in Waiting: Indonesia's search for stability*, Sydney: Allen & Unwin.

Scott, David 2005 *Last Flight out of Dili: Memories of an accidental activist in the triumph of East Timor*, North Melbourne: Pluto Press.

Scott, James C. 1998 *Seeing Like a State: How certain schemes to improve the human condition have failed*, New Haven, Conn.: Yale University Press.

Sebastian, Leonard C. 2006 *Realpolitik Ideology: Indonesia's use of military force*, Singapore: Institute of Southeast Asian Studies.

Security Sector Reform Monitor 2010 *Timor-Leste* (2) (May 2010), Waterloo, Ontario: Security Sector Reform Resource Centre.

Sen, Amartya 1997 'Human rights and Asian values: what Lee Kwan Yew and Le Peng don't understand about Asia', *The New Republic* 217(2–3), 33–41.

Severino, Rodolfo C. 2006 *Southeast Asia in Search of an ASEAN Community: Insights from the former ASEAN Secretary-General*, Singapore: Institute for Southeast Asian Studies.

Shackleton, Shirley 2010 *The Circle of Silence*, Millers Point, NSW: Pier 9.

Shawcross, William 2000 *Deliver us from Evil: Warlords and peacekeepers in a world of endless conflict*, London: Bloomsbury.

Shearing, Clifford 1997 'Violence and the changing face of governance: privatization and its implications', *Kolner Zeitschrift fur Soziologie und Sozialpsychologie* [*Cologne Journal of Sociology and Social Psychology*] 49(37), 263–78.

Shearing, Clifford and Jennifer Wood, with John Cartwright and Madeleine Jenneker 2003 'Nodal governance, democracy and the new "denizens": challenging the Westphalian ideal', *Journal of Law and Society* 30(3), 400–19.

Shoesmith, Dennis 2003 'Divided leadership in a semi-presidential system', *Asian Survey* 43(2), 231–52.

Shoesmith, Dennis 2008 'Legislative–executive relations in Timor-Leste: the case for building a stronger parliament', in David Mearns (ed.), *Democratic Governance in Timor-Leste: Reconciling the local and the national*, Darwin: Charles Darwin University Press.

Siapno, Jacqueline 2008 'Whispered confidences: articulating the female in the PNTL (police) and the F-FDTL (military) in Timor-Leste', *IIAS Newsletter: Women Warriors* (48), 7–8, viewed March 2011, <http://213.206.241.179/files/IIAS_NL48_0708.pdf>

Sikkink, Kathryn 2011 *The Justice Cascade: How human rights prosecutions are changing world politics*, New York: W. W. Norton.

Silva, Kelly 2010 'Processes of regionalisation in East Timor social conflicts', *Anthropological Forum* 20, 105–23.

Simonsen, Sven Gunnar 2006 'The authoritarian temptation in East Timor: national building and the need for inclusive governance', *Asian Survey* 46(4), 575–96.

Simpson, Brad 2004 'Solidarity in an age of globalization: the transnational movement for East Timor and US foreign policy', *Peace and Change* 29(3–4), 453–82.

Simpson, S. R. 1976 *Land Law and Registration*, Cambridge: Cambridge University Press.

Singh, Bilveer 1996 *East Timor, Indonesia and the World: Myths and realities*, [Revised edn], Singapore: Singapore Institute for International Affairs.

Skinner, Quentin 1983 'Machiavelli on the maintenance of liberty', *Politics* 18(3), 3–15.

Slaughter, Ann-Marie 2004 *A New World Order*, Princeton, NJ: Princeton University Press.

Smith, Michael G. with Moreen Dee 2003 *Peacekeeping in East Timor: The path to independence*, Boulder, Colo.; Lynne Rienner.

Smith, Michael G. with Moreen Dee 2006 'East Timor', in William Durch (ed.), *Twenty-First Century Peace Operations*, Washington, DC: United States Institute of Peace.

Soares, Adérito de Jesus 2011 'Combating corruption in Timor-Leste: avoiding "institutional ritualism"', in D. Kingsbury and M. Leach (eds), *The Politics of Timor-Leste: A decade of independence*, New York: Cornell University Press.

Sorensen, Eva 2006 'Metagovernance: the changing role of politicians in processes of democratic governance', *American Review of Public Administration* 36(1), 98–114.

Sorensen, Eva and J. Torfing 2006 'The democratic anchorage of governance networks', *Scandinavian Political Studies* 28(3), 195–218.

Stanley, Elizabeth 2009 *Torture, Truth and Justice: The case of Timor-Leste*, London: Routledge.

Steele, Janet 2007 'The voice of East Timor: journalism, ideology, and the struggle for independence', *Asian Studies Review* 31(3), 261–82.

Stephan, Maria J. and Erica Chenoweth 2008 'Why civilian resistance works: the strategic logic of nonviolent conflict', *International Security* 33(1), 7–44.

Stiglitz, J. E. 2002 *Globalization and its Discontents*, New York: W. W. Norton.

Sukma, Rizal 2002 'Securing East Timor: the military and external relations', in Hadi Soesastro and Landry Haryo Subianto (eds), *Peace Building and State Building in East Timor*, Jakarta: Centre for Strategic and International Studies.

Swaine, Aisling 2003 *Traditional Justice and Gender Based Violence*, International Rescue Society, <http://ssrn.com/abstract=1440231>

Sword Gusmão, Kirsty 2003 *A Woman of Independence: A story of love and the birth of a new nation*, Sydney: Pan Macmillan.

Tanner, C. 2002 *Law making in an African context: the 1997 Mozambiquan land law*, FAO Legal Papers Online No. 26, Food and Agriculture Organisation, Rome, viewed May 2008, <www.fao.org>

Taylor, John G. 1999 *East Timor: The price of freedom*, London: Zed Books.

Therik, Tom 2004 *Wehali: The female land—traditions of a Timorese ritual centre*, Canberra: Pandanus Books.

Thompson, Edwina 2008 *Principled Pragmatism: NGO engagement with armed actors*, Monrovia, Calif.: World Vision International.

Thompson, Mark 2001 'Whatever happened to "Asian values"?' *Journal of Democracy* 12(4), 154–65.

Tiffen, Rodney 2001 *Diplomatic Deceits: Government, media and East Timor*, Sydney: UNSW Press.

Timor-Leste Armed Violence Assessment (TLAVA) 2009a *Groups, gangs, and armed violence in Timor-Leste*, TLAVA Issue Brief No. 2, Timor-Leste Armed Violence Assessment, Dili.

Timor-Leste Armed Violence Assessment (TLAVA) 2009b *After the guns fall silent: sexual and gender-based violence in Timor-Leste*, TLAVA Issue Brief No. 5, Timor-Leste Armed Violence Assessment, Dili.

Toohey, Paul 2008 'Autopsy doubt on East Timor rebel Alfredo Reinado', *The Australian*, 13 August 2008.

Toulmin, C. and J. Quan 2000 'Registering customary rights', in C. Toulmin and J. Quan (eds), *Evolving Land Rights, Policy and Tenure in Africa*, London: DFID/HED/IIED/NRI.

Toulmin, C., P. Lavigne Delville and S. Traore 2002 'Introduction', in C. Toulmin, P. Lavigne Delville and S. Traore (eds), *The Dynamics of Resource Tenure in West Africa*, Portsmouth, NJ: Heinemann.

Traub, James 2000 'Inventing East Timor', *Foreign Affairs* 79(4), 74–89.

Trindade, José and Bryant Castro 2007 *Rethinking Timorese identity as a peace building strategy: the Lorosa'e–Loromonu conflict from a traditional perspective*, Final report for GTZ International Services, The European Union's Rapid

Reaction Mechanism Programme, Dili, viewed January 2008, <www.timorleste.org/nation_building/Trindade_Castro_Rethinking_Timorese_Identity_2007.pdf>

Trindade, Josh 2008 An ideal state for East Timor: reconciling the conflicting paradigms, Email communication discussing his February 2008 paper of this title.

Tsing, A. L. 2005 *Friction: An ethnography of global connection*, Princeton, NJ: Princeton University Press.

Unger, Roberto Mangabeira 1986 *The Critical Legal Studies Movement*, Cambridge, Mass.: Harvard University Press.

Unger, Roberto Mangabeira 1987 *False Necessity: Anti-necessitarian social theory in the service of radical democracy*, Cambridge, Mass.: Harvard University Press.

United Nations (UN) 1999 *Situation of human rights in East Timor: Report on the Joint Mission to East Timor undertaken by the Special Rapporteur on Extrajudicial, Summary or Arbitrary Executions, the Special Rapporteur on the Question of Torture, and the Special Rapporteur on Violence against Women, its Causes and Consequences*, UN Document A/54/660, 10 December 1999.

United Nations Development Programme (UNDP) 2004 *The Community Reconciliation Process of the Commission for Reception, Truth and Reconciliation*, Dili: United Nations Development Programme.

United Nations Development Programme (UNDP) 2006 *Timor-Leste Human Development Report 2006: The path out of poverty—integrated rural development*, Dili: United Nations Development Programme.

United Nations Development Programme (UNDP) 2007 *Justice for All? An assessment of access to justice in five provinces of Indonesia*, Jakarta: United Nations Development Programme.

United Nations Development Programme (UNDP) 2009 *Country Programme for Timor-Leste (2009–2013)*, Dili: United Nations Development Programme.

United Nations Development Programme (UNDP) 2011 *Timor-Leste Human Development Report: Managing natural resources for human development*, Dili: United Nations Development Programme.

United Nations Independent Special Commission 2006 *Report of the United Nations Independent Special Commission of Inquiry for Timor-Leste*, 2 October 2006, Geneva: United Nations.

United Nations Integrated Mission in Timor-Leste (UNMIT) 2007 *Report on human rights developments in Timor-Leste, August 2006 – August 2007*, UNMIT Human Rights and Transitional Justice Section, Dili.

USAID and Asia Foundation 2004 *Law and Justice in East Timor: A survey of citizen awareness and attitudes regarding law and justice in East Timor*.

van Klinken, Gerry 2007 *Communal Violence and Democratization in Indonesia: Small town wars*, London: Routledge.

Walsh, Pat 2011 *At the Scene of the Crime*, Preston, Vic.: Mosaic Press.

Wandita, Galuh 2007 Rape and sexual violence in the context of the popular consultation in East Timor 1999, Statement to the Commission of Truth and Friendship Public Hearing, Crowne Plaza Hotel, Jakarta, 29 March 2007.

Wandita, Galuh, Karen Campbell-Nelson and Manuela Long Pereira 2006 'Learning to engender reparations in Timor-Leste: reaching out to female victims', in Ruth Rubio-Marin (ed.), *Engendering Reparations: Recognizing and compensating women victims of human rights violations*, New York: Social Science Research Council.

Webber, Jeremy 1994 *Reimagining Canada: Language, culture, community and the Canadian Constitution*, Montreal: McGill University Press.

Weber, Max 1954 *Law in Economy and Society*, New York: Clarion.

Webster, David 2003 'Non-state diplomacy: East Timor 1975–99', *Portuguese Studies Review* 11(1), 1–28.

Wheeler, Nicholas J. and Tim Dunne 2001 'East Timor and the new humanitarian interventionism', *International Affairs* 77(4), 805–27.

White, Hugh 2008 'The road to INTERFET: reflections on Australian strategic decisions concerning East Timor, December 1998–September 1999', *Security Challenges* 4(1), 69–87.

Whittington, Sherrill 2003 'Gender and peacekeeping: the United Nations Transitional Administration in East Timor', *Signs: Journal of Women in Culture and Society* 28(4), 1283–8.

Wilson, Bu V. E. 2007 'Challenges to sustainable police-building: the development of the Policia Nacional Timor-Leste', in Lisa Palmer, Sara Niner and Lia Kent (eds), *Exploring the tensions of nation building in Timor-Leste*, SSEE Research Paper No. 1, University of Melbourne, Carlton, Vic.

Wilson, Bu V. E. 2008 'Smoke and mirrors: institutionalizing fragility in the Policia Nacional Timor-Leste', in David Mearns (ed.), *Democratic Governance in Timor-Leste: Reconciling the local and the national*, Darwin: Charles Darwin University Press.

Wilson, Bu V. E. 2010 Smoke and mirrors: the development of the East Timorese police 1999–2009, PhD dissertation, The Australian National University, Canberra.

Wilson, Bu V. E. and Nelson De Sousa C. Belo 2009 The UNPOL to PNTL 'handover': what exactly is being handed over? SSRC Conflict Prevention and Peace Forum, Dili, 3 December 2009.

Wise, Amanda 2006 *Exile and Return Among the East Timorese*, Philadelphia: University of Pennsylvania Press.

Wollstonecraft, Mary 1792 *A Vindication of the Rights of Women*, available at <http://www.bartleby.com/144/>

Woolcott, Richard 2000 'The consequences of the crisis over East Timor', in Bruce Brown (ed.), *East Timor: The consequences*, Wellington: New Zealand Institute of International Affairs.

Woolcott, Richard 2003 *The Hot Seat: Reflections on diplomacy from Stalin's death to the Bali bombings*, Sydney: HarperCollins.

World Bank 1993 *The East Asian Miracle*, Washington, DC: The World Bank.

World Bank 2004 *Village Justice in Indonesia: Case studies on access to justice, village democracy and governance*, Jakarta: The World Bank.

Wright, Warren L. 2009 'Witchcraft and murder in East Timor', *East Timor Law Journal* 6, viewed May 2011, <http://www.eastimorlawjournal.org/ARTICLES/2009/Witchcraft_and_Murder_in_East_Timor_Warren_L_Wright.html>

Zelter, Angie 2004 'Civil society and global responsibility: the arms trade and East Timor', *International Relations* 18(1), 125–40.

Zifcak, Spencer 2003 *Restorative Justice in East Timor: A case study of the nation's Truth and Reconciliation Commission*, Melbourne: La Trobe University.

Zifcak, Spencer 2005 'Restorative justice in Timor-Leste: the Truth and Reconciliation Commission', *Development Bulletin* 68, 51–4.

Index

Abrahms, Max 279
Abrantes, Laura Soares 265
Aceh 97, 108, 119, 242n.7, 287–8
Act of Free Choice 19, 40, 94
Action for World Development 70
Ad Hoc Human Rights Court on East Timor 198
adat 179, 188, 190, 205, 216, 217, 275
  see also lisan
Aditjondro, George J. 73, 266
Afaloikai 243, 244, 245
Africa 71, 76, 124, 181, 236, 241, 260, 280, 309
Ahmed, Eliza 32
Ahtisaari, Martti 288
Alatas, Ali 45, 77, 93, 94, 96
aldeia 120, 168, 188n.11, 266, 272
Alkatiri, Mari xi, 49, 71, 124, 127, 138, 153, 156, 157, 169, 194, 202, 224, 225, 236, 284, 295
  1975 generation 114
  and reconciliation 225, 226, 227, 228
  and Timor Sea 248, 251–2
  and violence in Dili (2006) 140, 141, 142, 144
  as founder of Fretilin 12
  as Prime Minister 120, 121, 122, 125, 126, 140, 141, 178, 180, 192, 223, 247
  conflict with Gusmão 125, 126, 127, 137, 168, 226
  criticism of 126, 127, 281
  diplomacy 3, 135, 280n.4
  enlisting African support 76, 280
  Fretilin leadership 187
  in opposition 125–6, 127
  interviews with 153, 154, 171n.18, 236, 285
  on National Council 120
  relations with Australia 171, 172
  relations with Indonesia 196
  renouncing violence 125
  resignation 140n.9, 144
Allen, Matthew 126, 139, 145, 160, 168, 173, 181
Alola Foundation 212, 269
Alves, Maria Domingas 225, 265, 309
Amnesty International 26n.12, 155, 299
AMP, see Parliamentary Alliance Majority
Anderson, Benedict R. O.'G. 27, 28
Anderson, Tim 253
Angola 76, 103
Annan, Kofi 35, 77, 96, 102, 107, 108, 191, 196, 197
anomie 91, 104, 149, 150, 151, 172, 173, 233, 296
Anti-Corruption Commission (CAC) xii, 186, 249n.9, 290, 294, 298
Anti-Corruption Commissioner 128, 129, 249, 297, 300
Apodeti (Associação Popular Democrática Timorense/Timorese Popular Democratic Association) 13, 47, 54, 124, 202
'Arab Spring' 3, 4, 35, 89, 90
Araujo, Elisia 190
Araujo, Father Jovito de Jesus 190n.13
Araujo, Rui 79
Arendt, Hannah 4, 134
Arndt, Heinz 72
Aroujo, Fernando 'La'Sama' 280n.2
ASDT (Associação Social-Democrata Timorense/Timorese Social Democratic Association) 12, 14
Asia 2, 9, 23, 30, 36, 73, 76, 240, 241, 258, 281, 309
  see also South-East Asia
Asia Foundation 114, 155, 156n.14, 177, 179, 181, 186, 188, 189n.12, 274, 275
Asia Pacific Coalition for East Timor 71
Asia Pacific Economic Cooperation (APEC) 68, 73, 102, 108
Asia Watch 80, 82, 85
Asian Development Bank (ADB) 119, 120, 242

343

Asian financial crisis 40, 91, 258
'Asian values' 29, 30n.16, 36
Aspinall, Edward 91, 92
Associação Popular Democrática Timorense, *see* Apodeti
Associação Social-Democrata Timorense, *see* ASDT
Association of Ex-Combatants 1975 (AC75) 137
Association of South-East Asian Nations (ASEAN) 26, 29, 30, 41, 72, 73
Aubrey, Jim 83
Aung San Suu Kyi 29, 31
Australian Broadcasting Corporation (ABC) 72, 80, 249
Australian Catholic Relief 70
Australian Council for International Development (ACFID) 70
Australian Council for Overseas Aid (ACFOA) 70
Australian Labor Party 25, 26, 42, 93, 196
Australian National University xi, xii, xiii, 28, 72, 234n.39
Australian Parliamentary East Timor Friendship Group 70
autonomy xii, 2, 10, 12, 74, 77, 92, 93, 96, 97, 264, 275, 277, 288
'axis of evil' 32, 34
Ayres, Ian xi, xii

Ba Futuru 225
Babo-Soares, D. xv, 198n.21, 201, 205, 216
BAKIN (Badan Koordinasi Intelijen Negara/State Intelligence Coordinating Agency of Indonesia) 18, 19, 22
Bali 3, 55, 66, 67, 79, 85, 98, 186
Balibo 24, 43
Ball, Desmond 23, 25, 95, 97, 98
Bangladesh 181, 242n.7, 253, 260, 307, 309
barlaque (bride price) 264, 265, 274, 276
Barnes, Susanna 180, 181, 182, 183

Barnett, Michael xv, 123, 128, 131, 132, 133, 134, 283, 287, 292, 299
Barreto, Emilio 200n.22
Baucau 48, 169, 170, 171, 172, 177, 243
Bayley, David H. 157, 159n.16, 164
Beauvais, Joel C. 115, 116, 117, 118, 119, 120n.1
Bell, Daniel 30n.16
Belo, Bishop 66, 74, 79, 80, 83, 84, 85, 225, 226, 281
Belo, Nelson De Sousa C. 154, 158–9, 160
Belun 165, 225
Bere, Maria Agnes 274
Bere, Maternus 212, 213, 301
Berger, Mark T. 92
Berger, Sandy 101, 107, 109
Bertrand, Jacques 13, 91, 92
Bevir, M. 8
Binswanger, H. P. 184n.7
Blair, Admiral Dennis 102, 104
Blair, Tony 101
Blix, Hans 35
Boavida, J. 296
Boege, Volker 114
Boll, Edward 29n.14
Bonaparte, Rosa Muki 48, 49, 265
Bougainville 7, 35, 160, 161, 181, 199, 221, 226
Braithwaite, John xi, xii, xiii, 1, 32, 33, 34, 36, 41, 85, 89, 91, 104, 109, 119, 126, 128, 139, 145, 152, 160, 168, 171n.18, 172, 173, 174, 181, 189, 196n.19, 198, 221, 226, 228, 229, 230, 231, 288, 291, 294, 305, 307
Braithwaite, Valerie 32, 33n.18, 36, 85, 89, 91, 104, 109, 119, 126, 139, 145, 160, 168, 173, 181, 230, 231, 288
Braz, Ruben 187
Brazil 76, 112, 114, 260
Brereton, Laurie 93
bride price, *see barlaque*
Brotherhood of Pentjak Silat, *see* PSHT
Brown, Anne 114

Brown, M. Anne 215
Bruce, J. W. 184n.7
Budiardjo, Carmel 71
Bueno de Mesquita, Bruce 122
Buffet, Warren 3
Burma 17, 29, 30, 31, 32, 34, 35, 36, 37, 39, 168, 260
Burr, William 23–4, 48
Bush, George H. W. ix, x
Bush, George W. 35

Caeiro, Olandina 271
Caetano, Marcelo 11
Cambodia 1, 25, 26, 103, 119, 283, 289
Campbell-Nelson, Karen 264, 265, 266, 268, 271, 272, 276
Cancio de Carvalho 100
cantonment, *see* Falintil—troops in cantonment
Caplan, Richard 114, 116
Carey, Peter 266, 267, 269
Carrascalão, Joao 120, 202
Carrascalão, Mario 120, 124, 227, 236
Carter, Jimmy x, 40, 42
Cartwright, John xi, 134
Castells, Manuel xii, 8
Castro, Bryant 151, 216, 231
Castro, Fidel 76, 252
Catholic Church 55, 59, 63–6, 70, 108, 126, 127, 133, 170, 226, 253, 254, 279n.1
Catholic Commission for Peace and Justice 225
Catholicism 9, 64, 136, 206, 243, 264, 292n.12
CAVR, *see* Commission for Reception, Truth and Reconciliation in East Timor
ceasefire 58, 59, 61, 62, 63, 77, 122, 123, 124, 142, 279n.1
Central Bank of Timor-Leste 248
Central Intelligence Agency (CIA) 25
centralisation 114, 125, 127, 169, 190, 242, 276, 295
see also decentralisation, re-centralisation
centralised power ix, 112–18, 124–7, 128, 129, 185
Centre for Strategic and International Studies (CSIS) 18, 28
Charlesworth, Hilary xiii, 1, 126, 139, 145, 160, 168, 171n.18, 173, 181, 221, 267, 268, 270, 307
chefe 217
chefe d'aldeia 158, 165, 188, 217, 222, 245, 246, 272, 294, 299
chefe de posto 222
chefe de suco 144, 158, 165, 170, 182, 188, 217, 222, 245, 246, 272, 275, 294, 299
Cheney, Dick ix, 36
Chenoweth, Erica 133, 279, 280
Chesterman, Simon 94, 103n.8, 119, 120, 125
China x, 1, 2, 5, 18, 25n.11, 29, 30, 42, 76, 129, 159, 168, 258, 259, 303, 307
Chinese 9, 10, 21, 42, 48, 55, 91, 106, 109, 113, 237, 239, 258, 259n.13, 304
Chinkin, Christine xiii
Chinn, Liam 152, 155, 162, 181, 225
Chopra, Jarat 100n.6, 115, 119, 120, 121, 282, 283
clandestine networks 61–77, 79, 83, 114, 120, 173, 193, 280, 286, 298, 307, 308, 309
  dedication of 58
  disaffected activists 137
  former leaders 236
  Gusmão's leadership from prison 59
  Indonesian organisations as cover for 56
  key actors xi, 87
  martial arts groups as cover for 148, 152
  mobilisation 58
  protection for members 58
  recruitment 62

resilience of 3, 167
success of 40, 58
support for 81
the Church as cover for 55
youth in 52, 79, 86, 109
see also Rede Clandestina, Renetil, women—clandestine networks
Clandestinos 61–3, 136, 148, 265, 266, 280n.2
Cleary, Paul 24, 153, 247, 250, 251
Clements, Kevin 114
Cliffe, Sarah 254
Clinton, Bill x, 68, 101, 102, 107, 108, 195, 196
Clinton, Hilary 17, 31, 34
CNRM (Conselho Nacional da Resistência Maubere/National Council of Maubere Resistance) 54, 59, 63, 64, 135
CNRT (Conselho Nacional de Resistência Timorense/National Council of Timorese Resistance) 4, 54, 94, 95, 114, 118, 119, 124, 126, 127, 244, 252, 269, 270, 285, 289
Cohen, David 177n.2, 192, 198
Cohen, William 102
Coki Nai Pos Pos 67
Cold War 2, 12, 15, 21, 76
Colimau 2000 133n.6, 136, 151
Collier, Paul 253, 302
colonialism 1, 10, 13, 18, 22n.4, 55, 56, 88, 93, 113, 115, 145, 155, 176, 179, 181, 182, 223, 237–41, 264, 288, 290
  anti-colonial 151, 265
  post-colonial 126, 259, 291
  pre-colonial 145, 151
Combs, Nancy Amoury 191n.14, 192, 207, 214, 215, 216
Comição Justiça 225
Comissão de Acolhimento, Verdade e Reconciliação, *see* CAVR
Commission for Reception, Truth and Reconciliation in East Timor (CAVR) 14, 175, 186, 199, 201, 202–5, 207, 212, 216, 267, 268, 271, 286n.9, 289, 292
  Report (2006) 14, 17, 18n.2, 22, 23, 24, 25n.11, 26, 42, 47, 48, 54, 57, 62, 63n.2, 64, 69, 79, 80, 81, 84, 95, 96, 97, 98, 99, 100, 145, 190n.13, 198, 201, 202, 203, 204, 205, 206, 211n.27, 212n.28, 212n.29, 214, 215, 238, 267, 272, 290
  Women's Justice Unit 186
Commission of Experts 215n.31
Commission of Truth and Friendship Indonesia–Timor-Leste 198, 199, 200, 201, 202, 203
Committee for the Popular Defence of the Democratic Republic of Timor-Leste 138
Committee on the Elimination of All Forms of Discrimination against Women (CEDAW) 255, 273, 276, 277
  Concluding observations on Timor Leste CEDAW/C/TLS/CO1 (2009) 271n.1, 273, 277
  see also Convention on the Elimination of All Forms of Discrimination against Women
communism 2, 12, 13, 15, 18, 48, 52, 55, 56, 63, 68, 71, 76, 110
Community Aid Abroad (now, Oxfam Australia) 70
Community Empowerment Project (CEP) 119, 120, 127, 240, 242, 243, 244, 246, 251
Community Reconciliation Process (CRP) 205–11, 212, 214, 215, 216, 218, 220
Conboy, Ken J. 23n.9, 58
Confucianism 258, 259n.13
Conselho Nacional da Resistência Maubere, *see* CNRM
Conselho Nacional de Resistência Timorense, *see* CNRT

Conselho Revolusionário da Resisténsia Nasional, *see* CRRN
Constituent Assembly, East Timor 121, 125, 218, 219, 270
Constitution, of Democratic Republic of Timor-Leste x, xiv, 121, 175, 183, 218–19, 249n.9, 271, 289, 296
constitution
  consultations on 269, 270
  democratic 131, 132
  drafting of 118, 121, 125, 126, 219, 307
  enforcement of 164
  republican 131, 291
  struggle for 5
constitutional
  balances xii
  debate 129
  democracy 282
  moment 6
  separation of powers 164, 223, 296
constitutionalism 5, 180, 236
  asymmetric 180
Convention on the Elimination of All Forms of Discrimination against Women (CEDAW) 271, 273, 276
  see also Committee on the Elimination of All Forms of Discrimination against Women
Conversi, Danielle 180n.4
Cookson, Michael 36, 85, 89, 91, 104, 109, 119, 181, 230, 231, 288
Corcoran-Nantes, Yvonne 266, 269, 270, 272, 273, 274, 275, 276
corruption 6, 18, 92, 129, 155, 157, 184, 185–8, 189, 220n.35, 236, 241n.3, 242n.7, 253–4, 288, 294, 296, 298, 300
  in Fretilin 133
  of power 5, 6, 130, 134, 168, 185, 252, 290
  see also Anti-Corruption Commission, Anti-Corruption Commissioner
Cosgrove, Peter 102, 103, 111, 196

crimes against humanity 32, 44, 84, 191, 192, 197, 198, 201, 212, 215, 239, 301
  see also war crimes
Cristalis, Irena 265
Cronin, Audrey Kurth 279
Crouse, Chadd 161
CRRN (Conselho Revolusionário da Resisténsia Nasional/ Revolutionary Council of National Resistance) 54, 55
Cuba 76, 235, 252, 253
Cummins, Deborah 222, 246
Curtain, Richard 286
Curthoys, Ann 264
Cusack, Agnes 101n.7

Daley, Paul 93, 212
Daly, Erin 203
Daly, K. xiii
Damiri, Adam 95
Daschle, Tom 70, 107
Davis, Thomas W. 242n.7
de Carvalho, Dementrio do Amaral 256, 257
de Mello, Sergio Vieira 112, 114, 115, 116, 117, 120, 126, 127, 192, 194, 201, 269, 270, 284, 287
decentralisation 116, 118, 119, 168, 173, 247
  see also re-centralisation
Dee, Moreen 48, 81, 99, 111, 121
Deininger, K. 184n.7
'democratic experimentalism' xiii, 185, 299n.13
Democratic Party (PD) 141, 147
Deng Xiaoping 258, 303
Department of Defence 102
Dili 21, 42, 61, 84, 87, 99, 113, 124, 139, 237, 239, 240, 241n.3, 242, 246, 247, 257, 269
  arrival of International Stabilisation Force 142
  as capital of Portuguese Timor 9

as seat of power 113, 114, 121, 126, 251, 260, 273, 276, 295
Australian personnel in 10
capture of Gusmão in 58–9
collapse of policing in 157–8, 165, 166, 169, 170
courts and law 177, 183, 186, 187, 188n.8, 207, 213, 214, 219n.33, 274, 293
demonstrations in 92
disputed property 120, 149, 150, 166
Falintil attack on (1980) 54
Gusmão in 87, 89, 105
Indonesian intelligence operatives in 12
Indonesian military in 6, 167
invasion of 47, 48
media in 74, 79, 85
Motael Church 79
Pope John Paul II's visit (1989) 265
Portuguese parliamentary delegation visit 79, 85
potential Soviet intrusion 18
rates of domestic violence 161
reconciliation 172–3, 193–4, 201, 231
signing of peace agreement in (1999) 96
street violence (2006–08) 18n.3, 140, 142, 143, 144, 145, 147, 148, 151, 169, 172–3, 240
United Nations in 116, 119, 158, 168, 174, 250, 268
see also Santa Cruz Cemetery massacre
Dinnen, Sinclair 126, 139, 145, 154, 157, 160, 168, 173, 181
Diogo, Tome 200n.22
Documents on Australian Foreign Policy 19, 22, 23n.8, 26n.12
Dodd, Mark 139
Dorf, Michael 185, 303
Downer, Alexander 92–3, 101, 103, 106, 226, 248, 250
Downes, George W. 122
Doyle, Michael W. 122
Drahos, Peter xi, 39, 41, 134, 196n.19
Drysdale, Jennifer 247, 249, 289

Dunn, James 9, 10, 14, 15, 21, 22, 25, 28, 49
Dunn, Leah 36, 85, 89, 91, 104, 109, 119, 181, 221, 230, 231, 288
Dunne, Tim 98n.3
Durkheim, Émile 150n.13, 151
Dutch 9, 10, 18, 49, 81

East Timor Action Network (ETAN) 70
East Timor Museum 100
East Timor NGO Forum 163
East Timorese Women's Network, *see* Rede
Easterly, William 184n.7
Eckstein, Harry 133, 287
Eide, Espen Barth 132n.4
Eisenhower, Dwight D. 5
Elle Sette (L-7) 136
Ellickson, Robert 189
Engel, Rebecca 254
Europe 106, 131, 241, 309
European Parliament 82
European Union ix, 72, 73, 76, 102, 194, 229, 257
European x, 9, 39, 70, 71, 186, 291
Evans, Gareth 1, 2, 3, 25, 31, 44, 45, 56, 83
Evans, Michael L. 23–4, 48
Everett, Silas 152, 155, 162, 181, 225
executive government 128, 129, 182, 202, 248, 249n.9, 289, 290, 291, 298
abuse of power 130, 131
as tripartite power xii, 5, 7, 128, 180, 263, 291, 296
checks and balances on xi, xii, 131, 292
corruption 129
domination xii, 127, 128, 290, 298
Fretilin control of 121
power of 125n.2, 300, 303
separation from other powers 115
executive policing 159, 160
Exposito, Leopoldino 153

Falintil (Forças Armadas da Libertação
        Nacional de Timor-Leste/Timorese
        Armed Forces for the National
        Liberation of East Timor) 15, 58,
        74, 81, 135, 232, 284
    action against Indonesian forces 49,
        73
    admiration for 168
    and clandestine movement 62, 67
    and communism 63
    and war crimes 194
    attack on Dili (1980) 54
    captured in counterinsurgency 54
    civilians living with 53
    commitment to equality 266
    contact with youth leaders 62, 64
    deaths 66
    demobilisation 289
    dispersal of forces 55
    identification of fighters by
        Indonesians 59, 61
    Indonesian strategy against 97, 98,
        146, 232
    interviews with members 49, 63, 65,
        86, 139, 308, 309
    involvement in politics 125, 134
    lack of external patronage 49
    rebuilding membership 54
    recruitment 61
    Reinsertion Assistance Program 137
    reintegration of fighters 135, 136–7
    restraint 65
    separation from Fretilin 54, 124, 296
    strategy 86
    strength of forces 81
    ties with the Church 64
    troops in cantonment 64, 65, 96, 100,
        135, 136, 148n.11, 194, 280n.3
    unofficial agreements with Indonesian
        commanders 58
    veterans 139, 152, 192
    see also women—in Falintil
Falintil-Forças de Defesa de Timor Leste,
        see F-FDTL
Farram, Steve 18n.1

Feder, G. 184n.7
Federer, Juan 81, 83, 122, 178
Feith, Herb 28
feminisation 81, 222
feminism 255, 257
    and justice 162
    Timorese 7
feminist
    advocacy 218, 219
    agenda 269
    checks on power 293
    civic republicanism 7, 264
    community response 255
    politics xiii, 5, 7, 255, 275, 305
    struggles 130–4, 277
    theory xiii, 7, 8
fence jumping into embassies to seek
        asylum 67, 68, 82
'fence of legs' campaigns 54, 55, 56
Fernandes Alves, Maria Domingas, *see*
        Alves, Maria Domingas
Fernandes, Alarico 47
Fernandes, Clinton 3, 18, 19, 67, 71, 94,
        97, 98, 101, 106, 279
Fernandes, Teresa de Jesus 190
F-FDTL (Falintil-Forças de Defesa de
        Timor Leste/Timor-Leste Defence
        Force) 133n.6, 135–42, 151, 152,
        164, 166, 168, 169, 223, 224n.37,
        226, 300, 308, 309, 310
Field, Annette 231
Fiji 30, 255, 307, 309
FitzGerald, Stephen 42
Fitzpatrick, Daniel xv, 149, 179, 180, 181,
        182, 183, 184n.7, 185, 292, 294,
        301
Fluri, Philipp H. 154
Fokupers 225, 269
Forças Armadas da Libertação Nacional
        de Timor-Leste, *see* Falintil
Ford, Gerald 23, 24, 40
Ford, John 42
Fortna, Virginia Page 122, 123, 248
Fox, James J. xv, 9, 207, 222
France 68, 93, 133

Franks, Emma 265, 268
Fraser, Malcolm x, 26, 27
Freedom House Index 299
FRELIMO (Frente de Libertação de Moçambique/Liberation Front of Mozambique) 72, 124
French 114, 150n.13, 151
Freney, Denis 52
Fretilin (Frente Revolucionária do Timor-Leste Independente/Revolutionary Front for an Independent Timor) 12, 14, 15, 52, 54 71, 109, 127, 137, 140, 148, 149, 155, 171, 179, 224, 236, 267, 284, 285, 296
 and Catholic Church 55, 63
 and communism 12, 15, 18, 25n.11, 52, 63, 76
 and Indonesian casualties 49
 and Korka 147
 and reconciliation 226
 anti-Fretilin groups 133n.6, 141
 areas of control 48, 52
 break with CNRT 118, 126
 cabinet members 120, 137, 138
 Central Committee 22n.4, 54, 74, 138
 civil war with UDT 4, 9, 13, 14, 21, 22, 122, 124, 193, 203
 clandestine supporters 3, 62
 corruption 133
 decapitation of 139
 declaration of independence 14
 elite 4, 294
 founders 12, 124
 government 22n.4, 121, 122, 136, 139n.8, 226, 294
 government in exile 136
 in opposition 125–6, 187, 249, 285
 Indonesian strategy against 6, 19, 22, 40, 47
 killings by 14, 15, 203
 lack of Australian support for 2, 22, 40
 leadership 53, 76, 104, 122, 124, 125, 126, 127, 128, 138, 141, 187
 military successes 47, 48
 networking by 8, 15
 policy towards civilians 53
 relations with Cuba 76
 relations with Russia 76
 relations with UDT 13, 63n.2, 77, 231
 retaliation against 48
 rioting (2007) 125, 155, 170
 seats in Constituent Assembly 121, 125
 showing of flags 67, 85
 support for 21, 42, 52, 63, 67, 76
 see also Falintil, women—in Fretilin
Fretilin Reform (Fretilin Mudansa) 187
Fry, Ken 22n.4
Fukuyama, Francis 122

Gaddafi, Moamar 247
Gandhi, Mahatma 45, 67, 88, 281, 290, 295
Garcia-Milà, Teresa 180n.4
gas 11, 76, 247
 see also oil, petroleum
Gender Resource Centre 273
gendered violence 161–3, 164, 218, 274, 293
 see also rape
Gephart, Richard 70, 107
Germany 10, 35, 71, 103
Ghai, Yashi 30n.16
Ghana 159
Giddens, Anthony 304
GMPTL (Grupo das Mulheres Parlamentares de Timor-Leste/ Women's Parliamentary Group of Timor-Leste) 273, 276
Goldsmith, Andrew xiv, 154, 157, 159, 307
Goldstone, Jack A. 300, 310
Golkar (Golongan Karya/Indonesian Golkar Party) 56, 63, 94, 146, 155
Gomes, Sebastião 79
Gorbachev, Mikhail 15
Graydon, Carolyn 216, 218, 219

Grenfell, Damian 160, 188n.8, 190, 235, 238
Grenfell, Laura 219n.32, 219n.33, 222
Guggenheim, Scott 254
Gunn, Geoffrey C. 192
Gusmão, Alex Freitas 215
Gusmão, Emilia Baptista 232
Gusmão, Xanana xi, 41, 47, 61, 93, 96, 110, 124, 133n.6, 142, 147, 157, 169, 171, 182, 191, 230, 236, 246, 270, 271, 279, 283n.6, 284
- and Catholic Church 55, 63, 279n.1
- and immunity 192–3, 194, 196, 197, 201, 202
- and non-state justice 222–3, 290, 294, 295
- and petitioners incident 140, 141, 144, 171
- and reconciliation 96, 225–6, 227, 228, 229
- and reconciliation with Indonesia 135, 193–4, 195, 196
- and reparations fund 203, 204, 205, 215
- and Santa Cruz massacre 79, 80, 81, 85, 86, 87, 88, 90
- and security sector 135, 137, 138, 139, 144, 164
- as Indonesian target 54
- as leader of insurgency 3, 6, 53, 54, 55, 58, 65, 136, 194, 280
- as President of Timor-Leste 54, 121, 125, 134, 225, 292
- as Prime Minister of Timor-Leste 125, 126, 128, 157, 178, 180, 187, 213, 294
- assassination attempt 153, 154
- attack on CAVR report 290
- autonomy proposal 93
- capture 58–9
- ceasefire negotiation 58, 124
- centralisation of power 4, 54, 120, 126, 127, 128, 134, 281–2
- closure of CNRT 118, 126
- commitment to democracy 168, 287
- criticism of 126, 213, 227, 281–2, 295
- diplomacy 74, 135
- imprisonment 77, 280n.2
- interview with 194, 282
- 'Message from the President' (2006) 246
- moral agony 87, 88, 90
- on UDT–Fretilin score settling 14
- political opponents 125, 126
- principled engagement 40
- prison cell as node 4, 59, 280–1
- prison visit by Mandela 59, 194, 281
- relations with Alkatiri 126, 137, 168, 226, 285
- resignation from Fretilin 54, 124, 296
- return to Timor-Leste 104, 105, 282
- shift from violence to non-violence 88
- *Timor Lives!* (2005) 192n.15, 195n.18
- *To Resist is to Win!* (2000) 53
- UN consultations with 114, 120, 126
- 'victory' speech 100
- view on war 67
Guterres, Antonio 101, 107, 108
Guterres, Eurico 98, 100, 198
Guterres, Isabel 271
Guterres, Luis 187
Gutteres, Aniceto 187

Habibie, B. J. 2, 3, 6, 75, 92, 93, 94, 95, 98, 102, 104, 107, 108, 193, 195
Haburas Foundation 257
Hackers Against Indonesia 69
HAK Association Peacebuilding Programme 225
Hallett, Brien 64
Hanreich, Herbert 30n.16
hansip (civil defence) units 55, 62
Harland, David 114, 116
Harrington, Andrew 149, 191, 201
Harris Rimmer, Susan 176, 192, 201, 205, 212, 231, 232, 233, 267, 274
Harris, Nathan 32
Harris, Vandra 154, 159
Hawke, Bob x, 25, 26

Hayden, Bill 1, 2, 3, 25, 31
Hicks, David 264
Higashi, Daisaku 157, 166, 285
Hill, Helen xv, 9, 12, 14, 253, 254n.10
Hirst, Megan 198
Hoeffler, A. 253
Hohe, Tanja 114, 120, 166, 167, 216, 217, 218, 219, 221, 242, 246
Holbrooke, Richard 26
Holliday, Ian 29
Holthouse, Kym 160, 188n.8, 190, 235, 238
Hood, Ludovic 154
Howard, John 11, 92, 93, 94, 98, 100, 101, 106, 107, 108, 112, 171, 196, 307
Huang, Reyko 192
Human Rights Watch 155, 299
Hunt, Greg 93n.1
hurting stalemate 58, 59
Hussein, Saddam 34, 35, 38
Hyland, Tom 239
Hynes, Michelle 161

Impettu (East Timorese Students and Youth Association) 66–7
impunity 36, 102, 161–3, 164, 175, 191, 194n.17, 198, 210, 211–15, 223, 226, 284, 285, 297, 301
India 29, 30, 291, 295, 307, 309
Indochina 26
'Indonesia lobby' 27, 28, 70, 72, 83, 109
Indonesian Armed National Forces, *see* TNI
International Committee for the Red Cross (ICRC) 52
International Court of Justice 11, 76
International Criminal Court 297
International Crisis Group (ICG) 1, 31, 112, 135n.1, 136, 138, 140, 141, 159, 276
International Federation for East Timor 279

International Force for East Timor (INTERFET) 102, 103, 104, 111–12, 135, 176, 196, 213, 279, 285n.8, 308
International Monetary Fund (IMF) 91
International Organisation for Migration (IOM) 135
International Stabilisation Force (ISF) 142–4, 160
Inter-Parliamentary Union (IPU) 193
Iran 2, 26, 32, 35, 89
Iraq 2, 34, 35, 38, 112, 132, 157
Ireland 70, 106

Japan 10, 27, 30, 38, 68, 71, 106, 170, 179, 194, 258
Jardine, Matthew 25, 55, 73, 75, 80, 82, 83, 84, 87, 279
Jefferson, Thomas 45, 131
Jenneker, Madeleine xi, 134
Johnston, Les xi, 134
Joint Committee for the Defence of East Timor 81
Jolliffe, Jill 49, 79, 80
Judicial System Monitoring Programme (JSMP) 178, 186, 219, 274, 275, 286
judicial power 125n.2, 129, 213, 303
judiciary 182, 201, 212, 222, 286
   as tripartite power xii, 5, 128, 180, 263, 291, 296
   domination by executive 127
   independence of 285
   male domination of 162
   separation from other powers 7, 115, 117, 128, 168, 180, 220n.35, 296, 297
   see also women—in judiciary
juramento (blood oath) 216, 291
justice
   restorative 32, 37, 112, 175, 189, 211, 215, 220n.35, 223, 290, 305
   separation of powers 206, 219, 220, 293, 297

United Nations 175, 176–9, 185, 189, 192, 193n.16, 197, 215, 218, 285, 286, 294, 299n.13
United States 294
see also adat, lisan
Jütersonke, Oliver 151, 229

Kaldor, Mary 167
Kammen, Douglas 9, 124, 217, 236
Karstedt, S. 35
Karzai, Hamid 131
Kaspersen, Anja Therese 132n.4
Keating, Paul x, 26, 34, 84
Kecamatan Development Program (KDP) 242n.7
Kehi, Balthasar 286
Kelly, Paul 93n.1, 95, 98, 102, 103, 107, 112
Kennedy, Edward (Ted) 70, 101, 107, 108, 196
Kenny, Charles 130
Kent, Lia xv, 210, 211, 214
Kent, Randolph 132n.4
Kie, Bian 22n.5
King, Angela 268
King's College Report 120, 135, 154, 158, 192n.15, 238
Kingsbury, Damien xv, 59, 84, 91, 95, 104, 113, 125, 133n.6, 141, 153, 154, 224, 225, 229, 289, 296
Kingston, Jeffrey 193n.16
Kissinger, Henry x, 23, 24, 44
Kivimäki, Timo 102
Knetsch, J. 184n.7
Koh, Harold 31n.17
Kohen, Arnold 22, 24, 27, 48
Kooijmans, Pieter 87
Kopassus, *see* Special Forces
Korka 147
Kosovo 101, 112, 118, 125n.2
Kostner, Markus 254
Kouwenberg, Saskia 81
Krugman, Paul 195
Krygier, Martin 292n.11
Kymlicka, Will 180

La'o Hamutuk Bulletin 154, 158
Laakso, Jennifer 188n.9, 202, 217, 219n.32, 223
Laka, Mau 49
Larke, Ben 205, 211, 212, 214
Lastaria-Cornhiel, S. 184n.7
Latour, Bruno 6n.2, 8
Lavigne Delville, P. 184n.7
Leadbeater, Maire 23n.7
Lee Kuan Yew 29
Lee, Lynn 211
legislative power 125n.2, 128, 129, 303
legislature 117, 291, 297
    as tripartite power xii, 5, 128, 180, 263, 296
    Fretitlin control of 121
    separation from other powers 7, 115, 116, 291, 296, 297
    see also women—in legislature
Lenin, Vladimir 4, 5
Leninism 54, 76
Lennox, Rowena 66
Leong, James 211
lia nain 206, 222, 246, 299
Liberation Front of Mozambique, *see* FRELIMO
Liberia 31
Libya 35, 247, 299n.13
Liquica 95, 96, 98, 188n.8, 200n.22, 267
lisan 179n.3, 182n.6, 188n.10, 190n.13, 206, 215–20, 222, 225, 226, 230, 284, 285, 290, 292, 293, 294, 299
    leaders 170, 205, 308, 309
    uma lisan 182n.6
    see also adat
liurai 10, 188n.8, 222
Lobato, Lúcia 273
Lobato, Nicolau 12, 49
Lobato, Rogerio 124, 125, 127, 136, 137, 138, 139, 141, 152, 154, 156, 157, 158, 159, 163, 224, 282
Loch, Alexander 225, 231
Long Pereira, Manuela 264, 265, 268, 271, 272, 276
Lopes da Cruz, Francisco 94, 95
Lopes, Monsignor 63n.2, 66

Los, Rai 141
Lospalos 48, 138n.5, 272, 273, 274, 275
Lowry, Bob 154, 157, 158
lulik 190, 222

MacAskill, Ewen 31
McCarthy, John 136, 137n.2
McCosker, Anthony 83
McCulloch, Lesley 59
McDonald, Hamish 23, 25, 95
McFarlane, John 154
McGuire, Therese J. 180n.4
McKenna, James 177, 178
Mackenzie, Catriona 264
Mackie, Jamie 72, 73
McLeod, Jason 67
McWilliam, Andrew 62, 180, 181, 182, 183, 217
Mahathir, Prime Minister 29
Makarim, Zacky Anwar 95
Makkai, Toni 33, 34
Maley, William 97, 98, 102, 103, 104, 154
Malik, Adam 14, 19, 39
Malik, Mohan 29
Mandela, Nelson 36, 40, 41, 45, 59, 88, 156, 157, 194, 197, 280–1, 282, 290
Mao Zedong 5, 258
Maoism 236, 259n.13, 279n.1, 295
Maoulidi, Salma 264
Maputo 4, 53, 72, 114, 124
Marcal, Guilhermina 167
Marcal, Hercules Rozario 239
Marcal, Sister Guilhermina 167
Marino, Pascal 240
Marker, Jamsheed 77
Marshall, Shane 177, 178
martial arts groups (MAG) 6, 56, 63, 133n.6, 144, 146–9, 151, 152, 155, 163, 169, 170, 171, 172n.19, 173, 174, 240, 308, 209, 310
Martin, Ian 99n.5, 111
Martinkus, John 141, 171
Marxism 13, 54, 76, 124

Mason, Christine 265, 266, 268
Mason, Whit 234n.39
Masters, Edward 52
Maubere 100, 217, 236, 279n.1, 293
Maubere Security 148
Mayer-Rieckh, Alexander 111
Mearns, David 220n.35, 221
media 24, 27, 35, 38, 40, 49, 52, 57, 66, 68, 79, 80, 81, 83, 85, 89, 90, 101, 109, 117, 128, 129, 241, 260, 280n.3, 287, 297, 298, 304
Melanesia 30
Melanesian Spearhead Group 30
Merry, Sally Engle xiii, 37, 218, 234, 255, 256, 257, 260
Michels, Robert 295
Milner, Anthony 29n.14
Molnar, Andrea 151
Monteiro, Longuinhos 239
Montesquieu, Baron Charles de Secondat 128, 131, 180, 291
Morrow, Jonathan 269, 270
Moxham, Ben 238
Moynihan, Daniel Patrick 75
Mozambique 53, 72, 74, 76, 124, 182
Muggah, Robert 151, 229
Mullet, Etienne 194
Munton, Alexander J. 247
Murdani, Benny 19, 22n.5, 28, 237, 238
Murdoch, Lindsay 163, 239
Murdoch, Rupert 68
Murray, Robin 151, 229
Murtopo, Ali 13, 19, 28, 48
Myrttinen, Henri 148, 155, 162, 172, 173, 240

nahe biti 165, 189, 205, 220, 230, 299
Nairn, Allan 79, 80
National Committee for Dialogue 225
National Consultative Council 119, 120, 269
National Council 118, 120, 269, 270
National Council of Maubere Resistance, *see* CNRM

National Council of Timorese Resistance, see CNRT
National Investigation Commission 84
National Police Force of Timor-Leste, see PNTL
National Statistics Directorate 161, 162, 232n.38
National Union of Primary School Teachers 15
National Union of Timorese Workers 14–15
National Women's Organisation 15
National Youth Organisation 15
NATO 101, 160
Nehru, Jawaharlal 295
Netherlands, the 68, 83, 240, 307
Neto, Felix 194
networked governance 235, 287, 302
    by the weak xi
    definition xii, 263
    for rule of law 6
    for freedom xiii, 4, 6, 7, 30
    nodes of xi
    of transition 279–305
    of tyranny 4, 6, 7, 263
    power of 8
    success of 4, 168
    theory 7–8, 263
    see also women—in networked governance
Neves, Guteriano 247
Nevins, Josèph 98, 99, 102, 199, 237
New Zealand 30, 68, 81, 95, 101, 106, 112, 142, 160–1, 259, 280, 285n.7, 307
Nicol, Bill 9, 14, 15
Nicolau, Guteriano 247
Niner, Sara 87, 88, 264, 265, 273, 275, 276, 281, 282
Nixon, Rod 179, 189, 216, 217, 219n.32, 221
Nobel Peace Prize 74, 226, 258, 281, 288
nodes xi, xii, 4, 8, 30, 39, 62, 70, 72, 134, 170, 263, 302
Nolan, Anna 114

Non-Aligned Movement 23n.6, 26, 36
non-domination xii, 5, 7, 220, 302, 304
    freedom as xii, 111, 130, 131, 196, 198, 235, 240, 250, 251, 252, 254, 263, 293, 298, 304
non-governmental organisation (NGO) xii, 29, 70, 81, 165, 241, 242, 251, 254, 286, 301, 308, 309
    accountability 285–6
    and reconciliation 224
    and separations of power 118, 254
    human rights 38, 198n.21, 199, 218, 286, 293, 308
    networks 7, 236
    observers 198
    Western 30
    youth 152
    see also names of organisations, women—non-governmental organisations
nonviolence 35, 61, 63–6, 67, 85, 88, 89, 90, 145, 147, 279–82, 290, 291, 296, 305
Noronha, Carmenesa Moniz 160, 188n.8, 190, 235, 238
Northern Ireland 35, 180n.4, 310

Obama, Barack 17, 31, 34
Oecussi 9, 10, 18, 162, 275
Oenarto, Josèph 100
oil 1, 11, 24, 26, 45, 58, 76, 235, 247–52
    see also gas, petroleum, Timor Gap Treaty
Okoth-Ogendo, H. 184n.7
Olsen, Tricia D. 197n.20
OMT (Organização de Mulher Timor/ Organisation of East Timorese Women) 244, 245, 246, 269, 273
OPMT (Organização Popular da Mulher Timor/Popular Organisation of East Timorese Women) 265, 266, 269, 273
Organisation of Petroleum Exporting Countries (OPEC) 1, 26

Ospina, Sofi 242, 246
Oxfam 70, 268, 273

Pacific Island Forum 30
Pacific region x, 18, 24, 26, 73, 102, 160, 253, 309
Pakistan x, 77, 309
Palmer, Lisa 256, 257
Panjaitan, Sintong 85
Papua New Guinea 1, 17, 30, 35
Paris, Roland 250
Parker, Christine xii, 305
parliament 297
    confidence in 188n.11
    de facto first x
    debates in 180n.5, 290, 299
    Falintil in 152
    first 307
    Indonesian 94, 95, 288
    members of 136, 166, 179, 309
    national 121, 125, 129, 215, 224, 227, 238, 246, 249
    passage of legislation 129, 275
    votes in 248
    weak 121
    see also women—in Parliament
Parliamentarians for East Timor 71
Parliamentary Alliance Majority (AMP) 187
Pascoe, Daniel 176, 192, 193n.16, 198, 202
Pateman, Carole 264
Patrick, Ian 254
Patterson, Gerard R. 34n.19
Payne, Leigh A. 197n.20
Paz 225
PD, see Democratic Party
Peace and Democracy Foundation 225
peacebuilding 112, 113, 132, 223, 232, 233, 287, 295
    analyses of 123, 131, 230, 232, 249
    and *lisan* 182n.6
    captured 131, 132
    compromised 131, 132, 134
    conflictive 131, 132
    confrontational 132
    cooperative 132
    corporate contribution to 241
    data 123
    in Bougainville 226
    in Indonesia 231, 287
    in Liberia 31
    in Solomon Islands 126, 294
    in Timor-Leste 151, 168, 227, 263
    leaders x, 201
    mechanisms 230
    pathology 177
    policy 148
    republican 287
    Timorese 5
    see also United Nations—peacebuilding, women—role in peacebuilding
Peacebuilding Compared Project 8, 14, 36, 77, 126, 180, 199, 253, 287, 294, 302
    methodology 307–10
Peacock, Andrew 26, 31
Peake, Gordon xv, 154
Peceny, Mark 122
Pedersen, Morten B. xi, 17, 29n.13, 30, 31
Pelosi, Nancy 70, 101, 107, 196
Pereira, Agio 289
Perito, Robert M. 157, 159n.16, 164
Persaudaraan Setia Hati Terate, see PSHT
Pessoa, Ana 120, 128, 187
petitioners 140, 141, 156, 164, 171, 224, 308
petroleum 17, 22, 24, 237, 239, 247, 248, 249n.9
    see also gas, oil, Timor Gap Treaty
Petroleum Fund 235, 236, 247, 248, 249, 261, 286, 289, 290, 291, 298
Pettit, Philip xi, xii, xv, 7, 130, 131, 152, 198, 240, 250, 251, 259, 293
Philippines, the 159, 242n.7
Phillips, Anne 264
Pickering, Jeffrey 122

Pilger, John 10, 43, 56, 57, 74, 80, 83, 84
Pinto, Constâncio 55, 73, 86, 87, 88
Pinto, Maria da Conceição 194
Pires, Angelita 141
Pires, Maria Helena 277
Platteau, J. P. 184n.7
Ploughshares for Peace 69
pluralisation of power 113, 129, 302
pluralism xii, 4, 54, 123, 124, 126, 127, 128, 134, 168, 185, 236, 279n.1, 284, 287, 291, 294, 295, 296, 302
PNTL (Policia Nacional de Timor-Leste/ National Police Force of Timor-Leste) 138n.6, 139, 140, 142, 144, 156n.15, 158–60, 162, 164, 165, 166, 168, 170, 175, 224n.37, 226, 300, 308, 309, 310
Pocock, J. G. A. 131
police, *see* PNTL, United Nations Civilian Police (UNPOL)
Policia Nacional de Timor-Leste, *see* PNTL
politics of hope 3, 4, 5, 279, 280, 281
Pope John Paul II 66, 79, 265, 281
Popular Organisation of East Timorese Women, *see* OPMT
Popular Organisation of Timorese Women 48
Portugal x, 11, 19, 23n.7, 23n.8, 113, 129, 177, 265
  alliance with United States 107
  and Fretilin 15
  and Oecussi 9, 10, 18
  and World War II 10
  asylum in 68
  autonomy under 12, 92
  challenge of Timor Gap Treaty 11, 24, 76
  criticism of 151, 202
  dialogue over East Timor 74, 75, 76
  disputes with Indonesia 79
  East Timorese refugees in 76, 176
  isolation of 72
  public opinion in 106
  response to Santa Cruz massacre 76, 83
  revolution in 11, 12
  solidarity movement in 71
  students returning from 14
  tripartite process 77, 79, 98
  women refugees in 41
Portuguese 8, 69, 83, 129, 142n.10, 178, 181, 182, 186
  citizenship 11
  colonialism 9, 10, 22n.4, 55, 76, 113, 145, 151, 155, 176, 179, 182, 254n.10, 264
  corporations 9, 237, 238, 240
  influence in Timor 10, 13
  language 65, 76, 82, 83, 114, 115, 169, 177, 269
  law 149, 176, 177, 180
  parliamentary delegation to East Timor 79, 87
  peacekeepers 106, 112, 142, 226
Portuguese Timor 9, 10, 18, 21, 23n.6, 24, 64, 76, 107, 238
Power, Samantha 116, 191
principled engagement xi, 7, 17, 29–31, 32–8, 39, 40, 41, 290
  see also unprincipled engagement
Prosecutor-General 128, 176, 187, 192n.15, 206, 294
Provedor 129, 180, 186, 294, 297
Prueller, Vanessa 225, 231
PSD, *see* Social Democratic Party
PSHT (Persaudaraan Setia Hati Terate/ Brotherhood of Pentjak Silat) 147, 148, 151, 170, 173, 240
Purdey, Jemma 91
Putnam, Robert D. 27, 30, 105, 106, 196

Quan, J. 182, 184n.7

Rae, James DeShaw 202
Ramos-Horta, Jóse xi, 4, 47, 71, 77, 110, 125, 127, 133, 141, 169, 201, 284, 295
  1975 generation 114

acknowledgment of mistakes 13, 14, 194
and Gareth Evans 2, 25
approach to reconciliation 193–4, 195–8, 203, 204, 205, 225, 228
as Foreign Affairs spokesman 14
as founder of Fretilin 12
as independence leader 124, 194, 236
as President of Timor-Leste 125
as Prime Minister of Timor-Leste 125, 126, 144, 180
assassination attempt 153, 154, 164, 223, 229, 239, 281
at United Nations 75, 76, 83
attitude to immunity 191, 192–3
autonomy proposal 93
criticism of 41, 126, 281
delivering solidarity 101–4
diplomacy 37, 42, 52, 74, 75, 280, 287
diplomacy with Indonesia 135, 193, 195
Funu: The unfinished saga of East Timor (1987) 25, 37
hacking threat 69
imprisonment 53
influence of 14
interview with 65, 101, 309
labelled traitor 53
negotiation with Reinado 153, 154
networking ability 8, 14, 27, 43
Nobel Peace Prize 74, 226
praise for 3, 68
principled engagement 40
reflections on Santa Cruz massacre 90
rejection of terrorism 67
resilience of 3, 74
return from exile 117
support for 58, 70, 76, 107, 196
rape 48, 55, 83, 86, 88, 90, 155, 162n.17, 163, 177, 188n.8, 190, 192, 198, 199, 204, 212, 218, 219, 220, 232, 233, 255, 266, 267, 275, 293
see also gendered violence
Reagan, Ronald x
realism xi, 1, 3, 23n.8, 45, 191, 194, 197, 263, 279, 282, 287

balanced 2, 3
defining features ix, x
error of misplaced realism 39, 43, 61, 63, 130, 309
in international politics 105
low integrity 27
misplaced 3, 7, 17–45, 107, 109, 290
opposite of 43
theory 27
realist
agenda 27
analysis 2, 4
anti-realist 6, 42, 195
decisions 66, 192, 196
diplomacy 13, 17, 26, 44, 45, 194, 195, 287
follies 209
game 133
Gusmão and Ramos-Horta as realists 195–8
international relations theory ix, x, xi, xii, 41, 45, 106, 112, 195, 287
lens 193, 263
politics 196
power ix, xi, 7, 42, 130, 305
pressures x
reintegrative shaming of realists 280
re-centralisation 119
see also centralisation, decentralisation
reconciliation 40, 59, 152, 167, 194, 195, 230, 231, 304, 309
and *adat* 275
and immunity 192n.15, 195n.18, 196
and truth 32, 199, 203, 206
and youth groups 148, 173
as central to peacebuilding 112
between Fretilin and UDT 77
between Gusmão and Alkatiri 126
between Gusmão and militia 96
between Timor-Leste and Indonesia 109, 182, 193–4, 201, 288
community 96, 189, 216, 223, 224, 225, 229, 231
culturally attuned 174
failure 149

'fatigue' 225, 226
gender balance in 271
in Bougainville 226
in Fiji 255
in rural areas 167
in security sector 139, 151, 164, 172, 173, 224
in urban areas 172–3
indigenous 173, 175
national 225, 292
rituals 151, 175, 199, 232, 233, 234
traditional 175, 225, 226, 261, 292, 299
value of 191
see also Commission for Reception, Truth and Reconciliation in East Timor, Community Reconciliation Process
Reddy, Peter 181, 221
Rede (Rede Feto Timor Lorosae/East Timorese Women's Network) 269, 270, 277
Rede Clandestina 6
Rees, Edward 137, 138, 151, 154, 165, 229
referendum 2, 3, 6, 11, 55, 61, 69, 74, 91–110, 125n.2, 176, 267, 284, 301
Reformasi 6, 91–110
Rei, Naldo 79, 81
Reiger, Caitlin 210n.26, 214
Reinado, Alfredo 140, 141, 144, 153, 154, 155, 157, 223, 239, 285
reintegrative shaming 32, 33, 34, 40, 280
Reis, Filomena B. 265
Reiter, Andrew G. 197n.20
Renetil (Resistencia Nacional dos Estudantes de Timor Leste/ Timor-Leste Students' National Resistance) x, 66, 67, 280n.2
Reno, William 139, 185
Report of the Alkatiri Initiative Review (2006) 129
republican 134, 218, 219, 235, 251, 260, 292, 299, 304
aid 252

analysis of feminism 5, 264, 275
anti-republican 195, 196, 258, 298
coercion 304
constitution 131, 290–1
craft 257
crowd 133
democracy 126, 129, 259, 296
finance 241
freedom fighters 197
freedom xii, 111, 250
ideal 195, 299, 304, 305
mobilisation 129
'peace' 133, 197, 215
peacebuilding 287
political theory xii, 4, 6, 7, 8, 130, 152, 240, 250, 251, 254
politics 196, 252, 305
polity 3
reform 133
revolution 293, 299n.13
values 196, 304
virtue 260, 286
see also non-domination, separation of powers—republican
republicanism xi, xii, 128, 304
and peacekeeping 122–3
civic xiii, 5, 7, 236, 243, 250, 252, 263, 264, 275
Resistencia Nacional dos Estudantes de Timor Leste, *see* Renetil
Responsibility to Protect doctrine 1, 299n.13
responsive regulation xi, 7, 17, 32–7, 41, 187
restorative justice, *see* justice—restorative
Revolutionary Council of National Resistance, *see* CRRN
Revolutionary Front for an Independent Timor, *see* Fretilin
Reynal-Querol, M. 282
Rhodes, Rod 8
Rinakit, Sukardi 91
Robalo, Mario 79
Robertson, Kathryn 161

Robinson, Geoffrey 52, 53, 95, 211, 212
Robinson, Mary 268
Rodrik, Dani 258, 259
Rodriques, Roqué 76
Roosa, John x
Ross, Michael L. 248
Roth, Dr Stanley 98
Roulston, Jim 26n.12
Ruak, Taur Matan (TMR) 65, 100, 136, 137, 141, 152, 153, 164, 227, 230, 280n.3
Rudd, Kevin 73, 93
Rudé, George F. E. 3, 133
rule of law xii, 6, 128, 149, 156, 164, 166, 175, 176, 179, 180, 185, 188n.11, 193n.16, 200, 212, 233–4, 285, 296, 297, 301, 304
Russia 2, 5, 68, 260
Rwanda 107, 132, 181, 191, 289
Ryan, Alan 111, 154

Sabel, Charles F. xii, 185, 299n.13, 303
Sachs, Jeffrey 247
Sagrada Familia 133n.6, 136, 138
Sakabe, Yukako 255
Salazar, Antonio de Oliveira 11
Salla, Michael 3, 49
Sambanis, Nicholas 122, 310
Santa Cruz Cemetery massacre 6, 29, 40, 45, 56, 61, 63, 68, 69, 73, 74, 76, 79–90, 114, 136, 265, 280n.3, 281
Sao Paulo Parliamentary Front for East Timor's Independence 76
Sarkin, Jeremy 203
Scambary, James 147, 148, 149, 151, 152, 173, 174, 229, 230
Scheeringa, Sandra 205, 207, 210
Scheiner, Charles 247
Schwartz, Adam 37
scorched-earth policy 11, 97, 99, 103, 107
Scott, Catherine 265
Scott, David 10, 11, 22, 23, 24, 25, 62, 66, 67, 68, 69, 203
Scott, James C. 100, 181

Scowcroft, Brent 23n.9
Sebastian, Leonard C. 54
Security Sector Reform Monitor 160
self-determination 2, 3, 12, 17, 24, 25, 26, 75, 92, 93, 98, 107, 270
Sen, Amartya 29n.14, 30n.16
separation of economic power 242–3, 259, 298, 301
separation of financial powers 240, 291
separation of powers xii, 128, 129, 133n.5, 184, 191, 215, 222, 223, 235, 257, 260, 263, 284, 288, 290–1, 292, 296, 299, 300–5
  abuse of 213
  and civil society 131, 133, 215, 281, 287
  and donors 251, 254, 260
  and elections 250
  and land tenure 180–5, 299
  and politics 236
  and religion 253, 254
  and rule of law 285, 287
  and security sector 155, 156, 164–7, 293, 297
  and the media 287, 298
  and the United Nations 137, 250, 282, 285, 295
  breaches of 126, 128, 187, 301
  civil xiii
  constitutional recognition of 175, 223, 236
  construction of 117
  corruption of 134, 290
  defence of 169
  developing-country 252
  difficulty of achieving 111, 115, 125, 126, 127
  domination of 169, 290, 301
  improvement of 7, 187, 283, 294, 299, 304
  institutionalisation of 7, 116, 118, 154, 164, 187, 284, 285, 297
  institutions of 249
  invigoration of xiii, 134, 178, 282, 299n.13

networked 235
problems with 115, 219, 237, 301
republican xii, 5, 130, 133, 134, 187, 195, 251, 259, 292, 293, 299, 302, 309
residual 223
struggle for 127–30, 134, 195
tools for 7
transitional 125, 215, 289, 290
value of 251, 254
variegation of xii, 5, 7, 128, 180, 189, 260, 294, 299, 302
Western doctrine of xiii
see also justice—separation of powers, Petroleum Fund, vernacularisation
separation of violence from politics 155, 156, 168, 296
Sereprosetil 147
Serious Crimes Panel 191, 203, 210, 212, 215, 289
Serious Crimes Unit 191, 192, 210, 211, 289
Severino, Rodolfo C. 81
Shackleton, Shirley 43, 44
Shawcross, William 35
Shearing, Clifford xi, 134, 167
Shoesmith, Dennis 121, 136, 139
Siapno, Jacqueline 275
Sikkink, Kathryn 197n.20
Silva, Kelly 140, 141
Simon, William H. xii, 299n.13
Simonsen, Sven Gunnar 122
Simpson, Brad 34, 71
Simpson, S. R. 184n.7
Simu Malu 225
Singh, Bilveer 68, 84, 85
Sjafei, Theo 84
Skinner, Quentin 131
Slaughter, Ann-Marie 7
Small Enterprise Project (SEP) 240
Smith, Michael G. 48, 81, 99, 111, 121
Soares, Adérito de Jesus x, xii, 58, 66, 120, 129, 130, 147, 187, 199, 282, 294, 307
Soares, Santina 247

Social Democratic Party (PSD) 141, 147
solidarity 148, 172n.19, 273
  as resource 101–4
  Australian network 27, 106
  East Timor movement 2, 28, 41, 66, 71, 72, 107–8, 241
  Indonesian 81
  international network xi, 40, 42, 43, 55, 57, 58, 61–77, 83, 84, 93, 106, 110, 280, 286, 298
Solomon Islands 7, 126, 145, 160, 168, 173, 181, 294
Somalia 112, 132
Sorensen, Eva 8
South Africa 35, 41, 86, 88, 156, 194, 197, 199, 280, 281, 291
South Pacific Forum 30
South-East Asia x, 24
Soviet Union x, 2, 12, 18, 21, 25n.11, 43, 76
Special Forces (Komando Pasukan Khusus/Special Forces Command of the Indonesian Army) 13, 19, 64, 95, 239
Special Representative of the Secretary-General (SRSG) 112, 119, 268, 269
Stahl, Max 80, 81, 82, 86, 90
Stanley, Elizabeth 203, 204, 205, 210, 211
Ståslett, Gunnar 225, 226
State Intelligence Coordinating Agency of Indonesia, *see* BAKIN
Steele, Janet 62
Stephan, Maria J. 133, 279, 280
Stiglitz, J. E. 258, 259
Stone, Gerard 22n.4
students 6, 14, 26n.12, 66, 67, 88, 91, 114, 236, 293, 308
Subianto, Prabowo 239
suco (village) 120, 165, 188n.8, 222, 236, 245, 246, 272, 286, 293, 294, 295, 299
Sudarso, Tyasno 95
Suharto, President 3, 34, 36, 92, 281n.5
  and economy 18, 91
  and Golkar 56, 63, 155

361

and integration of East Timor 10, 19, 22, 23, 24, 25, 39, 40
and Whitlam 19, 22, 23, 24, 25, 39
anti-Suharto forces 67, 73, 84, 196, 280n.2
cronies 6, 9, 236, 237, 238
demise of 54, 74, 91
family 55, 109, 193, 238, 239
New Order 67, 91, 146
post Suharto 91, 92, 104, 108
regime 3, 57, 59, 239
relations with Australia 26, 27, 34
succession 3, 6, 91, 92
Sukarno, President 5, 18
Sukarnoputri, Megawati 109
Sukma, Rizal 154
Summy, Ralph 64
Sutrisno, Try 84
Suzman, Helen 45
Swaine, Aisling 221
Sweden 71, 307
Sword Gusmão, Kirsty 192, 212, 269
Syahnakri, General Kiki 103

tais 207, 238, 305
Tanner, C. 182
TAPOL 71
Tara, Augusto 140
Tavares, João da Silva 100
Taylor, John 22, 24, 27, 48
Taylor, John G. 18, 19, 23, 24, 48, 84, 95, 237, 238, 267
Tentara Nasional Indonesia, *see* TNI
Tetum 64, 114, 115, 179n.3, 186, 240, 285n.7
Therik, Tom 9
Thompson, Edwina 29
Thompson, Mark 30n.16
Tiffen, Rodney 38n.21
Tilman, Marcus 140
Timor Gap Treaty 11, 44, 45, 56, 76
Timor Sea 17, 24, 45, 247, 248, 250, 251
Timor Talks Campaign 74

Timorese Armed Forces for the National Liberation of East Timor, *see* Falintil
Timorese Democratic Union, *see* UDT
Timorese Popular Democratic Association, *see* Apodeti
Timorese Social Democratic Association, *see* ASDT
'Timorisation' 116, 119, 120
Timor-Leste Armed Violence Assessment (TLAVA) 148, 161, 172
Timor-Leste Court of Appeal 176, 178, 227, 249
Timor-Leste Defence Force, *see* F-FDTL
Timor-Leste Students' National Resistance, *see* Renetil
Tjan, Harry 28
TNI (Tentara Nasional Indonesia/ Indonesian Armed National Forces) 95n.2, 97, 99, 102, 267
Toohey, Paul 153
Torfing, J. 8
torture 1, 53, 56, 62, 81, 83, 86, 87, 88, 139, 155, 156, 204, 266
Toulmin, C. 182, 184n.7
traditional justice, *see adat*, *lisan*
Transparency International 186, 299
Traore, S. 184n.7
Traub, James 112
Treaty of Lisbon (1859) 10, 18
Trebilcock, M. 184n.7
Trembath, Anna 160, 188n.8, 190, 235, 238
Trindade, José (Josh) 151, 216, 222, 231
Tsing, A. L. 183, 256
Tutu, Desmond 281, 290
UDT (União Democrática Timorense/ Timorese Democratic Union) 12, 13–15, 47, 53, 55, 63, 77, 124, 133n.6, 202–3, 231, 279n.1
civil war with Fretilin 4, 9, 21, 22, 122
Ulfelder, Jay 300, 310
uma lulik 181, 182, 183, 184, 185, 231
Unger, Roberto Mangabeira xii, 299n.13

União Democrática Timorense, *see* UDT
United Kingdom 23n.8, 38, 42, 45, 65, 68, 71, 89, 101, 102, 180n.4, 290, 307
United Nations x, 2, 17, 22n.4, 25, 35, 42, 76, 98, 103, 104, 124, 137, 153, 154, 156, 161, 168, 169, 173, 211n.27, 212, 216, 223, 224, 242, 251, 257, 260, 267, 270, 275, 287, 290, 300
  agenda 24, 76, 77
  analysis 95
  and East Timorese independence 75, 99, 100n.6, 103
  and human rights 132n.4, 176, 215n.31, 218, 297, 299
  and invasion of East Timor 25, 27, 38, 39
  and language 114
  and separation of powers 250, 282, 284, 285, 289, 295, 297, 301
  and West Papua 19
  and women's rights 7, 270
  betrayal of Timorese 10, 107
  budgeting 116
  ceasefire negotiation (2006) 142, 143, 144
  Charter 25
  Civilian Police (UNPOL) 61n.1, 111, 118, 142, 144, 158, 159, 160, 162, 165, 166, 168, 169, 170, 172, 174, 178, 226, 227, 229, 293, 308
  Commission on Human Rights 82, 83
  criticisms and failures 5, 127, 134, 137, 149, 154, 156, 158, 159, 160, 163, 166, 168, 176, 201, 202, 215, 282, 284, 285, 289, 295
  Department of Political Affairs 250
  Development Fund for Women (UNIFEM) 257, 273
  Development Programme (UNDP) 120, 189n.12, 214, 230, 235, 238, 240, 246, 252, 254, 255, 265, 273, 289, 295, 299
  exit from East Timor 160
  General Assembly 75
  Global Compact 297
  High Commissioner for Refugees (UNHCR) 112, 297
    in Cambodia 1, 26, 119
    in Iraq 35, 112
  Independent Special Commission 138, 139n.7, 141, 163
  infrastructure in East Timor 113, 116, 160, 239
  institutions xiii, 38, 129, 169
  Integrated Mission in Timor-Leste (UNMIT) 121, 186, 220n.34, 223, 225
  irrelevance 166
  killing under UN flag 142, 143, 163, 223
  Mission in East Timor (UNAMET) 97, 99n.5, 100, 111–12, 125n.2, 268
  Mission of Support in East Timor (UNMISET) 118, 121, 191
  Office in Timor-Leste (UNOTIL) 121
  oversight of Indonesian draw-down 74
  peace operations 98–101, 102, 104, 106, 109, 112, 115, 117, 130, 154, 160, 169, 267, 297, 300, 303, 309
  peacebuilding 1, 5, 77, 268, 282, 283, 284
  personnel 10, 165, 283, 284, 307, 308
  policy 166
  presence in East Timor 74, 98, 101, 102
  regulations 271
  resolutions 75
  screening of personnel 159–60
  Secretary-General 75, 77, 96, 99, 107, 191, 197, 202, 268
  Security Council 75, 102, 112, 115, 121
  Special Rapporteur on Torture 87
  Special Rapporteurs 267
  support for East Timor 8, 71, 73, 76

Transitional Administration in East Timor (UNTAET) 111, 112–17, 118–22, 124, 125, 126, 127, 136, 137, 139, 149, 158, 166, 168, 176, 177n.2, 179, 180, 192n.15, 202, 219, 238, 242, 244, 250, 250, 251, 256, 268, 269, 282, 283n.6, 286, 289
UNTAET Gender Affairs Unit 268, 269, 273
tripartite process 77, 79, 92, 98
University 29n.13
see also Committee on the Elimination of All Forms of Discrimination against Women, justice— and United Nations, Special Representative of the Secretary-General
United States ix, x, 5, 13, 22, 25, 28, 43, 44, 88, 98n.4, 107, 109, 115, 129, 131, 134, 148, 156, 193, 290, 291
alliance with Australia 26, 102, 112, 196
and Iraq 34, 35,
and realism 44, 107, 197
and separation of powers 290
as source of power 257, 260
Australian criticism of 101
Congress 71, 73, 82, 101, 107
criticism of 202, 290
critics of Indonesia 28
diplomacy 193, 194, 196
disengagement from Asia x, 23
East Timor as public issue in 106, 280n.3
Embassy 68
facilitation of abuse 53
foreign policy 31, 34
in Afghanistan 160
intelligence on Asia 23
interests in Indonesia 26
intervention in East Timor 23, 39, 66, 98, 102, 193
military support to Indonesia 22, 23, 24, 41, 42, 48, 53, 65, 70, 102, 196

mobilisation against Indonesia 102
National Security Council 23n.9
non-involvement in East Timor x, 23, 52, 75
security sector 65
support for East Timor in 8, 42, 70, 76, 280
support for Indonesia x, 2, 26, 38, 40, 41
withdrawal of support for Indonesia 102, 108, 196
unprincipled engagement xi, 17–45
see also principled engagement
Uren, Tom 27
USAID 137, 180n.5, 240, 274, 275, 308

van Klinken, Gerry 92
Vanuatu 30, 307
'vernacularisation' xiii, 37, 218, 234, 255–9, 260, 261, 299
Victorian Institute of Forensic Medicine 80
Victorian Trades Hall Council 106
Vietnam 21, 43
Vietnam War x, 1, 18, 49, 52, 93, 106
Viqueque 151, 243
von Hippel, Karen 132n.4

Wahid, President 3, 108, 109, 193, 195
Walsh, Mayra 160, 188n.8, 190, 235, 238
Walsh, Patrick xv, 70, 201, 286
Walters, Patrick 74
Wanandi, Jusuf 28
Wandita, Galuh 212, 264, 265, 268, 271, 272, 276
war crimes 163, 191–5, 196, 199, 215, 230, 234
see also crimes against humanity
Ward, Jeanne 161
Weaver, S. 75
Webber, Jeremy 180
Weber, Max 184, 303
Webster, David 72, 93

West Papua 18, 22, 40, 85, 89, 90, 94, 97, 108, 125n.2, 253
West Timor 9, 13, 18, 23, 47, 95, 104, 109, 111, 112, 135, 139, 161, 192, 193, 197, 200, 202, 207, 212, 214, 216, 232, 238, 241, 253, 267, 269, 274, 289, 309
Wheeler, Nicholas J. 98n.3
White, Hugh 94, 98, 99, 101
White, Rachel 269, 270
Whitlam, Gough x, 1, 4, 10, 17, 18, 19, 21, 22, 23, 24, 25, 26n.12, 27, 28, 39, 40, 41, 42, 44, 107, 241
Whittington, Sherrill 268, 269
Wierda, Marieke 210n.26, 214
Wilson, Bu V. E. 130, 154, 155, 158–9, 160, 162, 164, 239
Wilson, Woodrow ix
Winata, Tommy 239
Wiranto, General 3, 40, 94, 95n.2, 96, 98, 99n.5, 102, 103, 104, 108, 109, 192, 193, 197
Wise, Amanda 10, 11, 64, 76, 83, 281, 282
Wollstonecraft, Mary 7, 264, 275, 277
women
    clandestine networks 7
    in Falintil 265, 266
    in Fretilin 265
    in judiciary 277
    in legislature 276
    in networked governance 263–77
    in parliament xiii, 7, 121, 272–3, 276, 293
    non-governmental organisations (NGOs) 7, 162, 163, 255n.11, 273, 286, 293, 308, 309
    role in peacebuilding 230
    see also feminism, gendered violence, names of organisations
Women's Charter of Rights 270
Wood, Jennifer xi, 134
Wood, Mary 267, 268, 270
Woolcott, Richard 13, 14, 17, 23, 24n.10, 26, 28, 44, 72, 73, 112

World Bank 102, 108, 119, 137, 189n.12, 232n.38, 240, 242, 244, 251, 257, 258, 259, 260, 308
World Trade Organisation (WTO) 258
Wright, S. xiii
Wright, Warren L. 221

Xavier do Amaral, Francisco 12, 14, 47, 226, 227

Yeltsin, Boris 4
Yudhoyono, Susilo Bambang 109, 193n.16
Yugoslavia 191, 281, 289

Zelter, Angie 69
Zifcak, Spencer 207, 210, 214
Zürcher, Christoph 131, 132, 133, 134, 283

www.ingramcontent.com/pod-product-compliance
Lightning Source LLC
Chambersburg PA
CBHW040934240426
43670CB00033B/2975